The Rebirth of Classical
Political Rationalism

The Rebirth of Classical Political Rationalism

An Introduction to the Thought of Leo Strauss

Essays and Lectures by
Leo Strauss

Selected and Introduced by
Thomas L. Pangle

The University of Chicago Press
Chicago and London

Leo Strauss (1899–1973) was the Robert Maynard Hutchins Distinguished Service Professor in Political Science at the University of Chicago. He was the Scott Buchanan Distinguished Scholar in residence at St. John's College at the time of his death. His many books include *The Argument and the Action of Plato's Laws, The City and Man, Natural Right and History, The Political Philosophy of Hobbes, Socrates and Aristophanes, Studies in Platonic Political Philosophy,* and *Thoughts on Machiavelli.*

Thomas L. Pangle is professor of political science and chairman of the American Studies Committee at the University of Toronto. He is the author of *Montesquieu's Philosophy of Liberalism* and *The Spirit of Modern Republicanism,* and the translator of *The Laws of Plato.*

The University of Chicago Press, Chicago 60637
The University of Chicago Press, Ltd., London
© 1989 by The University of Chicago
All rights reserved. Published 1989
Printed in the United States of America

98 97 96 95 94 93 92 91 90 89 54321

Library of Congress Cataloging-in-Publication Data
Strauss, Leo.
    The rebirth of classical political rationalism.
    Bibliography: p.
    Includes index.
    1. Political science—History.   2. Rationalism—History.   I. Pangle, Thomas L.   II. Title.
JA81.S756   1989   320'.09   88-20614
ISBN 0-226-77714-6
ISBN 0-226-77715-4 (pbk.)

Contents

Contents

Editor's Introduction

Who was Leo Strauss? More to the point, what did he stand for? What political philosophy did he promulgate? Or must we not ask a more basic question: what did he mean by political philosophy? In the years between 1945 and 1970 Strauss seized a dull and dying academic discipline called "the history of political ideas" and transformed it into an enterprise of gripping significance and vitality. What gave the history of political thought, in his hands, such a powerful allure? What is it about his writings that continues to shatter respectable intellectual categories and rules, thereby arousing so much fascination and so much hatred?

Since his death in 1973, Strauss's influence has steadily grown; in the past few years it has become more and more widely recognized. But the enhancement of his reputation has been the occasion for an intensifying level of controversy among those who claim to know something about him and an almost equally intense bewilderment on the part of those who come to hear of him only through these heated disputes. It is perhaps not surprising to find Strauss's own students and followers disagreeing, often sharply, over the meaning of his work: after all, how many great thinkers have not left behind a legacy of more or less fruitful discord among their followers? What cannot help but seem amazing, however, is the frequency with which Strauss—as well as his students or followers—is the object of passionate, even bitter, attacks, especially from fellow scholars and intellectuals.

Those unbiased observers who turn to Strauss's books in order to seek the reasons for this reception are not likely to find quick answers, though with persistence they may begin to appreciate the paradoxical connection between the initial obscurity, or rather, alien character, of Strauss's writing and that writing's ultimately explosive critical impact.

The Past as Source of Liberation

Strauss typically expresses his thought in the form of detailed, painstaking, and new or unorthodox interpretations of the major texts of philosophers and theologians from the past—not only from the classical and early modern, but also from the medieval, worlds; and not only from the Latin-Christian, but also from the Judaic and the Islamic (Hebrew and Arabic), traditions. Strauss's interpretations culminate in searching dialogues with the thinkers under study; but the reader who wishes to grasp and follow the dialogues must first undertake the task of studying with care, and with new eyes, the texts to which Strauss addresses himself. This insistence on close analysis of philosophic works from the past is far more than a hallmark of Strauss's own personal or peculiar approach. According to Strauss, such study is an *essential* prerequisite of authentic philosophic thinking in our time. If we are to free our minds from the blinders and prejudices of our age and culture, Strauss argues, we must ceaselessly compel ourselves to encounter the challenge of profound modes of thought that do not share our modern presuppositions. Ours is of course not the first epoch in which self-critical study of old philosophic texts has been the principal path to spiritual liberation. But in our time this path has acquired an unprecedented importance (and difficulty) because the present age is one of almost unprecedented resistance to the claims to truth advanced in previous ages; and, partly as a consequence, ours is also an age of spiritual disintegration and intellectual crisis or decay. Strauss contends that contemporary thinkers (with a few exceptions) have become unwittingly enthralled by certain dubious but deceptively "unquestionable" philosophic assumptions whose effect is to make us progressively lose touch with the issues, the themes, and even the modes of writing or communication that constitute the rich intellectual core of the West in both its Biblical and its philosophic dimensions. Strauss claims to demonstrate that these questions that are being more and more forgotten are in fact *the* most important questions for human life, the questions that alone truly define and illuminate the human situation as such, in all times and places—even where the questions, and hence the fundamental human situation, are lost sight of. In short, the initially historical or even pedantic appearance of Strauss's writing reveals itself on closer inspection to be the sign of Strauss's painfully incisive critical stance towards almost every major feature of the contemporary intellectual and political landscape.

The Maverick vs. the Authorities

Where the criticism is so uncompromising, where the stakes are so high, where the demands—for openmindedness to an unfamiliar way of thinking, for sometimes agonizing self-questioning—are so great, it is perhaps natural for the conventional guardians of culture and academe to rush to try to stamp out the fire that threatens their established peace and quiet.

There have been some notable and admirable exceptions, though it is perhaps not surprising that these are interlocutors and critics whose own work challenges conventional scholarship and intellectual life, especially in the Anglo-American world. The great French left-Hegelian philosopher Alexandre Kojève wrote a richly provocative response to Strauss's presentation of the philosophy of Xenophon, inducing Strauss to respond in turn—thus creating one of the most brilliant debates to appear in print in the twentieth century.[1] The leading Marxist historian of English political thought, C. B. Macpherson, and Strauss published respectful and careful criticisms of one another's competing, unorthodox interpretations of Hobbes and Locke as the sources of modern liberalism.[2] Raymond Aron, the lonely intellectual apostle of liberalism in France in the postwar years, appealed to Strauss's *Natural Right and History* as an elaboration of a principled prudence that could provide a politically sober middle ground between radically individualistic Sartrean existentialism on the one hand and doctrinaire or authoritarian Marxism and natural-law moralism on the other.[3] Martin Heidegger's most gifted students, Hans-Georg Gadamer and Karl Löwith, each engaged Strauss in wide-ranging debates on the meaning and implications of the philosophy of history.[4] Arnaldo Momigliano, the foremost classical historiographer of the twentieth century, wrote a critical appreciation of Strauss[5] in an attempt to win him a hearing in the tight-knit world of classical scholarship—to little avail.

For the prevalent scholarly reaction to Strauss has been censorious. It is not easy to convey, without appearing to exaggerate, the tone and level of many of the published responses to Strauss's precedent-shattering books. As one surveys the amazingly varied and contradictory record of accusations levelled at Strauss, one is forced to wonder with a smile what moral and intellectual lapses this fellow has not been proven guilty of. On the one hand, Strauss and his followers are regularly accused of being idle, romantic antiquarians who somehow seduce very bright, but unfortunately very gullible, students into losing all productive interest in serious

issues that affect contemporary life. Thus a work of analytic political theory that enjoyed brief fame in the sixties dismissed Strauss
with this assessment: "To spend one's working life rolling the classics round the tongue like old brandy (as advocated by Leo Strauss
and disciples) hardly seems likely to advance the sum of human
knowledge."[6] In a similar vein, a Mr. Burnyeat assured readers of
the *Times Literary Supplement* (9 April 1976) that Strauss, despite his
pretensions to be a political theorist, "shows no interest at all
in the realities of political and social life, whether ancient or
modern."

But at the same time, and sometimes by the same critics,[7]
Strauss is accused of having a political impact that is demonic in
proportion. As the alarmed Mr. Burnyeat put it (10 October 1985),
"when he retired Strauss was arguably one of the most influential
thinkers in the United States." The wide appeal of Strauss's
thought was brought home by Strauss's student Allan Bloom,
whose *Closing of the American Mind* was surely one of the most intellectually demanding books ever to reach and remain for months
at the top of the *New York Times* best seller list.

It is now increasingly undeniable: Leo Strauss's thought speaks
to some of the deepest concerns of a wide public, especially (but
by no means exclusively) the as yet uncommitted young. The only
disputed question is: what is he up to? Strauss and those he influences are stirring up the students, getting them to read old classics
with a passionate seriousness, provoking them to ask all sorts of
unusual questions—about the books, about the soul, about God,
about morality, about democracy. The questions do not fit the conventional categories; they obviously presuppose a doubt of the established intellectual authorities, of their respectable interpretations, of their accepted ways of thinking. The "Straussians" are
teaching something funny: we can't figure out what they're up to,
and Strauss's books are so difficult, and it's so hard to puzzle out a
complex new way of thinking anyway; but we do know it's alien,
that it's hard to understand, that it challenges, in a very powerful
way, the opinions of right-thinking people, that it's therefore "elitist," or—yes!—"un-American." Thus "Leo Strauss and his followers" have been accused in the pages of the *American Political Science
Review* of "a kind of 'inverted agreement' with the most brashly
totalitarian of the leftists," and Strauss has been lumped with Marx
in his dedication to a "rejection of the values underlying the American experience."[8] Recently this sort of charge was introduced into
the popular conservative press, when the *National Review* pub-

lished in its issue of 22 March 1985 a cover story by a professor questioning whether the "Straussians" on campuses were not "un-American"; and, in what must be a rare salute from the left to charges from the right of un-American activities, a writer in the *New York Review of Books* (10 October 1985) praised the *National Review* accusation as "calmly argued." But then on the other hand, and again in the *American Political Science Review,* Strauss's thought has been explained as an expression of an exaggerated American patriotism obsessed with building American resistance to "the threat of 'communism' and an 'Eastern despotism.'"[9] In 1975, the journal *Political Theory* went much further, publishing an attack (entitled "Prophet and Inquisitor") which labelled Strauss a dogmatic moralist with "little sympathy for the skeptical temper," a man whose undeniable learning and intelligence were unfortunately devoted to an "inquisitorial" assault on anyone suspected of what Strauss was said to call "Machiavellianism," i.e., disbelief in God and natural law. Strauss himself, it was charged, might have had delusions of prophecy, and those who acknowledged his influence were compared to the members of a fundamentalist religious cult.[10] Ten years later, the same journal published an attack equally bitter, but this time charging that the previous attack in the journal had completely misunderstood Strauss: in fact, the journal's scholarly readership was now solemnly assured, Strauss was a conspiratorial, atheistic nihilist who denied all moral and religious standards and whose book on Machiavelli, if properly read, showed that he used Machiavelli as his "mouthpiece"![11]

I recite these accusations (and I have not mentioned some of the most irresponsible and frenzied), not only to give the flavor of the reception accorded Strauss in some of the leading scholarly journals, but also to show the height and thickness of the wall of hostile prejudice that blocks access to Strauss's thought. My wish, obviously, is to help the candid reader pierce or vault that wall; and I know of no way to do so without first bringing such a reader face to face with the wall.

Classical Political Rationalism

One may naturally, and quite reasonably, wonder: where there is so much scholarly smoke, must there not be some fire? There is; but it is the fire of genuinely critical philosophy. It is the fire of Socratic dialectic. The present book is intended to introduce the reader to the central preoccupation of Strauss's thought: the attempt to resuscitate—after centuries of neglect or well-intentioned patronizing—the disquieting and seductive challenge offered by Socrates' erotic skepticism. The classical political rationalism to which Strauss gave new life is in essence the moral, political, and theological justification or vindication of the Socratic way of life. Strauss dedicated himself to advancing and to testing in argument this seemingly outlandish series of suggestions: that in the life of Socrates, in his relentless but erotic or loving skepticism, is to be found the model of a truly free, truly awakened, truly rational human existence; that this way of life affords the firmest foundation for lasting friendship and true generosity; that despite an inevitable and continuing tension between Socrates' erotic skepticism and the loyalties, commitments, and attachments required by family, religion, and citizenship, a fragile and mutually fruitful coexistence in dialogue is possible; that from such dialogue—the supreme products of which are Aristotle's *Ethics* and *Politics*—there emerge norms of civic justice, of civic virtue and vice, which, while not absolute in the sense of being susceptible of articulation in the form of natural laws or categorical imperatives, are yet transhistorically valid because grounded in rational insight into the nature, the permanent and deepest needs, of mankind; and finally, that the highest potential of liberal democracy is its capacity to keep alive and even to revere the model of Socrates, the Socratic dialectic, and the Socratic way of life.

What is it about this espousal of classical political rationalism, so conceived, that arouses suspicion, or even hatred, in our time? I do not have an altogether satisfactory answer. But I am inclined to believe that at bottom what is decisive is the fact that this classical political rationalism appears, or can appear, as antidemocratic: as opposed to the egalitarian sentiments that are the deepest and most powerful moral sentiments of our age and culture. Now, it is certainly true that Socrates and his greatest students or spiritual descendents—Xenophon, Plato, and Aristotle—were critics of democracy. Strauss always insisted that this discomfiting feature of classical political rationalism must be faced squarely and honestly; he strongly rejected the attempts made at various times and in various quarters (including among some of his own followers or students) to obscure or belittle or explain away this crucial characteristic of classical political thought. What is more, Strauss himself continued the classical criticism of democracy and, indeed, applied and extended that criticism to the new or modern form of Western liberal democracy. But in his insistence on bringing to the fore and continuing the classical criticism of democracy, Strauss also insisted that by so doing one would show that this was a criticism that was *not* hostile to democracy, but instead favorable to democracy and, indeed, rooted in a genuine attachment to democracy—though a rational and sober attachment, a friendship controlled by the strict refusal to flatter democracy. To quote Strauss, "we are not permitted to be flatterers of democracy precisely because we are friends and allies of democracy" (*Liberalism Ancient and Modern*, p. 24). The truest friend of democracy or of the people will be the frequent, not to say constant, critic of the people—and, even more, the critic of the political and cultural flatterers of the people or the critic of the wisdom of the people. The truest friend of democracy or of the people will therefore not win many popularity contests (Socrates himself was put to death as a criminal by the Athenian democracy)—though he may win a kind of posthumous respect that is worth much more than popularity.

But to understand better just what the sources of the animosity Strauss arouses are, we must enter more deeply into the precise character of classical political rationalism and thence into the critique of democracy Strauss inherited from, and continued in the name of, classical political rationalism. At the same time, we must make more explicit the sharp contrast between classical political rationalism and modern political rationalism—the rationalism which, though increasingly beleaguered, still prevails today: the rationalism which has its origins in the Enlightenment.

The Theme of Virtue

The central theme of classical political philosophy is virtue, or human excellence. The questions that typically preoccupy Socrates and his followers are: What is virtue? Can it be taught, and if so, how? What is the education that makes a full citizen and human being? What is a virtuous statesman and citizen? What political regime best promotes virtue or excellence? What is a true friend? Who or what is worthy of passionate love?

Now, this kind of questioning and preoccupation immediately appears to characterize Socrates and his rationalism as far removed from, not to say alien to, the sophistication which tends to predominate in our contemporary culture. Every undergraduate "knows" that what Socrates is talking about, what he is groping unsuccessfully to express, is the idea of "values." The fact that Socrates never once in his life referred to "values" is a clear sign that stood at the dim dawn, the lisping babyhood, of science and scientific thinking. To know, as we are sure we do, that morals and principles of justice are values, is to know that Socrates' questions are deeply misconceived inasmuch as they express a search for truly rational or objectively valid answers; it is to know that values lack any ascertainable fixed meaning or status. Values are individual preferences, or subjective commitments, or cultural creations, or historical dispensations. Once this truth—this absolute and unquestionable truth—is recognized, the sophisticated response is one that turns its back on sustained argument over the "truth" of values and instead proceeds to "self-expression" and search for "community," based on the "clarification" of our tradition and its evolving, "considered moral judgments" (prejudices). This quest is to be regulated only by the absolute moral principle that we ought to express ourselves and seek community and values-clarification only in such ways as respect the equal right of all others to express themselves and seek community and values-clarification.

It is not very difficult to unmask the incoherence in this pseudo-sophistication: the denial of the possibility of absolute or universal truth rests on the assertion of an absolute or universal truth and is said to entail the assertion of universally valid moral imperatives or prohibitions—of human rights that transcend race, color, creed, or ethnic and historical background. It is more important to observe that no human being can actually live according to this pseudo-sophistication. This basis for loyalty to democracy and equality contradicts and thus undermines itself at every moment, in action as well as in logic. For as soon as one turns from the silly abstractions about values and relativism back to real life—back to elections, jury duty, hiring decisions, the forming of friendships, the choice of a spouse, the raising of children, the communion with one's own conscience—one sees the inescapable need and obligation to evaluate and judge the characters of other people at every turn. So long as we live, we cannot help but feel the urgency of our need to know what Socrates sought to know; for we see that what is at stake is the happiness of ourselves and those we love and, what is more, the obligation to be fair to others: the need to evaluate and respect, and hence to have some basis for knowing and judging, character and dignity in ourselves and others.

Just beneath the sophisticated veneer that distorts our moral experience there is to be found, then, overwhelming evidence of the primordial and permanent power of the concerns or questions that are the Socratic starting point. Moreover, there is evidence—in our most important experiences—of knowledge that points the way to a response to these questions and concerns. Life teaches all of us some considerable awareness of what Aristotle is referring to when he discusses, and carefully distinguishes and ranks, the various versions of the moral virtues (courage, moderation, generosity, magnanimity, integrity, delicacy of wit, friendship, self-control, clemency, prudence, and wisdom); when he distinguishes and ranks legal, distributive, commutative, and retributive justice; when he distinguishes and ranks the noble or beautiful and the good or advantageous. We may have grown unaccustomed to the rich and subtle moral discourse found in the classic works of political philosophy and poetry—our moral senses are rusty, and our moral discourse and consciousness have grown accordingly inarticulate and crude; but we can begin to cultivate those senses again, if only we will enter with open minds into the arguments and stories and characters of that humane old classical republican tradition.

The Socratic Questions

It is only when we do begin to enter into the classic arguments and dramas that we begin to recover the deep problems with which the classical tradition wrestled. Classical political philosophy originates with Socrates, and Socrates' knowledge was knowledge of ignorance—knowledge of the imperfect character of most of our moral knowledge. To say that our knowledge is imperfect is not, however, to say that it is insignificant. The Socratic political philosophers find, through their cross-examination and clarification of the discourse and moral awareness of serious citizens, much that is worthy of intellectual respect, much that can provide reasonable guidance for civic action and education. The codifications of these discoveries are found in works like Plato's *Laws*, Aristotle's *Ethics*, Cicero's *Offices*, and the great medieval commentaries which they spawned. But precisely these codifications and commentaries indicate, in unobtrusive ways, the deeply troubling puzzles or questions that lurk at the bottom of our powerful moral experiences. Let me try to state these fundamental Socratic questions, as simply as possible and within the limits of brevity required by the present occasion:

What is the relation and relative rank of, on the one hand, concern for the health and fulfillment of one's own soul and, on the other hand, dedication to others, especially to fellow citizens in the political community?

The splendor or nobility of virtue is most apparent at moments of sacrifice or self-transcendence; yet it is happiness that comes to sight as the ultimate goal of all human life: what then is the relation between nobility and happiness?

In the experience of friendship, love, and especially erotic love, what is the relation between the longing for personal happiness and the longing to devote oneself to, or even to sacrifice one's self and one's happiness for, the beloved?

Given that rational self-consciousness lies at the core of human excellence, given that knowledge, especially self-knowledge, is central to virtue, what exactly is the nature of human responsibility? Do not all human beings pursue what they believe to be good? If virtue is knowledge or is rooted in knowledge, is not vice ignorance or rooted in ignorance? How then can crime and punishment, praise and blame, honor and dishonor, be understood?

These are the sorts of questions which the Socratic philosopher takes upon himself the responsibility of pursuing intransigently. In doing so he at some point departs from or leaves behind the citizen and statesman, who must avoid, or at least suspend or curtail, this questioning in order to act. Yet the philosophic life, consumed by the uncompromising philosophic quest, is also a kind of deed or action, and, insofar as it more fully completes the rational self-consciousness that is man's highest attribute, this life emerges as a standard that supervenes upon and must in some degree guide the life devoted to civic and moral action.

The Philosopher's Civic Responsibility

The manner in which the philosophic life—demanding relentless questioning and the pursuit of moral wisdom—can or ought to transcend while yet guiding political and moral life is itself a question of the utmost importance and delicacy for classical political philosophy. For the philosopher's skepticism can easily undermine the dedication required by the civic and moral virtues. We today find it especially difficult to recover this dimension of classical republican thought, because we live in a new or modern kind of republican society that is permissive or tolerant to an unprecedented degree, and that appears or claims to demand very little in the way of collective religious or moral commitment and consensus. As we shall see in a moment, this new kind of republicanism is largely the product of a new or modern political rationalism. The sorts of republican (and nonrepublican) society the classical philosophers confronted were of a very different character from the society we inhabit—although even our society, the classical political philosophers would insist, requires more in the way of democratic moral consensus than we are perhaps initially aware of or inclined to admit. In every society, the philosophic life can pose some danger and can, if imprudently or irresponsibly pursued, provoke a fanatic response, which in turn endangers the philosophers.

But the full gravity of the tension between society and philosophy becomes clear only when we take into consideration the theological dimension of the philosopher's situation. For the questions raised by Socratic philosophers imply a dissatisfaction with all available authoritative responses; and the most authoritative traditional responses are those given by religion or by the voices of religious tradition—the poets, sacred texts, and authorized interpreters. Indeed, the religious tradition teaches, against the philosophers, that the unresolved conundrums of moral and civic life are properly understood as indications of the fact that the life of political and social action points beyond itself, to divinity or to a divine destiny before whose commandments and direction the human heart and mind must bow in humble obedience and resignation. The Socratic philosopher who is truly honest or open-minded cannot ignore these widely accepted authoritative teachings. As a matter of fact, one does not exaggerate when one says that the most urgent question for any truly self-conscious rationalist must be the question whether reason, unassisted by suprarational inspiration or revelation, or by obedience to such inspiration or revelation, can or ought to be the guide for human existence. The Socratic philosopher is therefore necessarily compelled to engage in a critical dialogue with religion or revelation or poetic inspiration; and this questioning or probing of religious authority obviously entails a new level of danger, both to that authority and to the philosopher who questions it.

The problem I am now trying to sketch—the problem that Strauss, following Spinoza, called the "theologico-political problem"—is *the* most fundamental of the permanent questions that define the human situation. It is not merely a prudential, it is above all a *moral*, problem for the philosopher—and ultimately for all thinking men who become aware of the possibility of philosophy. I quote from Strauss's essay "On Classical Political Philosophy" (chapter 4 of this volume):

> The philosophers, as well as other men who have become aware of the possibility of philosophy, are sooner or later driven to wonder, *Why* philosophy? *Why* does human life *need* philosophy? Why is it *good*, why is it *right*, that *opinions* about the nature of the whole should be replaced by *genuine knowledge* of the nature of the whole? . . . To justify philosophy before the tribunal of the political community means to justify philosophy *in terms of the political community*, that is to say, by means of a kind of argument which appeals, not to philosophers as such, but to citizens as such. (my italics)

In other words, the moral and prudential problem becomes at once also a problem of communication, of rhetoric. The classical political philosopher who follows in the wake of Socrates must become a "dialectician": he must learn to speak and argue *not* on his own terms, i.e., not on the premise that reason is the supreme guide and standard. He must justify the reliance on reason; and that means he must not start from premises that assume the sufficiency of reason. He must justify the authority of reason in the eyes, and in the terms, of men who do not begin by accepting such a standard as necessarily the supreme standard. And he must execute this task in full awareness of the fact that what he faces is not mere intellectual doubt but moral suspicion, and even the likelihood of moral persecution.

Yet this means that for the classical political rationalist, the study of rhetoric or communication is not merely or even mainly a theoretical study: it is a practical, a moral, a political, discipline. As a result of their own practical experience with rhetoric, the classical political rationalists do not believe in the existence, or even the possibility, of a general theory of rhetoric, or of "hermeneutics," or of "semiotics." In every society, in every historical situation, a somewhat different rhetoric, political sensibility, and psychological delicacy will be required; and, contrary to what is often said of Strauss, Strauss never ceased stressing that every text in political philosophy must therefore be approached with a view to its primary addressees and hence with a view to the unique, concrete, historical situation and circumstances within which it emerged. This was the thesis of Strauss's great work on communication, *Persecution and the Art of Writing*. But what set Strauss apart from all conventional, historicist students of the relation be-

tween thinkers and their historical milieu was his insistence that
the historical situation must be seen *as it was seen by the thinker
under study*. And in the case of the few truly politic thinkers, this
means that the text must be seen as deliberately accomodating itself, by rhetoric and even by what Plato called "noble lies," to the
most healthy of the reigning prejudices. The text, as well as the
thought contained in the text, responds to the specific historical
situation, but it is not wholly explicable in terms of that situation,
because the text does not simply reflect or grow out of the situation. Instead, the text of a truly politic philosopher, especially if it
is the text of a Socratic philosopher, may have to be seen as in part
a deliberate adaptation to the milieu—as a means of constructively
and responsibly criticizing and effecting liberation from the milieu.

Classical Political Rationalism and Democracy

Given the characterization of classical political rationalism that I
have just hastily sketched, what is that rationalism's view of democracy? As I have noted, the democracy with which the classics
were familiar was not today's mass, liberal democracy. Democracy
in its original form was the direct rule of the majority of freeborn
adult males in a small, pretechnological, urban society whose economic base was usually agricultural. Rule by such a majority in
such a society meant rule by the poor heads of households, men
who lacked the wealth and leisure to gain a good education or to
have much experience in public office, not to mention interna-
tional affairs. These severe deficiencies of the majority, caused by
the harsh scarcities and inequalities brought about by nature or by
chance, cast a long shadow over democracy. Nevertheless, the
classical political philosophers did not scorn democracy or charge
it with being unconcerned with virtue. On balance, Aristotle in his
Politics treats democracy, especially when rooted in the landown-
ing or yeoman peasantry, as more likely to foster both a sense of
fraternity and the sturdy, basic virtues of citizenship than its chief
competitor in most practical circumstances of republican life, oligarchy (the rule of the wealthy minority). But Aristotle and the
other classics observed that democracy was constantly prone to
overestimate and overemphasize those virtues (manly courage,
patriotism, piety) that were within the reach of the poor majority,
while neglecting those virtues or excellences requiring unusual capacity, education, leisure, and broad political experience. When
guided by enlightened statesmen, democracy judiciously incor-

porated some of the reasonable elements of oligarchy (elections rather than selection by lot, educational or other qualifications on eligibility for office, fixed terms of office and relative independence of magistrates during office, infrequent and carefully regulated assemblies, a senate, etc.), and thus tended toward a polity, or mixed regime, whose combination of some of the best features of oligarchy and democracy effected a synthesis that transcended both ingredients in the direction of aristocracy. In Strauss's discussion of the plays of Aristophanes, we will see him bring to vivid life some of the rollicking, rough-and-tumble strengths of this sort of democracy favored by the classics. Still, the excellences of democracy, like its weaknesses, are clearly viewed, are seen for what they truly are, only when democracy is studied in the light of the standard set by aristocracy.

Aristocracy is the form of government in which the most virtuous rule without having to make compromises; it is the regime which has as its unambiguous goal the promotion and cultivation of virtue to the fullest possible extent. Now, aristocracy in this strict sense is not intended to be a practical proposal: "the classics had no delusions regarding the probability of a genuine aristocracy's ever becoming actual" (*Liberalism Ancient and Modern*, p. 15). The classical political philosophers elaborated the idea of aristocracy, or what they called the best regime, not as a program for action, but as a standard, held in the mind's eye, by which the existing regimes might be measured and criticized, or made aware of their limitations. In practice, and wherever it was prudent to do so, the classical political rationalists favored and actively supported polity, or the democratic mixed regime. They did so, I should add, not only because of their support for moral and civic virtue, but also because their interests as philosophers made them more fond of life in democracy than in any other regime. For precisely the relative laxness or easygoingness of which democracy is susceptible allows greater freedom of thought and greater scope for the unorthodox ways of the philosopher or the young potential philosopher. Socrates, Plato, and Aristotle all preferred, for themselves, life in democratic Athens over life in the morally more elevated Greek or African cities (e.g., Sparta, Crete, Carthage; consider here the tribute Plato pays to "permissive" Athens in *Laws* 642c–d). We remark here another aspect of the complex and tense, or somewhat antagonistic, relationship between philosophic and moral or civic excellence.

The Crisis of Modern Rationalism

At the heart of *modern* political rationalism—the modern political philosophy that has its inception in the sixteenth and seventeenth centuries, in such philosophers as Machiavelli, Descartes, Bacon, Hobbes, Spinoza, and Locke—is a radically new and different interpretation of this relationship between philosophic virtue and moral or civic virtue. The new interpretation of the relation between theory and practice implies or goes hand in hand with a radically new and different conception of republicanism; and this new conception is the predominant, though certainly not the sole, source of contemporary liberal democracy. The new rationalism and the new republicanism which it inspires are by no means monolithic: there are sharp, and deep, divisions among the modern rationalists. But the disagreements take place on the basis of a more fundamental agreement. The modern rationalists claim to surmount or circumvent the tensions, the problems, the unresolved contradictions (above all, the tension or contradiction between the contemplative and the active life) that set Socratic rationalism in motion. The modern rationalists hold out the promise of a society that would be rational or uncontradictory to a degree and in a way considered impossible by classical political rationalism.

Precisely how the tensions are to be resolved is a matter of grave dispute among the diverse strands of modern rationalism; but in every case what is required can be briefly characterized as a similar sort of profound reinterpretation and recasting of the nature of both philosophy and republican society. On the one hand, philosophy is no longer to be publically defended as the highest good, above and beyond any service to society. The love or pursuit of the truth is to be understood as in the service of the gratification of other, more natural or deep-seated, needs and passions. Even where philosophy still comes to the fore, as in Spinoza, philosophy is understood to culminate in the teaching of a system of ethics for mankind. On the other side, society is no longer to be understood as pointing beyond itself, to a dimension of existence that transcends what can be attained or realized through rational social and political action. Accordingly, revealed religion or supra-rational piety is to play a secondary, or even more subordinate, role in politics and society. The God of nature or reason, the God demonstrated by empirical science, is to replace the God of scripture and revelation or mystery.

From the perspective of modern rationalism, the key difficulty
or inadequacy of the old rationalism and republicanism seems to
be their misguided attempt to discover, or to orient themselves by
the promise of, an objective happiness, or a *summum bonum* or utmost good, that would stand as the goal, the term, the guiding
pinnacle, of existence. Modern rationalism rejects this orientation
in the name of a new orientation: an orientation either by the
strongest passions (the fear of violent death, comfortable preser-
vation; vanity or pride or recognition) or by the formal attributes
of lawfulness and of reverence rooted in lawfulness (the general
will or categorical imperative).

These new compass points are said to have the enormous advantage of being based on what is powerfully active in, and therefore massively evident to, all human beings—whatever else they
may feel or seek. The new principles are the first principles of justice that can plausibly claim to be rooted in an insight into human
nature—into the indisputably permanent and necessary in man.
The new principles are therefore held up as the true natural laws
or natural rights, deriving from "nature and nature's God." These
new laws of nature hold out the promise of putting an end to the
interminable moral, political, and religious wars that have plagued
mankind and that will always plague mankind so long as it seeks
to take its bearings by that happiness or utmost good of which it
is evidently ignorant. The new rationalism promises to diminish
the need for political leadership or guidance by men of superior
insight into the ultimate goals; the new rationalism promises to
mute the interminable diputes among claimants to rule who base
their claims on such wisdom. Since the first principles are capable
of being made evident to all as the compellingly necessary basis
for action, democratic consent emerges as the sole legitimate foundation of government; and the government that ought to be established by such consent is arguably a new, enlightened, representative democracy, in which "rulers" are abolished, and replaced by
representatives compelled to be "public servants" of the popular
will. The new democracy does not claim to make virtue its end,
though it may well cultivate certain civic virtues understood as
means or tools and may provide the freedom in which individuals
may pursue moral virtue in their private lives; the new democracy
does not claim to provide the avenue to human fulfillment or happiness; it advances only the much more restricted and sober claim
to be the indispensable means for protecting each individual's per-

sonal or private liberty to "pursue happiness"—whatever that will-o'-the-wisp might appear to be—as he or she wishes, so long as the similar right in others to such pursuit is not abridged. The new republicanism takes its bearings, not from the ends of life, but from the prerequisites to the pursuit of ends—ends which may or may not have objective existence. But this means that more and more the means—property, power, prestige, civil liberties, law and order—become in fact the chief ends, first in public life and then, inevitably, in private life. Can human beings by nature rest satisfied with the ever-increasing trend toward a public life of purposeless purposefulness? Or is life in this new dispensation more and more what Strauss called, at the conclusion of his study of Locke, "the joyless quest for joy" (*Natural Right and History,* p. 251)?

Modern political rationalism held out the promise that the enlightened mass of men, once schooled in the new principles, would find peaceful consensus and sober satisfaction in those principles and in the life guided by them. Very great philosophers eventually began to speak, in the nineteenth century, of "the end of history," "perpetual peace," "the riddle of history solved." But it suffices to read the most superficial history of our century, nay, to read tomorrow's morning paper, in order to see that the promise of modern political rationalism has not been kept. In fact, the fundamental principles of modern natural right on which all enlightened men were supposed to agree have come to be viewed almost universally as no longer rooted in nature or in any permanently valid insight; what once were held to be natural laws and natural rights, grounded in objectively verifiable knowledge, are now widely or generally held to be no more than the values or worldview created by or mysteriously dispensed to a particular historical culture; and this culture of ours is more and more viewed, by the sophisticated among those who inhabit it, as in a state of decline or senescence. This is the most obvious meaning of what Strauss calls "the crisis of our time," "the crisis of the West," "the crisis of liberal democracy."

Strauss and Liberal Democracy

Yet Strauss was far from joining those among his great contemporaries, like Heidegger, who regarded modern political rationalism as bankrupt; still less did he believe that liberal, and especially

American liberal, democracy was tottering on its last legs. However distant liberal or mass democracy may be, in both its theoretical foundations and its daily practice, from the civic republicanism of antiquity, liberal democracy remains a vital form of republicanism. It remains, that is, a form of self-government by the citizenry. It therefore continues to require, and to inspire, some version (an attenuated version, to be sure) of the Greco-Roman ideal of an active, proud citizenry imbued with knowledgeable respect for outstanding statesmanship. Strauss consequently deplored the influence of those thoughtlessly egalitarian historians who debunk, rather than make more intelligible, the greatness of statesmen; he vigorously opposed the prevalent tendency among historians to downplay or belittle political history, to reduce the arguments and deeds of citizens and rulers to a merely ideological surface masking supposedly deeper, subpolitical economic or social forces; he ceaselessly challenged those among his social-science colleagues who focused on what they called behavior, and who thus treated the written opinions of judges, the deliberations of representatives, and the formation of public opinion as purely quantifiable and largely predictable elite-group or mass phenomena. He argued that these scholarly and teaching fashions not only undermined the already precarious respect for political debate and public-spirited leadership, but also falsified the empirical data, the reality of man as the political animal.

Still, in trying to keep glowing the embers of the older republican citizenship and statecraft, Strauss did not succumb to any kind of nostalgic longing for the polis and its *"vita activa,"* its "public space," or sense of community. In this Strauss differed sharply, not only from other philhellenic critics of liberal democracy like Hannah Arendt, but also from Machiavelli, Rousseau, Nietzsche, and other radical modern thinkers. Strauss's overriding allegiance was to Socratic philosophy, not to the classical city or even to classical art. Strauss was too deeply penetrated by Thucydides' dissection of all that is implied in the immoderation of Pericles' funeral oration to be able to celebrate the splendors of imperialistic Athens.

Partly as a result, it was not Strauss's habit to speak contemptuously of "bourgeois" individualism, or to spurn with ingratitude the unprecedented humanity, compassion, social welfare, and protection for diversity brought by the modern commercial republic. Strauss saw perhaps more clearly than anyone the disharmony in the American tradition between an older, nobler, but less influential classical or civic ideal and a new, ever more triumphant, permissive and individualistic order. But precisely for this reason he saw more clearly both the distinct virtues and the distinct vices of each component of the uneasy combination.

In particular, Strauss admired the tolerance and respect for personal liberty that are the hallmarks of liberalism, not only because they provide a haven for persecuted philosophy, but also because they allow, if they do not encourage, the emergence of invigorating political disputation that can sometimes extend far beyond current events and controversies. There is then room within liberalism of the modern sort for liberalism of the original or ancient sort. Strauss even found in modern liberalism a native place for the highest ingredient of that older liberalism—the liberalism that consists in liberation of the mind through study and debate of the alternative visions of human excellence developed in the great books. In the liberal university at its best the ancient idea of liberal education continues to shine as the crown jewel of modern liberalism—so long, that is, as the university resists the distorting pressures of democratic society's ceaseless demands for relevance, service to society, and the endorsement of current moral crusades and dogmas.

This threat to the idea of the liberal university is endemic, Strauss argued, because it is only the most acute manifestation of a threat to authentic freedom of the mind that everywhere haunts the steps of modern liberalism: the grave fact is, the very openness of the open society contains within itself a self-destructive germ. This disease to which Strauss pointed is not the one liberals see readily and often resist nobly—the persistence and frequent resurgence of unofficial persecution and discrimination. More insidious and hence more corrosive is the tendency of democratic tolerance to degenerate, first into the easygoing belief that all points of view are equal (hence none really worth passionate argument, deep analysis, or stalwart defense) and then into the strident belief that anyone who argues for the superiority of a distinctive moral insight, way of life, or human type is somehow elitist or antidemocratic—and hence immoral. This is the syndrome that Tocqueville characterized, in an earlier manifestation, as the new, soft, "tyranny of the majority": a subtle, unorganized, but all-pervasive pressure for egalitarian conformity arising from the psychologically chastened and intimidated individual's incapacity to resist the moral authority of mass "public opinion." In its most sublime expression, equality promises to every human being the opportunity to ascend to a just rank in the natural hierarchy of talents and attainments, of virtue and wisdom; but especially under the poisonous influence of the levelling moralism that disguises itself as relativism, equality all too easily degrades itself. Moreover, the problem is not alleviated, it is in fact aggravated, by the thoughtless lurch away from relativism; for contemporary democratic moralism in its overt forms, especially in its communitarian forms, tends to overstress the virtues of a rather soft or flaccid sociability:

> There exists a very dangerous tendency to identify the good man with the good sport, the cooperative fellow, the "regular guy," i.e., an overemphasis on a certain part of social virtue and a corresponding neglect of those virtues which mature, if they do not flourish, in privacy, not to say in solitude: by educating people to cooperate with each other in a friendly spirit, one does not yet educate nonconformists, people who are prepared to stand alone, to fight alone. . . . Democracy has not yet found a defense against the creeping conformism and the ever-increasing invasion of privacy which it fosters. (*What Is Political Philosophy?* p. 38)

There is, in Strauss's judgment, only one adequate response: "Liberal education is the counterpoison to mass culture . . . the ladder by which we try to ascend from mass democracy to democracy as originally meant"—i.e., "an aristocracy which has broadened into a universal aristocracy" (*Liberalism Ancient and Modern*, pp. 4–5). Strauss held out no expectation that such a society could be achieved, and he in fact insisted that one not entertain distorting illusions and hopes as to its achievement; but he contended that small steps in its direction could be taken, and that to take such steps was the highest calling of liberal democracy. Yet, to repeat, Strauss never tired of stressing the importance of distinguishing, especially in politics, between what is highest and what is most urgent; and what is most urgent as regards liberal democracy is not its improvement but its defense. In our aspirations to improve liberalism, Strauss argued, we must not lose our appreciation for the precious prosperity, humanity, and freedom we already possess.

The preceding reflections are not meant to be an adequate explanation, or even summation, of Strauss; in the pages that follow one will not find a thought that is easily summarized, or explained, or categorized. I venture to make this suggestion: that the reader now try to lay aside preconceptions, to suspend at least for a time the desire to categorize the thinker whose thoughts are here introduced—that the reader accept, in good will, an invitation to a feast of thinking and arguing.

The Present Volume

This book is an introduction to the philosophy of Leo Strauss in his own words, though not by his own intention. The selection, arrangement, and editing of the writings here assembled are entirely my responsibility and doing. Since Strauss left behind a rather large body of published writings, which presumably convey his thought more or less exactly as he intended it to be conveyed, the present enterprise may well appear questionable. To say the least, it is incumbent upon me to warn the reader at the outset that this book is not a book intended by Strauss, and it should therefore be taken as only a first introduction to his thought. Such an introduction—an inducement to further reading—is indeed my aim. My purpose will have been defeated if this book substitutes for Strauss's authentic books, or if this book does not induce its readers to ascend from it to Strauss's authentic books.

To be sure, a substantial portion of the writings here assembled (chapters 1, 2, 4, 5, and 10) have been previously published—some by Strauss himself (chapters 1, 2, and 4) and some under the aegis of his literary executor, Joseph Cropsey (chapters 5 and 10), who has given his sanction to the present collection. One of my subordinate aims has been to make more readily available these already published writings, which have been for the most part tucked away in rather obscure learned journals. The chapters made up of materials that have not been previously published comprise slightly edited versions of lectures Strauss delivered on various occasions. These lectures are characterized by an informality or directness that seems to me to make them especially appropriate as introductions. Moreover, these lectures do not simply foreshadow or recapitulate what is to be found in Strauss's publications. In selecting these particular lectures from the many that Strauss left behind, I sought to bring together, not only what seemed appropriate as an introduction, but also what seemed to contribute substantially to our understanding of Strauss's thought and the themes with which he was preoccupied. I would therefore justify this book on three grounds: it puts in print otherwise unavailable and important material; it makes conveniently accessible published writings that were previously difficult of access; and, above all, it affords an avenue or approach to Strauss's books by way of lectures Strauss himself gave.

I have divided this book into three parts. In the first I have assembled writings which convey Strauss's view of the spiritual crisis of our times, the crisis of modern rationalism that spurred Strauss to a fresh examination of the alternative, Socratic, or classical, political rationalism. Chapter 1 is a paper Strauss delivered at a conference on the state of the social sciences.[12] Strauss here concisely presents his vision of a humane social science, his conception of the civic duty and role of the practitioner of such a social science, and what he sees as the massive contemporary obstacle to such a humane and civic spirit in the social sciences. This massive obstacle is moral relativism. Moral relativism comes in many versions, ranging from the less to the more thoughtful and hence truly challenging or troubling. The second half of the first chapter and the succeeding two chapters ascend through confrontations with increasingly serious and rigorous philosophic relativists. In the latter half of chapter 1, Strauss tries to draw out the inhuman consequences and the logical absurdity of unqualified relativism; the chapter closes by raising the question whether a qualified relativism may not be a tenable middle ground between strict relativism and absolutism.

In chapter 2, which reproduces a substantial portion of a previously published essay,[13] Strauss begins to answer that question. He begins with a critique of Isaiah Berlin's famous "Two Concepts of Liberty." Strauss finds in Berlin's essay a well-articulated, and hence especially revealing, version of the kind of relativism that is most widespread among intelligent Anglo-American liberals. Having pointed out the appealing strengths, and yet the decisive flaws, in Berlin's attempt to defend liberalism, Strauss declares the essay to be "a characteristic document of the crisis of liberalism— of the fact that liberalism has abandoned its absolutist basis and is trying to become entirely relativistic." Berlin's essay is meant to stand the test of time, and it is so treated by Strauss; but at the time it was written the essay was also—and was also meant to be—one of the most important attempts at a defensible philosophic statement of the liberal anticommunist position in the midst of the Cold War. Strauss therefore turns from his diagnosis of the inadequacies of Berlin's argument to a brief confrontation with Georg Lukács, the thinker who represented for Strauss the most powerful Marxist critic of liberalism and liberal relativism. In the course of Strauss's argument with Lukács, it becomes clear that in

Strauss's judgment the deepest philosophic source of relativism is one version or another of "historicism," including contemporary Marxist historicism. "Historicism" is the embracing term for the various and diverse doctrines which have in common the teaching that humanity lacks a fixed nature and hence any universal or permanent norms. According to historicism, mankind, in the most important respects and in regard to its deepest needs and highest norms, changes and differs fundamentally from one historical epoch or culture to another. According to the most radical (existentialist) historicism, there is no objective truth, even in the sciences, and human consciousness at every level is in the final analysis embedded in and determined by an elusive, changing, and uncanny historical fate: every thinker, even the greatest, is a child of his times. At the end of the second chapter Strauss begins to indicate the power of radical historicism by showing that liberalism, Marxism, and positivism or contemporary philosophy of science are all unable to refute, or even avoid a steady slippage toward, radical historicism.

Chapter 3 is meant to convey at least the introductory outlines of Strauss's lifelong grappling with the awesome challenge of Martin Heidegger—in Strauss's eyes the greatest thinker of the twentieth century and the most powerful advocate of a truly radical historicism and relativism. The first three-quarters of this chapter derives chiefly from a typescript, apparently made by students from a recording, of a lecture Strauss delivered at the University of Chicago in the fifties—a lecture entitled "Introduction to Existentialism." The original typescript is in a few places garbled or uncertain, and I was compelled to omit several sentences and to edit for smoothness. I was aided by some corrections Strauss made on a copy that is lodged in the Strauss archives at the University of Chicago Library. I took the further liberty of adding a three-paragraph elaboration of Strauss's discussion of Heidegger's understanding of *Sein*, or *Being*, an elaboration that is to be found in a fragmentary typescript of a lecture by Strauss entitled "The Problem of Socrates."

Part 2 is meant to introduce Strauss's conception of classical political rationalism. At the heart of that rationalism stands Socrates, together with the political philosophizing he began—and which he may have brought to a kind of perfection. Strauss viewed Socrates in the light of Socrates' response to pre-Socratic philosophic and poetic thinking, as well as in the light of the Platonic, Xenophontic, and Aristotelian continuations of his political philosophizing. Strauss approached Socratic rationalism in a serious but testing or experimental spirit, passionately drawn to it in part because of its manifest human wisdom and in part because of the spiritual crisis of modern rationalism, sketched in part 1. As the discussion of Heidegger in chapter 3 shows, the contemporary crisis culminates in the severest doubts as to whether reason is adequate to, or appropriate for, the uncovering of the deepest and most important truths about the human condition. The crisis of modern rationalism reopens, to a degree unknown for centuries, the challenge to reason and science from revelation or divine inspiration. Strauss's investigation of classical rationalism is therefore especially attentive to the question of how Socrates, and the other classical rationalists from whom Socrates learned and whom he taught, dealt with the problem of the meaning and the place of the divine in human life.

Chapter 4, the first chapter of part 2, is a reprint of the general introduction to classical political philosophy that Strauss published as chapter 3 of *What Is Political Philosophy?* [14] This essay, with its numerous and wide-ranging textual references to the major works of the Greco-Roman tradition of political philosophy, affords the reader a kind of synoptic orientation for the more particular studies that follow. The chapter leads up to a preliminary discussion of the dangerous tension between philosophy, or the inevitable radicalism of philosophic questioning, and healthy civil society, with its need for authoritative moral opinions and sturdy loyalty to those opinions. Because classical rationalism is so acutely aware of the morally and politically problematic status of reason or rationalism, the study of communication or rhetoric is at the very heart of classical political rationalism.

Chapter 5 presents Strauss's introduction to the classical teaching on communication, especially philosophic dialectic or rhetoric. [15] Strauss himself was introduced to the buried or forgotten classical understanding of the problem of communication in part through the writings of Lessing, the great eighteenth-century German philosopher, dramatist, and art critic. Strauss's essay accordingly moves from Lessing to the ancient authors, especially Plato, whom Lessing interpreted in terms of what he called "exoteric teaching." Here Strauss's critique of the inadequacy and narrowness of the fundamental presuppositions of contemporary classical scholarship becomes explicit.

On the basis of the preceding general discussions of the substance and the manner of classical political philosophizing, we turn in chapter 6 to a lecture Strauss delivered on the greatest pre-Socratic political theorist, Thucydides. The discussion is explicitly introduced by a reflection on the danger involved in rushing back to antiquity, in flight from the contemporary crisis of modern rationalism, and with the hope of finding an unproblematic alternative rationalism. The philosophic superiority of classical antiquity consists, not in its freedom from problems, but in its penetrating awareness of the permanent problems, above all the permanently problematic character of reason. What is more, Strauss here stresses that for us today the claims of Socratic political philosophy must be examined critically in the light of our awareness of the competing claims of Biblical revelation: "We must be aware of the fact that the vitality and the glory of our Western tradition are inseparable from its problematic character. For that tradition has two roots. . . . We speak, and we speak rightly, of the antagonism between Jerusalem and Athens, between faith and philosophy."

But, strictly speaking, Greekness, and even Athenian Greekness, can certainly not be simply identified with rationalism: as we learn with especial poignancy from the pages of Thucydides, the Athenians were an extremely pious, sometimes even fanatically pious, people. Even or above all in Athens, the classical rationalists had to face what we would call "the religious question." And the classical rationalists were not obviously unified or agreed on the manner in which this question ought to be faced or comprehended. Socratic political philosophy is not the only manifestation of classical political rationalism; it finds a great rival, if a friendly rival, in Thucydidean political rationalism, the rationalism of the political historian: "Political history is as characteristic of the Western tradition as philosophy or science, on the one hand, and belief in revelation, on the other." And, "as the very terms politics and history show, political history is of Greek, not of Hebrew, origin." What is the meaning of political history in its original, pre-Socratic, but rationalist, sense? What is the key difference between the craft of the historian or political historian in our time and Thucydides' spiritually more ambitious conception of the task of political history? How does Thucydides conceive his relation to the poets, whose access to the muses made them the recognized spiritual authorities of Greece? What, according to Thucydides, is the relation between, and the relative ranking of, the activity of the political historian and the activity of the gifted statesman like Pericles? The attempt to shed light on these questions, i.e., on the original or classical meaning of political history, is the leading theme of

Strauss's lecture, which culminates in a provisional contrast between Thucydidean and Socratic political rationalism. I would like to emphasize the word "provisional" in the preceding sentence. The conclusion of this chapter especially, it seems to me, represents a statement which must be supplemented and even corrected in the light of Strauss's later, mature, published comparisons between Thucydidean and Socratic political rationalism.[16]

The lecture on Thucydides, which treats Thucydides in the light of the dialogue between faith and reason and raises the question of the nature of the revolution in thought effected by Socrates, sets the stage for the core of the book, chapter 7. This chapter comprises five of six lectures Strauss delivered in 1958 at the University of Chicago entitled "The Problem of Socrates." I have omitted the first lecture because it seems to me that most of its ideas have already been presented in the earlier chapters here assembled. The lectures as presented here begin with an examination of what Strauss regarded as the most direct, the most intelligent, the deepest, and the wittiest criticism of Socrates and Socratic rationalism ever written: the comedies of Aristophanes. Strauss moves from this attack, and in the light of this attack, to the presentations of Socrates and the Socratic way of life in Xenophon and Plato. Strauss argues that the works of Xenophon and Plato, centered on the dramatic portrayal of the Socratic way of life, must be understood as in some large measure responses to the great dramatic critique by Aristophanes. At issue is the contest between poetry at its wisest and philosophy at its humanly wisest: each contends that it possesses the fullest understanding of the human soul and hence the most correct assessment of the best way of life and of the relative ranking of the major alternative ways of life. The critical test, agreed to by each side, is the understanding of justice, divinity, and love. It is Strauss's goal to introduce us to this intense erotic dispute. Throughout these lectures, but especially in the discussion of the intellectual genius of Xenophon, Strauss accuses contemporary classical scholarship of overlooking or distorting the authentic philosophic drama and message found in the great texts committed by fate to the custodial care of our philologists.

We are ushered into Part 3 with a lecture Strauss delivered on Plato's dialogue *Euthyphron*, a dialogue whose theme is the moral and intellectual virtue of piety. The *Euthyphron* is a comic work; as Strauss emphasizes, it cannot possibly be regarded as Plato's last word on piety or divinity. The clearest sign of this is the fact that the dialogue never discusses, indeed conspicuously omits to men-

tion, the soul. But the *Euthyphron* is, let us say, Plato's first word
on piety and divinity. As such, and very characteristically, the dialogue raises some probing and discomfiting questions about piety,
or about the life suffused and sustained by piety. These questions
lead us into the heart of part 3, which consists of lectures in which
Strauss pursues thematically the fundamental question adum-
brated several times previously in this book: the debate or dialogue
between classical rationalism and Biblical revelation. This dispute,
which I believe Strauss regarded as perhaps the highest theme of
human self-consciousness, is today largely a matter of dim memory. It was Strauss's passionate aspiration to bring back to life this
high form of human life. Hence a book attempting to introduce
Strauss naturally culminates in an introduction to this dialogue.

There is a simple reason, or half-reason, why modern Western
man has forgotten the supreme intellectual challenge that absorbed his greatest ancestors: modern man has forgotten the supreme achievement of the Middle Ages. Oh, yes, in our time there
appear occasional historical novels and movies, usually dwelling
on the grotesque features of the Middle Ages; there is what is
called "appreciation" of the magnificent art of the Middle Ages;
there are in the universities history courses about the Middle
Ages, and, scattered here and there, a few Thomists nobly attempting to keep alive a great, but dying, intellectual tradition. But
since the twilight fell over romanticism, almost no one has seriously suggested that the answers to the most agonizing human
questions might be found in the Middle Ages, that is, in the
thought of the Middle Ages. But this is what Strauss suggested,
and without a trace of romanticism. The Middle Ages are today
generally regarded—and not without some considerable justification, to be sure—as the Dark Ages. But Strauss insisted that one
small corner, if you will, of the medieval experience reached a peak
of rational illumination that has not been rivalled since. That corner is medieval political philosophy, especially in the Muslim
world. Medieval political philosophy was devoted, with a kind of
uncanny intensity—in the spirit of a club of geniuses who goad
one another higher and higher up a path of argument—to meditation on the argument between classical rationalism and Biblical
revelation. One has only to hear the titles of the great works to get
a whiff of the passion, the daring, the ambition, that fueled the
debates of those forgotten thinkers: *The Decisive Treatise* (Averroës);
The Attainment of Happiness (Alfarabi); *The Healing: or the Sufficiency*
(Avicenna); *The Incoherence of the Philosophers* (Algazel); *The Incoher-*

ence of the "The Incoherence" (reply to Algazel, by Averroës); *The Book of Roots* (Albo); *The Guide of the Perplexed* (Maimonides). Chapter 9 of the present work is an introduction to this forgotten world of medieval, and especially Muslim and Jewish, political philosophy, by way of a lecture Strauss delivered in 1944. The decisive superiority of medieval to modern philosophy is articulated by Strauss in the following terms:

> One may say that the Platonic dialogues serve no more obvious purpose than precisely this one: to answer the question, Why philosophy? or, Why science? by justifying philosophy or science before the tribunal of the city, the political community. In fundamentally the same way, our medieval philosophers are compelled to raise the question, Why philosophy? or, Why science? by justifying philosophy or science before the tribunal of the law, or the Torah. This most fundamental question of philosophy, the question of its own legitimacy and necessity, is no longer a question for modern philosophy. Modern philosophy was from its beginning the attempt to replace the allegedly wrong philosophy or science of the Middle Ages by the allegedly true philosophy or science. It did not raise any longer the question of the necessity of philosophy or science itself; it took that necessity for granted. This fact alone can assure us, from the outset, that medieval philosophy is distinguished by a philosophic radicalism which is absent from modern philosophy, or that it is, in this most important respect, superior to modern philosophy.

The final chapter comprises a small portion of one lecture and almost all of two others Strauss originally delivered as a three-lecture series at the Hillel House of the University of Chicago in the fifties.[17] In these lectures, Strauss tries to set in motion again, in our time and with a view to our time, the meditation on the antagonism between Biblical faith and classical rationalism. Strauss approaches the great debate by way of the new questions and new perspective introduced by modern rationalism or the Enlightenment, and above all by Spinoza. The quarrel between reason and faith today comes to sight as a quarrel between the belief in "progress," on the one hand, and the call for "return" on the other.

> Return is the translation for the Hebrew word *t'shuvah. T'shuvah* has an ordinary and an emphatic meaning. Its emphatic meaning is rendered in English by "repentance." Repentance

is return, meaning the return from the wrong way to the right one. . . . Man is originally at home in his Father's house. He becomes a stranger through estrangement, through sinful estrangement. Repentance, return, is homecoming.

The belief in progress, progressivism, sums up modern rationalism. "The contemporary crisis of Western civilization may be said to be identical with the climactic crisis of the idea of progress in the full and emphatic sense of the term."

Strauss himself was in his youth a progressive: he began as an adherent, if a doubting adherent, of the neo-Kantian philosophy taught by the philosophic leader of German Judaism, Hermann Cohen. For Cohen, following with some modifications Kant, progress was not a matter of mere belief or hope or faith; it was a postulate of practical reason; it was an article of *rational* belief or of "the religion of reason," of "religion within the limits of reason alone." For the Marburg neo-Kantians progress had, within the moral realm, something like the status of the postulates of mathematics within the realm of natural science: the objective validity of the idea of progress was affirmed by the explanatory power of the system of concepts and laws—the moral, social, and political science—in which it issued. Progress was conceived of as an essential part of the rationalism which alone could make sense of human dignity and happiness, the rationalism that could and must withstand the most severe critical scrutiny by reason. In the last book he wrote, Strauss offered a final judgment on this great guide of his youth:

Cohen's thought belongs to the world preceding World War I. . . . The worst things that he experienced were the Dreyfus scandal and the pogroms instigated by Czarist Russia: he did not experience Communist Russia and Hitler Germany. . . . Catastrophes and horrors of a magnitude hitherto unknown, which we have seen and through which we have lived, were better provided for, or made intelligible, by both Plato and the prophets than by the modern belief in progress. (*Studies in Platonic Political Philosophy,* p. 168)

In the lecture printed here Strauss adds the following "massive" consideration, "perhaps the most massive one":

The idea of progress was bound up with the notion of the conquest of nature, of man making himself the master and owner of nature. . . . The means for that goal was the new science. We all know of the enormous successes of the new science and of technology which is based on it, and we all can witness the enormous increase of man's power. Modern man is a giant in comparison to earlier man. But we have also to note that there is no corresponding increase in wisdom and goodness. Modern man is a giant of whom we do not know whether he is better or worse than earlier man. More than that, this development of modern science culminated in the view that man is not able to distinguish in a responsible manner between good and evil—the famous "value judgment." Modern man is a blind giant. The doubt of progress led to a crisis of Western civilization as a whole, because in the course of the nineteenth century the old distinction between good and bad, or good and evil, had been progressively replaced by the distinction between progressive and reactionary. No simple, inflexible, eternal distinction between good and bad could give assurance to those who had learned to take their bearings only by the distinction between progressive and reactionary, as soon as these people had become doubtful of progress.

Today no thoughtful person can share Hermann Cohen's Kantian belief in the rational or scientific status of progress. Progress, or progressivism, has become a value judgment, a subjective commitment, a hope against hope, a matter of pure faith. But this means that what was once the core of modern rationalism has degenerated into a modern irrationalism of unprecedented degree. For this new religion or faith is in the crucial respect more contradictory and incoherent, i.e., more irrational, than any merely non- or anti- or supra-rational faith that has come before: the new faith is a rationally unjustifiable faith in principles that were supposed to supplant all faith that was rationally unjustifiable. Moreover, comparing this new faith with traditional faith, one is compelled to ask: Where is its ground? From what source does it get its inspiration? Where are its texts that give rich evidence of truth or insight? In short, how is it distinguishable from the most self-deluded longings of people who are too soft spiritually to face life for what it is?

Are we then left with a choice between the pathetically unfounded, progressive hopes of the relic of modern rationalism or the abandonment of any hope for progress, the surrender to tradition or the past? Strauss denies this dichotomy.

In the first place, Biblical religion, insofar as it is a messianic faith, is a kind of faith in progress—though not in a progress through man's unaided efforts, and not in a progress away from, or in opposition to, the Biblical past. Return in the emphatic sense may be the precondition for true progress; human reverence and humility may be the precondition for the discovery of true human dignity; a certain sense of homelessness may be the precondition for true homecoming. "I share the hope in America and the faith in America, but I am compelled to add that that faith and that hope cannot be of the same character as that faith and that hope which a Jew has in regard to Judaism and which the Christian has in regard to Christianity" (chap. 10, below).

In the second place, Plato "held that the fulfillment proper, namely full wisdom, is not possible, but only the quest for wisdom, which in Greek means philosophy. He also insisted that there are no assignable limits to that quest for wisdom, and therefore . . . that indefinite progress is possible in principle" (chap. 10). Yet Plato, like all the Socratics, was too keenly aware of the dangerous or problematic character of reason to suppose that intellectual progress necessarily implied or was accompanied by moral or social progress. Furthermore, Plato was inclined to the view that "the visible universe is of finite duration; it has come into being and it will perish again." And Aristotle, who taught the eternity of the visible order, taught also the eternal recurrence of catastrophes that had before and would always again wipe out human civilization and all its records.

From all this Strauss drew, in the name of classical rationalism, this momentous lesson: a human being cannot escape or compensate for his mortal limits by looking for solace to the collective efforts of mankind. A human being can only come to terms with his mortal limits, and he can do this only by trying to progress in understanding those limits and their necessity or permanence.

Yet, to repeat, the specific sort of commitment to progress in rational understanding that is central to classical rationalism is a commitment accompanied by a pervasive awareness of the problematic or challengeable character of reason. The possibility of progress in the classical sense is rooted in the awareness of the unfulfilled or incomplete character of human wisdom. It is therefore a commitment to a progress that must always return: "Because of the elusiveness of the whole, the beginning or the questions retain a greater evidence than the end or the answers; return to the beginning remains a constant necessity" (*The City and Man*, p. 21).

For the Socratic in our time, this return comprises two especially noteworthy dimensions. The return must be a return to a sympathetic dialogue with Biblical faith; and it must be a return from contempt for the senility of modern rationalism to respectful argument with its vigorous youth. For Strauss did not assume that the decay of rationalism in the nineteenth century was a necessary decay, or that modern rationalism necessarily entailed the ultimately irrational progressivism of the nineteenth and twentieth centuries. In the nineteenth century philosophers began to speak of a scientific or rational point of view from which the "realm of necessity" could be said to be abolishable in the name of the "realm of freedom." Against this view, which is Marxist but by no means solely Marxist, Strauss appeals in chapter 2 of the present collection to Machiavelli, the clear-eyed founder of modern rationalism. Strauss published his first book on Socrates only when he was in his sixties: only after he had written such works as *Spinoza's Critique of Religion*, *The Political Philosophy of Hobbes*, *Natural Right and History*, and *Thoughts on Machiavelli*. Strauss's revival of classical political rationalism was rooted in a decades-long, and always unfinished, sympathetic encounter with the great modern political philosophers. For we are all moderns; or, as Strauss said in a book published the year before he died, "we are all beginners" (*Xenophon's Socrates*, p. 3). "The wisdom which takes a serious interest in politics must then be the wisdom of men who are, or who have remained, children—in a way. The wise men of Greece were such men. An Egyptian priest said to a Greek: 'You Greeks are always children; you are young in soul, every one of you; for therein you possess not a single belief that is ancient and derived from old tradition, nor yet a single piece of learning that is hoary with age' (Plato *Timaeus* 22b)." The rebirth of classical rationalism cannot be the rebirth of a tradition without becoming self-defeating. The rebirth of classical rationalism requires a continuing return from, and on the basis of, that rationalism to a dialogue with its antagonists. Thus Strauss carried on the dialectic of Maimonides: that philosopher who, in Strauss's judgment, criticized most deeply, and therefore harvested most richly, classical rationalism.

Part I
The Spiritual Crisis of
Modern Rationalism

1
Social Science and Humanism

Humanism is today understood in contradistinction to science, on the one hand, and to the civic art, on the other. It is thus suggested to us that the social sciences are shaped by science, the civic art, and humanism, or that the social sciences dwell in the region where science, the civic art, and humanism meet and perhaps toward which they converge. Let us consider how this meeting might be understood.

Of the three elements mentioned, only science and humanism can be said to be at home in academic life. Science and humanism are not always on friendly terms. We all know the scientist who despises or ignores humanism, and the humanist who despises or ignores science. To understand this conflict, tension, or distinction between science and humanism, we do well to turn for a moment to the seventeenth century, to the age in which modern science constituted itself. At that time Pascal contrasted the spirit of geometry (i.e., the scientific spirit) with the spirit of *finesse*. We may circumscribe the meaning of the French term by referring to terms such as these: subtlety, refinement, tact, delicacy, perceptivity. The scientific spirit is characterized by detachment and by the forcefulness which stems from simplicity or simplification. The spirit of finesse is characterized by attachment or love and by breadth. The principles to which the scientific spirit defers are alien to common sense. The principles with which the spirit of finesse has to do are within common sense, yet they are barely visible; they are felt rather than seen. They are not available in such a way that we could make them the premises of our reasoning. The spirit of finesse is active, not in reasoning, but rather in grasping in one view unanalyzed wholes in their distinctive characters. What is meant today by the contrast between science and humanism represents a more or less profound modification of Pascal's contrast between the spirit of geometry and the spirit of finesse. In both cases the contrast implies that, in regard to the understanding of human things, the spirit of science has severe limitations—limitations which are overcome by a decidedly nonscientific approach.

What are these limitations as we observe them today within the social sciences? Social science consists of a number of disciplines which are specialized and which are becoming ever more specialized. There is certainly no social science in existence which could claim that it studies society as a whole, social man as a whole, or such wholes as we have in mind when we speak, for example, of this country, the United States of America. De Tocqueville and Lord Bryce are not representative of present-day social science. From time to time one or the other special and specialized science (e.g., psychology or sociology) raises the claim to be comprehensive or fundamental; but these claims always meet strong and justified resistance. Cooperation of the various disciplines may enlarge the horizon of the cooperating individuals; it cannot unify the disciplines themselves; it cannot bring about a true hierarchic order.

Specialization may be said to originate ultimately in this premise: In order to understand a whole, one must analyze or resolve it into its elements, one must study the elements by themselves, and then one must reconstruct the whole or recompose it by starting from the elements. Reconstruction requires that the whole be sufficiently grasped in advance, prior to the analysis. If the primary grasp lacks definiteness and breadth, both the analysis and the synthesis will be guided by a distorted view of the whole, by a figment of a poor imagination rather than by the thing in its fullness. And the elements at which the analysis arrives will at best be only some of the elements. The sovereign rule of specialization means that the reconstruction cannot even be attempted. The reason for the impossibility of reconstruction can be stated as follows: the whole as primarily known is an object of common sense; but it is of the essence of the scientific spirit, at least as this spirit shows itself within the social sciences, to be distrustful of common sense or even to discard it altogether. The commonsense understanding expresses itself in common language; the scientific social scientist creates or fabricates a special scientific terminology. Thus scientific social science acquires a specific abstractness. There is nothing wrong with abstraction, but there is very much wrong with abstracting from essentials. Social science, to the extent to which it is emphatically scientific, abstracts from essential elements of social reality. I quote from a private communication by a philosophically sophisticated sociologist who is very favorably disposed toward the scientific approach in the social sciences: "What the sociologist calls 'system,' 'role,' 'status,' 'role expectation,' 'situation,' and 'institutionalization' is experienced by the individual actor on the social scene in entirely different terms." This is not merely to say that the citizen and the social scientist mean the same things but express them in different terms. For "the social scientist qua theoretician has to follow a system of relevances entirely different from that of the actor on the social scene. . . . His problems originate in his theoretical interest, and many elements of the social world that are scientifically relevant are irrelevant from the point of view of the actor on the social scene, and vice versa." The scientific social scientist is concerned with regularities of behavior; the citizen is concerned with good government. The relevances for the citizen are values, values believed in and cherished, nay, values which are experienced as real qualities of real things: of man, of actions and thought, of institutions, of measures. But the scientific social scientist draws a sharp line between values and facts: he regards himself as unable to pass any value judgments.

To counteract the dangers inherent in specialization, as far as these dangers can be counteracted within the social sciences, a conscious return to commonsense thinking is needed—a return to the perspective of the citizen. We must identify the whole, in reference to which we should select themes of research and integrate results of research, with the overall objectives of whole societies. By doing this, we will understand social reality as it is understood in social life by thoughtful and broadminded men. In other words, the true matrix of social science is the civic art and not a general notion of science or scientific method. Social science must either be a mere handmaid of the civic art—in this case no great harm is done if it forgets the wood for the trees—or, if it does not want to become or to remain oblivious of the noble tradition from which it sprang, if it believes that it might be able to enlighten the civic art, it must indeed look farther afield than the civic art, but it must look in the same direction as the civic art. Its relevances must become identical, at least at the outset, with those of the citizen or statesman; and therefore it must speak, or learn to speak, the language of the citizen and of the statesman.

From this point of view, the guiding theme of social science in this age and in this country will be democracy, or, more precisely, liberal democracy, especially in its American form. Liberal democracy will be studied with constant regard to the coactual or co-potential alternatives and therefore especially to communism. The issue posed by communism will be faced by a conscientious, serious, and relentless critique of communism. At the same time, the dangers inherent in liberal democracy will be set forth squarely; for the friend of liberal democracy is not its flatterer. The sensitivity to these dangers will be sharpened and, if need be, awakened. From the scientistic point of view, the politically neutral—that which is common to all societies—must be looked upon as the clue to the politically relevant—that which is distinctive of the various regimes. But from the opposite point of view which I am trying to adumbrate, the emphasis is put on the politically relevant: the burning issues.

Social science cannot then rest satisfied with the overall objectives of whole societies as they are for the most part understood in social life. Social science must clarify those objectives, ferret out their self-contradictions and halfheartednesses, and strive for knowledge of the true overall objectives of whole societies. That is to say, the only alternative to an ever more specialized, an ever more aimless, social science is a social science ruled by the legitimate queen of the social sciences—the pursuit traditionally known by the name of ethics. Even today it is difficult, in dealing with social matters, consistently to avoid terms like "a man of character," "honesty," "loyalty," "citizenship education," etc.

This, or something like this, is, I believe, what many people have in mind when speaking of a humanistic approach, as distinguished from the scientistic approach, to social phenomena. We must still account for the term "humanism." The social scientist is a student of human societies, of societies of humans. If he wishes to be loyal to his task, he must never forget that he is dealing with human things, with human beings. He must reflect on the human as human. And he must pay due attention to the fact that he himself is a human being and that social science is always a kind of self-knowledge. Social science, being the pursuit of human knowledge of human things, includes as its foundation the human knowledge of what constitutes humanity, or, rather, of what makes man complete or whole, so that he is truly human. Aristotle calls his equivalent of what now would be called social science the liberal inquiry regarding the human things, and his *Ethics* is the first, the fundamental, and the directive part of that inquiry.

But, if we understand by social science the knowledge of human things, are we not driven to the conclusion that the time-honored distinction between social science and the humanities must be abandoned? Perhaps we must follow Aristotle a step further and make a distinction between the life of society and the life of the mind, and hence assign the study of the former to social science and the study of the latter, or a certain kind of study of the latter, to the humanities.

There is, finally, another implication of the term "humanism"—viz., the contradistinction of human studies to divinity. Provisionally I limit myself to the remark that humanism may be said to imply that the moral principles are more knowable to man, or less controversial among earnest men, than theological principles.

By reflecting on what it means to be a human being, one sharpens one's awareness of what is common to all human beings, if in different degrees, and of the goals toward which all human beings are directed by the fact that they are human beings. One transcends the horizon of the mere citizen—of every kind of sectionalism—and becomes a citizen of the world. Humanism as awareness of man's distinctive character as well as of man's distinctive completion, purpose, or duty issues in humaneness: in the earnest concern for both human kindness and the betterment and opening of one's mind—a blend of firm delicacy and hard-won serenity—a last and not merely last freedom from the degradation or hardening effected especially by conceit or pretense. One is tempted to say that to be inhuman is the same as to be unteachable, to be unable or unwilling to listen to other human beings.

Yet, even if all were said that could be said and that cannot be said, humanism is not enough. Man, while being at least potentially a whole, is only a part of a larger whole. While forming a kind of world and even being a kind of world, man is only a little world, a microcosm. The macrocosm, the whole to which man belongs, is not human. That whole, or its origin, is either subhuman or superhuman. Man cannot be understood in his own light but only in the light of either the subhuman or the superhuman. Either man is an accidental product of a blind evolution or else the process leading to man, culminating in man, is directed toward man. Mere humanism avoids this ultimate issue. The human meaning of what we have come to call Science consists precisely in this—that the human or the higher is understood in the light of the subhuman or the lower. Mere humanism is powerless to withstand the onslaught of modern science. It is from this point that we can begin to understand again the original meaning of science, of which the contemporary meaning is only a modification: science as man's attempt to understand the whole to which he belongs. Social science, as the study of things human, cannot be based on modern science, although it may judiciously use, in a strictly subordinate fashion, both methods and results of modern science. Social science must rather be taken to contribute to the true universal science into which modern science will have to be integrated eventually.

To summarize: to treat social science in a humanistic spirit means to return from the abstractions or constructs of scientistic social science to social reality, to look at social phenomena primarily in the perspective of the citizen and the statesman, and then in the perspective of the citizen of the world, in the twofold meaning of "world": the whole human race and the all-embracing whole.

Humanism, as I have tried to present it, is in itself a moderate approach. But, looking around me, I find that it is here and now an extreme version of humanism. Some of you might think that it would be more proper to present the median or average opinion of present-day humanistic social scientists rather than an eccentric one. I feel this obligation, but I cannot comply with it because of the elusive character of that median opinion. I shall therefore describe the extreme opposite of the view which appeals to me, or, rather, one particular expression, which is as good as any other, of that opposite extreme. Median social science humanism can be defined sufficiently for our purpose by the remark that it is located somewhere between these two extremes.

The kind of humanism to which I now turn designates itself as relativistic. It may be called a humanism for two reasons. First, it holds that the social sciences cannot be modeled on the natural sciences, because the social sciences deal with man. Second, it is animated, as it were, by nothing except openness to everything that is human. According to this view, the methods of science, of natural science, are adequate to the study of phenomena to which we have access only by observing them from without and in detachment. But the social sciences deal with phenomena whose core is indeed inaccessible to detached observation but discloses itself, at least to some extent, to the scholar who relives or reenacts the life of the human beings whom he studies or who enters into the perspective of the actors and understands the life of the actors from their own point of view as distinguished from both his point of view and the point of view of the outside observer. Every perspective of active man is constituted by evaluation or is at any rate inseparable from it. Therefore, understanding from within means sharing in the acceptance of the values which are accepted by the societies or the individuals whom one studies, or accepting these values "histrionically" as the true values, or recognizing the position taken by the human beings under consideration as true. If one practices such understanding often and intensively enough, one realizes that perspectives or points of view cannot be criticized. All positions of this kind are equally true or untrue: true from within, untrue from without. Yet, while they cannot be criticized, they can be understood. However, I have as much right to my perspective as anyone else has to his or any society to its. And, every perspective being inseparable from evaluation, I, as an acting man and not as a mere social scientist, am compelled to criticize other perspectives and the values on which they are based or which they posit. We do not end then in moral nihilism, for our belief in our values gives us strength and direction. Nor do we end in a state of perpetual war of everybody against everybody, for we are permitted to "trust to reason and the council table for a peaceful coexistence."

Let us briefly examine this position, which at first glance recommends itself because of its apparent generosity and unbounded sympathy for every human position. Against a perhaps outdated version of relativism one might have argued as follows. Let us popularly define nihilism as the inability to take a stand for civilization against cannibalism. The relativist asserts that objectively civilization is not superior to cannibalism, for the case in favor of civilization can be matched by an equally strong or an equally weak case in favor of cannibalism. The fact that we are opposed to cannibalism is due entirely to our historical situation. But historical situations change necessarily into other historical situations. A historical situation productive of the belief in civilization may give way to a historical situation productive of belief in cannibalism. Since the relativist holds that civilization is not intrinsically superior to cannibalism, he will placidly accept the change of civilized society into cannibal society. Yet the relativism which I am now discussing denies that our values are simply determined by our historical situation: we can transcend our historical situation and enter into entirely different perspectives. In other words, there is no reason why, say, an Englishman should not become, in the decisive respect, a Japanese. Therefore, our believing in certain values cannot be traced beyond our decision or commitment. One might even say that, to the extent to which we are still able to reflect on the relation of our values to our situation, we are still trying to shirk the responsibility for our choice. Now, if we commit ourselves to the values of civilization, our very commitment enables and compels us to take a vigorous stand against cannibalism and prevents us from placidly accepting a change of our society in the direction of cannibalism.

To stand up for one's commitment means among other things to defend it against its opponents, not only by deed but by speech as well. Speech is required especially for fortifying those who waver in their commitments to the values we cherish. The waverers are not yet decided to which cause they should commit themselves, or they do not know whether they should commit themselves to civilization or to cannibalism. In speaking to them, we cannot assume the validity of the values of civilization. And, according to the premise, there is no way to convince them of the truth of those values. Hence the speech employed for buttressing the cause of civilization will be not rational discourse but mere "propaganda," a propaganda confronted by the equally legitimate and perhaps more effective propaganda in favor of cannibalism.

This notion of the human situation is said to be arrived at through the practice of sympathetic understanding. Only sympathetic understanding is said to make possible valid criticism of other points of view—a criticism which is based on nothing but our commitment and which therefore does not deny the right of our opponents to their commitments. Only sympathetic understanding, in other words, makes us truly understand the character of values and the manner in which they are legitimately adopted. But what is sympathetic understanding? Is it dependent on our own commitment, or is it independent of it? If it is independent, I am commited as an acting man, and I am uncommited in another compartment of myself, in my capacity as a social scientist. In that latter capacity I am, so to speak, completely empty and therefore completely open to the perception and appreciation of all commitments or value systems. I go through the process of sympathetic understanding in order to reach clarity about my commitment, and this process in no way endangers my commitment, for only a part of my self is engaged in my sympathetic understanding. This means, however, that such sympathetic understanding is not serious or genuine and is, indeed, as it calls itself, "histrionic." For genuinely to understand the value system, say, of a given society, means being deeply moved and indeed gripped by the values to which the society in question is committed and to expose one's self in earnest, with a view to one's own whole life, to the claim of those values to be the true values. Genuine understanding of other commitments is then not necessarily conducive to the reassertion of one's own initial commitment. Apart from this, it follows from the inevitable distinction between serious understanding and histrionic understanding that only my own commitment, my own "depth," can possibly disclose to me the commitment, the depth, of other human beings. Hence my perceptivity is necessarily limited by my commitment. Universal sympathetic understanding is impossible. To speak crudely, one cannot have the cake and eat it; one cannot enjoy both the advantages of universal understanding and those of existentialism.

But perhaps it is wrong to assume that all positions ultimately rest on commitments, or at any rate on commitments to specific points of view. We all remember the time when most men believed explicitly or implicitly that there is one and only one true value system of universal validity, and there are still societies and individuals who cling to this view. They too must be understood sympathetically. Would it not be harsh and even inconsistent to deprive the Bible and Plato of a privilege which is generously accorded to every savage tribe? And will sympathetic understanding of Plato not lead us to admit that absolutism is as true as relativism, or that Plato was as justified in simply condemning other value positions as the relativist is in never simply condemning any value position? To this our relativist will reply that, while Plato's value system is as defensible as any other, provided it is taken to have no other support than Plato's commitment, Plato's absolutist interpretation of his value system, as well as any other absolutism, has been refuted unqualifiedly, with finality, absolutely. This means, however, that Plato's view as he understood it, as it reveals itself to us if we enter sympathetically into his perspective, has been refuted: it has been seen to rest on untrue theoretical premises. So-called sympathetic understanding necessarily and legitimately ends when rational criticism reveals the untruth of the position which we are attempting to understand sympathetically; and the possibility of such rational criticism is necessarily admitted by relativism, since it claims to reject absolutism on rational grounds. The example of Plato is not an isolated one. Where in fact do we find, outside certain circles of present-day Western society, any value position which does not rest on theoretical premises of one kind or another—premises which claim to be simply, absolutely, universally true, and which as such are legitimately exposed to rational criticism? I fear that the field within which relativists can practice sympathetic understanding is restricted to the community of relativists who understand each other with great sympathy because they are united by identically the same fundamental commitment, or rather by identically the same rational insight into the truth of relativism. What claims to be the final triumph over provincialism reveals itself as the most amazing manifestation of provincialism.

There is a remarkable contrast between the apparent humility and the hidden arrogance of relativism. The relativist rejects the absolutism inherent in our great Western tradition—in its belief in the possibility of a rational and universal ethics or of natural right—with indignation or contempt; and he accuses that tradition of provincialism. His heart goes out to the simple preliterate people who cherish their values without raising exorbitant claims on their behalf. But these simple people do not practice histrionic or sympathetic understanding. Lacking such understanding, they do not adopt their values in the only legitimate manner, that is, as supported by nothing except their commitment. They sometimes reject Western values. Therewith they engage in invalid criticism, for valid criticism presupposes histrionic understanding. They are then provincial and narrow, as provincial and narrow as Plato and the Bible. The only people who are not provincial and narrow are the Western relativists and their Westernized followers in other cultures. They alone are right.

It almost goes without saying that relativism, if it were acted upon, would lead to complete chaos. For to say in the same breath that our sole protection against war between societies and within society is reason, and that according to reason "those individuals and societies who find it congenial to their systems of values to oppress and subjugate others" are as right as those who love peace and justice, means to appeal to reason in the very act of destroying reason.

Many humanistic social scientists are aware of the inadequacy of relativism, but they hesitate to turn to what is called "absolutism." They may be said to adhere to a qualified relativism. Whether this qualified relativism has a solid basis appears to me to be the most pressing question for social science today.

2
"Relativism"

"Relativism" has many meanings. In order not to become confused by the "blind scholastic pedantry" that exhausts itself and its audience in the "clarification of meanings" so that it never meets the nonverbal issues, I shall work my way into our subject by examining the recent statement of a famous contemporary about "the cardinal issue," the fundamental political problem of our time. As a fundamental problem it is theoretical; it is not the problem of particular policies, but the problem of the spirit that should inform particular policies. That problem is identified by Isaiah Berlin as the problem of freedom (*Two Concepts of Liberty* [Oxford, 1958], p. 51; cf. p. 4.).

Berlin distinguishes two senses of freedom, a negative and a positive sense. Used in the negative sense, in which it was used by "the classical English political philosophers" or "the fathers of liberalism," "freedom" means "freedom *from*": "Some portion of human existence must remain independent of social control"; "there ought to exist a certain minimum area of personal freedom which must on no account be violated" (ibid., pp. 8, 9, 11, 46). Positive freedom, on the other hand, is "freedom *to*": the freedom of the individual "to be his own master" or to participate in the social control to which he is subject (ibid., pp. 15, 16). This alternative regarding freedom overlaps another alternative: freedom for the empirical self or freedom for the true self. Still, negative freedom, freedom from, is more likely to mean freedom for the empirical self; whereas positive freedom, freedom for, has to a higher degree the tendency to be understood as freedom only for the true self and therefore as compatible with the most extreme coercion of the empirical selves to become something that their true selves allegedly desire (ibid., p. 19).

The freedom that Berlin cherishes is the negative freedom for "our poor, desire-ridden, passionate, empirical selves" (ibid., p. 32): "a maximum degree of noninterference compatible with the minimum demands of social life" (ibid., p. 46), or the "freedom to live as one prefers" (ibid., p. 14 n.). He seems to cherish that freedom as "an end in itself" or "an ultimate value" (ibid., pp. 36, 50, 54). He certainly does not believe that the older reasoning in favor of negative freedom is valid. For, contrary to the older view, negative freedom is not the "necessary condition for the growth of human genius": "Integrity, love of truth and fiery individualism grow at least as often in severely disciplined communities or under military discipline, as in more tolerant or indifferent societies"; negative freedom is a peculiarly Western ideal and even a peculiarly modern Western ideal, and even in the modern Western world it is cherished by some individuals rather than by large masses; there is no necessary connection between negative freedom and democracy (ibid., pp. 13–15, 48).

Berlin finds the true justification of negative freedom in the absurdity of the alternative. The alternative is the notion that men can be free only by participating in *the* just, *the* rational or *the* perfect society in which all just or rational ends of all members of society are harmoniously satisfied or in which everyone obeys himself, i.e., his true self. This notion presupposes that there is a hierarchy, and therefore a fundamental harmony, of human ends. But this presupposition is "demonstrably false"; it is based on a "dogmatic and a priori certainty"; it is "not compatible with empiricism," i.e., with "any doctrine founded on knowledge derived from experience of what men are and seek"; it is the root of "the metaphysical view of politics" as opposed to the "empirical" view (ibid., pp. 39 n., 54, 57 n.). Experience shows us that "the ends of men are many, and not all of them in principle are compatible with each other. . . . The necessity of choosing between absolute claims is then an inescapable characteristic of the human condition. This gives its value to freedom . . . as an end in itself and not as a temporary need . . ." (ibid., p. 54).

Experience, knowledge of the observable Is, seems to lead in a perfectly unobjectionable manner to knowledge of the Ought. The allegedly empirical premise would seem to be the equality of all human ends. "Mill, and liberals in general, at their most consistent . . . wish the frontiers between individuals and groups of men to be drawn solely with a view to preventing collisions between human purposes, all of which must be considered to be equally ultimate, uncriticizable ends in themselves. Kant and the rationalists of his type do not regard all ends as of equal value." From the context it appears that the ends that are to be regarded as equal include "the various personal aims which their individual imagination and idiosyncrasies lead men to pursue" (ibid., p. 38 n.).

Interference with the pursuit of ends is legitimate only to the extent to which one man's pursuit of an end collides with another man's pursuit. Yet it appears that such collisions cannot possibly be prevented: "The possibility of conflict—and of tragedy—can never be wholly eliminated from human life, either personal or social" (ibid., p. 54). Not all collisions but only certain kinds of collisions can and ought to be prevented by social control: "there must be *some* frontiers of freedom which nobody should ever be permitted to cross" (ibid., p. 50, italics mine). The frontiers must be of such a character as to protect a reasonably large area; it would not be sufficient to demand that every man must have the freedom to dream of the pursuit of any end he likes.

Yet the primary question concerns, not the location of the frontiers, but their status. Those frontiers must be "sacred" (ibid., p. 57). They must be "absolute": "Genuine belief in the inviolability of a minimum extent of individual liberty entails some . . . absolute stand" (ibid., p. 50). "Relativism," or the assertion that all ends are relative to the chooser and hence equal, seems to require some kind of "absolutism." Yet Berlin hesitates to go quite so far.

> Different *names or natures* may be given to the rules that determine these frontiers: they may be called natural rights or the word of God, or Natural Law, or the demands of utility or of "the deepest interests of man"; I may believe them to be valid a priori, or assert them to be *my own subjective ends, or the ends of my society or culture*. What these rules or commandments will have in common is that they are accepted so widely, and are grounded so deeply in the actual human nature of men as they have developed through history, as to be, by now, an essential part of what we mean by being a normal human being. Genuine belief in the inviolability of a minimum extent of individual liberty entails *some such absolute stand* (ibid., p. 50, italics mine).

That is to say, the demand for the sacredness of a private sphere needs a basis, an "absolute" basis, but it has no basis; any old basis, any "such absolute stand" as reference to my own subjective will or the will of my society will do. It would be shortsighted to deny that Berlin's comprehensive formula is very helpful for a political purpose—for the purpose of an anticommunist manifesto designed to rally all anticommunists. But we are here concerned with a theoretical problem, and in this respect we are forced to say that Berlin contradicts himself. "Freedom from" and "freedom to" are "two profoundly divergent and irreconcilable attitudes to the ends of life . . . each of them makes absolute claims. These claims cannot both be fully satisfied. But . . . the satisfaction that each of them seeks is an ultimate value which . . . has an equal right to be classed among the deepest interests of mankind" (ibid., pp. 51–52). The absolute claim for a minimum private sphere cannot be fully satisfied; it must be diluted, for the opposite claim has an equal right. Liberalism, as Berlin understands it, cannot live without an absolute basis and cannot live with an absolute basis.

Let us consider more precisely the basis of liberalism as Berlin sees it. "What these rules and commandments [*sc.* that determine the frontiers of freedom that nobody should ever be permitted to cross] will have in common is that they are accepted so widely, and are grounded so deeply in the actual nature of men as they have developed through history, as to be, by now, an essential part of what we mean by being a normal human being" (ibid., p. 50). But Berlin has told us earlier that "the domination of this ideal has been the exception rather than the rule, even in the recent history of the West" (ibid., p. 13), i.e., that the ideal of negative freedom is not natural to man as man. Let, then, the rules in question be natural to Western man as he is now. But what about the future?

> It may be that the ideal of freedom to live as one wishes . . .
> is only the late fruit of our declining capitalist civilization: an
> ideal which . . . posterity will regard with . . . little compre-
> hension. This may be so; but no sceptical conclusions seem
> to me to follow. Principles are not less sacred because their
> duration cannot be guaranteed. (Ibid., p. 57)

But it is also true that principles are not sacred merely by virtue of the fact that their duration cannot be guaranteed. We are still waiting to hear why Berlin's principles are regarded by him as sacred. If these principles are intrinsically valid, eternally valid, one could indeed say that it is a secondary question whether they will or will not be recognized as valid in the future and that if future generations despise the eternal verities of civilization, they will merely condemn themselves to barbarism. But can there be eternal principles on the basis of "empiricism," of the experience of men up to now? Does not the experience of the future have the same right to respect as the experience of the past and the present?

The situation would be entirely different if one could assume the possibility of a peak of experience, of an absolute moment in history, in which the fundamental condition of man is realized for the first time and in principle fully. But this would also mean that in the most important respect history, or progress, would have come to its end. Yet Berlin seems to take it for granted that in the most important respect history is unfinished or unfinishable. Hence the ideal of negative freedom can only be "relatively valid" for him: it can be valid only for the time being. In entire accord with the spirit of our time, he quotes "an admirable writer of our time" who says: "To realize the relative validity of one's convictions and yet stand for them unflinchingly, is what distinguishes a civilized man from a barbarian" (ibid., p. 57).

That is to say, not only are all our primary ends of relative validity; even the end that suggests itself as necessary by virtue of the absolute insight into the relative validity of all our primary ends is likewise only relatively valid. On the other hand, the latter end, or the right position toward any primary end, is so absolutely valid that Berlin or his authority can build on it the absolute distinction between civilized men and barbarians. For this distinction, as set forth in the quoted passage, is obviously meant to be final and not to be subject to revision in the light of future experience.

Berlin cannot escape the necessity to which every thinking being is subject: to take a final stand, an absolute stand in accordance with what he regards as the nature of man or as the nature of the human condition or as the decisive truth, and hence to assert the absolute validity of his fundamental conviction. This does not mean, of course, that his fundamental conviction is sound. One reason why I doubt that it is sound is that if his authority were right, every resolute liberal hack or thug would be a civilized man, while Plato and Kant would be barbarians.

Berlin's statement seems to me to be a characteristic document of the crisis of liberalism—of a crisis due to the fact that liberalism has abandoned its absolutist basis and is trying to become entirely relativistic. Probably the majority of our academic colleagues will say that no conclusion can be drawn against relativism from the inadequacies of Berlin's statement because these inadequacies arise from his wish to find an impossible middle ground between relativism and absolutism; if he had limited himself to saying that liberalism is merely his "own subjective end," not intrinsically superior to any other subjective end, that since the belief in liberalism is based on a value judgment, no case or no conclusive case can be made for or against liberalism; in other words, if he had not rejected the nonliberal position as "barbarian," but had admitted that there is an indefinitely large variety of notions of civilization each of which defines barbarism in its own way; in brief, if he had remained within the confines of the positivism of our time, he would never have contradicted himself. Whether withdrawal to the citadel of that positivism or of unqualified "value relativism" overcomes the crisis of liberalism or whether it merely conceals that crisis is another question.

According to the positivist interpretation of relativism which prevails in present-day social science, reason is unable to show the superiority of unselfish gratification to selfish gratification and the absurdity of any attainable ends "which imagination and idiosyncracies lead men to pursue." From this it follows that a bachelor without kith and kin who dedicates his whole life to the amassing of the largest possible amount of money, provided he goes about this pursuit in the most efficient manner, leads, in principle, as rational a life as the greatest benefactor of his country or of mankind. The choice among attainable ends may be made *en pleine connaissance de cause*, i.e., in full clarity about the likely consequences of the choice; it cannot in itself be rational. Reason can tell us which means are conducive to which ends; it cannot tell us which attainable ends are to be preferred to other attainable ends. Reason cannot even tell us that we ought to choose attainable ends; if someone "loves him who desires the impossible," reason may tell him that he acts irrationally, but it cannot tell him that he ought to act rationally or that acting irrationally is acting badly or basely. If rational conduct consists in choosing the right means for the right end, relativism teaches in effect that rational conduct is impossible. Relativistic social science may therefore be said to be one branch of the rational study of nonrational behavior.

But in what sense is the study rational? Social science proceeds by inductive reasoning or is concerned with prediction or with the discovery of causes. Yet what is the status of the principle of causality in social science relativism? According to a widely accepted view, the principle of causality is a mere assumption. There is no rational objection to the assumption that the universe may disappear at any moment, not only into thin air, but into absolute nothingness, and that this happening may be a vanishing, not only into nothing, but through nothing as well. What is true of the possible end of the world is true also of its beginning. Since the principle of causality is not intrinsically evident, nothing prevents us from assuming that the world has come into being out of nothing and through nothing. Not only has rationality disappeared from the behavior studied by science; the rationality of that study itself has become radically problematic. All coherence has gone. We are then entitled to say that positivistic science in general, and therefore positivistic social science in particular, is characterized by the abandonment of reason or the flight from reason. The flight from scientific reason, which has been noted with regret, is the reasonable reply to the flight of science from reason.

A Marxist writer, Georg Lukács, has written a history of nineteenth- and twentieth-century German thought under the title *Die Zerstorung der Vernunft* ([Berlin, 1954] = *The Destruction of Reason,* trans. Peter Palmer [Atlantic Highlands, N.J., 1981]). I believe that many of us Western social scientists must plead guilty to this accusation. For obvious reasons we must be especially interested in Lukács's critique of Max Weber's conception of social science. One may summarize that critique as follows. Weber more than any other German scholar of his generation tried to save the objectivity of social science; he believed that to do so required that social science be made "value-free" because he assumed that evaluations are transrational or irrational; but the value-free study of "facts" and their causes admittedly presupposes the selection of relevant facts; that selection is necessarily guided by reference to values; the values with reference to which the facts are to be selected must themselves be selected; and that selection, which determines in the last analysis the specific conceptual framework of the social scientist, is in principle arbitrary; hence social science is fundamentally irrational or subjectivistic (cf. ibid., pp. 484–89 = pp. 612–19 of Palmer trans.).

According to Lukács, an objective and evaluating social science is possible provided social science does not limit itself to the study of arbitrarily selected "facts" or segments, but understands particular social phenomena in the light of the whole social situation and ultimately in the light of the whole historical process. "Historical and dialectical materialism is that comprehensive view in which the progressiveness and the rationally knowable lawfulness of history are expressed in the highest form, and in fact the only comprehensive view that can give a consistent philosophic foundation to progressivism and reasonableness" (ibid., p. 456 = p. 576 of Palmer trans.).

Hegel's attempt to demonstrate the progressive and rational character of the historical process was based on the premise that that process is in principle completed; for if it were not completed, one could not know, for instance, whether the future stages would not lead to the self-destruction of reason. Yet, according to Marx, the historical process is not completed, not to say that it has not even begun. Besides, Marx does not admit transhistorical or natural ends with reference to which change can be diagnosed as progress or regress. It is therefore a question whether by turning from Western relativism to Marxism one escapes relativism. "Historical materialism," Lukács had said,

> can and must be applied to itself. Yet this application of materialist method to materialism does not lead to complete relativism; it does not lead to the consequence that historical materialism is not the right method. The substantive truths of Marxism are of the same quality as the truths of classical economics according to Marx's interpretation of those truths. They are truths within a certain order of society and production. As such, but only as such, they possess absolute validity. This does not exclude the emergence of societies in which other categories, other connections of truth, will be valid as a consequence of the essential structure of these societies. (*Geschichte und Klassenbewusstsein* [Berlin, 1923], pp. 234–35 = *History and Class Consciousness*, trans. Rodney Livingstone [Cambridge, Mass., 1971], p. 228)

This would seem to mean that the substantive truths of Marxism are true until further notice; in principle we know already now that they will be replaced by different truths. Surely, the Marxist truths will be "preserved," in Hegel's sense of the term: "the 'objectivity' of the truth accessible on the lower planes is not destroyed: that truth merely receives a different meaning by being integrated into a more concrete, a more comprehensive totality" (*ibid.*, p. 206 = p. 188 of Livingstone trans.). That is to say, Marxism will reveal itself as a one-sided truth, a half-truth. Lukács compares the truth of Marxism also to the truth of the ideologies of the French Revolution. Marxism is as true today as those ideologies were in their time: both make or made intelligible a historical situation in such a way as to render visible for contemporaries the root of their difficulties and to show them the way out of those difficulties. But while the ideologists of the French Revolution saw clearly the rottenness of the *ancien régime* and the necessity of a revolution, they were utterly mistaken about the goodness of the new society that their revolution brought to birth.

The application to Marxism is obvious: even if Marxism were the last word regarding the ground of the rottenness of capitalist society and regarding the way in which that society can and will be destroyed, it cannot possibly be the last word regarding the new society that the revolutionary action of the proletariat brings to birth: the new society may be as rich in contradictions and oppressions as the old society, although its contradictions and oppressions will, of course, be entirely novel. For if Marxism is only the truth of our time or our society, the prospect of the class-less society too is only the truth of our time and society; it may prove to be the delusion that gave the proletariat the power and the spirit to overthrow the capitalist system, whereas in fact the proletariat finds itself afterwards enslaved, no longer indeed by capital, but by an ironclad military bureaucracy.

Yet perhaps Marxism must not be applied to itself and thus made relative. Perhaps its fundamental verities are objective, scientific truths, the validity of which cannot be understood in terms of their conditions or genesis. Marxism can then be regarded as a final truth of the same dignity as the theory of evolution. Yet since other truths of great importance will be discovered in the future, the "meaning" of Marxism will radically change.

But perhaps Marxism is the final truth, since it belongs to the absolute moment in history in which the realm of necessity can be surveyed in its entirety and therewith the outlines of the realm of freedom can come into view for the first time. The realm of necessity coincides with the division of labor. The realm of freedom emerges with the abolition of the division of labor. Yet the original form of the division of labor is "the division of labor" not in the generation of offspring, but "in the sexual act" (Marx and Engels, *Die Deutsche Ideologie* [Berlin, 1953], p. 28 = *The German Ideology*, ed. C. J. Arthur [New York, 1972], p. 51). It would seem that the realm of freedom, if brought to its perfection, will be the realm of homunculi produced in test tubes by homunculi, if it will not be, as is more likely, the earth of "the last man," of the one herd without a shepherd. For, to quote Machiavelli, "as has been written by some moral philosophers, man's hands and tongue, two most noble instruments for ennobling him, would not have done their work perfectly nor would they have carried the works of men to the height to which they are seen to have been carried, if they had not been driven on by necessity" [*Discourses on Livy* 3.12]: the jump from the realm of necessity into the realm of freedom will be the inglorious death of the very possibility of human excellence.

But let us return to that school which is externally the most powerful in the present-day West, to present-day positivism. That positivism is logical positivism. With some degree of truth it traces its origin to Hume. It deviates from Hume in two important respects. In the first place, deviating from Hume's teaching, it is a logical, i.e., not a psychological, teaching. The supplement added by logical positivism to the critique of reason is symbolic logic and the theory of probability; in Hume that supplement was natural belief and natural instinct. The sole or chief concern of logical positivism is the logical analysis of science. It has learned through Kant, the great critic of Hume, or through neo-Kantianism, that the question of the validity of science is radically different from the question of its psychological genesis.

The second important respect in which present-day positivism deviates from Hume is indicated by the fact that Hume was still a political philosopher. More particularly, he still taught that there are universally valid rules of justice and that those rules are not improperly called Laws of Nature. This means that "he thought and wrote before the rise of anthropology and allied sciences" (John Dewey, *Human Nature and Conduct*, Modern Library edition, p. vii), or, more precisely stated, before "the discovery of History." Hume still viewed human things in the light of man's unchangeable nature; he did not yet conceive of man as an essentially historical being. Present-day positivism believes it can evade the problem raised by "the discovery of History" by the same device by which it frees itself from Hume's or any other psychology: through the Kantian distinction between validity and genesis. Yet Kant was enabled to transcend psychology because he recognized an a priori; and an a priori does not have a genesis, at least not an empirical genesis. Logical positivism rejects the a priori. Hence it cannot avoid becoming involved in psychology, in the question of the empirical genesis of science out of what precedes science. One cannot stop at simply trying to answer the question, What is science? One cannot avoid raising the question, Why science? or, What is the meaning of science? Since positivism denies that there is a "pure reason" or a "pure mind," it can answer the question, Why science? only in terms of "the human organism." It must understand science as an activity of a certain kind of organism, as an activity fulfilling an important function in the life of that kind of organism. In brief, man is an organism that cannot live, or live well, without being able to predict, and the most efficient form of prediction is science.

This way of accounting for science has become extremely questionable. In the age of thermonuclear weapons the positive relation of science to human survival has lost all the apparent evidence that it formerly may have possessed. Furthermore, the high development of science depends on highly developed industrial societies; the predominance of such societies renders ever more difficult the survival of "underdeveloped societies." Who still dares to say that the development of those societies, i.e., their radical transformation, the destruction of their traditional way of life, is a necessary condition for those peoples' living or living well? Those people survived and sometimes lived happily without having an inkling of the possibility of science. While it becomes necessary to trace science to the needs of organisms of a certain kind, it is impossible to do so. For to the extent to which science could be shown to be necessary for man's living or living well, one would in fact pass a rational value judgment regarding science, and we know that, according to positivism, rational value judgments are impossible.

Some positivists avoid the difficulty indicated by finding the rationale of science in democracy, without being deterred by the fact that they thus merely appeal to the dogmatic premise or the inertia of established orders and without paying attention to the complications alluded to by Berlin, or else by conceiving of science as one of the most thrilling forms of spiritual adventure, without being able to tell us what they understand by the spiritual, how it differs in their opinion from the nonspiritual, and, in particular, how it is related to the rational. Positivism grants that science depends on conditions that science itself does not produce. They are produced by the unintended coming together of various factors that may diverge as they have converged. As long as they are together, science may progress by virtue of something that looks like an innate propensity. Yet science is not autonomous; as the saying goes, thinking does not take place in a vacuum. What renders the autonomy of science questionable is not primarily the fact that science presupposes the availability of conditions external to science. If one conceives of science as a spiritual adventure, one implies that there are other forms of spiritual adventure; one cannot exclude the possibility that, just as science influences those other forms, science itself undergoes their influence. Furthermore, one must assume that the spirit changes as a consequence of its adventures, hence that the spirit may well differ from age to age, and hence that science may depend, in the direction of its interests or of its hypotheses-forming imagination, on the spirit of the age. In other words, one cannot help raising the question of the relation between scientific progress and social progress. Given the positivistic verdict regarding value judgments, positivism can no longer speak properly, or with an easy conscience, of social progress; but it continues, even if in a more or less surreptitious manner, the older tradition that believed in the natural harmony between scientific progress and social progress.

Stated generally, by virtue of the distinction between validity and genesis, positivism tries to treat science as autonomous, but it is unable to do so; that distinction merely prevents it from giving due weight to the question of the human context out of which science arises and within which it exists. Positivism treats science in the way in which it would have to be treated if science were "the very highest power of man," the power by which man transcends the merely human; yet positivism cannot maintain this "Platonic" understanding of science. The question of the human context of science, which positivism fails and refuses to raise, is taken up by its most powerful present-day opponent in the West, radical historicism, or, to use the better-known name, existentialism.

Existentialism came into being through the meeting, which first took place in Germany, of Kierkegaard's and Nietzsche's thought. While being related to these two illustrious names, existentialism is as nameless as positivism or idealism. But this is misleading. Existentialism, like many other movements, has a flabby periphery and a hard center. That hard core, or that thought to which alone existentialism owes its intellectual dignity, is the thought of Heidegger. In Heidegger's first great publication, the influence of Kierkegaard was indeed as powerful as that of Nietzsche. But with the increased clarity that Heidegger achieved afterward, it became clear that the root of existentialism must be sought in Nietzsche rather than in Kierkegaard: existentialism emerged by virtue of the reception of Kierkegaard on the part of a philosophic public that had begun to be molded by Nietzsche.

Nietzsche is *the* philosopher of relativism: the first thinker who faced the problem of relativism in its full extent and pointed to the way in which relativism can be overcome. Relativism came to Nietzsche's attention in the form of historicism—more precisely, in the form of a decayed Hegelianism. Hegel had reconciled "the discovery of History"—the alleged insight into the individual's being, in the most radical sense, the son or stepson of his time, or the alleged insight into the dependence of a man's highest and purest thoughts on his time—with philosophy in the original meaning of the term by asserting that Hegel's time was the absolute moment, the end of meaningful time: the absolute religion, Christianity, had become completely reconciled with the world; it had become completely secularized, or the *saeculum* had become completely Christian in and through the postrevolutionary State; history as meaningful change had come to its end; all theoretical and practical problems had in principle been solved; hence, the historical process was demonstrably rational.

The decayed Hegelianism with which Nietzsche was confronted preserved Hegel's "optimism," i.e., the completedness of the historical process. In fact, its "optimism" was based on the expectation of infinite future progress or on the belief in the unfinishable character of history. Under this condition, as Nietzsche saw, our own principles, including the belief in progress, will become as relative as all earlier principles had shown themselves to be; not only the thought of the past but also our own thought must be understood to depend on premises which for us are inescapable, but of which we know they are condemned to perish. History becomes a spectacle that for the superficial is exciting and for the serious is enervating. It teaches a truth that is deadly. It shows us that culture is possible only if men are fully dedicated to principles of thought and action which they do not and cannot question, which limit their horizon and thus enable them to have a character and a style. It shows us at the same time that any principles of this kind can be questioned and even rejected.

The only way out seems to be that one turn one's back on this lesson of history, that one voluntarily choose life-giving delusion instead of deadly truth, that one fabricate a myth. But this is patently impossible for men of intellectual probity. The true solution comes to sight once one realizes the essential limitation of objective history or of objective knowledge in general. Objective history suffices for destroying the delusion of the objective validity of any principles of thought and action; it does not suffice for opening up a genuine understanding of history. The objective historian cannot grasp the substance of the past because he is a mere spectator, not dedicated or committed to substantive principles of thought and action, and this is a consequence of his having realized that such principles have no objective validity. But an entirely different conclusion may and must be drawn from the realization of this objective truth. The different values respected in different epochs had no objective support, i.e., they were human creations; they owed their being to a free human project that formed the horizon within which a culture was possible. What man did in the past unconsciously and under the delusion of submitting to what is independent of his creative act, he must now do consciously. This radically new project—the revaluation of all values—entails the rejection of all earlier values, for they have become baseless by the realization of the baseless character of their claim, by which they stand or fall, to objective validity. But precisely the realization of the origin of all such principles makes possible a new creation that presupposes this realization and is in agreement with it, yet is not deducible from it; otherwise it would not be due to a creative act performed with intellectual probity.

It is in this way that Nietzsche may be said to have transformed the deadly truth of relativism into the most life-giving truth. To state the case with all necessary vagueness, he discovered that the life-giving comprehensive truth is subjective or transtheoretical in that it cannot be grasped detachedly and that it cannot be the same for all men or for all ages. We can do no more than allude here to the difficulties in which Nietzsche became involved in trying to overcome the difficulties that afflict his solution. I have in mind his interpretation of human creativity as a special form of the universal will to power, and the question that this interpretation entails, namely, whether he did not thus again try to find a sufficient theoretical basis for a transhistorical teaching or message. I have in mind, in other words, his hesitation as to whether the doctrine of the will to power is his subjective project, to be superseded by other such projects in the future, or whether it is the final truth. We limit ourselves here to saying that the movement of Nietzsche's thought can be understood as a movement from the supremacy of history towards the supremacy of nature, a movement that bypasses the supremacy of reason throughout or tries to replace the opposition between the subjective and the objective (or between the conventional and the natural) by the opposition between the superficial and the profound. Existentialism is the attempt to free Nietzsche's alleged overcoming of relativism from the consequences of his relapse into metaphysics or of his recourse to nature.

3
An Introduction to Heideggerian Existentialism

Existentialism has reminded many people that thinking is incomplete and defective if the thinking being, the thinking individual, forgets himself as what he is. It is the old Socratic warning. Compare Theodorus in the *Theaetetus:* the purely objective man who loses himself completely in the contemplation of mathematical objects, who knows nothing about his fellow men and himself, and in particular about his own defects. The theoretical man is not a pure mind, a pointer-reading observer. For instance, the question, What am I? or, Who am I? cannot be answered by science, for this would mean that there are some self-forgetting Theodoruses who have gotten hold of the limits of this human soul by means of scientific method. For if they have not done so, if their results are necessarily provisional and hypothetical, it is barely possible that what we can find out by examining ourselves and our situation honestly, without the price and the pretense of scientific knowledge, is more helpful than science.

Existentialism is a school of philosophic thought. The name is not like Platonism, Epicureanism, and Thomism. Existentialism is a nameless movement like pragmatism or positivism. Yet this is deceptive. Existentialism owes its overriding significance to a single man: Heidegger. Heidegger alone brought about such a radical change in philosophic thought as is revolutionizing all thought in Germany and continental Europe and is beginning to affect even Anglo-Saxony. I am not surprised by this effect. I remember the impression he made on me when I heard him first as a young Ph.D., in 1922. Up to that time I had been particularly impressed, as many of my contemporaries in Germany were, by Max Weber: by his intransigent devotion to intellectual honesty, by his passionate devotion to the idea of science—a devotion that was combined with a profound uneasiness regarding the meaning of science. On my way north from Freiburg, where Heidegger then taught, I saw, in Frankfurt-am-Main, Franz Rosenzweig, whose name will always be remembered when informed people speak about existentialism, and I told him of Heidegger. I said to him that, in comparison with Heidegger, Weber appeared to me as an "orphan child" in regard to precision and probing and competence. I had never seen before such seriousness, profundity, and concentration in the interpretation of philosophic texts. I had heard Heidegger's interpretation of certain sections in Aristotle, and some time later I heard Werner Jaeger in Berlin interpret the same texts. Charity compels me to limit my comparison to the remark that there was no comparison. Gradually the breadth of the revolution of thought which Heidegger was preparing dawned upon me and my generation. We saw with our own eyes that there had been no such phenomenon in the world since Hegel. He succeeded in a very short time in dethroning the established schools of philosophy in Germany. There was a famous discussion between Heidegger and Ernst Cassirer in Davos which revealed the lostness and emptiness of this remarkable representative of established academic philosophy to everyone who had eyes. Cassirer had been a pupil of Hermann Cohen, the founder of the neo-Kantian school. Cohen had elaborated a system of philosophy whose center was ethics. Cassirer had transformed Cohen's system into a new system of philosophy in which ethics had completely disappeared. It had been *silently* dropped: he had not *faced* the problem. *Heidegger did face the problem.* He declared that ethics is impossible, and his whole being was permeated by the awareness that this fact opens up an abyss.

Prior to Heidegger's emergence the most outstanding German philosopher—I would say the only German philosopher—of the time was Edmund Husserl. It was Heidegger's critique of Husserl's phenomenology which became decisive: it became so precisely because that criticism consisted in a radicalization of Husserl's own question and questioning. Briefly, Husserl once said to me, who had been trained in the Marburg neo-Kantian school, that the neo-Kantians were superior to all other German philosophical schools, but they made the mistake of beginning with the roof. He meant the following. The primary theme of Marburg neo-Kantianism was the analysis of science. But science, Husserl taught, is derivative from our primary knowledge of the world of things: science is not the perfection of man's understanding of the world, but a specific modification of that prescientific understanding. The meaningful genesis of science out of prescientific understanding is a *problem:*

the primary theme is the philosophical understanding of the pre-scientific world, and therefore in the first place the analysis of the sensibly perceived thing. According to Heidegger, Husserl himself began with the roof: the merely sensibly perceived thing is itself derivative; there are not first sensibly perceived things and thereafter the same things in a state of being valued or in a state of affecting us. Our primary understanding of the world is not an understanding of things as objects but of what the Greeks indicated by *pragmata*. The horizon within which Husserl had analyzed the world of prescientific understanding was the pure consciousness as the absolute being. Heidegger questioned that orientation by referring to the fact that the inner time belonging to the pure consciousness cannot be understood if one abstracts from the fact that this time is necessarily finite, and even constituted by man's *mortality*.

The same effect which Heidegger produced in the late twenties and early thirties in Germany, he produced very soon in continental Europe as a whole. There is no longer in existence a philosophic position, apart from neo-Thomism and Marxism crude or refined. All rational liberal philosophic positions have lost their significance and power. One may deplore this, but I for one cannot bring myself to clinging to philosophic positions which have been shown to be inadequate. I am afraid that we shall have to make a very great effort in order to find a solid basis for rational liberalism. Only a great thinker could help us in our intellectual plight. But here is the great trouble: the only great thinker in our time is Heidegger.

The only question of importance, of course, is the question whether Heidegger's teaching is true or not. But the very question is deceptive because it is silent about the question of competence—of who is competent to judge. Perhaps only great thinkers are really competent to judge the thought of great thinkers. Heidegger made a distinction between philosophers and those for whom philosophy is identical with the history of philosophy. He made a distinction, in other words, between the thinker and the scholar. I know that I am only a scholar. But I know also that most people who call themselves philosophers are mostly, at best, scholars. The scholar is radically dependent on the work of the great thinkers, of men who faced the problems without being overpowered by any authority. The scholar is cautious: methodic, not bold. He does not become lost to our sight in, to us, inaccessible heights and mists, as the great thinkers do. Yet, while the great thinkers are so bold, they are also much more cautious than we are; they see pit-falls where we are sure of our ground. We scholars live in a charmed circle, light-living, like the Homeric gods—protected against the problems by the great thinkers. The scholar becomes possible through the fact that the great thinkers disagree. Their disagreement creates a possibility for us to reason about their dif-ferences—to wonder which of them is more likely to be right. We may think that the possible alternatives are exhausted by the great thinkers of the past. We may try to classify their doctrines and make a kind of herbarium and think we look over them from a vantage point. But we cannot exclude the possibility that other great thinkers might arise in the future—in 2200 in Burma—the possibility of whose thought has in no way been provided for in our schemata. For who are we to believe that we have found out the limits of human possibilities? In brief, we are occupied with reasoning about the little we understand about what the great thinkers have said.

I apply this to my situation in regard to Heidegger. A famous psychologist I saw in Europe, an old man, told me that in his view it is not yet possible to form a judgment about the significance as well as the truth of Heidegger's work. This work changed so radi-cally in its intellectual orientation that a long time will be needed in order to understand with even tolerable adequacy what this work means. The more I understand what Heidegger is aiming at, the more I see how much still escapes me. The most stupid thing I could do would be to close my eyes or to reject his work.

There is a not altogether unrespectable justification for doing so. Heidegger became a Nazi in 1933. This was not due to a mere error of judgment on the part of a man who lived on great heights high above the low land of politics. Everyone who had read his first great book and did not overlook the wood for the trees could see the kinship in temper and direction between Heidegger's thought and the Nazis. What was the practical, that is to say, seri-ous meaning of the contempt for reasonableness and the praise of resoluteness except to encourage that extremist movement? When Heidegger was rector of the University of Freiburg in 1933, he de-livered an official speech in which he identified himself with the movement which then swept Germany. Heidegger has not yet dared to mention that speech in the otherwise complete lists of his writings which appear from time to time on the book jackets of his recent publications. In 1953 he published a book, *Introduction to Metaphysics*, consisting of lectures given in 1935, in which he spoke of the greatness and dignity of the National Socialist movement. In the preface written in 1953 he said that all mistakes had been corrected. The case of Heidegger reminds one to a certain extent of the case of Nietzsche. Nietzsche, naturally, would not have sided with Hitler. Yet there is an undeniable kinship between Nietzsche's thought and fascism. If one rejects, as passionately as Nietzsche did, conservative constitutional monarchy, as well as democracy, with a view to a new aristocracy, the passion of the denials will be much more effective than the necessarily more subtle intimations of the character of the new nobility, to say nothing of the blond beast.

Passionate political action against the movements just referred to is absolutely in order, but it is not sufficient. It is not even politically sufficient. Are there no dangers threatening democracy, not only from without but from within as well? Is there no problem of democracy, of industrial mass democracy? The official high priests of democracy with their amiable reasonableness were not reasonable enough to prepare us for our present situation: the decline of Europe, the danger to the West, to the whole Western heritage, which is at least as great as and even greater than that which threatened Mediterranean civilization around 300 of the Christian era. Nietzsche once described the change which had been effected in the second half of the nineteenth century in continental Europe. The reading of the morning prayer had been replaced by the reading of the morning paper: not every day the same thing, the same reminder of man's absolute duty and exalted destiny, but every day something new with no reminder of duty and exalted destiny; specialization, knowing more and more about less and less; the practical impossibility of concentration upon the very few essential things upon which man's wholeness entirely depends; the specialization compensated by sham universality, by the stimulation of all kinds of interests and curiosities without true passion; the danger of universal philistinism and creeping conformism.

Or let me look for a moment at the Jewish problem. The nobility of Israel is literally beyond praise, the only bright spot for the contemporary Jew who knows where he comes from. And yet Israel dces not afford a solution to the Jewish problem. "The Judeo-Christian tradition"? This means to blur and to conceal grave differences. Cultural pluralism can only be had, it seems, at the price of blunting all edges.

It would be wholly unworthy of us as thinking beings not to listen to the critics of democracy—even if they are enemies of democracy—provided they are thinking men (and especially great thinkers) and not blustering fools.

Existentialism appeals to a certain experience, anguish or *angst*, as the basic experience in the light of which everything must be understood. Having this experience is one thing; regarding it as the basic experience is another thing. That is, its basic character is not guaranteed by the experience itself. It can only be guaranteed by argument. This argument may be invisible because it is implied in what is generally admitted in our time. What is generally admitted may imply, but only imply, a fundamental uneasiness which is vaguely felt but not faced. Given this context, the experience to which existentialism refers will appear as a revelation, as the revelation, as the authentic interpretation of the fundamental uneasiness. But something more is required which is equally generally admitted in our time: the vaguely felt uneasiness must be regarded as essential to man, and not only to present-day man. Yet this vaguely felt uneasiness is distinctly a present-day phenomenon. Let us assume, however, that this uneasiness embodies what all earlier ages have thought, or is the *result* of what earlier ages have thought. In that case the vaguely felt uneasiness is the natural fruit of all earlier human efforts; no return to an older interpretation of that uneasiness is possible. Now, this is a second view generally accepted today (apart from the fundamental uneasiness which is vaguely felt but not faced); this second element is the belief in progress.

I have already referred to the well-known expression: we know more and more about less and less. What does this mean? It means that modern science has not kept the promise which it held out from its beginning up until the end of the nineteenth century: that it would reveal to us the true character of the universe and the truth about man. You have in *The Education of Henry Adams* a memorable document of the change in the character and in the claim of science which made itself felt in the general public towards the end of the last century, and which has increased since in momentum and sweep. You all know the assertion that value judgments are impermissible to the scientist in general and to the social scientist in particular. This means certainly that, while science has increased man's power in ways that former men never dreamt of, it is absolutely incapable of telling men how to use that power. Science cannot tell man whether it is wiser to use that power wisely and beneficently, or foolishly and devilishly. From this it follows that science is unable to establish its own meaningfulness or to answer the question whether, and in what sense, science is good. We are then confronted with an enormous apparatus, whose bulk is ever increasing, which in itself has no meaning. If a scientist would say, as Goethe's Mephisto still said, that science and reason is man's highest power, he would be told that he was not talking as a scientist, but making value judgments, which from the point of view of science is altogether unwarranted. Someone has spoken of the flight from scientific reason. This flight is not due to any perversity but to science itself. I dimly remember the time when people argued as follows: to deny the possibility of scientific or rational value judgments means to admit that all values are of equal rank; and this means that respect for all values, universal tolerance, is the dictate of scientific reason. But this time has gone. Today we hear that no conclusion whatever can be drawn from the equality of all value, that science does not legitimate (nor, indeed, forbid) our drawing rational conclusions from scientific findings. The assumption that we should act rationally and therefore turn to science for reliable information—this assumption is wholly outside of the purview and interest of science proper. The flight from scientific reason is the consequence of the flight of science from reason—from the notion that man is a rational being, who perverts his being if he does not act rationally. It goes without saying that a science which does not allow of value judgments has no longer any possibility of speaking of progress except in the humanely irrelevant sense of scientific progress: the concept of progress accordingly has been replaced by the concept of change. If science or reason cannot answer the question, Why science? then science or reason says in effect that the choice of science is not rational: one may choose with equal right pleasing and otherwise satisfying myths. Furthermore, science does no longer conceive of itself as the perfection of the human mind; it admits that it is based on fundamental hypotheses which will always remain hypotheses. The whole structure of science does not rest on evident necessities. If this is so, the choice of the scientific orientation is as groundless as the choice of any alternative orientation. But what else does this mean except that the reflective scientist discovers as the ground of his science and his choice of science a groundless choice—an abyss. For a scientific interpretation of the choice between the scientific orientation and an alternative orientation presupposes already the acceptance of the scientific orientation. The fundamental freedom is the only nonhypothetical thing; everything else rests on that fundamental freedom. We are already in the midst of existentialism.

Someone might say that science by itself, as well as poor and stupid positivism, is of course helpless against the existentialist onslaught. But we do not have a rational philosophy which takes up the thread where science and positivism drop it, and for which poetic, emotional existentialism is no match. I have looked myself for a long time—where do I find that rational philosophy? If I disregard the neo-Thomists, where do I find today the philosopher who dares to say that he is in possession of the true metaphysic and the true ethics, which reveal to us in a rational, universally valid way the nature of being and the character of the good life? Naturally we can sit at the feet of the great philosophers of old, of Plato and of Aristotle. But who can dare to say that Plato's doctrine of ideas as he intimated it, or Aristotle's doctrine of the *nous* that does nothing but think itself and is essentially related to the eternal visible universe, is the true teaching? Are those like myself who are inclined to sit at the feet of the old philosophers not exposed to the danger of the weak-kneed eclecticism which will not withstand a single blow on the part of those who are competent enough to remind them of the singleness of purpose and of inspiration that characterizes every thinker who deserves to be called great? Considering the profound disagreement among the great thinkers of the past, is it possible to appeal to them without blunting all edges? The place of traditional philosophy is then more and more taken by what was called in the country of its origin *weltanschauungslehre.*

In this general approach, it is admitted that we cannot refer to the true metaphysical and ethical teaching available in any of the great thinkers of the past. It is admitted that there are N ways of answering the fundamental questions, that there are N types of absolute presuppositions, as Collingwood called them, none of which can be said to be rationally superior to any other. This means the abandonment of the very idea of the truth as rational philosophy has always understood it. It means, just as in the case of the social sciences, that the choice of any of these presuppositions is groundless and leads us again to the abyss of freedom—to say nothing of the fact that any such doctrine of comprehensive views presupposes that the fundamental possibilities are available, or that fundamental human creativity is at its end. Furthermore, there is a radical disproportion between the analyst of comparative views who does not face the fundamental questions directly and does not even recognize them in their primary meaning, viz., as pointing to one answer only, and the great thinkers themselves. He is separated from them by a deep gulf which is created by his pretended knowledge of the utopian character of original philosophy itself. How can we possibly believe him when he claims he is in a position to understand the thinkers as they want to be understood and as they must have been understood if one is to order and tabulate their teachings? We are sufficiently familiar with the history of philosophy in particular in order not to be taken in for a moment by the pious hope that while there may be profound disagreement among the rational philosophers in all other respects, they will happily agree regarding human conduct. There is only one possible way out of the predicament in which the doctrine of comprehensive views finds itself, and that is to find the ground of the variety of comparative views in the human soul, or, more generally stated, in the human condition. If one takes this indispensable step, one is again already at the threshold of existentialism.

There is another very common way of solving the so-called value problem. People say that we must adopt values, and that it is natural for us to adopt the values of our society. Yet our values are our highest principles, if the meaning of science itself depends on values. Now, it is impossible to overlook the relation of the principles of our society to our society and the dependence of the principles on the society. This means, generally stated, that the principles, the so-called categorical system or the essences, are rooted ultimately in the particulars, in something which exists. Existence precedes essence. For what else do people mean when they say, e.g., that the Stoic natural law teaching is rooted in or relative to the decay of the Greek polis and the emergence of the Greek empire?

Sometimes people try to avoid the difficulty indicated by saying that we have to adopt the values of our society. This is altogether impossible for serious men. We cannot help raising the question as to the value of the values of our society. To accept the values of one's society because they are the values of one's society means simply to shirk one's responsibility; it means not facing the situation, i.e., the fact that everyone has to make his own choice; it means running away from one's self. To find the solution to our problem in the acceptance of the values of our society because they are the values of our society means to make philistinism a duty and to make oneself oblivious to the difference between true individuals and whited sepulchres.

The uneasiness which today is felt but not faced can be expressed by a single word: relativism. Existentialism admits the truth of relativism, but it realizes that relativism, so far from being a solution or even a relief, is deadly. Existentialism is the reaction of serious men to their own relativism.

Existentialism begins, then, with the realization that as the ground of all objective, rational knowledge we discover an abyss. All truth, all meaning, is seen in the last analysis to have no support except man's freedom. Objectively there is in the last analysis only meaninglessness, nothingness. This nothingness can be experienced in anguish, but this experience cannot find an objective expression, because it cannot be made in detachment. Man freely originates meaning; he originates the horizon, the absolute presupposition, the ideal, the project within which understanding and life are possible. Man is man by virtue of such a horizon-forming project, of an unsupported project, of a thrown project. More precisely, man always lives within such a horizon without being aware of its character; he takes his world as simply given, i.e., he has lost himself; but he can call himself back from his lostness and take the responsibility for what he has in a lost, unauthentic way. Man is essentially a social being: to be a human being means to be with other human beings. To be, in an authentic way, means to be in an authentic way to others: to be true to oneself is incompatible with being false to others. Thus there would seem to exist the possibility of an existential ethics, which would have to be, however, a strictly formal ethics. However this may be, Heidegger never believed in the possibility of an ethics.

To be a human being means to be in the world. To be authentic means to be authentic in the world; to accept the things within the world as merely factual and one's own being as merely factual; to risk oneself resolutely, despising sham certainties (and all objective certainties are sham). Only if man *is* in this way do the things in this world reveal themselves to him as they are. The concern with objective certainty necessarily narrows the horizon. It leads to the consequence that man erects around himself an artificial netting which conceals from him the abyss of which he must be aware if he wants to be truly human. To live dangerously means to think exposedly.

We are ultimately confronted with mere facticity or contingency. But are we not able and even compelled to raise the question of the causes of ourselves and of the things in the world? Indeed we cannot help raising the questions of the whence and whither, or of the whole. But we do not know and cannot know the whence.

Man cannot understand himself in the light of the whole, in the light of his origin or his end. This irremediable ignorance is the basis of his lostness or the core of the human situation. By making this assertion, existentialism restores Kant's notion of the unknowable thing-in-itself and of man's ability to grasp the fact of his freedom at the limits of objective knowledge and as the ground of objective knowledge. But in existentialism there is no moral law and no other world.

It becomes necessary to make as fully explicit as possible the character of human existence; to raise the question: What is human existence? and to bring to light the essential structure of human existence. This inquiry is called by Heidegger analytics of *Existenz*. Heidegger conceived of the analytics of *Existenz* from the outset as the fundamental ontology. This means he took up again Plato's and Aristotle's question, What is Being? What is that by virtue of which any being is said to be? Heidegger agreed with Plato and Aristotle not only as to this—that the question of what is *to be* is the fundamental question; he also agreed with Plato and Aristotle as to this—that the fundamental question must be primarily addressed to that being which *is* in the most emphatic or the most authoritative way. Yet while according to Plato and Aristotle *to be* in the highest sense means to be *always*, Heidegger contends that *to be* in the highest sense means *to exist*, that is to say, *to be* in the manner in which man *is: to be* in the highest sense is constituted by mortality.

Philosophy then becomes analytics of *Existenz*. Analytics of existence brings to light the essential structures, the unchangeable character of *Existenz*. Is then the new philosophy, in spite of the difference of content, objective, rational philosophy, comparable to Kant's transcendental analytics of subjectivity? Does not the new philosophy too take on the character of absolute knowledge, complete knowledge, final knowledge, infinite knowledge? No—the new philosophy is necessarily based on a specific ideal of *Existenz*. One cannot analyze *Existenz* from a neutral point of view; one must have made a choice which is not subject to examination in order to be open to the phenomena of *Existenz*. Man is a finite being and incapable of absolute knowledge; his very knowledge of his finiteness is finite. One may also say: commitment can only be understood by an understanding which is itself committed, or which is a specific commitment. Or, existential philosophy is subjective truth about subjective truth. To speak in general terms, rational philosophy has been guided by the distinction between the objective, which is true, and the subjective, which is opinion (or an equivalent of this distinction). On the basis of existentialism what was formerly called objective reveals itself to be superficial (problematic); and what was formerly called subjective reveals itself as profound, assertoric—with the understanding that there is no apodicticity.

The great achievement of Heidegger was the coherent exposition of the experience of *Existenz*, a coherent exposition based on the experience of existing. Kierkegaard had spoken of existence, but within the traditional horizon, i.e., within the horizon of the traditional distinction between essence and existence. Heidegger tried to understand existence out of itself.

Yet the analytics of existence was exposed to serious difficulties which eventually induced Heidegger to find a fundamentally new basis, that is to say, to break with existentialism. I shall mention now some of these difficulties. First, Heidegger demanded from philosophy that it should liberate itself completely from traditional or inherited notions which were survivals of former ways of thinking. He mentioned especially concepts that were of Christian theological origin. Yet his understanding of existence was obviously of Christian origin (conscience, guilt, being unto death, anguish). Second, the fact that the analytics of existence was based on a specific ideal of existence made one wonder whether the analysis was not fundamentally arbitrary. Third, the analytics of *Existenz* had culminated in the assertion that the highest form of knowledge is finite knowledge of finiteness; yet how can finiteness be seen as finiteness if it is not seen in the light of infinity? Or in other words, it was said that we cannot know the whole; but does this not necessarily presuppose awareness of the whole? Professor Hocking stated this difficulty neatly as follows: *désespoir* presupposes *espoir*, and *espoir* presupposes love: is then not love rather than despair the fundamental phenomenon? Is therefore not that which man ultimately loves, God, the ultimate ground? These objections which Heidegger made to himself were fundamentally the same objections which Hegel had made to Kant. The relation of Heidegger to his own existentialism is the same as that of Hegel to Kant. The objections mentioned would seem to lead to the consequence that one cannot escape metaphysics: Plato and Aristotle. This consequence is rejected by Heidegger. The return to metaphysics is impossible. But what is needed is some repetition of what metaphysics intended on an entirely different plane. Existence cannot be the clue, the clue to the understanding of that by virtue of which all beings are. Existence must rather be understood in the light of that by virtue of which all beings are. From this point of view the analytics of existence appears still to partake of modern subjectivism.

I have compared the relation of Heidegger to existentialism with the relation of Hegel to Kant. Hegel may be said to have been the first philosopher who was aware that his philosophy belongs to his times. Heidegger's criticism of existentialism can therefore be expressed as follows. Existentialism claims to be the insight into the essential character of man, the final insight, which as such would belong to the final time, to the fullness of time. And yet existentialism denies the possibility of a fullness of time: the historical process is unfinishable; man is and always will be a historical being. In other words, existentialism claims to be the understanding of the historicity of man, and yet it does not reflect about its own historicity, about its belonging to a specific situation of Western man. It becomes therefore necessary to return from Kierkegaard's existing individual, who has nothing but contempt for Hegel's understanding of man in terms of universal history, to that Hegelian understanding. The situation to which existentialism belongs can be seen to be liberal democracy, or, more precisely, a liberal democracy which has become uncertain of itself or of its future. Existentialism belongs to the decline of Europe.

This insight has grave consequences. Let us look back for a moment to Hegel. Hegel's philosophy knew itself to belong to a specific time. As the completion or perfection of philosophy it belonged to the completion or fullness of time. This meant for Hegel that it belonged to the postrevolutionary state, to Europe united under Napoleon: nonfeudal, providing equality of opportunity, promoting free enterprise, but under a strong government not dependent on the will of the majority while yet expressive of the general will which is the reasonable will of each. In other words: recognition of the rights of man or of the dignity of every human being, and a monarchic head of state guided by a first-rate and highly devoted civil service. Society thus constructed was the final society. History had come to its end precisely because the completion of philosophy had become possible. The owl of Minerva commences its flight at the beginning of dusk. The completion of history is the beginning of the decline of Europe, of the West, and therewith, since all other cultures have been absorbed into the West, the beginning of the decline of mankind. There is no future for mankind. Almost everyone rebelled against Hegel's conclusion, and no one more powerfully than Marx. He pointed out the untenable character of the postrevolutionary settlement and the problem of the working class with all its implications. There arises the vision of a world society which presupposes and establishes forever the complete victory of the town over the country, or of the West over the East, which would make possible the full potentialities of each on the basis of man having become completely collectivized. The man of the world society who is perfectly free is so in the last analysis because all specialization, all division of labor has been abolished; all division of labor has been seen to be due ultimately to private property. The man of the world society goes hunting in the forenoon, paints at noon, philosophizes in the afternoon, works in his garden after the sun has set. He is a perfect jack-of-all-trades.

No one questioned this communistic vision with greater energy than Nietzsche. He identified the man of the communist world society as the last man, that is to say, as the extreme degradation of man. This did not mean, however, that Nietzsche accepted the noncommunist society of the nineteenth century or its future. Like all continental European conservatives, he saw in communism only the consistent completion of democratic egalitarianism and of that liberalistic demand for freedom which was not a freedom for but only a freedom from. But in contradistinction to the European conservatives, he saw that conservatism as such is doomed. For all merely defensive positions are doomed. The future was with democracy and with nationalism. And both were regarded by Nietzsche as incompatible with what he saw to be the task of the twentieth century. He saw the twentieth century to be the age of world wars, leading up to planetary rule. If man were to have a future, this rule would have to be exercised by a united Europe. And the enormous task of such an iron age could not possibly be discharged, he thought, by weak and unstable governments dependent upon democratic public opinion. The new situation required the emergence of a new aristocracy. It had to be a new nobility, a nobility formed by a new ideal. This is the most obvious meaning, and for this reason also the most superficial meaning, of his notion of the superman: all previous notions of human greatness would not enable man to face the infinitely increased responsibility of the planetary age. The invisible rulers of that possible future would be the philosophers of the future. It is certainly not an overstatement to say that no one has ever spoken so greatly and so nobly of what a philosopher is as Nietzsche. This is not to deny that the philosophers of the future as Nietzsche described them remind one much more than Nietzsche himself seems to have thought of Plato's philosopher. For while Plato had seen the features in question as clearly as Nietzsche, and perhaps more clearly than Nietzsche, he had intimated rather than stated his deepest insights. But there is one decisive difference between Nietzsche's philosophy of the future and Plato's philosophy. Nietzsche's philosopher of the future is an heir to the Bible. He is an heir to that deepening of the soul which has been effected by the Biblical belief in a God that is holy. The philosopher of the future, as distinct from the classical philosopher, will be concerned with the holy. His philosophizing will be intrinsically religious. This does not mean that he believes in God, the Biblical God. He is an atheist, but an atheist who is waiting for a god who has not yet shown himself. He has broken with the Biblical faith also and especially because the Biblical God as the creator of the world is outside the world: compared with the Biblical God as the highest good, the world is necessarily less than perfect. In other words, the Biblical faith necessarily leads, according to Nietzsche, to otherworldliness or asceticism. The condition of the highest human excellence is that man remains or becomes fully loyal to the earth; that there is nothing outside the world which could be of any concern to us—be it God or ideas or atoms of which we could be certain by knowledge or by faith. Every concern for such a ground of the world as is outside of the world, i.e., of the world in which man lives, alienates man from this world. Such concern is rooted in the desire to escape from the terrifying and perplexing character of reality, to cut down reality to what man can bear. It is rooted in a desire for comfort.

The First World War shook Europe to its foundations. Men lost their sense of direction. The faith in progress decayed. The only people who kept that faith in its original vigor were the communists. But precisely this showed to the noncommunist the delusion of progress. Spengler's *Decline of the West* seemed to be much more credible. But one had to be inhuman to leave it at Spengler's prognosis. Is there no hope for Europe? And therewith for mankind? It was in the spirit of such hope that Heidegger perversely welcomed 1933. He became disappointed and withdrew. What did the failure of the Nazis teach him? Nietzsche's hope of a united Europe ruling the planet, of a Europe not only united but revitalized by this new, transcendent responsibility of planetary rule, had proved to be a delusion. A world society controlled either by Washington or Moscow appeared to be approaching. For Heidegger it did not make any difference whether Washington or Moscow would be the center. America and Soviet Russia are metaphysically the same. What is decisive for him is that this world society is to him worse than a nightmare. He called it the "night of the world." It means indeed, as Marx had predicted, the victory of an ever more completely urbanized, ever more completely technological West over the whole planet—complete levelling and uniformity regardless of whether it is brought about by iron compulsion or by soapy advertisement of the output of mass production. It means unity of the human race on the lowest level, complete emptiness of life, self-perpetuating doctrine without rhyme or reason; no leisure, no concentration, no elevation, no withdrawal; nothing but work and recreation; no individuals and no peoples, but instead "lonely crowds."

How can there be hope? Fundamentally, because there is something in man which cannot be satisfied by the world society: the desire for the genuine, for the noble, for the great. The desire has expressed itself in man's ideals, but all previous ideals have proved to be related to societies which were not world societies. The old ideals will not enable man to overcome the power, to weaken the power, of technology. We may also say: a world society can be human only if there is a world culture, a culture genuinely uniting all men. But there never has been a high culture without a religious basis: the world society can be human only if all men are genuinely united by a world religion. But all existing religions are steadily undermined, so far as their effective power is concerned, by the progress towards a technological world society. There forms itself an open or concealed alliance of the existing religions which are united only by their common enemy (atheistic communism). Their union requires that they conceal from themselves and from the world that they are incompatible with each other—that each regards the other as indeed noble, but untrue. Man cannot make or fabricate a world religion. He can only prepare it by becoming receptive to it, and he becomes receptive to it if he thinks deeply enough about himself and his situation.

Man's humanity is threatened with extinction by technology. Technology is the fruit of rationalism, and rationalism is the fruit of Greek philosophy. Greek philosophy is the condition of the possibility of technology and therefore at the same time of the impasse created by technology. There is no hope beyond technological mass society if there are no essential limitations to Greek philosophy, which is the root of technology, to say nothing of modern philosophy. Greek philosophy was the attempt to understand the whole. It presupposed therefore that the whole is intelligible, or that the grounds of the whole are essentially intelligible and at the disposal of man as man—that they *are* always, and therefore in principle are always accessible to man. This view is the condition of the possibility of human mastery of the whole. But that mastery leads, if its ultimate consequences are drawn, to the ultimate degradation of man. Only by becoming aware of what is beyond human mastery can we have hope. Transcending the limits of rationalism requires the discovery of the limits of rationalism. Rationalism is based on a specific understanding of what being means, viz., that *to be* means primarily to be present, to be ready at hand, therefore that *to be* in the highest sense means to be always present, to be always. This basis of rationalism proves to be a dogmatic assumption. Rationalism itself rests on nonrational, unevident assumptions; in spite of its seemingly overwhelming power, rationalism is hollow; rationalism itself rests on something which it cannot master. A more adequate understanding of being is intimated by the assertion that *to be* means to be elusive or to be a mystery. This is the Eastern understanding of Being. Hence there is no will to master in the East. We can hope beyond technological world society, we can hope for a genuine world society, only if we become capable of learning from the East, especially from China. But China succumbs to Western rationalism.

Heidegger is the only man who has an inkling of the dimensions of the problem of a world society.

There is needed a meeting of the West and of the East. The West has to make its own contribution to the overcoming of technology. The West has first to recover within itself that which would make possible a meeting of West and East: its own deepest roots, which antedate its rationalism, which in a way antedate the separation of West and East. No genuine meeting of West and East is possible on the level of present-day thought—i.e., in the form of the meeting of the most vocal, most glib, most superficial representatives of the most superficial period of both West and East. The meeting of West and East can only be a meeting of the deepest roots of both.

The Western thinker can prepare for that meeting by descending to the deepest root of the West. Within the West the limitations of rationalism were always seen by the Biblical tradition. (Here lies the justification for the Biblical elements in Heidegger's earlier thought.) But this must be rightly understood. Biblical thought is one form of Eastern thought. By taking the Bible as absolute, one blocks the access to other forms of Eastern thought. Yet the Bible is the East within us, Western men. Not the Bible as Bible but the Bible as Eastern can help us in overcoming Greek rationalism.

The deepest root of the West is a specific understanding of Being, a specific experience of Being. The specifically Western experience of Being led to the consequence that the ground of grounds was forgotten, and the primary experience of Being was useful only for the investigation of beings. The East has experienced Being in a way which prevented the investigation of beings and therewith the concern with the mastery of beings. But the Western experience of Being makes possible, in principle, coherent speech about Being. By opening ourselves to the problem of Being and to the problematic character of the Western understanding of Being, we may gain access to the deepest root of the East. The ground of grounds which is indicated by the word "Being" will be the ground not only of the religion but even of any possible gods. From here one can begin to understand the possibility of a world religion.

The meeting of East and West depends on an understanding of Being. More precisely it depends upon an understanding of that by virtue of which beings are: *esse, être,* to be, as distinguished from *entia, étants,* beings. The ground of all being, especially of man, is said to be "Sein." "Sein" would be translated in the case of every writer other than Heidegger by "being." But for Heidegger everything depends on the radical difference between "being" understood as verbal-noun and "being" understood as participle, and in English the verbal-noun is indistinguishable from the participle. I shall therefore use the German terms after having translated them once into Greek, Latin, and French: "Sein" is *einai, esse, être;* "das Seinde" is *on, ens, étant.* "Sein" is not "das Seinde." But in every understanding of "das Seinde" we casually presuppose that we understand "Sein." One is tempted to say in Platonic language that "das Seinde" is, only by participating in "Sein." But in that Platonic understanding "Sein" would be a "Seinde." What does Heidegger mean by this? I can begin to understand it in the following manner: "Sein" cannot be explained by "das Seinde," as causality cannot be explained causally. Someone has said that "Sein" takes the place of the categories (surely in the Kantian sense). This change is necessary because the categories, the system of categories, the absolute presuppositions, change from epoch to epoch. This change is not "progress," nor is it rational. The change of the categories cannot be explained by or on the basis of one particular system of categories. Yet we could not speak of change if there were not something lasting in the change. That lasting which is responsible for the most fundamental thought is "Sein." "Sein," as Heidegger puts it, gives or sends in different epochs a different understanding of "Sein" and therewith of everything. This is misleading insofar as it suggests that "Sein" is only inferred. But of "Sein" we know through experience of "Sein." That experience presupposes, however, a leap. That leap was not made by the earlier philosophers, and therefore their thought is characterized by oblivion of "Sein." They thought only of and about "das Seinde." Yet they could not have thought of and about "das Seinde" except on the basis of some awareness of "Sein"; but they paid no attention to it. This failure was due not only to negligence on their part but also to "Sein" itself. The key to "Sein" is one particular manner of "Sein," the "Sein" of man. Man is "Project": everyone is who he is by virtue of the exercise of his freedom, his choice of a determinate idea of existence—his choosing a project, or his failure to do so. But man is finite; the range of his fundamental choices is limited by his situation, which he has not chosen. Man is a project which is "thrown" *somewhere*. The leap through which "Sein" is experienced is primarily the awareness or acceptance of being thrown, of finiteness, the abandonment of every thought of a railing, a support.

Earlier philosophy, and especially Greek philosophy, was oblivious of "Sein" precisely because it was not based on that experience. Greek philosophy was guided by an idea of "Sein" according to which "Sein" meant to be at hand, to be present, and therefore ("Sein" in the highest sense) to be always present, to be always. Accordingly the Greeks and their successors understood the soul as substance, as a thing, and not as a self which, if it is truly a self, if authentic, and not mere drifting or shallow, is based on the awareness, the acceptance, of the project as "thrown." No human life that is not mere drifting or shallow is possible without a project, without an idea of existence and dedication to it; "idea of existence" takes the place of respectable opinion of the good life. But opinion points to knowledge, whereas idea of existence implies that in this respect there is no knowledge possible but only what is much higher than knowledge (i.e., knowledge of what is), project or decision. The ground of all being, and especially of man, is "Sein"; this ground of grounds is coeval with man and therefore also not sempiternal or eternal. But if this is so, "Sein" cannot be the complete ground of man; the emergence of man, in contradistinction to the essence of man, would require a ground different from "Sein." In other words, "Sein" is not the ground of the fact. If we try to understand anything radically we come up against facticity, irreducible facticity. If we try to understand the fact of man, the fact that the human race is, by tracing it to its causes, to its conditions, we shall find that the whole effort is directed by a specific understanding of "Sein," of an understanding which is given or sent by "Sein." The conditions of man in this view are comparable to Kant's thing-in-itself, of which one cannot say anything and in particular not whether it contains anything sempiternal. Heidegger mentions this reply: one cannot speak of anything being prior to man in time, for time is or happens only while man is. Authentic or primary time is or arises only in man. Cosmic time, the time measurable by chronometers, is secondary or derivative and can therefore not be appealed to, or made use of, in a fundamental philosophical consideration. This argument reminds one of the medieval argument according to which the temporal finiteness of the world is compatible with God's eternity and unchangeability because, time being dependent on motion, there cannot have been time when there was no motion. But yet it seems that it is meaningful and even indispensable to speak of "prior to the creation of the world" and, in the case of Heidegger, "prior to the emergence of man." It seems that one cannot avoid the question as to what is responsible for the emergence of man and of "Sein," of what brings them out of nothing; for *ex nihilo nihil fit* (out of nothing nothing comes into being). This is a very big question for Heidegger. He says, "*Ex nihilo omne ens qua ens*" (out of nothing every being has being / comes out). This could remind one of the Biblical doctrine of creation out of nothing, but Heidegger has no place for the Creator God.

Esse, as Heidegger understands it, may be described crudely, superficially, and even misleadingly (but not altogether misleadingly) by saying that it is a synthesis of Platonic ideas and the Biblical God: it is as impersonal as the Platonic ideas and as elusive as the Biblical God.

Part II
Classical Political Rationalism

4
On Classical Political Philosophy

The purpose of the following remarks is to discuss especially those characteristic features of classical political philosophy which are in particular danger of being overlooked or insufficiently stressed by the schools that are most influential in our time. These remarks are not intended to sketch the outlines of an adequate interpretation of classical political philosophy. They will have fulfilled their purpose if they point to the way which, as it seems to me, is the only one whereby such an interpretation can eventually be reached by us.

Classical political philosophy is characterized by the fact that it was related to political life directly. It was only after the classical philosophers had done their work that political philosophy became definitely "established" and thus acquired a certain remoteness from political life. Since that time the relationship of political philosophers to political life, and their grasp of it, have been determined by the existence of an inherited political philosophy: since then political philosophy has been related to political life through the medium of a tradition of political philosophy. The tradition of political philosophy, being a tradition, took for granted the necessity and possibility of political philosophy. The tradition that originated in classical Greece was rejected in the sixteenth and seventeenth centuries in favor of a new political philosophy. But this "revolution" did not restore the direct relation to political life that had existed in the beginning: the new political philosophy was related to political life through the medium of the inherited general notion of political philosophy or political science, and through the medium of a new concept of science. The modern political philosophers tried to replace both the teaching and the method of traditional political philosophy by what they considered as the true teaching and the right method; they took it for granted that political philosophy as such is necessary and possible. Today, political science may believe that by rejecting or emancipating itself from political philosophy, it stands in the most direct relation to political life; actually it is related to political life through the medium of modern natural science, or of the reaction to modern natural science, and through a number of basic concepts inherited from the philosophic tradition, however despised or ignored.

It was its direct relation to political life which determined the orientation and scope of classical political philosophy. Accordingly, the tradition which was based on that philosophy, and which preserved its orientation and scope, preserved that direct relation to a certain extent. The fundamental change in this respect begins with the new political philosophy of the early modern period and reaches its climax in present-day political science. The most striking difference between classical political philosophy and present-day political science is that the latter is no longer concerned at all with what was the guiding question for the former: the question of the best political order. On the other hand, modern political science is greatly preoccupied with a type of question that was of much less importance to classical political philosophy: questions concerning method. Both differences must be traced to the same reason: to the different degree of directness in which classical political philosophy, on the one hand, and present-day political science, on the other, are related to political life.

Classical political philosophy attempted to reach its goal by accepting the basic distinctions made in political life exactly in the sense and with the orientation in which they are made in political life, and by thinking them through, by understanding them as perfectly as possible. It did not start from such basic distinctions as those between the "state of nature" and "the civil state," between "facts" and "values," between "reality" and "ideologies," between "the world" and "the worlds" of different societies, or between "the I, Me, Thou, and We"—distinctions which are alien, and even unknown, to political life as such and which originate only in philosophic or scientific reflection. Nor did it try to bring order into that chaos of political "facts" which exists only for those who approach political life from a point of view outside of political life, that is to say, from the point of view of a science that is not itself essentially an element of political life. Instead, it followed carefully and even scrupulously the articulation which is inherent in, and natural to, political life and its objectives.

The primary questions of classical political philosophy, and the terms in which it stated them, were not specifically philosophic or scientific; they were questions that are raised in assemblies, councils, clubs and cabinets, and they were stated in terms intelligible and familiar, at least to all sane adults, from everyday experience and everyday usage. These questions have a natural hierarchy which supplies political life, and hence political philosophy, with its fundamental orientation. No one can help distinguishing among questions of smaller, of greater, and of paramount importance, and between questions of the moment and questions that are always present in political communities; and intelligent men apply these distinctions intelligently.

Similarly it can be said that the method, too, of classical political philosophy was presented by political life itself. Political life is characterized by conflicts between men asserting opposed claims. Those who raise a claim usually believe that what they claim is good for them. In many cases they believe, and in most cases they say, that what they claim is good for the community at large. In practically all cases claims are raised, sometimes sincerely and sometimes insincerely, in the name of justice. The opposed claims are based, then, on opinions of what is good or just. To justify their claims, the opposed parties advance arguments. The conflict calls for arbitration, for an intelligent decision that will give each party what it truly deserves. Some of the material required for making such a decision is offered by the opposed parties themselves, and the very insufficiency of this partial material—an insufficiency obviously due to its partisan origin—points the way to its completion by the umpire. The umpire *par excellence* is the political philosopher.[1] He tries to settle those political controversies that are both of paramount and of permanent importance.

This view of the function of the political philosopher—that he must not be a "radical" partisan who prefers victory in civil war to arbitration—is also of political origin: it is the duty of the good citizen to make civil strife cease and to create, by persuasion, agreement among the citizens.[2] The political philosopher first comes into sight as a good citizen who can perform this function of the good citizen in the best way and on the highest level. In order to perform his function he has to raise ulterior questions, questions that are never raised in the political arena; but in doing so he does not abandon his fundamental orientation, which is the orientation inherent in political life. Only if that orientation were abandoned, if the basic distinctions made by political life were considered merely "subjective" or "unscientific" and therefore disregarded, would the question of how to approach political things in order to understand them, that is to say, the question of method, become a fundamental question, and, indeed, *the* fundamental question.

It is true that political life is concerned primarily with the individual community to which the people happen to belong, and mostly even with individual situations, whereas political philosophy is concerned primarily with what is essential to all political communities. Yet there is a straight and almost continuous way leading from the prephilosophic to the philosophic approach. Political life requires various kinds of skills, and in particular that apparently highest skill which enables a man to manage well the affairs of his political community as a whole. That skill—the art, the prudence, the practical wisdom, the specific understanding possessed by the excellent statesman or politician—and not "a body of true propositions" concerning political matters which is transmitted by teachers to pupils, is what was originally meant by "political science." A man who possesses "political science" is not merely able to deal properly with a large variety of situations in his own community; he can, in principle, manage well even the affairs of any other political community, be it "Greek" or "barbarian." While all political life is essentially the life of this or that political community, "political science," which essentially belongs to political life, is essentially "transferable" from one community to any other. A man like Themistocles was admired and listened to not only in Athens, but, after he had to flee from Athens, among the barbarians as well; such a man is admired because he is capable of giving sound political advice wherever he goes.[3]

"Political science" designated originally the skill by virtue of which a man could manage well the affairs of political communities by deed and by speech. The skill of speaking takes precedence over the skill of doing, since all sensible action proceeds from deliberation, and the element of deliberation is speech. Accordingly, that part of political skill which first became the object of instruction was the skill of public speaking. "Political science" in a more precise sense, that is, as a skill that is essentially teachable, appeared first as rhetoric, or as a part of it. The teacher of rhetoric was not necessarily a politician or statesman; he was, however, a teacher of politicians or statesmen. Since his pupils belonged to the most different political communities, the content of his teaching could not possibly be bound up with the particular features of any individual political community. "Political science," on the level which it reached as a result of the exertions of the rhetoricians, is more "universal," is to an even higher degree "transferable," than is "political science" as a skill of the excellent statesman or politician: whereas strangers as statesmen or political advisers were an exception, strangers as teachers of rhetoric were the rule.[4]

Classical political philosophy rejected the identification of political science with rhetoric; it held that rhetoric, at its best, was only an instrument of political science. It did not, however, descend from the level of generality that had been reached by the rhetoricians. On the contrary, after that part of political skill which is the skill of speaking had been raised to the level of a distinct discipline, the classical philosophers could meet that challenge only by raising the whole of "political science," as far as possible or necessary, to the rank of a distinct discipline. By doing this they became the founders of political science in the precise and final sense of the term. And the way in which they did it was determined by the articulation natural to the political sphere.

"Political science" as the skill of the excellent politician or statesman consists in the right handling of individual situations; its immediate "products" are commands or decrees or advices effectively expressed, which are intended to cope with an individual case. Political life knows, however, a still higher kind of political understanding, which is concerned not with individual cases but, as regards each relevant subject, with all cases, and whose immediate "products"—laws and institutions—are meant to be permanent. The true legislators—"the fathers of the Constitution," as modern men would say—establish, as it were, the permanent framework within which the right handling of changing situations by excellent politicians or statesmen can take place. While it is true that the excellent statesman can act successfully within the most different frameworks of laws and institutions, the value of his achievement depends ultimately on the value of the cause in whose service he acts; and that cause is not his work, but the work of him or those who made the laws and institutions of his community. The legislative skill is, therefore, the most "architectonic" political skill[5] that is known to political life.

Every legislator is primarily concerned with the individual community for which he legislates, but he has to raise certain questions which regard all legislation. These most fundamental and most universal political questions are naturally fit to be made the subject of the most "architectonic," the truly "architectonic," political knowledge: of that political science which is the goal of the political philosopher. This political science is the knowledge which would enable a man to teach legislators. The political philosopher who has reached his goal is the teacher of legislators.[6] The knowledge of the political philosopher is "transferable" in the highest degree. Plato demonstrated this *ad oculos* in his dialogue on legislation, by presenting in the guise of a stranger the philosopher who is a teacher of legislators.[7] He illustrated it less ambiguously by the comparison, which frequently occurs in his writings, of political science with medicine.

It is by being the teacher of legislators that the political philosopher is the umpire *par excellence*. All political conflicts that arise within the community are at least related to, if they do not proceed from, the most fundamental political controversy: the controversy as to what type of men should rule the community. And the right settlement of that controversy appears to be the basis of excellent legislation.

Classical political philosophy was related to political life directly, because its guiding subject was a subject of actual political controversy carried on in prephilosophic political life. Since all political controversies presuppose the existence of the political community, the classics are not primarily concerned with the question of whether and why there is, or should be, a political community; hence the question of the nature and purpose of the political community is not the guiding question for classical political philosophy. Similarly, to question the desirability or necessity of the survival and independence of one's political community normally means to commit the crime of treason; in other words, the ultimate aim of foreign policy is not essentially controversial. Hence classical political philosophy is not guided by questions concerning the external relations of the political community. It is concerned primarily with the inner structure of the political community, because that inner structure is essentially the subject of such political controversy as essentially involves the danger of civil war.[8]

The actual conflict of groups struggling for political power within the community naturally gives rise to the question what group should rule, or what compromise would be the best solution—that is to say, what political order would be the best order. Either the opposed groups are merely factions made up of the same type of men (such as parties of noblemen or adherents of opposed dynasties), or each of the opposed groups represents a specific type. Only in the latter case does the political struggle go to the roots of political life; then it becomes apparent to everyone, from everyday political life, that the question as to what type of men should have the decisive say is the subject of the most fundamental political controversy.

The immediate concern of that controversy is the best political order for the given political community, but every answer to that immediate question implies an answer to the universal question of the best political order as such. It does not require the exertions of philosophers to lay bare this implication, for the political controversy has a natural tendency to express itself in universal terms. A man who rejects kingship for Israel cannot help using arguments against kingship as such; a man who defends democracy in Athens cannot help using arguments in favor of democracy as such. When they are confronted with the fact that monarchy is the best political order, say, for Babylon, the natural reaction of such men will be that this fact shows the inferiority of Babylon, and not that the question of the best political order does not make sense.

The groups, or types, whose claims to rule were considered by the classical philosophers were "the good" (men of merit), the rich, the noble, and the multitude, or the poor citizens; in the foreground of the political scene in the Greek cities, as well as in other places, was the struggle between the rich and the poor. The claim to rule which is based on merit, on human excellence, on "virtue," appeared to be least controversial: courageous and skillful generals, incorruptible and equitable judges, wise and unselfish magistrates, are generally preferred. Thus "aristocracy" (rule of the best) presented itself as the natural answer of all good men to the natural question of the best political order. As Thomas Jefferson put it, "That form of government is the best, which provides the most effectually for a pure selection of [the] natural *aristoi* into offices of the government."[9]

What is to be understood by "good men" was known also from political life: good men are those who are willing, and able, to prefer the common interest to their private interest and to the objects of their passions, or those who, being able to discern in each situation what is the noble or right thing to do, do it because it is noble and right and for no ulterior reason. It was also generally recognized that this answer gives rise to further questions of almost overwhelming political significance: that results which are generally considered desirable can be achieved by men of dubious character or by the use of unfair means; that "just" and "useful" are not simply identical; that virtue may lead to ruin.[10]

Thus the question guiding classical political philosophy, the typical answer that it gave, and the insight into the bearing of the formidable objections to it, belong to prephilosophic political life, or precede political philosophy. Political philosophy goes beyond prephilosophic political knowledge by trying to understand fully the implications of these prephilosophic insights, and especially by defending the second of them against the more or less "sophisticated" attacks made by bad or perplexed men.

When the prephilosophic answer is accepted, the most urgent question concerns the "materials" and institutions which would be most favorable to "the rule of the best." It is primarily by answering this question, by thus elaborating a "blueprint" of the best polity, that the political philosopher becomes the teacher of legislators. The legislator is strictly limited in his choice of institutions and laws by the character of the people for whom he legislates, by their traditions, by the nature of their territory, by their economic conditions, and so on. His choosing this or that law is normally a compromise between what he would wish and what circumstances permit. To effect that compromise intelligently, he must first know what he wishes, or, rather, what would be most desirable in itself. The political philosopher can answer that question because he is not limited in his reflections by any particular set of circumstances, but is free to choose the most favorable conditions that are possible—ethnic, climatic, economic and other—and thus to determine what laws and institutions would be preferable under those conditions.[11] After that, he tries to bridge the gulf between what is most desirable in itself and what is possible in given circumstances, by discussing what polity, and what laws, would be best under various types of more or less unfavorable conditions, and even what kinds of laws and measures are appropriate for preserving any kind of polity, however defective. By thus erecting on the "normative" foundation of political science a "realistic" structure, or, to speak somewhat more adequately, by thus supplementing political physiology with political pathology and therapeutics, he does not retract or even qualify, he rather confirms, his view that the question of the best polity is necessarily the guiding question.[12]

By the best political order the classical philosopher understood that political order which is best always and everywhere.[13] This does not mean that he conceived of that order as necessarily good for every community, as "a perfect solution for all times and for every place": a given community may be so rude or so depraved that only a very inferior type of order can "keep it going." But it does mean that the goodness of the political order realized any-where and at any time can be judged only in terms of that political order which is best absolutely. "The best political order" is, then, not intrinsically Greek: it is no more intrinsically Greek than health, as is shown by the parallelism of political science and med-icine. But just as it may happen that the members of one nation are more likely to be healthy and strong than those of others, it may also happen that one nation has a greater natural fitness for political excellence than others.

When Aristotle asserted that the Greeks had a greater natural fitness for political excellence than the nations of the north and those of Asia, he did not assert, of course, that political excellence was identical with the quality of being Greek or derivative from it; otherwise he could not have praised the institutions of Carthage as highly as the institutions of the most renowned Greek cities. When Socrates asked Glaucon in the *Republic* whether the city that Glaucon was founding would be a Greek city, and Glaucon an-swered emphatically in the affirmative, neither of them said any more than that a city founded by Greeks would necessarily be a Greek city. The purpose of this truism, or rather of Socrates' ques-tion, was to induce the warlike Glaucon to submit to a certain mod-eration of warfare: since a general prohibition of wars was not fea-sible, at least warfare among Greeks should keep within certain limits. The fact that a perfect city founded by Glaucon would be a Greek city does not imply that any perfect city was necessarily Greek: Socrates considered it possible that the perfect city, which certainly did not exist at that time anywhere in Greece, existed at that time "in some barbarian place."[14] Xenophon went so far as to describe the Persian Cyrus as *the* perfect ruler, and to imply that the education Cyrus received in Persia was superior even to Spar-tan education; and he did not consider it impossible that a man of the rank of Socrates would emerge among the Armenians.[15]

Because of its direct relation to political life, classical political philosophy was essentially "practical"; on the other hand, it is no accident that modern political philosophy frequently calls itself po-litical "theory."[16] The primary concern of the former was not the description, or understanding, of political life, but its right guid-ance. Hegel's demand that political philosophy refrain from con-struing a state as it ought to be, or from teaching the state how it should be, and that it try to understand the present and actual state as something essentially rational, amounts to a rejection of the *raison d'être* of classical political philosophy. In contrast with present-day political science, or with well-known interpretations of present-day political science, classical political philosophy pursued practical aims and was guided by, and culminated in, "value judgments." The attempt to replace the quest for the best political order by a purely descriptive or analytical political science which refrains from "value judgments" is, from the point of view of the classics, as absurd as the attempt to replace the art of making shoes, that is, good and well-fitting shoes, by a museum of shoes made by apprentices, or as the idea of a medicine which refuses to distinguish between health and sickness.

Since political controversies are concerned with "good things" and "just things," classical political philosophy was naturally guided by considerations of "goodness" and "justice." It started from the moral distinctions as they are made in everyday life, although it knew better than the dogmatic skeptic of our time the formidable theoretical objections to which they are exposed. Such distinctions as those between courage and cowardice, justice and injustice, human kindness and selfishness, gentleness and cruelty, urbanity and rudeness, are intelligible and clear for all practical purposes, that is, in most cases, and they are of decisive importance in guiding our lives: this is a sufficient reason for considering the fundamental political questions in their light.

In the sense in which these distinctions are politically relevant, they cannot be "demonstrated," they are far from being perfectly lucid, and they are exposed to grave theoretical doubts. Accordingly, classical political philosophy limited itself to addressing men who, because of their natural inclinations as well as their upbringing, took those distinctions for granted. It knew that one can perhaps silence but not truly convince such people as have no "taste" for the moral distinctions and their significance: not even Socrates himself could convert, though he could silence, such men as Meletus and Callicles, and he admitted the limits set to demonstrations in this sphere by taking recourse to "myths."

The political teaching of the classical philosophers, as distinguished from their theoretical teaching, was primarily addressed not to all intelligent men, but to all decent men.[17] A political teaching which addressed itself equally to decent and indecent men would have appeared to them from the outset as unpolitical, that is, as politically, or socially, irresponsible; for if it is true that the well-being of the political community requires that its members be guided by considerations of decency or morality, the political community cannot tolerate a political science which is morally "neutral" and which therefore tends to loosen the hold of moral principles on the minds of those who are exposed to it. To express the same view somewhat differently, even if it were true that when men are talking of right they are thinking only of their interests, it would be equally true that that reserve is of the essence of political man, and that by emancipating oneself from it one would cease to be a political man or to speak his language.

Thus the attitude of classical political philosophy toward political things was always akin to that of the enlightened statesman; it was not the attitude of the detached observer who looks at political things in the way in which a zoologist looks at the big fishes swallowing the small ones, or that of the social "engineer" who thinks in terms of manipulating or conditioning rather than in terms of education or liberation, or that of the prophet who believes that he knows the future.

In brief, the root of classical political philosophy was the fact that political life is characterized by controversies between groups struggling for power within the political community. Its purpose was to settle those political controversies which are of a fundamental and typical character in the spirit not of the partisan but of the good citizen, and with a view to such an order as would be most in accordance with the requirements of human excellence. Its guiding subject was the most fundamental politically controversial subject, understood in the way, and in the terms, in which it was understood in prephilosophic political life.

In order to perform his function the philosopher had to raise an ulterior question which is never raised in the political arena. That question is so simple, elementary, and unobtrusive that it is, at first, not even intelligible, as is shown by a number of occurrences described in the Platonic dialogues. This distinctly philosophic question is, What is virtue? What is that virtue whose possession—as everyone admits spontaneously or is reduced to silence by unanswerable arguments—gives a man the highest right to rule? In the light of this question the common opinions about virtue appear at the outset as unconscious attempts to answer an unconscious question. On closer examination their radical insufficiency is more specifically revealed by the fact that some of them are contradicted by other opinions which are equally common. To reach consistency the philosopher is compelled to maintain one part of common opinion and to give up the other part which contradicts it; he is thus driven to adopt a view that is no longer generally held, a truly paradoxical view, one that is generally considered "absurd" or "ridiculous."

Nor is that all. He is ultimately compelled to transcend not merely the dimension of common opinion, of political opinion, but the dimension of political life as such; for he is led to realize that the ultimate aim of political life cannot be reached by political life, but only by a life devoted to contemplation, to philosophy. This finding is of crucial importance for political philosophy, since it determines the limits set to political life, to all political action and all political planning. Moreover, it implies that the highest subject of political philosophy is the philosophic life: philosophy—not as a teaching or as a body of knowledge, but as a way of life—offers, as it were, the solution to the problem that keeps political life in motion. Ultimately, political philosophy transforms itself into a discipline that is no longer concerned with political things in the ordinary sense of the term: Socrates called his inquiries a quest for "the *true* political skill," and Aristotle called his discussion of virtue and related subjects "a *kind* of political science."[18]

No difference between classical political philosophy and modern political philosophy is more telling than this: the philosophic life, or the life of "the wise," which was the highest subject of classical political philosophy, has in modern times almost completely ceased to be a subject of political philosophy. Yet even this ultimate step of classical political philosophy, however absurd it seemed to the common opinion, was nevertheless "divined" by prephilosophic political life: men wholly devoted to the political life were sometimes popularly considered "busybodies," and their unresting habits were contrasted with the greater freedom and the higher dignity of the more retired life of men who were "minding their own business."[19]

The direct relation of classical political philosophy to prephilosophic political life was due not to the undeveloped character of classical philosophy or science, but to mature reflection. This reflection is summed up in Aristotle's description of political philosophy as "the philosophy concerning the human things." This description reminds us of the almost overwhelming difficulty which had to be overcome before philosophers could devote any serious attention to political things, to human things. The "human things" were distinguished from the "divine things" or the "natural things," and the latter were considered absolutely superior in dignity to the former.[20] Philosophy, therefore, was at first exclusively concerned with the natural things. Thus, in the beginning, philosophic effort was concerned only negatively, only accidentally, with political things. Socrates himself, the founder of political philosophy, was famous as a philosopher before he ever turned to political philosophy. Left to themselves, the philosophers would not descend again to the "cave" of political life, but would remain outside in what they considered "the island of the blessed"—contemplation of the truth.[21]

But philosophy, being an attempt to rise from opinion to science, is necessarily related to the sphere of opinion as its essential starting point, and hence to the political sphere. Therefore the political sphere is bound to advance into the focus of philosophic interest as soon as philosophy starts to reflect on its own doings. To understand fully its own purpose and nature, philosophy has to understand its essential starting point, and hence the nature of political things.

The philosophers, as well as other men who have become aware of the possibility of philosophy, are sooner or later driven to wonder, Why philosophy? Why does human life need philosophy? Why is it good, why is it right, that opinions about the nature of the whole should be replaced by genuine knowledge of the nature of the whole? Since human life is living together, or, more exactly, is political life, the question, Why philosophy? means, Why does political life need philosophy? This question calls philosophy before the tribunal of the political community: it makes philosophy politically responsible. Like Plato's perfect city itself, which, once established, does not permit the philosophers to devote themselves any longer exclusively to contemplation, this question, once raised, forbids the philosophers any longer to disregard political life altogether. Plato's *Republic* as a whole, as well as other political works of the classical philosophers, can best be described as an attempt to supply a political justification for philosophy by showing that the well-being of the political community depends decisively on the study of philosophy. Such a justification was all the more urgent since the meaning of philosophy was by no means generally understood, and hence philosophy was distrusted and hated by many well-meaning citizens.[22] Socrates himself fell victim to the popular prejudice against philosophy.

To justify philosophy before the tribunal of the political community means to justify philosophy in terms of the political community, that is to say, by means of a kind of argument which appeals, not to philosophers as such, but to citizens as such. To prove to citizens that philosophy is permissible, desirable, or even necessary, the philosopher has to follow the example of Odysseus and start from premises that are generally agreed upon, or from generally accepted opinions:[23] he has to argue *ad hominem* or "dialectically." From this point of view the adjective "political" in the expression "political philosophy" designates not so much a subject matter as a manner of treatment;[24] from this point of view, I say, "political philosophy" means primarily not the philosophic treatment of politics, but the political, or popular, treatment of philosophy, or the political introduction to philosophy—the attempt to lead the qualified citizens, or rather their qualified sons, from the political life to the philosophic life. This deeper meaning of "political philosophy" tallies well with its ordinary meaning, for in both cases "political philosophy" culminates in praise of the philosophic life. At any rate, it is ultimately because he means to justify philosophy before the tribunal of the political community, and hence on the level of political discussion, that the philosopher has to understand the political things exactly as they are understood in political life.

In his political philosophy the philosopher starts, then, from that understanding of political things which is natural to prephilosophic political life. At the beginning the fact that a certain habitual attitude or a certain way of acting is generally praised is a sufficient reason for considering that attitude, or that way of acting, a virtue. But the philosopher is soon compelled, or able, to transcend the dimension of prephilosophic understanding by raising the crucial question, What is virtue? The attempt to answer this question leads to a critical distinction between the generally praised attitudes which are rightly praised, and those which are not; and it leads to the recognition of a certain hierarchy, unknown in prephilosophic life, of the different virtues. Such a philosophic critique of the generally accepted views is at the bottom of the fact that Aristotle, for example, omitted piety and sense of shame from his list of virtues,[25] and that his list starts with courage and moderation (the least intellectual virtues) and, proceeding via liberality, magnanimity, and the virtues of private relations, to justice, culminates in the dianoetic virtues.[26] Moreover, insight into the limits of the moral-political sphere as a whole can be expounded fully only by answering the question of the nature of political things. This question marks the limit of political philosophy as a practical discipline: while essentially practical in itself, the question functions as an entering wedge for others whose purpose is no longer to guide action but simply to understand things as they are.[27]

5

Exoteric Teaching

The distinction between exoteric (or public) and esoteric (or secret) teaching is not at present considered to be of any significance for the understanding of the thought of the past: the leading encyclopedia of classical antiquity does not contain any article, however brief, on *exoteric* or *esoteric* (*Real-Encyclopaedie der classischen Altertumswissenschaft*, ed. Pauly and Wissowa). Since a considerable number of ancient writers had not a little to say about the distinction in question, the silence of the leading encyclopedia cannot possibly be due to the silence of the sources; it must be due to the influence of modern philosophy on classical scholarship; it is that influence which prevents scholars from attaching significance to numerous, if not necessarily correct, statements of ancient writers. For while it is for classical scholars to decide whether and when the distinction between exoteric and esoteric teaching occurs in the sources, it is for philosophers to decide whether that distinction is significant in itself. And modern philosophy is not favorable to an affirmative answer to this philosophic question. The classical scholar Zeller may have believed himself to have cogent reasons for rejecting the view that Aristotle "designedly chose for [his scientific publication] a style obscure and unintelligible to the lay mind"; but it must be doubted whether these reasons would have appeared to him equally cogent, if he had not been assured by the philosopher Zeller that the rejected view "attributes to the philos-

63

opher a very childish sort of mystification, wholly destitute of any reasonable motive."[1]

As late as the last third of the eighteenth century, the view that all the ancient philosophers had distinguished between their exoteric and their esoteric teaching was still maintained; and its essential implications were still fully understood by at least one man. Gotthold Ephraim Lessing united in himself in a unique way the so divergent qualities of the philosopher and of the scholar. He discussed the question of exotericism clearly and fully in three little writings of his: in "Leibniz von den ewigen Strafen" (1773), in "Des Andreas Wissowatius Einwürfe wider die Dreieinigkeit" (1773), and in "Ernst und Falk" (1777 and 1780).[2] He discussed it as clearly and as fully as could be done by someone who still accepted exotericism not merely as a strange fact of the past, but rather as an intelligible necessity for all times and, therefore, as a principle guiding his own literary activity.[3] In short, Lessing was the last writer who revealed, while hiding, the reasons compelling wise men to hide the truth: he wrote between the lines about the art of writing between the lines.

In "Ernst und Falk," a character called Falk, who expresses himself somewhat evasively and sometimes even enigmatically, tries to show that every political constitution, and even the best political constitution, is necessarily imperfect; the necessary imperfection of all political life makes necessary the existence of what he calls "free-masonry," and he does not hesitate to assert that "free-masonry," which is necessary, was always in existence and will always be. Falk himself is a "free-mason," if a heretical "free-mason," and in order to be a "free-mason," a man must know truths which ought better to be concealed.[4] Which is then the concealed reason for his view that all political life is necessarily imperfect?[5] The intention of the good works of the "free-masons" is to make good works superfluous (First Dialogue, at the end, and Third Dialogue, p. 39 = pp. 19 and 28 of Maschler trans.), and "free-masonry" came into being[6] when someone who originally had planned a scientific society, which should make the speculative truths useful for practical and political life, conceived of a "society which should raise itself from the practice of civil life to speculation" (Fifth Dialogue, toward the end = p. 47 of Maschler trans.). The concealed reasons for the imperfection of political life as such are the facts that all practical or political life is essentially inferior to contemplative life, or that all works, and therefore also all good works, are "superfluous" insofar as the level of theoretical life, which is self-sufficient, is reached; and that the requirements of the lower are bound from time to time to conflict with, and to supersede in practice, the requirements of the higher. Consideration of that conflict is the ultimate reason why the "free-masons" (i.e., the wise or the men of contemplation) must conceal certain fundamental truths. It may be added that Lessing points out in "Ernst und Falk" that the variety of religions is due to the variety of political constitutions (Second Dialogue, pp. 34ff. = pp. 22ff. of Maschler trans.): the religious problem (i.e., the problem of historical, positive religion) is considered by him as part and parcel of the political problem.

In "Leibniz von den ewigen Strafen" and in "Wissowatius," Lessing applies these views to an explanation of Leibniz's attitude toward religion. The explicit purpose of these two little treatises is to discuss "the motives and reasons" which had induced Leibniz to defend certain orthodox beliefs—the belief in eternal damnation and the belief in the trinity (*Werke* 21:143, 181). While defending Leibniz's defense of the belief in eternal damnation, Lessing states that Leibniz's peculiar way of assenting to received opinions is identical with "what all the ancient philosophers used to do in their exoteric speech" (ibid., 147). By making that statement, he not only asserts that all the ancient philosophers made use of two manners of teaching (an exoteric manner and an esoteric manner); he also bids us to trace back all essential features of Leibniz's exotericism to the exotericism of the ancients. What, then, are the essential features of Leibniz's exotericism? Or, in other words, what are the motives and reasons which guided Leibniz in his defense of the orthodox or received opinion (see ibid., 146)? Lessing's first answer to this question is that Leibniz's peculiar way of assenting to received opinions is identical with "what all the ancient philosophers used to do in their exoteric speech. He observed a sort of prudence for which, it is true, our most recent philosophers have become much too wise."[7] The distinction between exoteric and esoteric speech has then so little to do with "mysticism" of any sort that it is an outcome of prudence. Somewhat later on Lessing indicates the difference between the esoteric reason enabling Leibniz to defend the orthodox doctrine of eternal damnation, and the exoteric reason expressed in his defense of that doctrine (ibid., 153ff.). That exoteric reason, he asserts, is based on the mere possibility of eternally increasing wickedness of moral beings. And then he goes on to say: "It is true, humanity shudders at this conception although it concerns the mere possibility. I should not, however, for that reason raise the question: why frighten with a mere possibility? For I should have to expect this counterquestion: why not frighten with it, since it can only be frightful to him who has never been earnest about the betterment of himself." This implies that a philosopher who makes an exoteric statement asserts, not a fact, but what Lessing chooses to call "a mere possibility": he does not, strictly speaking, believe in the truth of that statement (e.g., the statement that there is such a thing as eternally increasing wickedness of human beings which would justify eternally increasing punishments). This is indicated by Lessing in the following remark introducing a quotation from the final part of Plato's *Gorgias:* "Socrates himself believed in such eternal punishments quite seriously; he believed in them at least to the extent that he considered it expedient to teach such punishments in terms which do not in any way arouse suspicion and which are most explicit."[8]

Before proceeding any further, I must summarize Lessing's view of exoteric teaching. To avoid the danger of arbitrary interpretation, I shall omit all elements of that view which are not noticed at a first glance even by the most superficial reader of Lessing, although the obvious part of his view, if taken by itself, is somewhat enigmatic. (1) Lessing asserts that all the ancient philosophers, and Leibniz,[9] made use of exoteric presentation of the truth, as distinguished from its esoteric presentation. (2) The exoteric presentation of the truth makes use of statements which are considered by the philosopher himself to be statements, not of facts, but of mere possibilities. (3) Exoteric statements (i.e., such statements as would not and could not occur within the esoteric teaching) are made by the philosopher for reasons of prudence or expediency. (4) Some exoteric statements are addressed to morally inferior people, who ought to be frightened by such statements. (5) There are certain truths which must be concealed. (6) Even the best political constitution is bound to be imperfect. (7) Theoretical life is superior to practical or political life. The impression created by this summary, that there is a close connection between exotericism and a peculiar attitude toward political and practical life, is not misleading: "free-masonry," which as such knows of secret truths, owes its existence to the necessary imperfection of all practical or political life.

Some readers might be inclined to dismiss Lessing's whole teaching at once, since it seems to be based on the obviously erroneous, or merely traditional,[10] assumption that *all* the ancient phi-

losophers have made use of exoteric speches. To warn such readers, one must point out that the incriminated sentence permits of
a wholly unobjectionable interpretation: Lessing implicitly denies
that writers on philosophical topics who reject exotericism deserve
the name of philosophers.[11] For he knew the passages in Plato in
which it is indicated that it was the sophists who refused to conceal
the truth.

After Lessing, who died in the year in which Kant published his
Critique of Pure Reason, the question of exotericism seems to have
been lost sight of almost completely, at least among scholars and
philosophers as distinguished from novelists. When Schleiermacher introduced that style of Platonic studies in which classical
scholarship is still engaged, and which is based on the identification of the natural order of Platonic dialogues with the sequence
of their elaboration, he still had to discuss in detail the view that
there are two kinds of Platonic teaching, an exoteric kind and an
esoteric one. In doing this, he made five or six extremely important
and true remarks about Plato's literary devices,[12] remarks the
subtlety of which has, to my knowledge, never been surpassed or
even rivalled since. Yet he failed to see the crucial question. He
asserts that there is *only one* Platonic teaching—the teaching presented in the dialogues—although there is, so to speak, an infinite
number of levels of the understanding of that teaching: it is the
same teaching which the beginner understands inadequately, and
which only the perfectly trained student of Plato understands adequately. But is then the teaching which the beginner *actually* understands *identical* with the teaching which the perfectly trained student *actually* understands? The distinction between Plato's exoteric
and esoteric teaching had sometimes been traced back to Plato's
opposition to "polytheism and popular religion" and to the necessity in which he found himself of hiding that opposition; Schleiermacher believes he has refuted this view by asserting that "Plato's
principles on that topic are clear enough to read in his writings, so
that one can scarcely believe that his pupils might have needed
still more information about them" (Schleiermacher, *Platons Werke*
1.1.14). Yet "polytheism and popular religion" is an ambiguous
expression: if Schleiermacher had used the less ambiguous "belief
in the existence of the gods worshipped by the city of Athens," he
could not have said that Plato's opposition to that belief is clearly
expressed in his writings. As a matter of fact, in his introduction
to his translation of Plato's *Apology of Socrates*, he considers it "a
weak point of that writing that Plato has not made a more ener-

getic use of the argument taken from Socrates' service to Apollo, for refuting the charge that Socrates did not believe in the old gods" (ibid., 185). If Plato's Socrates believed in "the old gods," is not Plato himself likely to have believed in them as well? And how can one then say that Plato's opposition to "polytheism and popular religion" as such is clearly expressed in his writings? Schleiermacher's strongest argument against the distinction between two teachings of Plato appears to be his assertion that Plato's real investigations are hidden, not absolutely, but only from the inattentive readers, or that attention is the only prerequisite for a full understanding of his real investigations as distinguished from those investigations which are merely the "skin" of the former.[13] But did any man in his senses ever assert that Plato wished to hide his secret teaching from all readers or from all men? Did any man whose judgment can claim to carry any weight in this matter ever understand by Plato's esoteric teaching anything other than that teaching of his dialogues which escapes the inattentive readers only? The only possible difference of opinion concerns exclusively the meaning of the distinction between inattentive and attentive readers: does a continuous way lead from the extremely inattentive reader to the extremely attentive reader, or is the way between the two extremes interrupted by a chasm? Schleiermacher tacitly assumes that the way from the beginning to the end is continuous, whereas, according to Plato, philosophy presupposes a real conversion,[14] i.e., a total break with the attitude of the beginner: the beginner is a man who has not yet for one moment left the cave, and who has never even turned his eyes away from the shadows of man-made things toward the exit of the cave, whereas the philosopher is the man who has left the cave and who (if he is not compelled to do otherwise) lives outside of the cave, on "the islands of the blessed." The difference between the beginner and the philosopher (for the perfectly trained student of Plato is no one else but the genuine philosopher) is a difference not of degree but of kind. Now, it is well known that, according to Plato, virtue is knowledge or science; therefore, the beginner is inferior to the perfectly trained student of Plato not only intellectually, but also morally. That is to say, the morality of the beginners has a basis essentially different from the basis on which the morality of the philosopher rests: their virtue is not genuine virtue, but vulgar or political virtue only, a virtue based not on insight, but on customs or laws (*Republic* 430c3–5 and *Phaedo* 82a10–b8). We may say, the morality of the beginners is the morality of the "auxiliaries" of the *Republic*, but not yet the morality of the "guardians." Now, the "auxiliaries," the best among whom are the beginners, must believe "noble lies" (*Republic* 414b4ff.; see also *Laws* 663d6ff.), i.e., statements which, while being useful for the political community, are nevertheless lies. And there is a difference not of degree but of kind between truth and lie (or untruth). And what holds true of the difference between truth and lies holds equally true of the difference between esoteric and exoteric teaching; for Plato's exoteric teaching is identical with his "noble lies." This connection of considerations, which is more or less familiar to every reader of Plato, if not duly emphasized by all students of Plato, is not even mentioned by Schleiermacher in his refutation of the view that there is a distinction between Plato's exoteric and esoteric teaching. Nor does he, in that context, as much as allude to Lessing's dialogues ("Ernst und Falk" and Lessing's conversation with F. H. Jacobi) which probably come closer to the spirit of Platonic dialogues and their technique than any other modern work in the German language. Therefore Schleiermacher's refutation of the view in question is not convincing. A comparison of his *Philosophic Ethics* with the *Nicomachean Ethics* would bring to light the reason[15] why he failed to pay any attention to the difference between the morality of the beginner and the morality of the philosopher, i.e., to the difference which is at the bottom of the difference between exoteric and esoteric teaching.

I return to Lessing. How was Lessing led to notice,[16] and to understand, the information about the fact that "all the ancient philosophers" had distinguished between their exoteric and their esoteric teaching? If I am not mistaken, he rediscovered the bearing of that distinction by his own exertion after having undergone his conversion, i.e., after having had the experience of what philosophy is and what sacrifices it requires. For it is that experience which leads in a straight way to the distinction between the two groups of men, the philosophic men and the unphilosophic men, and therewith to the distinction between the two ways of presenting the truth. In a famous letter to a friend (to Moses Mendelssohn, 9 January 1771), he expresses his fear that "by throwing away certain prejudices, I have thrown away a little too much that I shall have to get back again."[17] That passage has sometimes been understood to indicate that Lessing was about to return from the intransigent rationalism of his earlier period toward a more positive view of the Bible and the Biblical tradition. There is ample evidence to show that this interpretation is wrong.[18] The context of the passage makes it clear that the things which Lessing had "thrown away" before and which, he feels, he ought to "fetch back" were truths which he descried "from afar" in a book by Ferguson, as he believed on the basis of what he had seen in the table of contents of that book. He also descried "from afar" in Ferguson's book "truths in the continual contradiction of which we happen to live and we have to go on living continually in the interest of our quietude." There may very well be a connection between the two kinds of truth: the truths which Lessing had formerly thrown away may have been truths contradictory to the truths generally accepted by the philosophy of enlightenment and also accepted by Lessing throughout his life. At any rate, two years later he openly rebuked the more recent philosophers who had evaded the contradiction between wisdom and prudence by becoming much too wise to submit to the rule of prudence which had been observed by Leibniz and all the ancient philosophers. External evidence is in favor of the view that the book referred to by Lessing is Ferguson's *Essay on the History of Civil Society.*[19] The "truths in the continual contradiction of which we have to live," which had been discussed by Ferguson and which are indicated to a certain extent in the table of contents of his *Essay,*[20] concerned the ambiguous character of civilization, i.e., the theme of the two famous early writings of Rousseau, which Lessing, as he perhaps felt, had not considered carefully enough in his youth.[21] Lessing expressed his view of the ambiguous character of civilization some years later in these more precise terms: even the absolutely best civil constitution is necessarily imperfect. It seems then to have been the political problem which gave Lessing's thought a decisive turn away from the philosophy of enlightenment—yet not, indeed, toward romanticism of any sort (toward what is called a deeper, historical view of government and religion) but towards an older type of philosophy. How near he apparently came to certain romantic views on his way from the philosophy of enlightenment to that older type of philosophy, we may learn from what F. H. Jacobi tells us in an essay of his which is devoted to the explanation of a political remark made by Lessing. According to Jacobi, Lessing once said that the arguments against papal despotism are either no arguments at all, or else they are two or three times as valid against the despotism of princes.[22] Could Lessing have held the view that ecclesiastical despotism is two or three times better than secular despotism? Jacobi elsewhere says in his own name, but certainly in the spirit of Lessing, that that despotism which is based "exclusively" on superstition is less bad than secular despotism.[23] Now, secular despotism could easily be allied with the philosophy of enlightenment, and therewith with the rejection of exotericism strictly speaking, as is shown above all by the teaching of the classic of enlightened despotism: the teaching of Hobbes. But "despotism based exclusively on superstition," i.e., not at all on force, cannot be maintained if the nonsuperstitious minority does not voluntarily refrain from openly exposing and refuting the "superstitious" beliefs. Lessing did not, then, have to wait for the experience of Robespierre's despotism to realize the relative truth of what the romantics asserted against the principles of Rousseau (who seems to have believed in a political solution of the problem of civilization): Lessing realized that relative truth one generation earlier, and he rejected it in favor of the way leading to absolute truth, the way of philosophy. The experience which he had in that moment enabled him to understand the meaning of Leibniz's "prudence" in a manner infinitely more adequate than the enlightened Leibnizians among his contemporaries did and could do. Leibniz, then, is that link in the chain of the tradition of exotericism which is nearest to Lessing. Leibniz, however, was not the only seventeenth-century thinker who was initiated. Not to mention the prudent Descartes, even so bold a writer as Spinoza had admitted the necessity of *"pia dogmata, hoc est, talia quae animum ad obedientiam movent"* as distinguished from *"vera dogmata"* (*Tractatus Theologico–Politicus*, cap. 14, sec. 20 [Bruder ed.]). But Lessing did not have to rely on any modern or medieval representatives of the tradition: he was familiar with its sources. It was precisely his intransigent classicism—his considered view that close study of the classics is the only way in which a diligent and thinking man can become a philosopher[24]—which had led him, first, to notice the exotericism of some ancient philosophers and, later on, to understand the exotericism of all the ancient philosophers.

6
Thucydides: The Meaning of Political History

This lecture forms part of a series: The Western Tradition—Its Great Ideas and Issues. The Western tradition is threatened today as it never was heretofore. For it is now threatened not only from without but from within as well. It is in a state of disintegration. Those among us who believe in the Western tradition, we Western-ers—we *Sapadniks*, as Dostoevski and his friends used to call the Westerners among the Russians—must therefore rally around the flag of the Western tradition. But we must do it in a manner, if not worthy of that noble tradition, at least reminding of it: we must uphold the Western principles in a Western manner; we must not try to drown our doubts in a sea of tearful or noisy assent. We must be aware of the fact that the vitality and the glory of our Western tradition are inseparable from its problematic character. For that tradition has two roots. It consists of two heterogeneous elements, of two elements which are ultimately incompatible with each other—the Hebrew element and the Greek element. We speak, and we speak rightly, of the antagonism between Jerusalem and Athens, between faith and philosophy. Both philosophy and the Bible assert that there is ultimately one thing, and one thing only, needful for man. But the one thing needful proclaimed by the Bible is the very opposite of the one thing needful proclaimed by Greek philosophy. According to the Bible, the one thing needful is obe-dient love; according to philosophy, the one thing needful is free inquiry. The whole history of the West can be viewed as an ever repeated attempt to achieve a compromise or a synthesis between these two antagonistic principles. But all these attempts have failed, and necessarily so; in every synthesis, however impressive, one element of the synthesis is sacrificed, however subtly, but nonetheless surely, to the other. Philosophy is made, against its meaning, the handmaid of theology, or faith is made, against its meaning, the handmaid of philosophy. The Western tradition does not allow of a synthesis of its two elements, but only of their tension: this is the secret of the vitality of the West. The Western tradition does not allow a final solution of the fundamental contradiction, a society without contradiction. As long as there will be a Western world, there will be theologians who distrust philosophers, and there will be philosophers who are annoyed by theologians. While rallying around the flag of the Western tradition, let us beware of the danger that we be charmed or bullied into a conformism which would be the inglorious end of the Western tradition.

I must leave it open whether the very principles underlying the Western tradition, i.e., whether philosophy and theology, would allow us to speak of "the Western tradition" in the terms which I have used. Permit me to declare that it is impossible to do so in the last analysis. But it is foolish even to try always to speak in terms which could stand the test of precise analysis. Most of the time our maxim must be that expressed in the words of a Greek poet: "I do not want these highbrow things, I want what the city needs" (Euripides, frag. 16, Nauck ed.; quoted in Aristotle *Politics* 1277a 19–20). As long as we speak politically, i.e., crudely, we are indeed forced to speak of the Western tradition more or less in the terms which I have used.

Now, one of the great ideas or issues of the Western tradition is political history. Political history is as characteristic of the Western tradition as philosophy or science, on the one hand, and belief in revelation, on the other. Since the Western tradition consists of two heterogeneous elements, we must first determine to which of these two elements political history belongs. There cannot be the slightest doubt as regards the answer. As the very terms "politics" and "history" show, political history is of Greek, not of Hebrew, origin.

One may say that the theme of political history is human power, but power viewed sympathetically. Power is a very imprecise term. Let us therefore speak rather of freedom and empire. Political history presupposes that freedom and empire are, not unreasonably, mankind's great objectives—that freedom and empire are legitimate objects of admiration. Freedom and empire elicit the greatest efforts of large bodies of men. That greatness is impressive. That greatness can be seen or felt by everyone, and it is a greatness which affects the fate of everyone. The theme of political history is massive and popular. Political history requires that this massive and popular theme call forth a massive and popular response. Political history belongs to a political life in which many participate. It belongs to a republican political life, to the polis. Political history will be important only if politics is important. Political history will reach its full stature, it will be of decisive importance, only if politics is of decisive importance. But politics will be of decisive importance only to men who prefer (as some Florentines did) the salvation of their city to the salvation of their souls: to men who are dominated by the spirit of republican virtue, by the spirit of the polis.

Yet men dominated by the spirit of the polis will not be able to be political historians in the full sense of the term. An ancient critic has said that the political historian must be *apolis*, cityless, beyond the city. The political historian must be more than a citizen or even a statesman: he must be a wise man. Political history presupposes that wise men regard political life as sufficiently important to describe it with care and with sympathy, and this presupposition involves a paradox. Wise men will always be inclined to look down on political life, on its hustle and bustle, its glitter and glory. Above all, they will regard it as dull. The political man is constantly forced to have very long conversations with very dull people on very dull subjects. Ninety-nine percent, if not more, of politics is administration. And as for the exciting part, the decision-making, it is inseparable from long periods of mere waiting—of an action which consists in the suspension of doing as well as of thinking. Wise men will always be inclined to see in political life an element of childishness. The wisdom which takes a serious interest in politics must then be the wisdom of men who are, or who have remained, children—in a way. The wise men of Greece were such men. An Egyptian priest said to a Greek: "You Greeks are always children; you are young in soul, every one of you; for therein you possess not a single belief that is ancient and derived from old tradition, nor yet a single piece of learning that is hoary with age" (Plato *Timaeus* 22b). It was the coming together of Greek republicanism with Greek wisdom which generated political history.

Political history presupposes, then, the belief that political activity is of vital importance, and, in addition, a wisdom which enlightens that belief. But while this is the necessary condition of political history, it is obviously not its sufficient condition. Plato and Aristotle were wise men, and they believed that political activity is of vital importance. Yet they were not political historians. What then is the precise character of that wisdom, of that Greek wisdom, which issues in political history?

We are not in the habit of raising this question. We take political history for granted. A tradition of millennia has accustomed us to the existence of political history; political history is a part of the furniture amidst which we have grown up. And for many centuries there was indeed no urgent need for raising the question we have raised. But certain changes which have taken place during the last two centuries force us to be more exacting than our predecessors have been. Since the eighteenth century or so, there has been an ever growing concern with history and an ever growing expansion of history. Political history is at present only one branch among many branches of history and by no means more fundamental or central than any other branch. The comprehensive theme of history is now no longer the political deeds and speeches, but something called "civilization" or "culture." Everything human is thought to be a part of a civilization or of a culture: everything—and hence in particular philosophy. Now if philosophy is essentially part and parcel of a civilization or a culture, philosophy is no longer philosophy in the strict sense. For philosophy in the strict sense is man's effort to liberate himself from the particular premises of any particular civilization or culture.

The development of history in the last two centuries has then led to the consequence that philosophy as truly free inquiry has ceased to be intelligible—that it has ceased to be intelligible as a legitimate and necessary pursuit. For reasons which are too obvious to be in need of being stated, we cannot leave it at that. And since the danger to philosophy stems from history, we are forced to reconsider the whole problem of history. History as such has become a problem for us. To clarify that problem we have to go back to the origin of the tradition of history: we cannot take for granted what the tradition of history has taken for granted. We must raise the question, What originally led wise men to become historians? It is in this spirit that we turn to Thucydides.

Of the many, but not very many, great historians which the West has produced, Thucydides is said to be the most political historian, the greatest political historian of all times, the man who has grasped and articulated most fully the essence of political life, the life of politics as it actually is: i.e., not the application of the principles of the Declaration of Independence but the operation of the principles which were operative in the Louisiana Purchase— "power politics" in its harsh grandeur. At the same time, Thucydides was an urbane Athenian, humane, even gentle—as his portrait indeed shows him to have been. If there is wisdom behind political history, if there is a wisdom justifying political history, it is most likely to be found in the pages, or between the pages, of Thucydides.

The admiration for Thucydides, which all people of judgment and taste feel, is today qualified by the awareness of some real or alleged deficiencies of Thucydides as a historian. This criticism can be condensed to three points: (a) A political historian is thought to be a man who describes particular situations or particular events; the universal seems to be the domain of the philosopher, or perhaps of the psychologist, the student of human nature. Thucydides' work is primarily devoted to a series of particular events (the Peloponnesian War). At the same time, it is meant to lay bare the eternal or permanent character of political life as such. It is with a view to this fact that Thucydides called his work "a possession for all times": all future generations shall be enabled to understand the substance of the political life of their times by understanding Thucydides' account of the political life of his time.

Thucydides seems to be at the same time and, as it were, in the same breath a historian and a political philosopher. The unity of the particular and the universal makes Thucydides' history singularly attractive, but at the same time singularly annoying. For he does not tell us how this unity of the universal and the particular has to be conceived, how the account of the Peloponnesian War and of nothing but the Peloponnesian War can be an account of political life as such. Thucydides gives an account of something which happened once in one part of the world, but he claims that that account will make intelligible what will happen at any time and anywhere; and he does not explain how this is possible.

(b) No modern political historian would write political history as Thucydides did. I take as an example the best American historian I know, Henry Adams. His history of the first Jefferson administration begins, of course, with a description of the situation in the United States at the time when Jefferson took office. Adams describes at appropriate length the intellectual, social, cultural, and economic conditions of the country at that time. Thucydides is practically silent about such things. He limits himself severely to politics—war, diplomacy, and civil strife. Was he blind to these other things? This would seem to be impossible. Does he then regard these other things—tragedy, comedy, philosophy, painting, sculpture, etc.—as unimportant, or at least as less important than the political things? Apparently. But what were his reasons for holding this view? He does not state them.

(c) There is another embarrassing feature of Thucydides' work.

He records both deeds and speeches. As for the deeds or events, he records them substantially in the way in which a modern historian would. But as for the speeches, he composes them himself. He claims that the speeches which he composed agree with the gist of the speeches as actually delivered. But Thucydides edits them. From the point of view of the present-day historian, this is a kind of forgery. Moreover, Thucydides edits his speeches according to certain canons of rhetoric: all his speakers speak just as Thucydides himself would have spoken; the individuality of the speaker, the local color, etc., are lacking. The speeches are not "natural." They are the speeches not of passionate and inerudite men, but of the perfect orator who has the time and the training to elaborate first-rate speeches and who complies with rules of art that claim to be of universal validity.

These three objections would seem to express the main difficulties which obstruct at present the understanding of Thucydides' work. We must try to overcome these difficulties. But we must try to do something more. The three objections mentioned are typically modern objections. They are based on the assumption that the manner in which the modern historian proceeds is the right manner. They measure Thucydides' work by the standards of modern historiography. But since modern history has brought us into very serious troubles, we cannot accept it as our standard. History as such has become a problem for us. Let us not hesitate, therefore, to wonder whether we are at all entitled to speak of Thucydides' work as a history—and of course also whether we are entitled to ascribe to Thucydides a political philosophy in particular, or a philosophy in general. From all we know prior to a fresh investigation, his enterprise may antedate any possible distinction between history and philosophy. We can safely say no more than this: that Thucydides intended to give a true or a clear or a precise or a detailed account of the war between the Peloponnesians and the Athenians. And we have to raise the question, Why did he decide to write such an account?

The question is apparently answered by the following statement of Thucydides: "I have gone out of my way to speak of [the interval between the Persian and the Peloponnesian War] because the writers who preceded me treat either of Greek affairs previous to the Persian War, or of that war itself. The period following the Persian War has been omitted by all of them with the exception of Hellanicus; and he, when he touched upon it in his *Attic Chronicle*, is very brief and inaccurate in his chronology" (1.97). Here Thucydides implies that the Greeks ought to have at their disposal a continuous, sufficiently detailed and chronologically correct account of Greek affairs—an account to be composed by successive writers. If history means merely this, Thucydides was obviously familiar with the idea of history, and he accepted it. But the question is whether his own work can be understood in these terms. It suffices to remark that Thucydides makes the statement quoted in order to explain or to excuse what might seem to be an unnecessary digression from his self-chosen task; he does not make that statement when he sets forth the reasons for writing his account of the Peloponnesian War. If it is seen within the context of Thucydides' whole work, the statement quoted almost reads like an emphatic rejection of the view of history which it presupposes. And it is not difficult to see why Thucydides rejects this notion of history, the vulgar notion of history. When he gives his reason for writing the account of the Peloponnesian War, he stresses the singular importance of that event. The vulgar notion of history does not make allowance for the difference between the important and the unimportant; it lets its light shine with perfect impartiality or indifference on all periods, on the unimportant as well as the important ones.

Why then did Thucydides choose his theme? He states in the beginning of his work that he wrote it because he believed that the Peloponnesian War was the most noteworthy of all wars up to now, that it was the biggest war in which Greeks were involved. The bigness of the war is not only the reason for writing a true and detailed account of the war; it is also a most important element of that account itself. One does not know the truth about the Peloponnesian War if one does not know that it was the biggest war, or at any rate the biggest Greek war. The proof given in the first twenty or so chapters of Thucydides' history that the Peloponnesian War is the biggest war is an essential element of that history, and not merely an introduction to that history.

Now, it is one thing to *believe* that the Peloponnesian War is the biggest war and another thing to know it. This knowledge can only be acquired by argument. For the superior bigness of the Peloponnesian War is not self-evident. After all, the contemporaries of every war believe that their war was the biggest. Fifty years prior to the Peloponnesian War there had been the Persian War, another big war. In fact the Persian War would seem to us to be the only competitor of the Peloponnesian War in regard to bigness, and indeed a most serious competitor. Thucydides disposes of the claim of the Persian War to superior bigness in two sentences. The issue seems to be settled: the Peloponnesian War is the biggest war. Yet Thucydides wrote at least nineteen chapters in order to prove his contention that the Peloponnesian War is the biggest war. Obviously the Peloponnesian War had another serious competitor. But what other war could possibly be thought to be bigger than the Peloponnesian War? There can be only one answer: the Trojan War. Both the Trojan War and the Peloponnesian War were common enterprises of all Greece; both lasted very long; and both caused very great sufferings. A generation after Thucydides, Isocrates still maintained that the Trojan War was the biggest Greek war. It was then absolutely necessary for Thucydides to prove that the Trojan War was definitely less big than the Peloponnesian War. He proved this by proving the weakness of the ancients: the Greeks of the time of the Trojan War were utterly incapable of waging war on a big scale.

Now the fame of the Trojan War was decisively due to the poems of Homer. The prestige of the Trojan War was due to the prestige of Homer; therefore, by questioning the prestige of the Trojan War, Thucydides questions the prestige of Homer. By proving the weakness of the ancients—their weakness in regard to power, to wealth, and to daring—Thucydides proves that the stories of the ancients are unreliable and untrue: he proves the weakness of the ancients in regard to wisdom, and in particular the weakness of Homer in regard to wisdom. By proving this superiority of the Greeks who were engaged in the Peloponnesian War, Thucydides proves the superiority of his own wisdom. Except for Thucydides' work, the glamor of the past—a glamor decisively enhanced by Homer's charm—would always overshadow the true superiority of the present. Thucydides confronts us, then, with the choice between Homeric wisdom and Thucydidean wisdom. Just as his contemporary Plato, he engages in a contest with Homer.

Homer was a poet, and in fact *the* poet. What is a poet? The term "poet" does not yet occur in Homer. We do find in Homer singers or minstrels. The difference between the singer or minstrel and the poet consists in this: that the poet is known to be a maker or producer of things which exist only by virtue of his making or producing, although they present themselves as if they existed without the poet's making. Poetry is fiction. Poetry, as distinguished from song, presupposes an awareness of the difference between fiction and truth, and concern with that difference, i.e., concern with the truth. The poet tells the truth—the truth about man—through fiction. The fiction consists primarily in magnify-ing and adorning, therewith concealing most important truths about men. To take an example from Thucydides: "I am inclined to think that Agamemnon succeeded in collecting the expedition [against Troy] not because the suitors of Helen had bound them-selves by oath to Tyndareus, but because he was the most powerful king of his age. . . . And it was, I believe, because Agamemnon inherited this power and also because he was the greatest naval potentate of his time that he was able to assemble the expedition, and the other kings followed him, not from generosity or grati-tude, but from fear" (1.9). Homer obscures the fact that political life—the relations between cities and kings—is characterized by the absence, by the almost complete absence, of *charis*, which is the opposite of necessity or compulsion. Hence, considering the fact that all higher human life is life in cities, Homer gives us a wholly untrue picture of human life as such: human life exists al-ways in the shadow of that dread compulsion.

The new wisdom is then superior to the old wisdom as wisdom, as knowledge of the truth. But Homer was admired because he revealed the truth which he knew in a way that was most pleasing or enjoyable. It is important to note that Thucydides does not simply deny that his wisdom will be enjoyable too: "The non-storylike character of my account will perhaps appear to be less pleasing to the ear" (1.22): i.e., it will not appear less pleasing than Homer's poetry to those whose ears have been properly trained. Thucydides' severe and austere wisdom too is music; it is inspired by a muse, by a higher, and therefore by a severer and austerer, muse than was Homer's.

We have raised the question, What is the character of that Greek wisdom which issues in political history? We have seen that Thu-cydides' wisdom presents itself as a substitute for Homeric wis-dom, or rather as the consummation of Homeric wisdom. Homeric wisdom reveals the character of human life by presenting deeds and speeches which are magnified and adorned. Thucydides's wis-dom reveals the character of human life by presenting deeds and speeches which are not magnified and adorned. This is obviously quite insufficient as an answer to our question. Even granting that Thucydides has successfully challenged the superiority of the *Iliad* by his account of the war, what about the *Odyssey?* Above all, granted that the unity of the universal and the particular in Thu-cydides is fundamentally the same as the unity of the universal and the particular in Homer, why does wisdom require such unity? Is not wisdom understanding of the universal, of the universal character of human life? Why is it then necessary that wisdom should appear in the presentation of deeds and speeches? We must then repeat our question: What is the character of that Greek wisdom which issues in political history? What is the character of that concern with the universal character of human life which issues in the true and detailed account of the Peloponnesian War? The question is identical with the question as to why Thucydides chose as his theme the Peloponnesian War. For by raising the question of why Thucydides chose his theme, we imply that he had alternatives and that these alternatives have something in common with the theme actually chosen (otherwise they would not be alternatives to it): i.e., we discover something in Thucydides' theme which is common to the Peloponnesian War and other possible themes; we discover something more general than the Peloponnesian War, we raise it to the general and even to the universal.

Thucydides chose the Peloponnesian War because it was the most noteworthy of all wars up to his time, or because it was the biggest of all Greek wars up to his time. He presupposed that war is a theme worthy of the attention of a wise man. Since his account of the Peloponnesian War is meant to be a guide for the understanding of all future wars, the Peloponnesian War must have had a particular fitness for the understanding of war as such, and this must be due to the fact that it was the biggest Greek war known to Thucydides. First, what is the virtue of bigness? We find the answer in Plato's *Republic*. Socrates is seeking the truth about justice together with his young friends. At his suggestion they look at a just city and not at a just individual because the city is larger or bigger than the individual: "There is likely to be more justice in the larger thing, and hence justice will be there more easy to apprehend" (368e). By looking at the larger or bigger thing, they will see justice written large. Similarly, by looking at the largest or biggest war, Thucydides is studying war writ large: the universal character of war will be more visible in the biggest war than in smaller wars, and there will be more war in the biggest than in smaller wars.

But future Greek wars might be still bigger than the Peloponnesian War and might therefore reveal the character of Greek war still more fully than the Peloponnesian War. Thucydides sets our mind at rest: the Greeks were at their peak in every respect at the time of the Peloponnesian War. The Peloponnesian War is the complete Greek war. No future Greek war can bring to light anything relevant regarding Greek wars which was not observable clearly in the Peloponnesian War.

But the nature of Greek war is one thing; the nature of war as such is another thing. Yet let us assume that it is impossible to grasp the true character of the complete Greek war without grasping the character of non-Greek war, of barbarian war—in that case, grasping the character of the complete or final Greek war would be tantamount to understanding the character of war as such. Thucydides makes precisely this assumption; he calls the biggest Greek war the most noteworthy war simply.

But even a complete understanding of the nature of war would seem to be a far cry from understanding the nature of human life. After all, man's true life, as no one knew better then Thucydides, is a life of peace. If Thucydides challenged Homer, if he believed that his wisdom should supersede Homeric wisdom, he must have believed that by understanding the nature of war one understands the nature of human life.

Thucydides calls the biggest war by a more general term: the biggest *kinesis*, the biggest movement. War is a kind of movement, just as peace is a kind of rest. Movement is opposed to rest. The biggest movement is the opposite of the biggest rest. The biggest movement presupposes that the antagonists possess the maximum of power and wealth. This maximum of power and wealth has been built up or stored up during a very long period—during a much longer period than the biggest movement lasted. It was built up and stored up, not in and through movement, but in and through rest. This means: the biggest movement is preceded in time by the biggest rest. But rest is not the primary or initial situation of man. If we go back to the past, we see that earlier man had much less power and wealth than present man, and that this weakness and poverty was due to the preponderance of movement in the olden times. In the beginning, in the oldest times, there was complete absence of rest, there was nothing but movement: no settlement, no fearless or quiet intercourse, no order. Wealth and power emerged through rest. The movement from the beginning up to the Peloponnesian War was on the whole a progress—a progress in power and wealth. The initial movement or unrest lasted for a very long time. Compared with the span of time involved, the progress through rest is of very short duration, though of much longer duration than the climactic movement (i.e, the Peloponnesian War). The biggest movement is a movement in which the peak of power and wealth is used and used up. The biggest movement presupposes the biggest rest. Therefore it is impossible to understand the biggest movement without understanding simultaneously the biggest rest. One cannot understand the biggest war without understanding the biggest peace, the peace which, as it were, culminates in the biggest war. But, as Homer has shown by his *Iliad* and *Odyssey,* and as the greatest epic poet of modern times has shown by the very title of his greatest work, war and peace comprise the whole of human life. To understand the biggest war means, then, to grasp fully the whole of human life. Everything becomes visible in the biggest movement, and it becomes visible only now—with the emergence of the biggest movement itself. The biggest Greek war is the most noteworthy war: it is the most noteworthy war simply because it is the biggest Greek war. For one cannot understand the biggest Greek war without understanding at the same time all possibilities of non-Greek wars—for the same reason for which one cannot understand the biggest war without understanding at the same time the biggest peace.

The Greek is distinguished from, and opposed to, the barbaric or barbarian, just as war is opposed to peace. The process in which power and wealth were stored up or built up is also the process in which the Greeks became distinguished from the barbarians. The very name "Greek" is recent. So is the Greek way of life. Originally the Greeks lived like barbarians; originally they *were* barbarians. In the beginning there were no Greeks, and therefore no distinction between Greeks and barbarians. In the beginning, in the initial, complete unrest or movement, all men were indiscriminately barbarians. Rest, long rest, and the biggest rest, is the condition not only for building up power and wealth, but for the emergence of Greekness as well. Yet there are many more barbarians in the world than there are Greeks: Greekness is the exception, just as the period of initial unrest was so much longer than the period of rest. Rest and Greekness are the exception, an island in the ocean of unrest and barbarism. The biggest rest is that rest in which Greekness not only emerges but reaches its peak. Thucydides' own work, no negligible element of the peak of Greekness, required some rest in the very midst of the biggest unrest. The initial unrest is characterized by weakness, poverty, barbarism, noise, confusion, and fear. At the peak of the biggest rest, which partly extends into the biggest unrest, there is power, wealth, the arts, refinement, order, daring, and even the overcoming of poetic magnification by the sober quest for truth.

The Peloponnesian War is the climactic Greek war. As such it reveals completely both all possibilities of war and of peace, and all possibilities of barbarism and of Greekness. All human life moves between the poles of war and peace, and between the poles of barbarism and Greekness. Thus by understanding the Peloponnesian War, one grasps the limits of all human things. One understands the nature of all human things. One understands all human things completely.

Thucydides gives a detailed account of the Peloponnesian War, which was a particular event. But this particular event is the only phenomenon in which the nature of human things or of human life becomes fully visible because in it the peak of Greekness, and therewith the peak of humanity, becomes fully visible; we see the beginning of the descent. We see the limitation of the peak. For war, or movement, is destructive. And that particular movement which is the Peloponnesian War is destructive of the highest. The biggest rest finds not its culmination but its end in the biggest movement. The biggest movement weakens and endangers, nay, destroys, not only power and wealth but Greekness as well. The biggest movement leads very soon to that unrest within cities, that *stasis*, which is identical with re-barbarization. The most savage and murderous barbarism, which was slowly overcome by the building up of Greekness, reappears in the Peloponnesian War. The war brings murderous barbarians into the midst of Greece as allies of the Greeks engaged in fratricidal war. Thracians murder the children attending a Greek school. The Peloponnesian War reveals the extremely endangered character of Greekness. Original *kinesis*, original chaos, comes into its own. It reveals itself as the permanent basis of derivative rest, of derivative order, of derivative Greekness. By understanding the biggest unrest Thucydides understands the limits of human possibilities. His knowledge is final knowledge. It is wisdom.

The fact that barbarism is primary and ultimately victorious, or that Greekness is derivative, does not prove that Greekness is merely apparent and not real. Greekness is not reducible to barbarism; it cannot be conceived of as a modification of barbarism. When Thucydides describes the emergence of Greekness in the first twenty chapters, he does not mention justice. But he mentions justice immediately when he starts his detailed account of the peak of Greekness. Justice is not operative in the emergence of civilization, but it is there just as soon as there is civilization.

To understand the character of Greekness we must look at it as it unfolds its being in the pages of Thucydides. The war which he narrates is a war between the Peloponnesians and the Athenians. On the one side, we see one city and its subject cities; on the other side we see many cities. But we learn soon that the core of the Peloponnesian confederacy is one city: Sparta. The war is the war between Athens and Sparta. Greekness at its peak has two poles, Sparta and Athens—just as human life moves between the two poles of war and peace, and of barbarism and Greekness. To understand Greekness means therefore to understand the difference between Sparta and Athens—to understand the character of Sparta and Athens, the specific limitations of Sparta and Athens, the specific virtues of Sparta and Athens.

Thucydides exercises great restraint in speaking of virtues and of vices, in praising and in blaming. It is therefore easy to mistake his meaning. Mistakes are inevitable if one follows one's impressions instead of following the signposts erected by Thucydides himself. These signposts are the words of praise and blame which he utters in his own name.

Probably the most famous section of Thucydides' work is Pericles' funeral speech, this noble praise of Periclean Athens. Thucydides seems to identify himself completely with Periclean Athens, and therewith with Pericles himself. In addition Thucydides bestows his praise on Pericles. Yet Thucydides never says that Pericles was the best or the most virtuous man of his age: his praise of Pericles is qualified. And as for the funeral speech, it is delivered by Pericles, not by Thucydides. The funeral speech is a political action of Pericles. It must be read accordingly. In the funeral speech, the leading Athenian citizen characterizes Athens by contrasting her with Sparta. This speech is closely parallel to the speech delivered by the Corinthians in Sparta, in which they too contrast Sparta and Athens. In the situation in which the Corinthians found themselves in Sparta, it was impossible for them to praise Sparta unqualifiedly, for they were dissatisfied with Sparta: their speech served the function of bringing about a change of Spartan policy. But Pericles' funeral speech serves precisely the function of defending Athenian policy, of keeping Athenian policy unchanged. As a result, we find in Thucydides an Athenian praising Athens unqualifiedly, whereas we do not find anyone praising Sparta accordingly. No Spartan praises Sparta in the way in which Pericles praises Athens. This proves indeed that Sparta was less articulate or infinitely more laconic than Athens. It does not prove at all that Sparta did not deserve the highest praise. Sparta is inarticulate; she is praised by others, therefore she is not praised unqualifiedly, because the others, having different political interests than she, are naturally not enthusiastic about her.

Thucydides has stated the principles which guided him in judging of human things in the section on civil strife in the third book. When describing civil strife and its effect, the disintegration of the city, the diseases of the city, the decay of civilization, he makes clear which preferences correspond to the healthy city and which preferences correspond to the decayed city. One point only needs to be mentioned in the present context. The healthy city esteems most highly the virtue of moderation; the diseased city is enamored of daring, of what is called manliness, which it prefers to moderation. Moderation is akin to peace; daring and manliness belong to war. These statements allow us to assert without hesitation that the moral taste of Thucydides is identical with the moral taste of Plato. I dare say that it is identical with the moral taste of all wise men, i.e., of all great thinkers prior to the modern era.

How then must we judge of Sparta and Athens in the light of the fundamental distinction between moderation and daring? The Spartans above all others, Thucydides says, preserved moderation in prosperity. By this statement, Thucydides subscribes to what some of his characters say in praise of the Spartans—of their moderation, their slowness, their hesitancy, their quietude, their reliability, their sense of dignity—in brief, their old-fashioned habits. Sparta, Thucydides says again in his own name, obtained good laws at an earlier period than any other city and has never been subject to tyrants; she has preserved the same regime for more than four hundred years. The infrequency of Thucydides' explicit praise of Sparta does not prove its irrelevance. The value of a statement of a thoughtful man is not increased by his repeating it often. It is obvious what the praise of Spartan moderation implies: the Athenians did not preserve moderation in prosperity. Athens was animated by a spirit of daring innovation, at least since the time of Themistocles. No one could say in praise of Athens that she had never been subject to tyrants or always preserved the same regime. But nevertheless Thucydides might still have regarded the Periclean regime as the best which Athens ever had. In fact he did not; he definitely prefers the short-lived regime of 411, which was a good mixture of oligarchy and democracy, to the Periclean regime. As all wise men of classical antiquity, Thucydides favored a mixed or moderate regime. And Athenian democracy was not moderate. It is true that Pericles kept it in a tolerable shape, but this merely means that the fate of Athens depended entirely on one man's virtue. It means that Athenian democracy had to rely constitutionally on utterly unreliable chance. A sound regime is one in which a fairly large group that lives on a reasonably high level of civic virtue, and above all of moderation, is in control: a moderate regime. Thus, however great the merits of Pericles, his rule is inseparable from Athenian democracy; it belongs to Athenian democracy; the political judgment on Pericles' rule must be based on a clear understanding of the unsolid character of the foundation of that rule. The political preferences of Thucydides—I am speaking now of politics, not of political philosophy—are the same as Plato's. Now, Pericles, as Thucydides saw him, did not only belong to democracy; he was even in profound harmony with the democracy which he served and saved as well as he could. It is significant that Thucydides' Pericles never uses the term moderation. Especially the funeral speech shows that Pericles' preferences agree in substance with those which Thucydides himself ascribes to the diseased city: Pericles too prefers daring to moderation. There is a close link connecting the funeral speech, and even the first speech of the Athenians in Thucydides' history, with what the Athenians say in their famous, or infamous, dialogue with the Melians.

Thucydides has indicated his view of Sparta and Athens most clearly in the following form. The first group of speeches in his history are the speeches of the Corcyreans and the Corinthians in Athens; the second group of speeches are the speeches of the Corinthians, the Athenians, a Spartan king, and a Spartan *ephor* in Sparta. In the first group, the speeches delivered in Athens, Thucydides records no speech of the Athenians, but two contradictory decisions of the Athenians; in Athens there was no deliberation but hasty, fickle decisions—in fact, the decision which brought on the Peloponnesian War. In the second group of speeches, the speeches delivered in Sparta, Thucydides records two speeches of the Spartans and one decision of the Spartans: deliberation followed by a firm decision. Later on in the first book Thucydides gives the record of an assembly in Athens: there is only one speech; the speaker is Pericles; Pericles' monarchical rule gives Athens her direction. But Pericles will die soon.

Yet Thucydides cannot have been blind to the glory which was Athens, a glory which is inseparable from the spirit of daring innovation and from that madness, that *mania*, which rises far above moderation. In fact, Thucydides draws our attention to another facet of the difference between Sparta and Athens by contrasting the Spartan individual and the Athenian individual. In a sense Thucydides' history begins with the confrontation of the Spartan Pausanias and the Athenian Themistocles. This confrontation has been misunderstood as a digression into biography. In fact, it is not so much Pausanias and Themistocles in whom Thucydides is interested, as Sparta and Athens as manifested in these two men. Both men are individuals, and this means primarily men who deviate from the norm, i.e., criminals: both men were traitors to their city. Their crimes were connected with the Persian War, i.e., with another big movement. Yet in this earlier movement, which was less big than the Peloponnesian War, demoralization was still limited to particularly exposed individuals. Now, Thucydides is silent about Pausanias' nature and character. But he dwells on Themistocles' extraordinary gifts. He is silent about Themistocles' character and willpower in order to bring out more clearly the amazing intellectual power of the originator of the Athenian Empire. Sparta is the better polis; but Athens is outstanding as regards natural gifts, and this means regarding the gifts of individuals.

Moreover we cannot help noting a close parallel between Pericles' speeches and Thucydides' history. Thucydides' account at the beginning of his work of the increase of power and wealth which had been taking place at an ever accelerated pace for at least two generations is repeated by Pericles at the beginning of his funeral speech. Thucydides and Pericles agree in their consciousness of an amazing progress achieved—in their consciousness that they are living on a peak. Thucydides himself is an Athenian: the peak on which he stand is the peak of Athens. Pericles looks down, just as Thucydides himself, on the exaggerated glamor of the heroic age sung by Homer. And Pericles observes, just as Thucydides himself, icy silence about the gods. Thucydides' own work is a work of daring innovation. What he described in his section on civil strife as an essential characteristic of political decay, viz., the loss of awe of the divine law, is an essential element of his own manner of looking at things. Rest leads necessarily to admiration of antiquity. By freeing himself from the admiration of antiquity, Thucydides reveals his kinship with the spirit of restless daring or of impiety.

Yet there is a subtle and therefore decisive difference between Thucydides and Pericles, and therewith between Thucydides and Periclean Athens. Both Thucydides and Pericles are concerned with inextinguishable fame. Pericles says that "we Athenians have left everywhere behind us eternal memorials of evil things and of good things" (2.43). Thucydides says of the work which he has left behind that it is to be an eternal possession which is useful, i.e., which is good (1.22). I shall not insult your intelligence by belaboring the difference between memorials which can only be looked at and possessions which are meant to be owned; the difference between memorials which are meant for show and a possession which is for use, for the noblest use, for understanding; and the difference between an achievement which is partly bad and partly good and an achievement which is simply good. The spirit of daring innovation, that *mania* which transcends the limits of moderation, comes into its own, or is legitimate, or is in accordance with nature, only in the work of Thucydides—not in Periclean Athens as such. Not Periclean Athens, but the understanding that is possible on the basis of Periclean Athens, is the peak. Not Periclean Athens, but Thucydides' history, is the peak. Thucydides redeems Periclean Athens. And only by redeeming it does he preserve it. As little as there would be an Achilles or an Odysseus for us without Homer, so little would there be a Pericles for us without Thucydides. There is a disproportion between the politically best and the humanly best: the humanly best, wisdom, is akin to the politically inferior or an offspring of it. This is the meaning of the kinship between Thucydides and Periclean Athens.

The subtle and decisive difference between Thucydides and Pericles confirms our contention that Thucydides regarded Sparta as superior to Athens from a political point of view. Or in general terms, Thucydides held the view that political virtue or political health is identical with the spirit of moderation or of respect for the divine law. Certainly Thucydides did not believe that the gods avenge injustice. He did not believe in a power of justice. The first speech recorded in his work begins with the word justice; the immediately following contradictory speech begins with the word necessity. Thucydides is impressed by the conflict between justice and necessity, a conflict in which necessity proves to be stronger. Necessity does not allow the cities always to act justly. The men who open their speech with the word justice are the Corcyreans; the men who open their speech with the word necessity are the Corinthians. The Corcyreans are definitely less just than the Corinthians. But with a view to necessity the Athenians may have acted wisely by allying themselves with the unjust Corcyreans against the tolerably just Corinthians. Necessity means involvement: Potidaea is a colony of Corinth and an ally of Athens; Potidaea is forced to break her promises in case of conflict between Corinth and Athens.

Thucydides does not say that necessity simply rules the relation between cities. For example, he does not say that the Peloponnesian War was simply necessary. There exist alternatives. There is room for choice between sensible and mad courses, between moderate and immoderate courses; there is room even, within limits, for choice between just and unjust courses. Still, the virtue which can and must control political life, as Thucydides sees it, is not so much justice as moderation. Moderation is something more than long-range calculation. It is, to use the language of Aristotle, a moral virtue. In most cases moderation is produced by fear of the gods and of the divine law. But it is also produced by true wisdom. In fact, the ultimate justification of moderation is exclusively true wisdom. For, by denying the power of the gods, Thucydides does not deny the power of nature, or more specifically the limitations imposed on man by his nature. There are then natural sanctions to immoderate courses. Immoderate courses may succeed, for chance is incalculable. But precisely for this reason, for the reason that an immoderate policy counts on chance, it is bad: it is not according to nature. "Thus ended the great expedition of the Athenians and their allies against Egypt" (1.110): It ended in disaster. "This was the end of Pausanias the Spartan and of Themistocles the Athenian, the two most famous Greeks of their day" (1.138): they ended in disaster. The extreme courses end in disaster. The right thing is the mean.

We can now venture to suggest an answer to the question as to why Thucydides is silent about what is at present called Athenian culture and why he limits his narrative so severely to things political. What we call culture would have been called by Thucydides, I suppose, love of the beautiful and love of wisdom. As Thucydides' strictures on Homer show, he assigned the highest place not to the beautiful but to wisdom. The question therefore is, Why was Thucydides silent about the wisdom that had found its home in Athens? Through his history Thucydides makes us understand movement and rest, war and peace, barbarism and Greekness, Sparta and Athens: he makes us understand the nature of human life; he makes us wise. By understanding Thucydides' wisdom, we ourselves become wise; but we cannot become wise through understanding Thucydides without realizing simultaneously that it is through understanding Thucydides that we are becoming wise, for wisdom is inseparable from self-knowledge. By becoming wise through understanding Thucydides, we see Thucydides' wisdom. But we know from Thucydides himself that he was an Athenian. And through understanding him we see that his wisdom was made possible by Athens—by her power and wealth, by her defective polity, by her spirit of daring innovation, by her active doubt of the divine law. By understanding Thucydides' history we see that Athens was the home of wisdom. For only through becoming wise ourselves can we recognize wisdom in others, and particularly in Thucydides, and also, in a way, in Athens. Wisdom cannot be presented as a spectacle, in the way in which military and political transactions can be presented. Wisdom cannot be said. It can only be done or practiced. Wisdom can only be seen by indirection, by reflection: by reflecting on our being or becoming wise. Only through understanding Thucydides' history can we really see that Athens was the school of Greece. From Pericles' mouth we merely hear it asserted. Wisdom canot be said. It cannot be presented by being spoken of. An indirect proof of this is the insipid, or at best boring, character of the chapters on the intellectual life of the various periods which occur in otherwise good modern political histories. If someone were to draw the conclusion that intellectual history is, strictly speaking, impossible, that intellectual history is an absurd attempt to present descriptively what is by its nature incapable of being described, I would be forced to agree with that man. Fortunately for us students of intellectual history, there is no such man.

By answering the question as to why Thucydides is silent about Athenian culture, we have found, not indeed the answer, but the thread which will eventually lead to the answer to another question: the question regarding the status of the speeches in Thucydides.

Wisdom cannot be shown by being spoken of. How then can it be shown at all? Wisdom is the highest form of the life of man. How can the life of man be shown? The life of man, or, if you wish, the inner life of man, man's awareness in the widest sense, shows itself in deeds and in speeches, but mostly in such a manner that neither the deeds by themselves nor the speeches by themselves suffice to reveal it. To take the most simple example: one man makes just speeches and does just deeds; another man makes just speeches and does unjust deeds; a third one makes unjust speeches and does unjust deeds; and a fourth one makes unjust speeches and does just deeds. In every case we see the man only when we both hear his speeches and see his deeds. And in every case the contribution made by the perception of the speeches on the one hand, and by the perception of the deeds on the other, is different. What is true of men applies also to measures or policies. Every policy proceeds from deliberation, from speech; speech is the cause of deed. Yet the speech, the deliberation, is itself based on consideration of facts, of deeds. Speech is neither the beginning nor the end, but a station on the way, or rather a beacon which illumines the way. Only through speech are the deeds or the facts revealed. Yet while revealing, speech also conceals or deceives. The speech, or the deliberation, does not control the outcome: it has no power over chance. The speech may be based on misapprehension of one kind or another. And the speech may be meant to deceive. The speech is meant to reveal the causes or reasons of the deed, but it states only the defensible reasons, which may or may not be the true reasons. The deeds without the speeches are meaningless, or at best wholly ambiguous. But the speeches add an ambiguity of their own. The light which the speeches throw on the deeds is not the light of truth. Speech distorts reality. But this distortion is part of reality. It is part of the truth.

Speeches are not only inseparable from deeds. They are even, in an important respect, primary. Thucydides sometimes uses the distinction between speech and deed synonymously with the distinction between speech and secrecy: what comes first to perception, what is least concealed, is what people openly say. The first word of the first speech in Thucydides is justice. If we knew only what the agents say about their policies, we would be forced to believe that all policies are just and all actors perfect gentlemen. Political speeches are primarily justifications. Justification is not limited to considerations of justice; policies are also justified by their expediency. To judge rightly of political life means to judge rightly of the relative importance of justice on the one hand and of expediency on the other. Sound judgment requires that we view the speeches in the light of the deeds. But on the other hand, we could not perceive the light of the deeds if we did not view the deeds in the light of the speeches, i.e., of the claim to justice. It might seem that as a result of a critical examination of deeds and speeches, justice loses its status. Yet this is not quite true. One kind of speech is a treaty or a promise. The value of a treaty or promise depends on the reliability of the partners, on the agreement or disagreement between their previous deeds and speeches, on their previous performance, i.e., on their justice. And all cities are forced to conclude treaties from time to time.

There are things which can be revealed only by speeches. These are the virtues and vices which belong essentially to the element of speech; e.g., cleverness in speaking, elegance of expression, frankness, both noble and shameless, and, above all, wisdom itself.

Human life moves between the poles of war and peace, of barbarism and Greekness, and of deed and speech. But the relationship of deed and speech is much more complex than the relationship of war and peace on the one hand and of barbarism and Greekness on the other. One may wonder whether the dualism of deed and speech is not the very core of human life. Be this as it may, when Thucydides set out to give a true account of the biggest unrest and therewith to lay bare the nature of human life, he was bound to have at his disposal an adequate articulation of the dualism of deed and speech. He had to present that dualism in action, in deed—by speech. He had to imitate that dualism appropriately. Thus he imitated the primacy of speech as follows. He makes a distinction between the spoken or avowed reasons for the Peloponnesian War and its concealed reason. He describes first the facts referred to in the avowed reasons (the Corcyrean and the Potidaean affairs) and thereafter the fact referred to in the concealed reason (the fear of Athenian power). He thus incidentally inverts the chronological order of events. This is a measure of the importance he attaches to the primacy of speech. He leads us to expect that the real reason for the Peloponnesian War is the concealed reason. But a closer study shows that the avowed reasons were much more real than they seemed to be at first (i.e., the Corcyrean affair was the decisive cause of the Peloponnesian War). Thucydides thus warns us of the danger which consists in trusting implicitly our distrust, our reasonable distrust, of what people say. The warning is, of course, only noticeable to those who harbor such reasonable distrust. For others the warning would be meaningless: they will not notice it in Thucydides.

A further example of Thucydides' imitation of the dualism of deed and speech: Thucydides refrains from giving us his complete judgments on men and politics. All his judgments are incomplete and therefore conceal as much as they reveal. He presents to us the deeds and the speeches just as reality presents them. He does not tell us how we should judge of the speeches in the light of the deeds and vice versa. Since we primarily understand speeches, Thucydides misleads us by presenting speeches to us, just as reality misleads us by the speeches we hear. Furthermore his characters say things which Thucydides does not say: the reader must find out for himself what Thucydides thought on the subject in question, i.e., what the wise judgment on the subject in question is. Thucydides imitates the enigmatic character of reality. By imitating the dualism of speech and deed, Thucydides reveals the true character of human life to those who can become wise, i.e., to those who can possibly understand the true character of human life.

We may thus understand why Thucydides presented to us both the deeds and the speeches. But we do not yet see clearly why he composed the speeches of his characters himself. After all, he intended to give an exact or true account of the war, and hence of both the deeds and speeches. Accordingly, he ought to have presented the speeches in indirect form, or else, if he had at his disposal something like stenograms, he ought to have transcribed the stenograms without making any other changes. But in fact he preserved only the gist of the speeches actually delivered. Everything else, i.e., the speeches as we read them in his history, are his own work: he himself expressed the gist of the speeches actually delivered as he saw fit. The case of the deeds is entirely different. Deeds cannot migrate from the battlefield into books except by being narrated. Deeds must necessarily be transposed into the element of speech. But speeches exist from the outset in the element of speech. They can migrate from the forum into a book as they are, without being transposed into another element. If any proof were needed it would be supplied by the fact that Thucydides incorporates texts of treaties verbatim. (In fact this proves that the treaties are not speeches but deeds.)

Two observations suggest themselves immediately. In the first place, Thucydides edited the speeches because he was certain that only by such editing could the speeches become true: the verbatim report of the speech would not be the true speech. Secondly, the deeds too are edited by Thucydides. Their presentation consists not merely in their being told, but above all in their being selected and arranged. Only through proper selection and proper arrangement do we get a true picture of the Peloponnesian War. Now, if a speech were left in its original condition, i.e., in the condition in which every citizen present had heard it, it would be as untrue as, say, a battle as observed by every soldier. The true battle is the battle as seen by the man of the highest military understanding. The true speech is the speech as heard by the man of the highest political understanding. The transposition of the deeds through narration, selection, and arrangement must be paralleled by a corresponding transposition of the speeches.

Yet could the transposition not have been effected if Thucydides had presented the speeches in the form of indirect speech? Such presentation would, however, blur the most important fact that the speeches exist in the same element as Thucydides' history, i.e., Thucydides' own *logos*, his own speech. And Thucydides was very anxious to emphasize this kinship between the speeches of his characters and his own speech. The speeches are present in Thucydides' history to a much higher degree than are the deeds: we do not see the deeds, but we hear the speeches. The speeches are present because they can be present, because they belong to the same element as Thucydides' speech. Thucydides was very anxious to emphasize the kinship between the speeches of his characters and his own speech because he was very anxious to bring out the difference between the speeches of his own characters and his own speech. The specific difference cannot be brought to light if the community of the genus is not seen in full clarity. What then is the specific difference between the speeches of Thucydides' characters and Thucydides' own speeches? And why does the specific character of the speeches of the characters require that these speeches be edited by Thucydides in order to become true? The speeches of the characters are political speeches: each speech presents a particular policy of this city to this audience. Each speech is radically partial. As such it does not properly reveal the whole. Yet it exists only within the whole, within the true whole, i.e., within the whole as Thucydides saw it. The man who delivered the actual speech did not see what he said in its true place within the whole: Thucydides sees it within the whole, i.e., as part of the biggest unrest, which was the complete unrest or unrest incarnate, and therewith completely revealing of the biggest rest as well or of barbarism and Greekness, or of the true character of human life. The true account of the true character of human life is Thucydides' own *logos*. Editing a political speech means to integrate it into the true and comprehensive speech. It means therefore to make the political speech visible as something fundamentally different from the true speech. The political speech is essentially untrue because of the necessarily limited horizon of the political actor. Connected with this difference is the following one: the political speech exercises much less reserve in praising and blaming than does the true speech.

I will try to indicate the virtues of the Thucydidean speeches by discussing briefly one example: the speech of the Athenian ambassadors in Sparta. Thucydides prefaces that speech with a statement as to what the Athenians meant to say: i.e., he tells us what he usually does not tell us, what the gist of the speech actually delivered was. He thus enables us to see clearly the character of his own editorial work. Thucydides says that the Athenians "also desired to set forth the power of their city" (1.72). But how do they set forth the power of Athens in the speech composed by Thucydides? Only indirectly. They justify Athenian policy, i.e., Athenian imperialism, by frankly confessing the very *principle* of imperialism. It is only by doing this that they reveal the power of Athens. They thus reveal the power of Athens much more convincingly than if they had enumerated her resources. For only the most powerful can afford to utter the principles which they utter. By thus editing the speech, Thucydides lets us see that Athens in whose name the ambassadors spoke. I can here merely note that the same speech proves, proves by itself, the amazing resourcefulness, the fastidious urbanity, and the greatness of the soul of Athens, and therewith one reason, never stated, why the Athenians were so offensive to their neighbors. It is safe to assume that Thucydides surpassed in fastidiousness these nameless Athenians. And we can perhaps guess how Thucydides would have praised Athens if he had thought it proper to praise Athens. He left this job to Pericles. The difference between Pericles' funeral speech, which Thucydides wrote, and Thucydides' praise of Athens, which Thucydides wrote only between the lines of his work, gives us an inkling of the gulf separating the political speech from the true speech. The true speech is deliberately incomplete. Thucydides' praise of Athens, and generally the full truth as he saw it, is located in the space between the deeds and the speeches. The full truth is pointed to by the dualism of the deeds and speeches. It is not pointed out.

It would then not be altogether wrong to say that Thucydides' speech, as it is written, is ultimately as untrue as Homer's. But if Homer's speech is untrue because Homer magnifies and adorns, Thucydides' speech is untrue because Thucydides understates the truth. It is possible that this is what Thucydides himself thought. Whether this thought does justice to Homer is a question which it is not improper to raise. This question is identical with the question as to whether or not poetry is more philosophic than history.

We have insensibly returned to our guiding question—the question regarding the specific character of that Greek wisdom which issues in political history. For all practical purposes, this question coincides with the question regarding the difference between Thucydides and Plato. Whereas Thucydides' wisdom issues in political history, Plato's wisdom issues in political philosophy. I have spoken of the agreement between Plato and Thucydides as regards specific moral and political judgments. Both regard moderation as higher than daring and manliness. Both regard the mixture of oligarchy and democracy as the best practical regime. The recognition of this broad practical agreement makes it all the more urgent that we define, however tentatively, their profound disagreement.

We must compare comparable things. Thucydides did not write Socratic dialogues on justice and the like, and Plato did not write history. But both Plato's dialogues and Thucydides' history have something most important in common: both present the universal truth in inseparable connection with particulars. The role played in Thucydides by the Peloponnesian War was played in Plato by Socrates. Thucydides starts from the experience of the biggest unrest; Plato starts from the experience of the serene citizen philosopher. To explain what this means, we start from a less comprehensive phenomenon. While Plato did not write a history, he has given us the sketch of a history covering the period from the barbarism of the beginnings up to Periclean democracy. I am referring to the third book of the *Laws*. The third book of the *Laws* is the only part of Plato's work which lends itself to a simple confrontation with Thucydides' history.

In the third book of the *Laws* Plato gives a strange account of how the good Athenian regime which obtained at the time of the Persian War, the ancestral regime, was transformed into the extreme democracy of the Periclean age. Plato traces this profound change to the willful disregard of the ancestral laws regarding music and the theater: by making not the best and the wisest but the audience at large the judges of songs and plays, Athens transformed herself from an aristocracy into a democracy. In the same context Plato contends that the significance of the naval victory of Salamis (as distinguished from the land victories of Marathon and Plataea) was negligible. We may say: Plato falsifies history. We must say even more: Plato deliberately falsifies history. This is one reason why he repeatedly calls his historical sketch a myth. Why does he falsify history? In what precisely does the falsification consist? The true reason for the emergence of Athenian democracy was that the Athenians had practically no choice but to wage the naval battle of Salamis and, one thing leading to another, they were practically compelled to build a powerful navy; for the navy they needed the poor as oarsmen; therefore they had to give the poor a much greater stake in Athens than they previously enjoyed: they were forced to embark on their democratic venture. The true account of what happened between the Persian War and the Peloponnesian War would have shown that the democratization of Athens was not a matter of willful folly, not a matter of choice, but rather a matter of necessity. In general terms, the true account would show that the margin of choice in regard to regimes is extremely limited, or, to paraphrase Plato himself, that it is nature and chance rather than man, rather than human wisdom or folly, which establishes regimes or which legislates (see *Laws* 709a–b). The correct statement of what has happened would incline one to believe in the absolute preponderance of fatality over choice.

We shall then tentatively describe the difference between Plato or political philosophy on the one hand, and Thucydides or political history on the other, as follows: the former puts the emphasis on human choice, the latter puts the emphasis on fatality.

Yet Plato admits implicitly by his falsification of Athenian history, and he admits it later on explicitly, that Thucydides' estimate of the situation is correct: that fatality is preponderant. He only adds that, within very narrow limits, man does have a choice between different regimes. Thucydides does not deny this. Thus there seems to be a perfect agreement between Thucydides and Plato. However, Plato regards the existence of the very small margin of choice in regard to regimes as of decisive importance for understanding political life, whereas Thucydides does not. Man as Plato sees him is distinctly less involved in fatality than man as Thucydides sees him. What is the essential difference behind this apparent difference of degree?

Plato starts from the fact that all political life is characterized by alternatives between better and worse policies, between policies which are believed to be better and policies which are believed to be worse. But it is impossible to believe that something is better without believing at the same time that something is simply good. In other words, every belief that a given policy is preferable is based on reasons which, if duly elaborated, would reveal a belief in what constitutes the best regime. Now, it is necessary to transform this belief into knowledge. It is necessary to seek knowledge of what constitutes the best regime. This quest is political philosophy. Political life is a kind of groping for the best regime. Political life points therefore to political philosophy, which is the conscious quest for the best regime. Now, the quest for the best regime is only the political form of the quest for the good life. Regarding the good life, there is ultimately only one alternative among serious people: does the good life consist in political action or in philosophy? The question of how to live is a grave practical problem for everyone and hence also for the city.

Thucydides denies that the question of how to live is a grave practical problem for the city. The goals which the city pursues are obvious and cannot be questioned without questioning the city itself. These goals are such things as stability, freedom from both foreign domination and tyranny, and prosperity. The framework within which these goals can be pursued is in each case given. Experience suffices to show that the framework most conducive to the wise pursuit of these goals is a moderate or mixed regime. Statesmanship is the wise or prudent pursuit of the obvious objectives mentioned. It is much more difficult to discern in each case what the statesman-like course of action is than to see what the best regime is and what the ultimate objectives of political life are. But statesmanship consists in the wise handling of individual situations. What can be said about statesmanship without regard to the individual situations is trivial and hardly worthwhile. No problem of principle arises among sensible and moderate statesman. Hence the right kind of political life can only be shown in action. The only question for the wise speaker about politics is: in what action, in what circumstances, can political life be shown in the best manner, i.e., in such a manner that the presentation will reveal most fully the character of political life? The answer is: action on the peak of political life.

We shall now say: Plato regards the ultimate goals of political action as fundamentally problematic, and Thucydides does not. What is the reason for this difference? As I believe I have shown, Thucydides is fully aware of the significance of the conflict between the political life and the life devoted to understanding. But contrary to Plato, Thucydides believes that while the thinker, and only the thinker, can fully understand political life, he cannot guide political life. Philosophy has no point of entrance into political life. Political life is impervious to philosophy. The Peloponnesian War, the biggest unrest, as well as the biggest rest which preceded it, is wholly independent of philosophy. Plato, however, believed that political life is not impervious to philosophy. This explains why his criticism of both Sparta and Athens is much harsher than Thucydides' criticism. Plato expects much more of political life than Thucydides does. According to Plato, the ultimate alternative—political life or philosophical life—affects political life itself; according to Thucydides, it does not. This is the reason why for Plato the ultimate goals of political life are fundamentally problematic, whereas they are not for Thucydides.

Plato had tried to show that political life points to the philosophical life. He started from the fact that political life needs excellence, or virtue, and he followed the dialectics of virtue: we may take any notion of virtue, however low and narrow (and there is no political life, however low and narrow, without such notions); we shall be led inevitably by the sheer demand for consistency to the insight that virtue is knowledge, and therefore that political life needs philosophy in order to be truly political life. Thucydides admits the obvious political relevance of virtue. But he insists all the more strongly on the fact that virtue, as far as it is politically relevant, is not, as indeed it presents itself in political speech, the end of political life, but only a means. He thus cuts off the dialectic movement leading up from the political life to the philosophic life. For Plato all human life, even on the lowest level, is directed toward philosophy, toward the highest. Even the most despicable actions of the most despicable demagogue or tyrant can ultimately be understood only as an extreme perversion, due to ignorance, of the same longing for the simply good which in its unperverted form is philosophy. The lower exists only by virtue of the attraction exerted by the higher, by virtue of the power of the higher. Thucydides, on the other hand, denies this directedness of the lower toward the higher. It is for this reason that he regards politics as impervious to philosophy. The lower is impervious to the higher. Whereas the Peloponnesian War and its antecedents are wholly independent of philosophy, philosophy is dependent on them. The lower is independent of the higher, but the higher is dependent on the lower. The high is weak; the low is strong.

Plato had no illusions about the fact that if we limit our observation to human affairs in the narrow sense, Thucydides is right: political life proves again and again its imperviousness to philosophy. But Plato demanded that we take a comprehensive view, that we see human affairs in their connection with human nature, and human nature as a part of the whole; and he contended that if we do this, we shall arrive at the conclusion that the higher is stronger than the lower. The ultimate reason why Plato and Thucydides disagree has to be sought, not in a different estimate of human affairs as such, but in a different view of the whole.

Thucydides held that the primary or fundamental fact is movement or unrest, and that rest is derivative; that the primary and fundamental fact is barbarism, and that Greekness is derivative; in a word, that war, and not peace, is the father of all things. Plato, on the other hand, believed in the primacy of rest, Greekness, harmony. Plato and Thucydides agree as to this—that for man, rest and Greekness and peace are the highest. But according to Plato, the highest for man and the highest in man is akin to the highest simply, to the principle or principles governing the whole; whereas according to Thucydides, the highest in man is not akin to the highest simply. According to Plato, the highest in man, man's humanity, has direct cosmic support. According to Thucydides, the highest in man lacks such support: man's humanity is too remote from the elements to be capable of receiving such support.

This difference explains the difference of moods conveyed by the Platonic dialogues on one hand and Thucydides' history on the other. The serenity of Plato corresponds to his gay science, to his comforting message that the highest is the strongest. A light veil of sadness covers Thucydides' somber wisdom; the highest is of extreme fragility.

For Thucydides the cause of the wisdom which found its home in Periclean Athens is Periclean Athens. For Plato, Periclean Athens is merely the condition, and not the cause, of Athenian wisdom. Thucydides, we may say, identifies condition and cause; Plato distinguishes between condition and cause. Hence politics is of decisive importance for Thucydides and is not of decisive importance for Plato. According to Plato, the cause of wisdom is the unknown god whose puppets we are.

The difference between Thucydides and Plato is identical with the difference between Thucydides and Socrates. Thucydides, we shall say, is a pre-Socratic. His work can only be understood against the background of pre-Socratic philosophy, and especially against the background of Heraclitus' thought. Pre-Socratic philosophy was a quest for an understanding of the whole which was not identical with understanding of the parts of the whole. It is for this reason that pre-Socratic philosophy did not know of a relatively independent study of the human things as such. Pre-Socratic philosophy needed, therefore, something like Thucydides' history as its supplement: a quest for the truth which was primarily a quest for the truth about the human things.

Socrates identified the understanding of the whole with understanding of the parts of the whole. Socratic philosophy allowed, therefore, a study of the nature of human things as such. With the emergence of Socratic philosophy, political history in the full Thucydidean sense loses its *raison d'être*. This explains why Xenophon continued Thucydides' history in such a different spirit and in such a different style. Xenophon's center of gravity lies no longer in political history but in his recollection of Socrates. This explains the apparent frivolity of Xenophon's account of things political. Xenophon could no longer take politics as seriously as Thucydides had done. His apparent frivolity as a historian is the reflection of Socratic serenity. By virtue of the Socratic revolution, political history became eventually a specialty, ancillary to philosophy and distinguished from it, a highly respectable specialty, but none the less a specialty. According to the traditional notion, political history provides examples, whereas moral and political philosophy provide the precepts.

The subordinate status into which history declined owing to the Socratic revolution remained unchanged for many centuries. History remained, however, political history. It is only since the eighteenth century or so that history has become the history of civilization. This change presented itself as an enormous progress, as an enormous step forward towards the comprehension of human life or of society as it really is or has been. This change finds its clearest expression in the fact that whereas for classical philosophy the comprehensive theme of social science is the best regime, the comprehensive theme of modern social science is civilization or culture. If we ask our contemporaries what constitutes a culture or a civilization, we do not receive a clear answer. Instead we are told how we could tell one civilization from another. Civilizations, we are told, can be distinguished from each other most clearly by the differences of artistic styles. This means that civilizations are distinguished from each other least ambiguously by something which is never in the focus of interest of societies: societies do not wage war and do not make revolutions on account of differences of artistic style. The orientation by civilizations thus appears to be based on a remarkable estrangement from those life-and-death issues which animate societies and keep them in motion. What presents itself as an enormous progress, as an enormous enlargement of our views, is in fact the outcome of the oblivion of the most fundamental things, and ultimately of the oblivion of the one thing needful. History is still primarily political history.

7
The Problem of Socrates:
Five Lectures

First Lecture

Of the four chief sources on which we depend if we wish to understand the thought of Socrates, Aristophanes' *Clouds* is the first in time. The first impression which anyone may receive of Socrates from the *Clouds* was expressed by Nietzsche in terms like these. Socrates belongs to the outstanding seducers of the people who are responsible for the loss of the old Marathonian virtue of body and soul, or for the dubious enlightenment which is accompanied by the decay of virtue of body and soul. Socrates is in fact the first and foremost sophist, the mirror and embodiment of all sophistic tendencies. This presentation of Socrates fits perfectly into the whole work of Aristophanes, the great reactionary who opposes with all means at his disposal all the new-fangled things, be it the democracy, the Euripidean tragedy, or the pursuits of Socrates. The point of view from which Aristophanes looks at contemporary life is that of justice, old-fashioned justice. Hence that novel phenomenon, Socrates, appears to him as a teacher of injustice and even of atheism. Aristophanes' Socrates is not only extremely evil but extremely foolish as well—and hence utterly ridiculous. He meets his deserved fate: a former disciple whose son has been completely corrupted by Socrates burns down Socrates' think tank, and it is only a lucky and ridiculous accident if Socrates and his disciples do not perish on that occasion; they deserve to perish. The *Clouds* is, then, an attack on Socrates. The Platonic Socrates, when defending himself against his official accusation, almost goes so far as to call the Aristophanean comedy an accusation of Socrates— the first accusation, which became the model and the source of the second and final accusation. But even this expression may well appear to be too mild. Especially if the comedy is viewed in the light of its apparent consequences and of its wholly unfounded character, one must describe Aristophanes' action as calumny. As Socrates says in Plato's *Apology*, he did none of the things which Aristophanes attributed to him. In the *Clouds*, Socrates appears as a sophist and a natural philosopher, whereas Socrates knew nothing of natural philosophy and was of course the sworn enemy of sophistry. And, finally, Aristophanes' comic treatment of Socrates, a treatment characterized by the utmost levity, must appear to be shocking to the highest degree if one looks forward to Socrates' tragic end.

To speak first of the striking dissimilarity between Aristophanes' Socrates and the true Socrates, i.e., the Socrates whom we know through Plato and Xenophon, there is Platonic and Xenophontic evidence to the effect that Socrates was not always the Socrates whom these disciples have celebrated. Plato's Socrates says on the day of his death (*Phaedo* 96aff.) that he was concerned with natural philosophy in an amazing way and to an amazing degree when he was young. He does not give any dates, and hence we do not know for how long this preoccupation with natural philosophy lasted—whether it did not last till close to the time at which the *Clouds* was conceived. As for Xenophon's Socrates, he was no longer young when he was already notorious as a man who was "measuring the air," or as a man resembling Aristophanes' Socrates, and had not yet raised the question of what a perfect gentleman is, i.e., the kind of question to which he seems to have dedicated himself entirely after his break with natural philosophy (*Oeconomicus* 6.13–17 and 11.1–6; *Symposium* 6.6–8). It follows that it is not altogether the fault of Aristophanes if he did not present Socrates as the same kind of philosopher as did Plato and Xenophon. Besides, if Socrates had always been the Platonic or Xenophontic Socrates, his selection by Aristophanes for one of his comedies would become hard to understand: Socrates would have been politically in the same camp as Aristophanes. And while a comic poet is perhaps compelled to caricature even his fellow partisans, the caricature must have some correspondence with the man being caricatured.

After we have begun to wonder whether there was not perhaps a little bit of fire where there was so much smoke, we go on and begin to wonder whether Aristophanes was after all an accuser, an enemy of Socrates. There is only one Platonic dialogue in which Aristophanes participates, the *Banquet*. That dialogue is presented as having taken place about seven years after the performance of

the *Clouds*. The occasion was a banquet at the end of which only
three men were still sober and awake, two of them being Aristophanes and Socrates. The three men were engaged in a friendly conversation ending in agreement about a subject than which none
was more important to Aristophanes, the subject of comedy. The
agreement was an agreement of Aristophanes to a thesis pro-
pounded by Socrates. In accordance with this is the Platonic Socrates' complicated and strange analysis, given in the *Philebus*
(48a8–50a10), of the condition of the soul at comedies. In that analysis we discern the following strand. The condition of the soul at
comedies is a mixture of the pleasure derived from the misfortunes
of one's friends, or their innocuous overestimation of their wisdom, with the pain of envy. Envy of what? The most natural explanation would seem to be envy of one's friend's wisdom. The
friend's wisdom may not be as great as he believes, and therefore
he may be somewhat ridiculous, but his wisdom may be substantial enough to afford cause for envy. This analysis of comedy is
monstrously inadequate as an analysis of comedy in general, but
it makes sense as Socrates' explanation of one particular comedy,
the comedy *par excellence,* the *Clouds*. In brief, on the basis of the
Platonic evidence it is no more plausible to say that the *Clouds* is
an accusation of Socrates than to say that it is a friendly warning
addressed to Socrates—a warning informed by a mixture of admiration and envy of Socrates. This interpretation is perfectly compatible with the possibility that the primary object of Aristophanes' envy is not Socrates' wisdom but Socrates' complete
independence from that popular applause on which the comic
poet necessarily depends, or Socrates' perfect freedom.

As in all cases of this kind, the differences of interpretation ultimately proceed less from the consideration or the neglect of this
or that particular fact or passage than from a primary and fundamental disagreement. In our case the fundamental disagreement
concerns tragedy. According to the view which is now predominant, tragedy at its highest is truer and deeper than comedy at its
highest, since life is essentially tragic. In the light of this assumption, Socrates' fate appears to be simply tragic. On the basis of this
assumption, scholarship tends to see much more clearly the connection of the Platonic dialogues with tragedy than their connection with comedy. We need not go into the question whether this
assumption is sound; we can be content with raising the question
whether it was Plato's assumption. Plato was familiar with the assumption; the prejudice in favor of tragedy is not peculiar to mod-

ern times. No one was more aware than Plato of the fact that tragedy is the most deeply moving art. But from this, he held, it does not follow that tragedy is the deepest or the highest art. He silently opposes the popular preference for tragedy. He suggests that the same man must be both tragic and comic poet. When his Adeimantus simply equates dramatic poetry with tragedy, he makes his Socrates unobtrusively correct Adeimantus by imputing to Adeimantus the assertion that dramatic poetry embraces comedy as well (*Republic* 394b–c). If we do not disregard the fact that the difference between tragedy and comedy corresponds somehow to the difference between weeping and laughing, we can bring out the issue involved in this way. Socrates laughed once, but never do we find that he wept so much as once. He left us no example of weeping, but on the other side he left us an example of laughing. He left us many examples of his joking and none of his indignation. His irony is a byword. He is not a tragic figure, but it is easy to see how he can become a comic figure. The philosopher who falls into a ditch while observing the heavenly things or the philosopher who, having left the cave of ordinary life, returns to it and cannot find his way in it, is of course ridiculous, as Plato's Socrates himself points out. Viewed in the perspective of the nonphilosophers the philosopher is necessarily ridiculous, and viewed in the perspective of the philosopher the nonphilosophers are necessarily ridiculous; the meeting of philosophers and nonphilosophers is the natural theme of comedy. It is, as we shall see, the theme of the *Clouds*. It is then not altogether an accident that our oldest and hence most venerable source regarding Socrates is a comedy.

These remarks are merely made for the purpose of counteracting certain prejudices. The decision of the question under discussion can be expected only from the interpretation of the *Clouds* itself. Such an interpretation will be facilitated, to say the least, by a consideration of the Aristophanean comedy in general.

In glancing at modern interpretations of the Aristophanean comedies, one is struck by the preoccupation of modern scholars with the political background and the political meaning of the comedies. It is as if these scholars were about to forget, or had already forgotten, that they are dealing with comedies. When about to enter a place at which we are meant to laugh and to enjoy ourselves, we must first cross a picket line of black-coated ushers exuding deadly and deadening seriousness. No doubt they unwittingly contribute to the effect of the comedies. Still, it is simpler to remember what Hegel has said about the Aristophanean comedies: "If one has not read Aristophanes one can hardly know how robustly and inordinately gay, of what beastlike contentment, man can be."

Hegel's statement reminds us of the obstacles which one has to overcome when reading the Aristophanean comedies. For if we desire to understand, to appreciate, and to love the Aristophanean comedy, it is necessary that we should first be repelled by it. The means which Aristophanes employs in order to make us laugh include gossip or slander, obscenity, parody, and blasphemy. Through this ill-looking and ill-smelling mist we see free and sturdy rustics in their cups; good-natured; sizing up women, free or slave, as they size up cows and horses; in their best and gayest moments the fools of no one, be he god or wife or glorious captain, and yet less angry than amused at having been fooled by them ever so often; loving the country and its old and tested ways, despising the new-fangled and rootless which shoots up for a day in the city and among its boastful boosters; amazingly familiar with the beautiful so that they can enjoy every allusion to any of the many tragedies of Aeschylus, Sophocles, and Euripides; and amazingly experienced in the beautiful so that they will not stand for any parody which is not in its way as perfect as the original. Men of such birth and build are the audience of Aristophanes, or (which is the same for any non-contemptible poet) the best or authoritative part of his audience. The audience to which Aristophanes appeals or which he conjured is the best democracy as Aristotle has described it: the democracy whose backbone is the rural population. Aristophanes makes us see this audience at its freest and gayest, from its crude and vulgar periphery to its center of sublime delicacy; we do not see it equally well, although we sense it strongly, in its bonds and bounds. We see only half of it, apparently its lower half, in fact its higher. We see only one half of humanity, apparently its lower half, in fact its higher. The other half is the preserve of tragedy. Comedy and tragedy together show us the whole of man, but in such a way that the comedy must be sensed in the tragedy and the tragedy in the comedy. Comedy begins at the lowest low, whereas tragedy dwells at the center. Aristophanes has compared the comic muse, or rather the Pegasus of the comic poet, to a dung beetle, a small and contemptible beast which is attracted by everything ill-smelling, which seems to combine conceit with utter remoteness from Aphrodite and the Graces—which, however, when it can be induced to arise from the earth, soars higher than the eagle of Zeus: it enables the comic poet to enter the world of the gods, to see with his own eyes the truth about the gods and to communicate this truth to his fellow mortals. Comedy rises higher than any other art. It transcends every other art; it transcends in particular tragedy. Since it transcends tragedy, it presupposes tragedy. The fact that it presupposes and transcends tragedy finds its expression in the parodies of tragedies which are so characteristic of the Aristophanean comedy. Comedy rises higher than tragedy. Only the comedy can present wise men as wise men: men like Euripides and Socrates, men who as such transcend tragedy.

This is not to deny that the Aristophanean comedy abounds with what is ridiculous on the lowest level. But that comedy never presents as ridiculous what only perverse men could find ridiculous. It keeps within the bounds of what is by nature ridiculous. There occur spankings but no torturings and killings. The genuinely fear-inspiring must be absent, and hence that which is most fear-inspiring: death, i.e., dying, as distinguished from being dead in Hades. Therefore there must be absent also what causes compassion, and also the truly noble. Whereas in Aristophanes' *Frogs* Aeschylus and Euripides are presented as engaged in violent name-calling, Sophocles remains silent throughout. The Aristophanean comedy, while abounding with what is by nature ridiculous on the lowest level, always transcends this kind of the ridiculous; it never remains mere buffoonery. That which is by nature not ridiculous is not omitted; it comes to sight within the comedy. The Aristophanean comedy owes its depth and its worth to the presence within it of the solemn and the serious.

We must try to find the proper expression for that regarding which Aristophanes is serious. The proper expression, i.e., the authentic expression, is Aristophanes' own expression. Here a difficulty arises. In a drama, the author never speaks in his own name. The dramatic poet can express what he is driving at by the outcome of his play. Aristophanes avails himself of this simple possibility: he makes those human beings or those causes victorious which in his view ought to be victorious, given the premises of the plot. For the triumph of the unpleasing and the defeat of the pleasing is incompatible with the required gratifying effect of the comedy. However this may be, a drama is a play; certain human beings, the actors, pretend to be other human beings; they speak and act in the way in which those human beings would act. The dramatic effect requires that this play, or pretending, be consistently maintained. If this effect is disturbed because the actors cease

to act their parts and become recognizable as actors in contradistinction to the characters they are meant to represent, or because
the poet ceases to be invisible or inaudible except through his characters, this is annoying or ridiculous. Hence, whereas the destruction of the dramatic illusion is fatal to the tragic effect, it may
heighten the comic effect. Aristophanes is then able in his comedies to speak to the audience directly; his chorus or his characters
may address not only one another but the audience as well. It is
even possible that the hero of a comedy, e.g., Dicaiopolis in the
Acharnians, reveals himself to be the comic poet himself. At any
rate Aristophanes can use his chorus or his characters for stating
to the audience, and hence also to his readers, his intention. Thus
he tells us that it is his intention to make us laugh, but not through
buffoonery. He claims that he is a comic poet who has raised
comedy to its perfection. But much as he is concerned with the
ridiculous, he is no less concerned with the serious, with making
men better by fighting on behalf of the city against its enemies and
corruptors, by teaching what is good for the city or what is simply
the best, and by saying what is just. Through his work, well-being
and justice have become allies. He also makes a distinction between the wise element of his comedies and their ridiculous element: the former should appeal to the wise, the latter to the laugh-
ers. These *ipsissima verba poetae* compel us to wonder regarding the
relation of justice and wisdom: are they identical or different? The
problem is clearly expressed in the poet's claim that he made the
just things a matter for comedy. However much the poet may succeed in reconciling the claims of the ridiculous on the one hand
and the serious on the other, or of the ridiculous on the one hand
and justice on the other, a fundamental tension must remain. In a
word, justice as Aristophanes understands it consists in preserving or restoring the ancestral or the old. The quality of a comedy,
on the other hand, depends very much on the inventiveness of the
poet, on his conceits being novel. Aristophanes may have been an
unqualified reactionary in political things; as a comic poet he was
compelled to be a revolutionary.

While the tension between the ridiculous and the serious is essential to the Aristophanean comedy, the peculiar greatness of that
comedy consists in its being the total comedy or in the fact that in
that comedy the comical is all-pervasive: the serious itself appears
only in the guise of the ridiculous. This must be intelligently
understood. Just as literally speaking there can be no complete
falsehood, given the primacy of truth, there cannot be a ridiculous

speech of some length which does not include serious passages, given the primacy of the serious. Within these inevitable limitations Aristophanes succeeds perfectly in integrating the serious or the just into the ridiculous. The comical delusion is never destroyed or even impaired. How does he achieve this feat?

It is easy to see how the castigation of the unjust can be achieved by ridicule. In order to show up the sycophants, the demagogues, the over-zealous jurymen, the would-be heroic generals, the corrupting poets and sophists, it is obviously useful to make a judicious use of gossip or slander about the ridiculous looks and the ridiculous demeanor of the individuals in question. Furthermore, one can hold up a mirror to the prevailing bad habits by exaggerating them ridiculously, by presenting their unexpected and yet, if one may say so, logical consequences. For instance, one may present an entirely new-fangled Athens, run by women, which is characterized by communism of property, women, and children as the final form of extreme democracy; one can show how the complete equality of the communist order conflicts with the natural inequality between the young and beautiful and the old and ugly; one may show how this natural inequality is corrected by a legal or conventional equality in accordance with which no youth can enjoy his girl before he has fulfilled the onerous duty of satisfying a most repulsive hag: the serious conclusion from this ridiculous scene is too obvious to be pointed out. The very fact that the injustice of the demagogues and the other types mentioned is publicly revealed shows how little clever those fellows are: it reveals their injustice as stupid and hence ridiculous. The ridicule is heightened by the fact that the ridiculed individuals are probably present in the audience. For the folly ridiculed by Aristophanes is contemporary folly. The contemporary vices are seen as vices in the light of the good old times, of the ancestral polity—in the perspective of the simple, brave, rural, and pious victors of Marathon, of those who prefer Aeschylus to Euripides. Contemporary injustice might arouse indignation and not laughter if it were not presented as defeated with ease, as defeated by ridiculous means: as the war-like Greek manhood is defeated by the wives' abstinence from intercourse, and the super-demagogue Cleon is defeated with his own means by the still baser sausage seller who is boosted by the upper-class people, Cleon's mortal enemies.

Yet how can one present the defeat of the unjust by ridiculous means without making ridiculous the victorious justice? Or, in other words, how can one present the just man without destroying the effect of the total comedy? Aristophanes solves this difficulty as follows. The victory of the just, or the movement from the ridiculousness of contemporary political folly to ancient soundness, is a movement toward the ridiculous of a different kind. The just man is a man who minds his own business, the opposite of a busybody, the man who loves the retired, quiet, private life. Living at home, on his farm, he enjoys the simple natural pleasures: food, drink, and, last but by no means least, love. He enjoys these pleasures frankly. He gives his enjoyment a frank, a wholly unrestrained, expression. He calls a spade a spade. If he does this as a character on the stage, he says in public what cannot be said in public with propriety: he publishes that private which cannot with propriety be published; and this is ridiculous. Hence the victory of justice is comically presented as a movement from the ridiculousness of public folly to the ridiculousness of the publication of the essentially private, of the improper utterance of things which everyone privately enjoys because they are by nature enjoyable.

A major theme, the first theme of the Aristophanean comedy, is then the tension between the city, the political community, and the family or the household. The bond of the family is love, and in the first place the love of husband and wife, legal eros. The love of the parents for the children appears most characteristically in the case of the mother, who suffers most when her sons are sent into wars by the city. No such natural feelings bind mothers to the city. Thus one might think that the family should be the model for the city. In his *Assembly of Women* Aristophanes has shown the fantastic character of this thought; there he presents the city as transformed into a household. Such a city therefore lacks private property of the members and is therefore ruled by women. Nevertheless the importance which Aristophanes assigns to the tension between family and city leads one to surmise that his critique is not only directed against the decayed city of his time but extends also to the healthy city or the ancestral polity. The hero of the *Acharnians*, Dicaiopolis, who is clearly identified with the poet himself, privately makes peace with the enemy of the city while everyone else is at war. He is persecuted for this act of high treason, not only by the war party, but precisely by his rustic neighbours who are wholly imbued with the old spirit of the Marathon fighters. Dicaiopolis makes a speech in his defense with his head on the executioner's block and using devices which he had borrowed from Euripides; he thus succeeds in splitting his persecutors into two parties and therewith in stopping the persecution; as a consequence he enjoys the pleasures of peace, of farm life, while everyone else remains at war. It is only another way of expressing the same thought if one says with Aristophanes that it was not, as Aeschylus and Euripides agree in the *Frogs*, the ancient Aeschylus, the political tragic poet *par excellence*, but the modern Euripides who gave her due to Aphrodite. For, as Socrates says in Plato's *Banquet* (177e), Aphrodite is the goddess to whom, together with Dionysus, the Aristophanean comedy is wholly devoted.

Incidentally, this agreement between Aristophanes and Euripides and this disagreement between Aristophanes and Aeschylus confirms our previous contention that Aristophanes was aware of the essentially novel or revolutionary character of his whole enterprise. The action of at least some of his comedies expresses this characteristic of Aristophanes' thought. In the *Knights*, the *Wasps*, the *Peace*, the *Birds*, the *Thesmophoriazusae*, and the *Assembly of Women*, the restoration of soundness in politics is effected by radically novel means, by means which are incompatible with the end, i.e., the ancestral polity and its spirit. Aristophanes did not, then, have any delusions about the politically problematic character of his political message.

But to return to the argument at hand, the phenomenon in the light of which Aristophanes looks critically at the city as such is the family or the household. His comedies may be said to be one commentary on the sentence in the *Nicomachean Ethics* (1162a17–19) which reads: "Man is by nature a pairing animal rather than a political one, for the family is earlier and more necessary than the city, and the begetting and bearing of children is more common to all animals [*sc.* than living in herds]."

The two poles between which the Aristophanean comedy moves have hitherto appeared to be contemporary public folly, on the one hand, and, on the other, the retired and easy life of the household as a life of enjoyment of the pleasures of the body. The transition from the one pole to the other is effected in the comedies by means which are ridiculous or wholly unprecedented or extreme. In the *Peace* the hero, Trygaeus, who is the comic poet himself in a thin disguise, succeeds in stopping the horrors of an insane, fratricidal war by ascending to heaven on the back of a dung beetle. He believes that Zeus is responsible for the war, and he wants to rebuke him for this unfriendly conduct. Having arrived in heaven, he finds out from Hermes that Zeus is responsible, not for the war itself, but for the continuation of the war: Zeus has put savage War in charge. War has interred Peace in a deep pit, and

Zeus has made it a capital crime to disinter her. The hero bribes
Hermes with threats and promises—the chief promise being that
Hermes will become the highest god—into assisting him in disinterring Peace. Trygaeus, acting against the express command of
the highest god, succeeds in disinterring Peace and thus brings
peace to all of Hellas. He does nothing, of course, to perform his
promise to Hermes. Hermes is superseded completely by Peace,
who alone is worshipped. By rebelling against Zeus and the other
gods, Trygaeus becomes the savior. The just and pleasant life of
ease and quiet cannot be brought about except by dethroning the
gods.

The same theme is treated from a somewhat different point of
view in the *Wasps*. In that comedy a zealous old juryman is prevented by his sensible son, first through force and then through
persuasion, from attending the sessions of the law court and from
acting there unjustly. The son wishes his father to stay at home
and thus not to hurt his fellow men, to feast and to enjoy the pleasures of refined, modern society. The son partly succeeds. The father is prevailed upon to stay away from the court and to go to a
party. But he is not fit for refined enjoyments: he merely gets
drunk, becomes entangled with a flute girl, and enjoys himself in
committing acts of assault and battery. His savage nature can be
directed into different channels, but it cannot be subdued. The father is not a typical juryman, the typical juryman being a poor
fellow who depends for his livelihood on the pay which the juryman received in Athens. He is extremely eager to attend the court
because he loves to condemn people. He traces his inhuman desire
to an injunction of the Delphic oracle. When his son deceives him
into acquitting a defendant, he is afraid of having committed a sin
against the gods. What makes him savage is, then, his fear of the
savagery of the gods. It is surprising that the gods should be more
punitive than men, for, as Trygaeus found out when he had as-
cended to heaven, men appear to be less evil (than they are) when
they are viewed from above, from the seat of the gods. The underlying notion of the savagery of the gods is nowhere contradicted
in the *Wasps*. To make men somewhat more humane one must free
them from the gods. As Plato's Aristophanes puts it in the *Banquet*
(189c–d), Eros is the most philanthropic god. The other gods are
not characterized by love of men. In the *Thesmophoriazusae* the poet
shows how Euripides is persecuted by the Athenian women because he had maligned women so much. There is no question as
to the truth of what Euripides had said about the female sex; Aris-

tophanes expresses the same view throughout the plays. But the women are a force to be reckoned with. To save himself, Euripides, who is said to be an atheist, commits an enormous act of sacrilege. It is not followed by any punishment. The only concession which he is compelled to make is that he must promise the women that he will no longer say nasty things about them. In contradistinction to the *Clouds*, the *Thesmophoriazusae* has a happy ending; a poet succeeds where the philosopher fails.

In the *Birds* we see two Athenians who have left their city because they are sick of lawsuits which they do not wish to pay and are in search of a quiet, soft, and happy city where a man does not have to be a busybody. Having arrived at the place where they expect to get the necessary information about the location of that city, one of the Athenians hits upon the thought of founding a city comprising all birds—a democratic world state. That city, he explains to the birds, will make the birds the rulers of all men and all gods, for all traffic between men and gods (the sacrifices) has to pass through the region in which the birds dwell. The proposal is adopted; the gods are starved into submission; the birds become the new gods; they take the place of the gods. The ruler of the birds is our clever Athenian. But he must make some concessions to the universal democracy of the birds. The birds praise themselves as the true gods: they are the oldest and wisest of all beings; they are all-seeing, all-ruling, and altogether friendly to men. Their life is altogether pleasant; what is "base by convention" among men is noble among the birds: desertion, abolition of slavery, and last but not least the beating of one's father. However, when a man who is given to beating his father wishes to join the city of the birds in order to be able to indulge his inclination with impunity—for the laws of the birds are said to permit the beating of one's father—he is told by the Athenian founder of the city of the birds that according to those laws the sons may not only not beat their fathers but must feed them when they are old. This is to say, it is possible to establish a universal democracy, and hence universal happiness, by dethroning the gods, provided one preserves the prohibition against beating one's father, provided one preserves the family. Eros, which inspires the generating of men, requires in the case of men the sacredness of the family. The family rather than the city is natural. While the city of the birds is in the process of being founded, the Athenian founder is visited by five men: by a poet who receives a gift, by a soothsayer, by a supervisor and a seller of decrees or laws (both of whom are thrown out and spanked), and, in the central place, by the Athenian astronomer Meton, who wishes to "measure the air." The founder admires Meton as another Thales and loves him; but he warns him of the fact that the citizens will beat him, and Meton is in fact beaten up by the citizens—of course, the birds. The founder's admiration and love cannot protect the astronomer against the popular dislike. Even in the perfectly happy city, even in the city which seems to be in every respect the city according to nature, one cannot be openly a student of nature.

Both obscenities and blasphemies consist in publicly saying things which cannot be said publicly with propriety. They are ridiculous and hence pleasing to the extent to which propriety is sensed as a burden, as something imposed, as something owing its dignity to imposition, to convention, to *nomos*. In the background of the Aristophanean comedy we discern the distinction between *nomos* and *physis*. Hitherto we have recognized the locus of nature in the family. But Aristophanes takes a further step. That step is indicated by the frequent nonindignant references to adultery as well as by facts like these: the hero of the *Birds* is a pederast, and the sensible son who corrects his foolish father to some extent in the *Wasps* uses force against his aged father. In brief, Aristophanes does not stop at the sacredness or naturalness of the family. One is tempted to say that his comedies celebrate the victory of nature, as it reveals itself in the pleasant, over convention or law, which is the locus of the noble and the just. Lest this be grossly misunderstood, one must add immediately two points. In the first place, if *nomos* is viewed in the light of nature, the Aristophanean comedy is based on knowledge of nature and therefore on consciousness of the sublime pleasures accompanying knowledge of nature. Above all, Aristophanes has no doubt as to the fact that nature, human nature, is in need of *nomos*. Aristophanes does not reject *nomos*, but he attempts to bring to light its problematic and precarious status, its status in between the needs of the body and the needs of the mind; for if one does not understand the precarious status of *nomos*, one is bound to have unreasonable expectations from *nomos*.

The profoundest student of Aristophanes in modern times was Hegel. His interpretation of the Aristophanean comedy occurs in the section of the *Phenomenology of the Mind* entitled "Religion" in the subsection entitled "The Art-Religion" (the religion expressing itself completely by art). By the Art-Religion Hegel means the Greek religion, which he regarded as the highest religion outside of revealed religion. The Art-Religion finds its end and culmination, or it achieves full self-consciousness, in the Aristophanean comedy. In that comedy, Hegel says, "The individual consciousness having become conscious of itself presents itself as the absolute power." Everything objective—the gods, the city, the family, justice—has become dissolved into the self-consciousness or taken back into it. The comedy presents and celebrates the complete insubstantiality of everything alien to the self-consciousness, the complete freedom from fear of everything transcending the individual. The comedy celebrates the triumph of "the subjectivity in its infinite security." Man has made himself the complete master of everything which he formerly regarded as the substantial content of his knowledge or action. This victory of subjectivity is one of the most important symptoms of the corruption of Greece. For our present purpose it is not necessary to dwell on the fact that in his lectures on aesthetics Hegel does not consistently maintain this view. But we must note that what Hegel calls the triumph of subjectivity is achieved in the Aristophanean comedy only by virtue of the knowledge of nature, i.e., the opposite of self-consciousness. Let us then turn to Plato's interpretation of the Aristophanean comedy, which we find in the speech he puts into the mouth of Aristophanes at the banquet. Only a few points can be mentioned here.

Aristophanes was supposed to make his speech in honor of Eros after Pausanias had made a pause. But Aristophanes got a hiccough—he did not possess perfect control of his body, or perfect self-control—and the physician Eryximachus had to take his place. Aristophanes proves to be interchangeable with a physician who was a student of nature in general. Aristophanes begins with the remark that men do not seem to have experienced the power of Eros, for if they had, they would build for him the greatest temples and altars and bring him the greatest sacrifices, since Eros is the most philanthropic of all gods. He then tells the following story. In the olden times human nature was different from what it is now. Each human being consisted of two human beings; it had four hands, four ears, etc. In this state men were of exceeding strength and pride so that they undertook to ascend to heaven in order to attack the gods. The gods did not know what to do, for they could not kill man, since by doing so they would deprive themselves of honors and sacrifices. Zeus discovered this way out: to weaken men by cutting each in two, so that man became as he is now; after this division, each half is longing for the other. This longing for the original unity, for a wholeness, is *eros*. The original whole was either androgynous, or male, or female. Those present human beings who stem from the original androgynes seek the opposite sex; an outstanding part of them are the adulterers. Those present human beings who stem from an original female are female homosexuals. Those present human beings who stem from an original male are male homosexuals; they are the best among the boys and youths because they are the most manly; they are born to become true statesmen. This is the story to which the Platonic Aristophanes appends an explanation of perfect propriety. But taken by itself the myth teaches that by virtue of eros men, and especially the best part of the male sex, will approach a condition in which they become a serious danger to the gods. We record here the fact that the hero of the *Birds*, who succeeds in dethroning the gods and in becoming the ruler of the universe through the birds, is the pederast Peisthetaerus.

Second Lecture

These lectures represent an attempt to go back to the origins of rationalism, and therefore to Socrates. The oldest document regarding Socrates is Aristophanes' comedy the *Clouds*. For an adequate understanding of the *Clouds* it is necessary to consider the Aristophanean comedy in general, or to understand the spirit of his comedy. I repeat a few points I made last time. Aristophanean comedy has a twofold function: to make us laugh and to teach us justice; to be ridiculous, and to be serious. Yet at the same time the Aristophanean comedy is the total comedy; the comical is all-pervasive. Hence not only injustice, or contemporary public folly, but justice itself is presented in such a way as to afford opportunity to laugh. How does Aristophanes achieve this feat? The just life, as he sees it, is the retired life, life on the farm, enjoying the pleasures of farm life, enjoying the pleasures of the body, especially of love. These pleasures are given in the comedy a frank, unrestrained expression. The characters use the language which, as I have learned through my frequent readings in the *American Journal of Sociology*, is called in this country the language of the stag party. The movement from the ridiculousness of public folly to the praise of public soundness is therefore a movement from the ridiculousness of public folly to the ridiculousness of impropriety, not to say obscenity. If one analyses this state of things one recognizes as the basis of Aristophanes' thought a polarity, the polarity of the polis, or the city, and the family, and in this context the family appears to be more natural than the polis. The comedy may be said to be one great appeal from the polis to the more natural family. In other words, Aristophanes presupposes the fundamental distinction between nature and law or convention. On the basis of this fundamental distinction he questions the family itself, and not only the city. For instance, the beating of one's father, *the* crime from the point of view of the family, is presented as not absolutely wrong in one of the comedies, the *Wasps*. Hence the more proper description of the fundamental polarity would be this: the conflict between the pleasant on the one hand and the just and noble on the other. Now, this life of gaiety, peace, and enjoyment—the natural life—requires, according to Aristophanes' presentation, the successful revolt against the gods, for the gods are punitive and harsh. This comes out most clearly in the *Birds* and in the *Peace*. Here is a place for the famous blasphemies in Aristophanes.

I concluded my general interpretation of the Aristophanean comedy by contrasting it with the interpretation given by the greatest mind who has devoted himself in modern times to Aristophanes, and that is Hegel. Hegel sees in the Aristophanean comedy the triumph of subjectivity over everything objective and substantial—over the city, the family, morality, and the gods. The subject, the autonomous subject, recognizes itself as the origin of everything objective, and takes the objective back into itself. This does justice to almost everything in Aristophanes except to one thing of, indeed, decisive importance. The basis of this taking back (or however we call it), of this subjectivism, is in Aristophanes not the self-consciousness of the subject, but knowledge of nature, and the very opposite of self-consciousness. Aristophanes has brought this out most clearly in a scene in the *Birds* in which the founder of a natural city is confronted by an astronomer, a student of nature, and the founder of this city-according-to-nature admires and loves that student of nature, but he cannot protect him against the enmity of the citizen body, or the populace. In this case the populace consists of birds, but the application to human beings does not require a very great effort of the intelligence or the imagination. The basis of Aristophanean comedy is knowledge of nature, and that means, for the ancients, philosophy. But philosophy is a problem; philosophy does not have a political or civic existence. Here is where the problem of the *Clouds* comes in, to which I turn now.

At the beginning of the *Clouds* it is dark. Strepsiades, the hero of the comedy, the man who causes Socrates' downfall, is lying on his couch and cannot find sleep. He longs for the day, for light in a literal sense. We may take this as a clue to the comedy. Socrates owes his downfall to a man who seeks light in the most literal sense, to a kind of Sancho Panza, to a rustic who has lost his bearings or has gone astray. It will do no great harm if this comparison suggests a similarity between Aristophanes' Socrates and Don Quixote. Strepsiades is not an embodiment of stern, old-fashioned justice; he is rather a crook. He is a simple rustic, a man of the common people who has married a patrician lady. The offspring of the marriage, their son Pheidippides, has inherited the expensive tastes of his mother's line. He is a passionate horseman. He has run his father into exorbitant debt. In order to get rid of his debts, Strepsiades has decided to send his spendthrift son to Socrates, the owner and manager of a think tank, so that he might learn how to talk himself out of his debts at law courts. Strepsiades knows this much of Socrates, that Socrates talks about the heavens and, besides, teaches people for money how they can win every lawsuit, by fair means or foul. But although he lives next door, Strepsiades does not know Socrates' name, whereas his sophisticated son knows it as a matter of course. His son refuses to become Socrates' pupil. The elegant young horseman has nothing but contempt for Socrates and his companions, "those pale-faced and ill-dressed boasters and beggars" (ll. 102–3); hence Strepsiades himself is compelled to become Socrates' pupil.

Let us reflect for a moment about this situation, as it comes to sight right at the beginning of the *Clouds*. The common people know nothing of Socrates, not even his name. The patricians do know of Socrates, but they despise him as a ridiculous sort of beggar. Socrates does not run any danger from the two most powerful sections of society. If Strepsiades had remained within his station, Socrates would never have gotten into trouble. Socrates does get into trouble through a certain inbetween type of man, who is not distinguished by honesty. Here we remind ourselves of the fact that the old juryman of the *Wasps*, who is such a savage condemner because he believes that the gods look askance at acquittals, is also socially an inbetween type. Needless to say, the demagogues too belong to the inbetween type.

Strepsiades, then, sends his son to Socrates so that he might learn dishonest practices for him. Strepsiades is ultimately responsible for a possible corruption of his son, and yet this will not prevent him from making Socrates alone responsible.

A word about Socrates' think tank or school. Misled by what the Platonic Socrates says in his apology addressed to the Athenian people about his spending all his time in the marketplace, some people think that the schoolhouse of Socrates is a pure or impure invention of Aristophanes. Yet there is Xenophontic evidence to the effect that Socrates used to sit together with his friends and to study with them the books of the wise men of old (*Memorabilia* 1.6.14), and that he never ceased considering with them what each of the beings is (Ibid., 4.6.1). Given that Socrates was the leader in these gatherings, and that the activities mentioned cannot well be engaged in at the marketplace, Xenophon tells us, then, in effect, that Socrates was a teacher, if a perfect teacher. And a teacher has pupils, and the community of teachers and pupils, rather than the building, is the school.

Strepsiades enters Socrates' think tank in order to become his pupil. He is received by a pupil of Socrates. It takes considerable time before he meets Socrates. Socrates is not as easy of access as Euripides is, in a comparable scene in the *Acharnians*. The pupil tells Strepsiades that what is going on in the think tank may not be divulged to anyone except to pupils. But Strepsiades' mere declaration that he intends to become a pupil induces the pupil to blurt out all the secrets he knows. Socrates' security arrangements are most inept. We learn through the pupil that Socrates and his pupils study mathematics and natural science. For example, they investigate how many feet of its own a flea can jump. They need not leave the tank in order to catch the flea. Then Strepsiades becomes aware of Socrates aloft, suspended in a basket, walking on air, and looking over the sun, or looking down on it. At Strepsiades' request, Socrates descends and learns of Strepsiades' desire to learn to talk himself out of his debts. Socrates initiates him immediately, without having given a moment's thought to the question of pay. In fact, nowhere in the play, after Strepsiades has knocked at Socrates' door, do we find any reference to Socrates taking any pay for his teaching. Only once is there a very casual reference to some sort of gift which Strepsiades offers to Socrates out of his gratitude. Socrates is not a sophist in Aristophanes. Socrates is no money-maker, but a needy fellow who makes his companions needy as well and yet is insensitive to his and his companions' neediness. Socrates' first words addressed to Strepsiades had been, "Why do you call me, you ephemeral one?" (l. 223). Socrates shows himself throughout as the despiser of everything ephemeral, and hence in particular of money. He is induced to converse with Strepsiades not by greed or vanity, but rather by a desire to talk, which is prompted either by the desire to reduce the volume of stupidity in the world, or else by sheer enthusiasm for his pursuit.

Socrates teaches two things, natural science and rhetoric. The duality of natural science and rhetoric corresponds to a duality of principles. The first principle is aether, which is the original whirl or chaos, the highest cosmic principle; and the other principle is the Clouds, which give understanding and power of speech and inspire the choruses. The Clouds correspond to rhetoric, since they can take any shape they like, or since they can imitate everything, or since they can reveal the nature of all things—and since at the same time they conceal the sky, they conceal the aether, or heaven, or the highest reality. Rhetoric is essentially both revealing and concealing. The Clouds are the only gods recognized and worshipped by Socrates. They are worshipped by him as gods because they are the origin of the greatest benefit to men, whereas the highest cosmic principle, aether, is responsible for both good and evil. The Clouds love lazy or inactive people and demand abstinence from bodily exercises. Socrates does not hesitate to make clear what he means by worshipping only the Clouds: "Zeus does not exist." (l. 367). He demands from Strepsiades that he no longer recognize the gods worshipped by the city, and Strepsiades, mind you, complies with this request without any hesitation. The strange thing is that Socrates blurts out these shocking things before he has tested Strepsiades regarding his worthiness to hear of them and his ability to understand them. The Aristophanean Socrates is characterized by an amazing lack of *phronesis*, of practical wisdom or prudence. Still, since Strepsiades has no interest beyond cheating his creditors, Socrates limits himself to teaching him speech, grammar, etc. He does not even attempt to teach him natural science. But Strepsiades proves to be too stupid even for the lower or easier branch of knowledge. He is therefore compelled to force his son to become Socrates' pupil. He is particularly anxious that Socrates should teach Pheidippides the Unjust Speech, the Unjust Argument (Just and Unjust Argument are personified in the *Clouds*). Socrates merely replies that Pheidippides will hear both speeches, the Just Speech and the Unjust Speech. Socrates himself will be absent while the two speeches have their exchange. Socrates does not teach injustice; he merely exposes his pupils to the arguments between justice and injustice. He cannot be held responsible for the fact that Justice cannot hold her own by argument against Injustice.

The Unjust Speech denies the existence of right on the grounds that justice is not "with the gods" (ll. 903–5). Zeus did not perish for having done violence to his father, but rather was rewarded for it. The Just Speech is unable to reply to this point. The Just Speech points out that the Unjust Speech does harm to the city, while the city feeds the Unjust Speech. It praises old-fashioned temperance. The Unjust Speech replies in the spirit of the Aristophanean comedy. It refers to the necessities of nature, which are stronger than the demands of temperance. It encourages people to make use of nature, that is to say, to regard nothing as base, for one cannot help being defeated by eros and by women. The proof is again supplied by the conduct of Zeus. In a word, the ancestral morality, *the* standard of the external Aristophanes, is contradicted by the ancestral theology on which it is based. At the end of the exchange the Just Speech admits its defeat and deserts to the camp of the Unjust Speech.

Pheidippides learns the art of speaking. Trusting in his son's accomplishments, Strepsiades refuses to pay his debts and, in addition, insults his creditors. He heaps ridicule on his former oaths regarding his debts and on the very gods. Then a controversy arises between father and son. The son despises Aeschylus, and the father admires him. The son prefers Euripides, who, he says, is the wisest poet, and he quotes from Euripides a description of incest between brother and sister. Strepsiades is deeply shocked. The son goes so far as to beat his father, but he proves to his father's satisfaction, through the Just Speech, that he acts justly in beating his father. But then, when Pheidippides declares that he can also prove by the Unjust Speech that he is entitled to beat his mother, Strepsiades' patience snaps. Cursing himself and his dishonesty, he repents, turns passionately against Socrates and his school, recognizes the existence of Zeus and the other gods, and burns down Socrates' think tank. He justifies this action as the punishment for the impiety of Socrates. But let us not forget that it was not Socrates' impiety or lessons, but Socrates' alleged teaching that a son may beat his own mother, which aroused Strepsiades' unquenchable ire and brought about Socrates' downfall. If we wish to understand Aristophanes' case against Socrates, we must overcome our natural revulsion to this kind of subject and raise the question as to the particular significance of the permission to beat one's mother as distinguished from beating one's father. An indication is given by the fact that Strepsiades was already about to rebel when he heard of Euripides' presentation of incest between brother and sister. We shall express the underlying thought as follows. Granted that the family is more natural than the city, yet the family cannot be secure and flourish except by becoming a part of the city. The prohibition against incest compels the family to transcend itself and, as it were, to expand into the city. The prohibition against incest is a quasi-natural bridge between the family and the city. By rebelling against the alleged outrageous teaching of Socrates, Strepsiades merely acts in the spirit of his love for his son, which has inspired his escapades into dishonesty. Given the delicate and complicated character of the relation between family and city, and ultimately between nature and convention, the gulf between the two poles can only be bridged if convention is consecrated by reference to the gods. For the reason I indicated, the gods cannot fulfill their function without harshness. Yet since the gods are not human beings and therefore cannot be bound by the laws to which they subject men—Hera is both Zeus's wife and sister—a great difficulty remains. Men must do what the gods tell them to do, but not what the gods themselves do. This is not altogether satisfactory for those who long with all their heart to imitate the gods.

It is necessary to consider the conduct of Socrates' goddesses, the Clouds. The Clouds do not express Socrates' sentiment regarding the non-existence of the other gods—very far from it. They present themselves as being on the friendliest terms with the other gods. But they listen silently to Socrates' denial of the existence of the other gods. They are highly pleased with Socrates' worshipping the Clouds. They congratulate Strepsiades on his desire for great wisdom and promise him perfect happiness, provided he has a good memory, indefatigable dedication to study, and extreme continence, and—last but not least—provided he honors the Clouds. They promise him in particular that he will surpass all Greeks in the art of public speaking, and certainly in that kind of public speaking which he needs in order to get rid of his debts. They hand him over to Socrates. When Strepsiades proves to be too dumb, they advise him to send his son to Socrates in his stead. While Strepsiades fetches Pheidippides they remind Socrates of their great generosity toward Socrates and advise him to take the fullest advantage of Strepsiades' willingness to do everything Socrates says. A change makes itself felt during the exchange between the Just Speech and the Unjust Speech. When the Just Speech praises the ancient system of education, the Marathonian system, they applaud. They never applaud the Unjust Speech. When Strepsiades scoffs at his creditors and insults them in every way, the Clouds express the direst warnings regarding Strepsiades' future fate, and especially as to what he may have to expect from his sophisticated son. After Strepsiades has come to his senses and repented, the Clouds tell him that he got only what was coming to him because he had turned to dishonesty. Strepsiades replies, with some justice, that the Clouds had encouraged him. But the goddesses reply that it is their constant practice to guide men intent on evils into misfortune, so that they may learn to fear the gods. Needless to say, the Clouds do not raise a finger, if Clouds can raise a finger, in defense of Socrates and his think tank. I suggest this explanation. The Clouds' only worshipper in Athens up to now is Socrates. Hence they favor him for the time being. They claim that they help the city more than all other gods, although they are the only gods which are not worshipped in Athens. There is this alternative before them. Either Socrates, whom they favor as their sole worshipper, becomes a success—and the Clouds will be worshipped by the whole city; or Socrates fails—and they will be instrumental, if only by permission, in his destruction. The Clouds will be worshipped again by the whole city. If I may use a very vulgar expression, they are sitting pretty.

After Socrates has introduced the new divinities into the city, they desert him when they see how unpopular he is bound to become. They change their position as soon as they see how the Strepsiades case, the test case, is developing. Their conduct proves their divinity. They are wiser than Socrates. The Clouds are wise because they act with prudent regard to both Socrates' virtue and his vice. His virtue consists in his daring, his intrepidity, his nonconformity, which virtue enables him not to worship the divinities worshipped by the city and to worship new divinities worshipped by no one but himself. His vice is his lack of practical wisdom, or of prudence. For it would be wrong to say of Aristophanes' Socrates that he is unjust. He is indifferent to justice. The fact that he does not rebuke Strepsiades for his dishonesty may very well mean that once you enter the life of business and action you have already made a decision to use dishonest means. Besides, it is by no means clear whether the creditors who sold Pheidippides the expensive horses and expensive chariots did not cheat him in the first place. And it is not Socrates' fault if the common view of justice, based as it is on mythology, is intellectually inferior to the open plea for injustice. If all men dedicated themselves to the pursuit to which the Aristophanean Socrates is dedicated, i.e., the study of nature, no one would have the slightest incentive for hurting anyone else. Yet, and this seems to be the beginning to Socrates' error, not all men are capable of leading a life of contemplation. As a consequence of this grave oversight the Aristophanean Socrates is wholly unaware of the devastating effect which his indifference to practical matters must have on the city if nontheoretical men should become influenced by Socrates' sentiments. Socrates is unaware of the setting within which his think tank exists. He lacks self-knowledge. His lack of prudence proceeds from his lack of self-knowledge. It is because of his lack of self-knowledge that he is so radically unpolitical. If one remembers the fact that the Aristophanean comedies are dedicated to the praises of Aphrodite and Dionysus, or to the praise of eros, one observes immediately, with great surprise, Socrates' complete immunity to wine and to love. The Aristophanean Socrates is altogether unerotic. It is for this reason that he is thoroughly amusic. However closely he may be linked with Euripides, there is a gulf between him and Euripides precisely because Socrates has nothing in common with the poetic muse. As a necessary consequence of this, when Euripides is persecuted in the *Thesmophoriazusae*, he is capable of saving himself, whereas when Socrates is persecuted in the *Clouds*, he has no means of defense. Socrates' pursuit, the precise study of nature and of rhetoric, is not a public power, whereas poetry is a public power. Aristophanes' comical presentation of Socrates is the most important statement of the case for poetry in that secular contest between poetry and philosophy of which Plato speaks at the beginning of the tenth book of the *Republic*.

Plato's *Republic* may be said to be the reply *par excellence* to Aristophanes. The political proposals of the *Republic* are based on the conceits underlying Aristophanes' *Assembly of Women*. The complete communism, communism not only regarding property but regarding women and children as well, is introduced in Plato's *Republic* with arguments literally taken from Aristophanes' *Assembly of Women*. There is this most important difference between the best city of the *Assembly of Women* and that of the *Republic*. Plato contends that complete communism requires as its capstone or its foundation the rule of philosophy, about which Aristophanes is completely silent. This difference corresponds to a difference indicated in Plato's *Banquet*. According to Aristophanes the direction of eros is horizontal. According to Plato the direction of eros is vertical. While the *Republic* makes important use of the *Assembly of Women*, it is at least equally much directed against, and indebted to, the *Clouds*. Thrasymachus represents the Unjust Speech, and

Socrates takes the place of the Just Speech. And the Just Speech is in Plato, of course, victorious. The chief interlocutors in the *Republic* are the erotic Glaucon and the musical Adeimantus. As for music, Socrates demands in the name of justice that the poet as free poet be expelled from the city. As for eros, the tyrant, injustice incarnate, is revealed to be eros incarnate. The Socrates of the *Republic* reveals his kinship with the unerotic and the amusic Socrates of the *Clouds*.

What, then, do we learn from Aristophanes regarding the origin of political science? Aristophanes presents Socrates in about the same light in which Aristotle presents Hippodamus from Miletus, as a student of nature as a whole who fails to understand the political things. The concern of philosophy leads beyond the city in spite, or because, of the fact that philosophy is concerned with rhetoric. Philosophy is unable to persuade the nonphilosophers, or the common people, and hence philosophy is not a political power. Philosophy, in contradistinction to poetry, cannot charm the multitude. Because philosophy transcends the human and ephemeral, it is radically unpolitical, and therefore it is amusic and unerotic. It cannot teach the just things, whereas poetry can. Philosophy is then in need of being supplemented by a pursuit which is political because it is musical and erotic, if philosophy is to become just. Philosophy lacks self-knowledge. Poetry is self-knowledge. Plato did not deny that there is a problem here. In the *Laws* (804b) his Athenian Stranger gives occasion to a political man to say to him, "Stranger, you hold our human race very cheap." To which the Stranger, the philosopher, replies, "Marvel not, but forgive me; for having looked away toward the god and having had the experience going with this, I said what I just said. But if you prefer, be it granted that our race is not despicable but worthy of some seriousness." The recognition by philosophy of the fact that the human race is worthy of some seriousness is the origin of political philosophy or political science. If this recognition is to be philosophic, however, this must mean that the political things, the merely human things, are of decisive importance for understanding nature as a whole. The philosopher who was the first to realize this was Socrates, the Socrates who emerged out of the Socrates of the *Clouds*. Of this Socrates we know through Xenophon and Plato. I shall speak first of the Xenophontic Socrates.

At first glance Xenophon's Socratic writings appear to be the most reliable source for establishing the character of a Socratic teaching. Among the four authors of the chief sources regarding

Socrates, Xenophon alone combined the two most important qualifications. He was an acquaintance of Socrates, and he has shown
by deed that he was able and willing to be a historian. In spite of
this, Xenophon's testimony does not enjoy in our time the respect
it so patently deserves. The reason for this anomaly can be stated
as follows. Xenophon is not very intelligent, not to say that he is a
fool. He has the mind of a retired colonel rather than of a philosopher. He was much more attracted by dogs, horses, battles, and
recollections of battles than by the truth. John Burnet, one of the
most outstanding scholars in this field, has stated this view in the
most extreme form and therefore in a particularly enlightening
form. Burnet contended (*Plato's Phaedo* [Oxford, 1963], p. xv) that
Xenophon did not know Socrates well, seeing that Xenophon himself practically says that he was a youth in 401, that is to say, when
he had already left Athens for good and was with Cyrus in Asia
Minor. Burnet suggested that Xenophon was attracted by Socrates,
not on account of Socrates' wisdom or intelligence, but on account
of Socrates' military reputation (Ibid., pp. xvii–xviii, and *Greek Philosophy* [London, 1928], 1:137 n. 2). The most obvious difficulty for
this theory is the fact that we owe all our specific information
about Socrates' military exploits to Plato, and even in the case of
Plato the most detailed report is given by an intoxicated man. Xenophon barely alludes to these things. In his two lists of Socrates'
virtues he does not even mention Socrates' military virtue, his
courage, or manliness (*Memorabilia*, end; *Apology of Socrates to the
Jury*, secs. 14 and 16). He leaves it at an occasional reference to
Socrates' having shown his justice both in civil life and in cam-
paigns. Besides, the term "youth" or "young man," which is applied to Xenophon by an emissary of the Persian king, means in
the context (*Anabasis* 2.1.13), "you clever young man." The term is
used in order to counteract a remark which Xenophon had made.
It cannot be used for fixing Xenophon's date of birth. The prejudice
against Xenophon is based, not on a sober study of his writings,
but on the fact that the prevailing notions of the greatness of a man
and the greatness of an author do not leave room for the recognition of the specific greatness of the man and the author Xenophon.
Romanticism, in all its forms, has rendered impossible the true
understanding of Xenophon. As for Burnet in particular, his dissatisfaction with Xenophon had a special reason. He was uncom-
monly sensitive to the presence in Socrates' thought of natural science, and Xenophon flatly denies that Socrates had anything to do
with natural science (see, e.g., John Burnet, *Plato's Euthyphro, Apol-*

ogy of Socrates, and *Crito* [Oxford, 1963]). While the modern criticism of Xenophon is of no value, its sheer power may incline us to reconsider our first impression. Despite the fact that Xenophon was a historian, this impression is an exaggeration. Xenophon wrote one historical work, the *Hellenica*, but his most extensive book, the *Education of Cyrus*, which presents itself as a historical book, is rightly regarded, and has always been regarded, as a work of fiction. Xenophon's achievement as a historian was only a part of his literary activity. In order to describe his literary activity as a whole it is wise to make use of a description which is sometimes found in the manuscripts of his writings. There he is sometimes called the Orator Xenophon. As for the close relationship between oratory and history in antiquity, it suffices to refer to Cicero's rhetorical writings. The expression, the Orator Xenophon, means less that Xenophon was a public speaker than that he was a man who fully possessed the art of public speaking, or that one can learn that art by studying his writings. The expression means here less the art of Pericles or Demosthenes than the art of Isocrates. Anticipating the result of this lecture, I shall say that Xenophon's rhetoric was Socratic rhetoric.

The art of public speaking exhibited in Xenophon's writing is an art of writing. Tradition tells us that Xenophon was a bashful man, a man with a strong sense of shame. This description certainly fits the writer Xenophon, or Xenophon's art of writing. A man who possesses a strong sense of shame will refrain as much as possible from hearing, seeing, and speaking of the ugly, the evil, and the bad. To quote his own words, "It is noble and just and pious and more pleasant to remember the good things rather than the bad ones" (*Anabasis* 5.8.26). For instance, Xenophon would prefer to say of a given town that it was big, rather than that it was big, deserted, and poor. But of a town in a good condition he would without hesitation say that it was big, inhabited, and well-off (ibid., 1.2). He would say of a given individual that he was brave and shrewd, rather than that he was a brave and shrewd crook. He expects the reader of his praises to think as much of the virtues which he mentions as of those virtues about which he is silent because of their absence. Lest we be shocked by the fact that an abominable traitor was highly regarded by the king who was benefited by the act of treason, Xenophon would suggest that that king had the traitor tortured to death throughout a whole year for his treason. But since Xenophon desires, not only not to shock our feelings, but also to indicate the truth, he will add the remark that he cannot be certain that such a fitting retribution for the act of treason actually took place. He says this act is said to have taken place (ibid., 2.6.29). Going a step further in the same direction, Xenophon would say of a man that his father is said to be X, but as for his mother there is agreement that she was Y (*Education of Cyrus* 1.2.1). One of the reasons why he entitled his so-called "Expedition of Cyrus" the *Anabasis*, i.e., *Cyrus's Ascent*, is that the only part of the story which was happy as far as Cyrus was concerned was the ascent, the way up from the coast to the interior, as distinguished from the battle which took place after the completion of the ascent and which was most unhappy for Cyrus. These examples must here suffice for showing that Xenophon's maxim regarding the preferability of remembering the good things rather than the bad ones circumscribes what is now generally known as irony. The ironical is a kind of the ridiculous.

In one of Xenophon's Socratic writings Socrates describes the general opinion about himself in terms reminiscent of the *Clouds.* In some way Aristophanes is present in Xenophon's work. One of the most striking differences between Xenophon's Socrates and Aristophanes' Socrates is that the former is urbane and patient, whereas the Aristophanean Socrates shows a complete lack of urbanity, and even of politeness, and also of patience. The only man whom Xenophon's Socrates ever addresses most impolitely is Xenophon himself. This occurs in the only conversation between Xenophon and Socrates which is recorded in Xenophon's Socratic writings (*Memorabilia* 1.3.8–13). Xenophon's Socrates calls Xenophon, "You fool!", "You wretch!" That is to say, Xenophon's Socrates treats Xenophon, and only Xenophon, in the same way in which Aristophanes' Socrates treats Strepsiades. In the *Clouds* Pheidippides says in a dream to a friend, "Take the horse home when you have given him a good roll" (l. 32). In Xenophon's *Oeconomicus* the interlocutor of Socrates says, "My slave takes the horse home when he has given him a good roll"—in the same meter (*Oeconomicus* 11.18). Could the interlocutor of Socrates in the *Oeconomicus*, the perfect gentleman Ischomachus, be Xenophon's substitute for Aristophanes' Pheidippides? Pheidippides comes to sight in the *Clouds* as Socrates' pupil in injustice. Ischomachus, however, is Socrates' teacher in justice, just as in Xenophon's work Xenophon takes the place which in the *Clouds* was throughout occupied by Strepsiades. Through the use of ridiculous things Socrates is shown by Xenophon to be in harmony with respectability and with the city, and to contribute through his activities to civic or political excellence of the highest order. Xenophon's Socratic writings, one might dare to say, constitute a reply to Aristophanes' *Clouds* on the level of the *Clouds,* and with a most subtle use of the means of Aristophanes. We could use this observation as a clue to Xenophon's Socratic writing if we were not wholly averse to paradoxes. Let us rather turn to the most obvious, to the surface, and cling to it as much as we can.

Fifteen writings have come down to us as writings of Xenophon. Four of them are the Socratic writings; then there is the "Expedition of Cyrus," the *Education of Cyrus,* the *Greek History,* or rather *Hellenica,* and the Minor Writings. The titles of some of these writings are strange. The title of the so-called "Expedition of Cyrus," the *Ascent of Cyrus,* fits only the first part of the work. The bulk of the work deals not with the ascent of Cyrus but with the descent of Xenophon: the descent, originated and organized by Xenophon, of the Greek mercenaries who had followed Cyrus on his ascent. The title of the *Education of Cyrus* fits only the first book of the work. The bulk of the work deals, not with Cyrus's education, but with the exploits of Cyrus after his education had been completed. The title of the largest of the Socratic writings, *Memorabilia* in the Latin translation, *Recollections,* is also somewhat strange. The strangeness was recognized by some editors as well as translators, who called the book *Memorabilia Socratis, Recollections of Socrates,* for the book is entirely devoted to what Xenophon remembered of Socrates. By calling the book *Recollections* simply, Xenophon indicated that his recollections simply, or his recollections *par excellence,* are not his recollections of his deeds in Asia Minor, which are recorded in the "Expedition of Cyrus," but his recollections of Socrates. The name of Socrates occurs in the title of only one of his four Socratic writings, in the title of the *Apology of Socrates*—just as the name of Socrates occurs in the title of only one of Plato's works—again, the *Apology of Socrates.* The Socratic writings constitute, as it were, one pole of Xenophon's work. The other pole is constituted by the *Education of Cyrus.* A reference by Xenophon's Socrates to Cyrus shows that Cyrus is not absent from Xenophon's Socratic writings. It could not be otherwise. Cyrus is presented by Xenophon as the model of a ruler, and especially of a captain. But Xenophon's Socrates possesses perfect command of the art of the captain, as Xenophon shows. And since according to a principle of both Xenophon's and Plato's Socrates the necessary and sufficient condition for being a perfect captain is possessing perfect command of the art of the captain, Xenophon's Socrates too is a perfect captain. On the other hand, Socrates is present in the three most extensive Xenophontic writings which are not devoted to Socrates, the *Hellenica*, the "Expedition of Cyrus," and the *Education of Cyrus*. In each of these writings there occurs a single reference, explicit or allusive, to Socrates. The characteristic feature of Xenophon's work as a whole can be said to be the presence in it of the two poles, Cyrus and Socrates.

There is a radical difference between Cyrus and Socrates in spite of the fact that both are excellent captains, a difference which on reflection proves to be an opposition. Xenophon indicated this difference most simply by failing to mention courage, or military virtue, among the virtues of Socrates. Cyrus exercises, and Socrates does not exercise, the royal or political art, since Cyrus is eager to exercise it and Socrates does not wish to exercise it. Since there is, then, an opposition between Cyrus and Socrates, there is needed a link between Cyrus and Socrates. This link is Xenophon himself. Xenophon can be a link between Cyrus and Socrates because he is a pupil of Socrates and not of the sophists. Xenophon was induced to accompany Cyrus the younger, the namesake of the great empire builder Cyrus, by his friend Proxenus, who had been a pupil of Gorgias, the famous teacher of rhetoric. Proxenus left the school of Gorgias in the belief that he was able to acquire a great name, great power, and great wealth by just and noble means alone. But he had the defect that he could rule only gentlemen and was incapable of making himself feared by the soldiers; for he believed that praise and withholding praise sufficed for the governance of men. He did not appreciate the power of punishment or of harshness. But Xenophon, the pupil of Socrates, was able to rule both gentlemen and those who were not gentlemen. He was as excellent at castigating the bad and base, and at beating them, as he was at praising the good and noble. Hence he could have become the sole commander of the Greek army if he had desired it. Hence he could seriously desire to become the founder of a city in Asia Minor. Xenophon shows by his deeds the radical difference between Socrates and the other wise men of his age. Socrates was the political educator *par excellence*. Socrates was the opposite of a mere speculator about the things in heaven and beneath the earth. Socrates, and not Gorgias, for example, was the political educator *par excellence* because he had recognized the power of that in man which is recalcitrant to reason and which therefore cannot be persuaded into submission, but must be beaten into it. Socrates understands the nature of political things, which are not simply rational. Accordingly, the Socratic student of politics can learn something important by observing the training of dogs and of horses. Therefore there exists a relation between Xenophon's Socratic writings and those of his minor writings which deal with dogs and horses. It is perfectly fitting, for more than one reason, that his writing on dogs, or rather on hunting with dogs, almost ends with a blame of the sophists and a praise of the philosophers.

I must now turn to a more detailed analysis of the political teaching of Xenophon's Socrates. There are four Socratic writings, the *Memorabilia*, the *Oeconomicus*, the *Banquet*, and the *Apology of Socrates*. Next time I will try to show that the *Memorabilia* are meant to be a presentation of Socrates' justice, while the three other Socratic writings present Socrates simply, without a limited regard to his justice. The *Oeconomicus* presents Socrates as a speaker, the *Banquet* presents Socrates as a doer, and the *Apology of Socrates* presents Socrates as a silent deliberator or thinker. The literary principle of the *Memorabilia*, the largest of these four books, is to indicate the character of Socrates' true activity, but not to set it forth. If one considers these indications carefully, one comes to see that the Xenophontic Socrates did not limit himself to the study of the human things but was concerned, as every other philosopher, with the whole—only he thought that the human things are the clue to the whole. For Xenophon's Socrates, as well as for the Platonic Socrates, the key for the understanding of the whole is the fact that the whole is characterized by what I shall call noetic heterogeneity. To state it more simply, the whole consists of classes or kinds, the character of which does not become fully clear through sense perception. It is for this reason that Socrates could become the founder of political philosophy, or political science. For political philosophy, or political science, is based on the premise that political things are in a class by themselves, that there is an essential difference between political things and things which are not political. Or, more specifically, that there is an essential difference between the common good and the private or sectional good. Socrates is the first philosopher who did justice to the claim of the political, the claim which is in fact raised by the polis, the political society. This means that he also realized the limitations of that claim. Hence he distinguished between two ways of life, the political life, and one which transcends the political life and which is the highest.

Now, while according to Xenophon and his Socrates the transpolitical life is higher in dignity than the political life, they did everything in their power to instill respect for the claims of the city and of political life and of everything connected with it. Moderation proves to be the characteristic quality of Socrates. Here as well as in other respects, recognition of the essential difference between the political and the nonpolitical, or, more fundamentally, recognition of the existence of essential differences, or of noetic heterogeneity, appears as moderation—as opposed to the madness of the philosophers preceding Socrates. But Socratic moderation means also, and in a sense even primarily, the recognition of opinions which are not true, but which are salutary for political life. Socrates, Xenophon says, did not separate from each other wisdom and moderation. The political is indeed not the highest, but it is the first, because it is the most urgent. It is related to philosophy as continence is related to virtue proper. It is the foundation, the indispensable condition. From here we can understand why Socrates could be presented in a popular presentation as having limited himself, his study, entirely to the human and political things. The human or political things are indeed the clue to all things, to the whole of nature, since they are the link or bond between the highest and the lowest, or since man is a microcosm, or since the human or political things and their corollaries are the form in which the highest principles first come to sight, or since the false estimate of human things is a fundamental and primary error. Philosophy is primarily political philosophy because philosophy is the ascent from the most obvious, the most massive, the most urgent, to what is highest in dignity. Philosophy is primarily political philosophy because political philosophy is required for protecting the inner sanctum of philosophy.

Third Lecture

Plato's and Xenophon's presentations of Socrates can be understood, *can* be understood, as replies to Aristophanes' presentation of Socrates. Aristophanes' presentation is not a piece of buffoonery; it goes to the root of the matter, not in spite but because of the fact that it is a comedy. The *Clouds,* read in conjunction with the other plays of Aristophanes, especially the *Birds* and the *Thesmophoriazusae,* is one of the greatest documents of the contest between philosophy and poetry for supremacy and of the case for the supremacy of poetry. The Aristophanean comedy is based on the fundamental distinction between nature and convention. It is therefore based on philosophy. Philosophy, or the science of nature, or "physiology" in the Greek sense of the word, as represented by Socrates, is allied with rhetoric. It recognizes two principles corresponding to the difference between natural science on the one hand and rhetoric on the other. These principles are Aether and the Clouds. Now, in spite of this alliance with rhetoric, philosophy, the investigation of what is in heaven and beneath the earth, is radically unpolitical. It simply transcends the political. It is oblivious of man, or rather of human life, yet human life is its basis. Hence it does not understand itself. It lacks self-knowledge, and therefore it lacks practical wisdom. Because it is unconcerned with human life it is unerotic and amusic. Philosophy must therefore be integrated into a whole which is ruled by poetry. Poetry is both the foundation and the capstone of wisdom within which philosophy finds its place, or through which philosophy is protected and at the same time perfected.

The Xenophontic, and especially the Platonic, theses assert exactly the opposite. Philosophy, not indeed the "physiology" of the Aristophanean Socrates, but a certain psychology, Platonic psychology let us say, is both the foundation and the capstone of wisdom within which poetry finds its place or through which poetry becomes good. Socrates was eminently political. He was *the* philosopher of self-knowledge, and therefore of practical wisdom. He was the erotician *par excellence*. This is the general reply of Plato and Xenophon to Aristophanes. Yet it remains a question whether Socrates was as musical as the greatest poets. Perhaps it was only Plato who decided the contest between poetry and philosophy in favor of philosophy through the Platonic dialogue, the greatest of all works of art.

I shall speak first of Xenophon. The great theme of Xenophon may be said to be this. Socrates was *the* citizen, *the* statesman, *the* captain. Socrates was political as no philosopher ever was, nay, as no statesman ever was. Yet Socrates is only one pole of Xenophon's thought. The other pole is Cyrus, be it the founder of the Persian Empire or the younger Cyrus whom Xenophon accompanied in his ascent to Asia Minor. The difference between Socrates and Cyrus indicates that while Socrates is profoundly political he is also something else. I stated last time what I believe to be characteristic of Xenophon's way of writing. To put it very colloquially and provisionally, one can compare Xenophon's manner to that of Jane Austen: not to speak about the sad and terrible things, but at any rate to remember the good things (not exactly matchmaking in Xenophon's case) rather than the bad things. It is preferable to speak of the good things rather than the bad things, as Xenophon explicitly says. Now, good is, however, here an ambiguous term. Good may mean what is truly good, or good may mean what is generally thought to be good. In the defense of Socrates especially, Xenophon is very anxious to show that Socrates was good according to the general notion of goodness; and that is perhaps not the deepest level in Socrates, as we shall see.

Now, Xenophon's Socratic writings consist of four pieces, the *Memorabilia*, the *Oeconomicus*, the *Banquet*, and the *Apology of Socrates*. As for the *Memorabilia*, the largest of these books, it consists of two main parts, a short first part, in which Xenophon refutes the indictment of Socrates, and a much more extensive second part, in which Xenophon shows that Socrates greatly benefited everyone who came into contact with him. Just as Plato in his *Apology of Socrates* (24b–c), Xenophon explicitly refrains from quoting the indictment with complete literalness (*Memorabilia* 1.1.1). The indictment was to the effect that "Socrates commits an unjust act by not recognizing the gods which the city recognizes, but introduces other divinities which are new. He also commits an unjust act by corrupting the young" (Diogenes Laertius 2.40). By refuting the indictment, Xenophon shows that Socrates did not commit these unjust acts of which he was accused, nor any other unjust act. He proves that Socrates acted justly in the sense of legal justice. In the bulk of the *Memorabilia* Xenophon proves that Socrates greatly benefited everyone who came into contact with him. But to benefit one's fellow men is, according to Xenophon, identical with being just, although perhaps not with being merely legally just. Hence the purpose of the *Memorabilia* as a whole is to prove Socrates' justice, both legal and translegal.

The three other Socratic writings can then be expected to deal with Socrates simply: without special regard to his justice, but rather with his activity simply. Now, the activity of man consists, according to Xenophon, of speaking, doing, and thinking or deliberating. In accordance with this tri-partition, Xenophon has divided his three smaller Socratic writings, as can be seen from the openings of these writings. The *Oeconomicus* deals with Socrates' speaking, the *Banquet* with his deeds, and the *Apology of Socrates* with his silent deliberation. Two special remarks are indispensable at this point. First, the *Banquet* deals with the deeds not only of Socrates, but of a number of other gentlemen as well. Moreover, it deals with deeds not performed in earnest or with seriousness, but performed playfully. We are therefore entitled to look somewhere for Xenophon's presentation of deeds which gentlemen performed in earnest. I am inclined to believe that we have this presentation in his Greek history, the *Hellenica*. In accordance with this he treats his narrative of tyrants, which occur in the Greek history, and only the narratives of tyrants, as excursuses: that is to say, as parts not properly belonging to the work (for the tyrant is, of course, the opposite of a gentleman). Secondly, the *Memorabilia* on the one hand, and the three other Socratic writings on the other, fulfill fundamentally different functions. The *Memorabilia* establishes the justice of Socrates, the three others deal with Socrates simply. Now, the *Apology of Socrates*, the last and shortest, is to a considerable extent a repetition of the last chapter of the *Memorabilia*. There are a number of minor divergences of which some editors have tried to get rid by assimilating the text of the *Apology of Socrates* to the text of the last chapter of the *Memorabilia*, a dangerous undertaking since it is based on the complete disregard of the possibility that subtle stylistic differences, to say nothing of others, may be required by the two different purposes of the two writings. To illustrate this, one may adduce the fact that certain sections of the *Hellenica* are used by Xenophon in his writing *Agesilaus*, with many minor stylistic changes. The differences between the *Agesilaus* and the corresponding sections of the *Hellenica* must be viewed in the light of the fact that the *Hellenica* is a history and the *Agesilaus* is a eulogy. And as every college boy knows, or should know, the style required for history differs from the style required for eulogy. And the editors also in this case correct the text of the *Agesilaus* because this simple idea did not occur to some of them.

The *Memorabilia*, to repeat, are devoted to the subject of Socrates' justice, and their first part to Socrates' legal justice. The accuser had charged Socrates with corrupting the young. He had specified this somewhat vague charge by contending, among other things, that Socrates induced his companions to look down on the established laws by saying to them that it is foolish to elect the magistrates of the city by lot. No one would choose a pilot, a builder, or a flute player by lot, and yet these kinds of people cannot do any serious harm compared with the harm which the rulers of the city can do. By such speeches, the accuser said, Socrates induced his companions to look down with contempt on the established regime, that is to say, on the democracy, and made them men of violence. Xenophon goes out of his way to show that a man like Socrates was bound to be opposed to the use of violence, but he does not even attempt to deny the charge that Socrates made his companions look down with contempt on the established regime and its accompaniment, the established laws. He does not deny this charge because he cannot deny it. Socrates was an outspoken critic of the Athenian democracy. If legal justice includes full loyalty to the established political order, Socrates' legal justice was deficient in a point of utmost importance. He was not, then, unqualifiedly just.

The accuser also referred to Socrates' relation with two of the most outstanding political criminals of the age, Critias the tyrant and Alcibiades. Xenophon shows that Socrates was in no way responsible for what these men did after they had left Socrates, whom they had left precisely because Socrates disapproved of their ways. In order to show the wickedness of Alcibiades in particular, Xenophon records many other things, among them the conversation which Alcibiades once had with his guardian, Pericles. Alcibiades asked Pericles, What is a law? Pericles fittingly defined law in such a way as to fit democratic law as such: law is an enactment of the assembled multitude as to what should be done or not be done. Alcibiades proceeded to force Pericles to grant that the enactments of the ruling few in an oligarchy or of a tyrant in a tyranny are equally law and, on the other hand, that the law merely imposed by the rulers on the ruled, therefore in particular a law merely imposed by the democratic majority on the minority, is an act of violence rather than a law. A law owes its lawfulness, not to its democratic origin, but to its goodness. The democratic origin in itself is no better than the tyrannical origin. Xenophon's Socrates never raises the grave and dangerous question, What is a law? This question is raised only by Xenophon's young and rash Alcibiades. Yet the young and rash Alcibiades who raises this question in the style characteristic of Socrates had not yet left Socrates, but was still a companion of Socrates at the time he raised this Socratic question. The accuser also charged Socrates with frequently quoting the verses from the *Iliad* in which Odysseus is described as using different language when speaking to outstanding men on the one hand, and when speaking to men of the common people on the other. Xenophon does not even attempt to deny this charge.

Yet the first and most important part of the charge against Socrates concerns his alleged impiety. As Xenophon makes clear, the charge of impiety was graver than the charge of injustice, or of corrupting the young. Only "*some* Athenians" believed that Socrates corrupted the young, whereas "*the* Athenians" believed that

Socrates was not sound as regards the gods. Yet Xenophon devotes more than three times as much space to proving that Socrates did not corrupt the young as to proving that Socrates was pious. In order to prove that Socrates was pious, Xenophon mentions that Socrates sacrificed frequently and that he relied on divination, especially on his "demonic thing." Lest there be any suspicion that Socrates acted differently in private than in public, he adds the remark that Socrates was always in the open, in places where he could meet the largest number of people. Still, a man may have no privacy of any kind, and yet have private thoughts. Xenophon adds, therefore, that Socrates was always in the open and talked almost constantly, yet no one ever heard him say anything impious. Immediately afterwards, however, he admits that Socrates' thought would not necessarily become known through what he said in the market-place. There is one, and only one, universally known fact which according to Xenophon proves Socrates' piety. This is Socrates' conduct at the trial of the generals after the battle of the Arginusae, where Socrates alone upheld his sworn duty not to permit an illegal vote. It is clear that while this action proves Socrates' justice, it does not necessarily prove Socrates' piety in the sense of sincere belief in the existence of the gods worshipped by the city of Athens.

At the end of Xenophon's refutation of the indictment of Socrates, we have come to realize that Socrates' legal justice and his legal piety could not be proven, or that Socrates was not unqualifiedly just. This, however, is perfectly compatible with the fact that he possessed translegal justice, which consists in benefiting one's fellow men. Socrates benefited his fellow men to the highest degree by leading them to excellence or to virtue, that is to say, to that kind or degree of virtue of which the individual in question was capable. For the difference among men in this respect was crucially important to Socrates—as he indicated by frequently quoting the Homeric verses in which Odysseus is presented as having conducted himself in an entirely different way when confronted with entirely different kinds of people. The bulk of the *Memorabilia* is meant to show how beneficent Socrates was. The fourth book of the *Memorabilia* is the only part of the work which can be said to present Socrates as a teacher rather than as an advisor or exhorter. The fourth book opens with the remark that Socrates helped those who spent their time with him not only by being serious but by joking as well, and that he did not approach all men in the same manner. He was naturally attracted by the good natures, that is to say, by the most gifted, who revealed themselves as such through the quickness with which they learned, through their memory, and through their desire for all worthwhile subjects of learning. Not all men possess good natures. Xenophon enumerates some other human types. The greatest part of the fourth book is devoted to Socrates' conversations with the handsome Euthydemus, whose characteristic was, not natural gifts, but conceit. Xenophon refrains from presenting the teacher Socrates as engaged in conversation with first-rate men. Hence we do not learn from Xenophon how Socrates, who talked differently to different kinds of people, talked to first-rate men.

Socrates taught only by conversation. His art consisted in the art, or the skill, of conversation. The Greek word for the skill of conversation is dialectics. As for Socrates' dialectics, we learn from Xenophon that it was twofold (*Memorabilia* 4.6.13–15). When someone contradicted Socrates, Socrates brought back the subject matter to its basic presupposition, that is to say, he raised the question, What is? regarding the subject under discussion, and he answered with the participation of the contradictor. Thus the contradictor himself came to see the truth clearly. This, we may say, is the higher form of dialectics. But, Xenophon goes on, when Socrates discussed something on his own initiative, that is to say, when he talked to people who merely listened, he did not raise the question, what is? but proceeded through generally accepted opinions, and thus he produced agreement among the listeners to an extraordinary degree. This latter kind of dialectics, which leads to agreement as distinguished from truth, is the most important part of the political art. It is the art which Homer ascribes to Odysseus. Socrates applied the scientific kind of dialectics when he talked to contradictors, that is to say, to men capable of contradicting intelligently, to people who are capable of going beyond the accepted opinions, or who possess good natures. Socrates applied the political or rhetorical dialectics in his conversations with the majority of people. Xenophon gives us hardly any specimen of Socrates' exhibiting the higher kind of dialectics. For it goes without saying that the mere use of the formula "what is" does not yet guarantee that the question will be handled appropriately. If we want to find the serious thought of Socrates as Xenophon understood it, we must translate Socrates' statements *ad hominem* into the form they would take if they were addressed to contradictors, or to men possessing good natures.

Xenophon is very sparing in his explicit praise of Socrates. And when he praises Socrates, he shrinks from using superlatives. The strongest expression which he ever uses in this connection is his statement that when he heard Socrates make a certain statement, "he seemed to me to be blessed." The statement of Socrates was to the effect that while others derived pleasure from horses, dogs, or birds, he derived pleasure from good friends: "together with my friends I scan the treasures of the wise men of old which they have left behind in writing and if we see something good, we pick it out, and we regard it as a great gain when we become useful to one another" (*Memorabilia*, 1.6.14). Of Socrates' studying with his friends the works of the wise men of old and of their selecting the best from them, Xenophon does not give us a single example. He draws our attention to what he regarded as Socrates' most praise-worthy activity, but he demands from a certain kind of his readers that they transform the intimation into clear knowledge. In the passage quoted Socrates speaks of his friends, or his good friends. We may say that Xenophon never records conversations between Socrates and his friends in the strict sense. Of course, "friends" is an ambiguous term. It may be applied to friends strictly speaking, as well as to mere acquaintances, and hence also to the interme-diate forms of relationship. Seven chapters of book 2 of the *Memorabilia* are devoted to the subject of Socrates and friendship. Xen-ophon records conversations between Socrates and acquaintances, interlocutors, and comrades of Socrates, but no conversation be-tween Socrates and a friend of Socrates. The most instructive case is a conversation between Socrates and Crito. The wealthy Crito complains to Socrates about being blackmailed by informers. Soc-rates draws Crito's attention to the fact that Crito, a landed gentle-man, uses dogs to keep wolves away from his sheep. In the same way, he says, he should use the informers to keep other informers away from his property. Crito would, of course, have to make the arrangement worthwhile to the protecting informer. Crito acts on Socrates' advice. They find a certain Archedemus who is excellent for this purpose: "Henceforth Archedemus was one of Crito's friends and was honored by the other friends of Crito" (*Memora-bilia* 2.9.8). We have here a choice between saying that Crito did not belong to Socrates' friends, and saying that Socrates honored a useful informer. I suggest that we choose the former alternative.

The third book of the *Memorabilia* shows how Socrates dealt with those who long and strive for the fair or noble. It ascends from conversations of Socrates with anonymous individuals, via conversations with acquaintances, to a conversation with Glaucon, the hero of Plato's *Republic*, the son of Ariston, to whom Socrates was benevolent for the sake of Charmides the son of Glaucon and for the sake of Plato. Immediately after the conversation with Glaucon, Xenophon records a conversation with Charmides, Charmides being one of the men for the sake of whom Socrates took an interest in Glaucon. We thus expect to be treated next to a conversation between Socrates and the other man for the sake of whom Socrates took an interest in Glaucon, this is to say, a conversation between Socrates and Plato. Instead we get a conversation between Socrates and another philosopher, Aristippus. Thereafter the descent begins, which leads us via outstanding craftsmen, a venal beauty, and a sickly youth, again to anonymous people. That is to say, Xenophon builds up the argument in such a way as to point toward a peak, to suggest a peak—anonymous people up to very close people and then again down to anonymous people. Xenophon suggests a peak of the third book, or, for that matter, of the whole work. He points to that peak, a conversation between Socrates and Plato, but he does not supply it. The peak is missing. This formula can be applied to Xenophon's Socratic writings as a whole. The highest does not become visible or audible, but it can be divined. The unsaid is more important than what is said. For the reader this means that he must be extremely attentive, or extremely careful.

Among all the passages in which Xenophon subtly alludes to Socrates' chief preoccupation, the most important one is that in which he says that Socrates "never ceased considering what each of the beings is" (*Memorabilia* 4.6.1). It appears from the context that this Socratic consideration is connected with distinguishing things according to their kinds or classes. But, to say the least, Xenophon gives very few examples of this constant preoccupation of Socrates. It is also hard to see how Socrates could constantly consider what each of the beings is and, at the same time, constantly be in public places and almost constantly talk about subjects other than what each of the beings is. At any rate Socrates' constant preoccupation was the concern with what is, with the essence of all things. It is true, the same Xenophon tells us also that Socrates limited his interest entirely to the human things, but one must consider the context within which Xenophon makes the latter assertion (ibid., 1.1.11ff.). He asserts that Socrates did not discuss the nature of all things, or what the sophists call the cosmos, in order to prove that no one had ever heard Socrates say something impious or irreligious, for the study of nature was sus-

pect as the presumptuous attempt to pry into the secrets of the
gods. But I have already indicated what one has to think about the
legal piety of Xenophon's Socrates. When asserting that Socrates
limited his study to human things, Xenophon makes his Socrates
wonder whether the students of nature, that is to say, the philosophers preceding Socrates, now called the pre-Socratics, did not
realize that man cannot discover the truth regarding nature, for
the various philosophers, says Socrates, contradict each other and
behave like madmen. Some of them believe that being is one, but
others that there are infinitely many beings. Some say that all
things change, but others say that nothing changes. Some say that
everything comes into being and perishes, but others say that
nothing comes into being or perishes. The characterization of
these contentions as mad permits us to see clearly which contentions about the whole Socrates regards as sound and sober,
namely, that there is a finite number of beings, that there are some
unchangeable and some changeable things, and that there are
some things which do not come into being and perish. Xenophon's
remark about Socrates' chief preoccupation permits us to render
this implication more precise. While there are infinitely many
things, there is only a finite number of kinds or classes of things,
that is to say, the beings which we intend when we raise the question, "what is." Those kinds or classes, as distinguished from the
individual things, are unchangeable and do not come into being
or perish.

Socrates is distinguished from all philosophers who preceded
him by the fact that he sees the core of the whole, or of nature, in
noetic heterogeneity. The whole is not one, nor homogeneous, but
heterogeneous. Yet the heterogeneity is not sensible heterogeneity,
like the heterogeneity of the four elements, for example, but noetic
heterogeneity, essential heterogeneity. It is for this reason that Socrates founded political science. Only if there is essential heterogeneity can there be an essential difference between political things
and things which are not political. The discovery of noetic heterogeneity permits one to let things be what they are and takes away
the compulsion to reduce essential differences to something common. The discovery of noetic heterogeneity means the vindication
of what one could call common sense. Socrates called it a return
from madness to sanity or sobriety, or, to use the Greek term,
sophrosynē, which I would translate as moderation. Socrates discovered the paradoxical fact that, in a way, the most important
truth is the most obvious truth, or the truth of the surface. Further-

more, the fact that there is a variety of being, in the sense of kinds or classes, means that there cannot be a single total experience of being, whether that experience is understood mystically or romantically, the specifically romantic assertion being that feeling, or sentiment, or a certain kind of sentiment, is this total experience. There is indeed mental vision, or perception, of this or that kind or pattern, but the many mental patterns, many mental perceptions, must be connected by *logismos*, by reasoning, by putting two and two together.

By recognizing the fact that the political is irreducible to the nonpolitical, that the political is *sui generis*, Socrates does justice to the claim raised on behalf of the political, or by the political itself, namely by the political community, by the polis. The polis presents itself as exalted far above the household and the individual. Yet this does not necessarily mean that Socrates recognized the claim of the polis to be the highest simply, or, which amounts to the same thing, to be the authoritative interpreter of the highest simply, or to be beyond the peak. The judgment on the status of the political will depend on the result of the analysis of the political. Socrates' analysis of the political may be said to start from the phenomenon of law, for laws appear to be the specifically political phenomenon. The reason is this. The political appears to be the domain of the most resplendent activity of adult freemen—and who is more resplendent than adult freemen?—and that which gives adult freemen as such their character, or that which limits them, is law, and law alone. Law means primarily the utterance of the assembled citizens which tells everyone, including the full citizens, what they ought to do and what they may not do, not until further notice, or for a given time, but forever. The well-being of the city, nay, its being, depends on law, on law-abidingness, or justice. Justice in this sense is the political virtue *par excellence*. Justice as law-abidingness comes to sight as a virtue by the consideration of the alternatives, which are force and law.

It is with a view to law that the distinction between legitimacy and illegitimacy is primarily made. "Kingship is rule over willing human beings and in accordance with the laws of the city, whereas the rule over unwilling human beings and according to the will of the ruler is tyranny" (*Memorabilia* 4.6.12). This remark seems to apply only to monarchs, but Socrates goes on to say, "The regime in which the magistracies are filled from among those who complete the laws or the customs is aristocracy. The regime in which the magistracies are filled on the basis of property qualification is plutocracy. The regime in which the magistracies are filled from all is democracy." This may be thought to mean that republics too can either be royal or tyrannical, the decisive point being whether the rulers are limited by law or not. Yet there is this obvious difficulty, that the rulers who ought to be subject to the law are themselves the cause or the origin of the law, and the cause or origin of the law cannot as such be subject to the law—the famous problem of sovereignty in modern times. Still, lawgivers cannot act arbitrarily. They are supposed to enact good laws. Hence we may have to make a distinction other than that between legitimate and illegitimate regimes. One may have to make a distinction between good regimes, as regimes most likely to produce good laws, and bad regimes, as regimes most likely to produce bad laws. If the quality enabling men to make good laws is wisdom, the good regime will be the rule of the wise. In other words, the only sound title to rule is knowledge; not inheritance, nor election, nor force, nor fraud, but only knowledge of how to rule can make a man a king or a ruler. The man of the highest political wisdom is superior to any law, not only because he alone can be the origin of excellent laws, but likewise because he has a flexibility which laws, however wise, necessarily lack. The man of highest political wisdom is a seeing law, whereas every law proper is blind to some extent. The justice of the true ruler cannot consist, then, in law-abidingness or in legal justice. He must be guided by translegal justice, by the habit of benefiting human beings, the habit of helping them to become as good as possible and to live as happily as possible. He must assign to everyone not necessarily what a possibly foolish law declares to be his, but what is good or fitting for him. To use a Xenophontic example, if a big boy owns a small coat, and a small boy owns a big coat, we must take away the big coat from the small boy and give it to the big boy, and vice versa (*Education of Cyrus*, 1.4.16–17). That is to say, by questioning the ultimacy of law, we question also the ultimacy of legal property.

At the beginning of Xenophon's *Oeconomicus* Socrates leads the argument from the view that the property of a man is the totality of his possessions, via the view that the property of a man is the totality of his useful possessions, or possessions useful to him, to the view that only that can be regarded as a man's property which he knows how to use, that is to say, how to use well. So heroin could not possibly be the property of a juvenile delinquent. We are thus brought up against the question as to whether unwise men can possess any property except under the strictest supervision of the wise. There is a simple formula expressing the view that the political art at its highest transcends law as such, namely, the thesis of Socrates that the political or royal art is identical with the economic art, that is to say, the art by means of which the father, husband, master rules his children, wife, and slaves. Neither Xenophon's Socrates nor Xenophon himself ever speaks of natural law, or natural right, *eo nomine*. But his Socrates once speaks of unwritten law (*Memorabilia* 4.4.19ff.). One example of unwritten law, that is to say, of laws which are self-enforcing since their transgression damages the transgressor without any human intervention, is the prohibition against incest between parents and children. As little as Plato's Socrates in the *Republic* does Xenophon's Socrates refer in this crucial context to the prohibition against incest between brothers and sisters.

Summarizing the analysis of the political given by Xenophon's Socrates, we may say that there is fundamental agreement between that analysis and the analysis given in the Platonic dialogues, especially the *Republic* and the *Statesman*. But Xenophon is much more laconic, reserved, or bashful than Plato.

Now we have followed Xenophon's Socrates up to the point where the absolute rule of the wise appeared to be the only wise solution to the political problem. The wise would assign to every unwise man the thing which he is best fitted to use and the work which he is best fitted to do. He would exercise his rule by virtue of his wisdom, i.e., of the recognition of his wisdom by the unwise. He would sway the unwise by persuasion alone. But will the unwise be able to recognize the wisdom of the wise? Is there no limit to the persuasive power of the wise? Socrates, who lived what he thought, illustrated this difficulty by his relation to the city of Athens. Socrates failed to persuade the city of Athens of his goodness. He illustrated it in a more homey way by his relation to his wife Xanthippe. In Xenophon's *Banquet* (2.10), Socrates is asked by a companion why he did not educate Xanthippe but had a wife who, of all the women present, past, and future, is probably the most difficult. Socrates replies that just as a man who wants to become good at handling horses will learn to handle the most spirited horse, for if he can handle such a horse he will be able to handle any horse, in the same way he, Socrates, desiring to live with human beings, acquired Xanthippe, well knowing that if he could control her, he could easily get along with all other human beings. The utmost one could say is that Socrates succeeded somehow in living with Xanthippe; he certainly did not succeed in educating her, or in ruling her by persuasion. When his son Lamprocles was angry with his mother because of the abominable things she had said to him out of her wild temper, Socrates talked to Lamprocles and silenced him. He did not even try to silence, to say nothing of appease, Xanthippe (*Memorabilia* 2.2). If it is then impossible that the wise can rule the unwise by persuasion, and since it is equally impossible, considering the numerical relation of the wise and the unwise, that the wise should rule the unwise by force, one has to be satisfied with a very indirect rule of the wise. This indirect rule of the wise consists in the rule of laws, on the making of which the wise have had some influence. In other words, the unlimited rule of undiluted wisdom must be replaced by the rule of wisdom diluted by consent. Yet laws cannot be the rulers, strictly speaking; they must be applied, interpreted, administered, and executed. The best solution of the political problem is then the rule of men who can best complete the laws, supplementing the essential deficiency of the law. The completion of the laws is equity. The best solution of the political problem is then the regime in which power rests with the equitable, in Greek the *epieikes*, which means in Greek at the same time "the better people," and this means, for all practical purposes, the landed gentry. Xenophon has given a sketch of what he regarded as the best regime in the first book of his *Education of Cyrus*, his political work *par excellence*. Xenophon tacitly claims that he has found the best regime in Persia, prior to the emergence of Cyrus, the founder of the Persian Empire. The best regime is a greatly improved Sparta. Every free man is a citizen and has access to all offices, with the exception of hereditary kingship, under the condition that he has successfully attended the public schools, public schools in the American sense. The regime seems then to be a democracy. But, unfortunately, the poor need their young sons on their small farms, and therefore only the sons of the well-to-do are in a position to acquire the right to the holding of public office. The best regime is then an aristocracy disguised as democracy. The principle animating this best regime comes to sight when Cyrus is about to destroy it, or to transform it into an absolute monarchy. Cyrus urges the gentlemen, the ruling class, to think no longer merely of decency, excellence, or virtue, but above all of the things which one can acquire through virtue, that is to say, of increasing their wealth. The principle of the best regime is then the cultivation of human excellence, as opposed to the increase of wealth.

As Xenophon indicates by presenting his utopia in a work of

fiction, the *Education of Cyrus*, he does not believe that the best regime as he understood it ever was actual, and thence that it is likely ever to become actual, in spite of its being possible. Political life as it always was, and as it always will be, is more or less imperfect. For all practical purposes, political greatness is generous and effective leadership in a tolerably good republic. The greatest example which Xenophon himself exhibits is that of the Spartan general, Dercylidas, the predecessor in Asia Minor of the somewhat pompous martinet, Agesilaus (see *Hellenica* 3 and 4). People called Dercylidas "Sisyphus" with a view to his outstanding resourcefulness. He was once punished by the Spartan authorities for what they regarded as lack of discipline, and he always loved to be away from home. Xenophon indicates other compromise solutions which are important given the practical impossibility of the best regime. There is no question for him that the life most fitting a gentleman is that of administering one's wealth rather than increasing it, that is to say, one's inherited landed estate. But after his Socrates has set forth this view with all possible emphasis, he reports the divergent practice of an Athenian whose son was particularly well known as a gentleman (*Oeconomicus* 20). In the opinion of that gentleman's son the father was an enthusiastic lover of farming. He could not see a run-down farm without buying it and making it flourish. When told this story by the son, Socrates asks, "Did your father keep all the farms which he cultivated, or did he sell them, when he could get much money?" The son replied, "He sold, by Zeus!" The compromise between the gentlemanly self-restraint regarding money, on the one hand, and greed, on the other, or between farming and trade, is trading in farms. It is not necessary to discuss here the extreme concession to human frailty which Xenophon considered, namely, beneficent tyranny (see *Hiero, Or, On Tyranny*). Generally speaking, by acting consistently on his literary principle of saying as little as possible about the highest, Xenophon was compelled or enabled, more than any other classic, to pave the way for Machiavelli, who, incidentally, generously acknowledged his debt (see esp. *The Prince*, chap. 14 end). But what in Xenophon had been a principle of writing became in Machiavelli a principle of thinking.

The crucial result of Socrates' analysis of the political, as Xenophon presents it, is that the political is essentially imperfect, the essence of the political being the dilution of wisdom by consent on the part of the unwise, or the dilution of wisdom by folly. Hence the claim of the political to be beyond the peak, or to be simply the highest, proves to be unfounded. Man's true excellence or virtue exists beyond the political, or is transpolitical. Xenophon's Socrates is the representative of man's transpolitical excellence, whereas his Cyrus is the representative of that life which is highest if the principle which is characteristic of the political is adhered to and thought through. The polarity of Socrates and Cyrus corresponds to the fundamental tension between philosophy and the polis. Xenophon has presented the tension between the two ways of life, the political and the transpolitical, most clearly in the *Oeconomicus*, which is his Socratic speech *par excellence*.

The *Oeconomicus* is a conversation between Socrates and Crito's son Critobulus, a young man who did not do too well. Socrates encouraged Critobulus to dedicate himself to the management of the household, of which farming is a distinguished, if subordinate, part. Socrates acts as a teacher of the art of farming, or of the art of managing the household in general. This contrasts with what he does when he is confronted with a young man eager to learn the art of a general (*Memorabilia* 3.1). Xenophon's Socrates appears to possess the art of the general, but he declines to teach it, whereas he is perfectly willing to teach the peaceful art of farming.

Socrates had acquired his command of the art of farming, not by farming, but by having had, once in his life, an extended conversation with a gentleman farmer called Ischomachus. He had learned that art in one sitting, which took place in the cloister of a temple in Athens, rather far away from any farm. His teaching of the art of farming consisted in transmitting to a young man a teaching which he had acquired in one day, in one sitting, just by listening. Yet, as has been indicated, what Socrates teaches is not merely the art of farming, but the whole economic art, or the art of managing the household, which includes above everything else the art of educating and managing one's wife, an art which Socrates had also learned at that single session with Ischomachus. More than this, what Socrates teaches young Critobulus is the way of life of the perfect gentleman, or perfect gentlemanship, a subject which comprises the economic art, and which was the primary and comprehensive theme regarding which Socrates consulted the gentleman farmer, Ischomachus, on the occasion of that single session once upon a time. Socrates did not learn perfect gentlemanship by thinking or by dialectics, but merely by listening, just as he transmits this art of gentlemanship to a young man who merely listens. Perfect gentlemanship is not a science, nor is it based on a science, but it is guided by opinions alone, by things which you understand fully by listening. In other words, no intellectual effort is required for grasping the principles of ordinary morality. Ordinary morality consists not in knowing, but in doing, whereas as regards the highest morality, the transpolitical morality, virtue is knowledge.

The first part of the teaching which Socrates transmits to Critobulus concerns, as I said, the education and management of one's wife. Ischomachus is very proud of the way in which he has educated his. He could not know at that time at which he gave Socrates his glowing report about the way in which he had educated his wife that in later years this woman would have a love affair with their son-in-law Callias, the son of Hipponicus, less than a year after Callias had married their daughter, and that as a consequence of this Callias would have Ischomachus' wife and Ischomachus' daughter together in his house, just as Pluto or Hades had Demeter and her daughter Persephone together in his house. Callias was, therefore, called Hades in Athens, and Plato's *Protagoras* is based in its setting on this story, the *Protagoras* taking place in the house of Callias, and there are quite a few allusions to the fact that we are there in Hades. But this only in passing. Now, this is not merely a joke, but indicates the great problem of the relation between theory and practice, or between knowledge and virtue. Ischomachus teaches his wife—theory. What she will do is a different story. However this may be, the center of the *Oeconomicus* is occupied by a direct confrontation of the life of the perfect gentleman, Ischomachus, and the life of Socrates. The two ways of life are presented as incompatible. One most obvious difference between the two ways of life is that one must be well off, or, as Aristotle puts it, one must be properly equipped, in order to be a perfect gentleman, whereas Socrates was rather poor. Since these remarks occur in a work on economics, one must raise the question regarding the economic basis of Socrates' life, Socrates' means of support. The answer conveyed through the work is that Socrates did not have to worry since he had friends. There is this nice passage (1.14) in which the question comes up whether from all the preceding things it follows that friends are money, and the answer given is, "By Zeus, they are."

I will devote the next lecture to the main thread of Plato's *Republic*, and the last one to the subject of Plato and the poets. I think you have seen by now that this is an absolutely crucial subject for Plato: the relative relation or status of poetry and philosophy. One could venture to say that the alternative to philosophy, to Platonic philosophy, is not any other philosophy, be it that of the pre-Socratics or of Aristotle, or what-not; the alternative is poetry, and therefore we really deal with the crucial issue by raising the question of how Plato conceives of the relation between philosophy and poetry.

Fourth Lecture

Among those who approach Plato in order to become enlightened by him about Socrates, it has become customary to pay the greatest attention to certain dialogues called the early dialogues, and especially to the *Apology of Socrates*. The *Apology of Socrates* may be said to be Socrates' own account, given on the most solemn occasion, of his way of life; and its solemnity may be thought to be increased by the fact that that account is a public account, an account given in public to the public *par excellence*, whereas Socrates' own account of his way of life which he gave on the day of his death in the *Phaedo* lacks the solemnity of the public and, in addition, is Plato's own writing. This consideration, or any consideration of this kind, suffers from the defect that it expresses a plausible thought which cannot lay claim to be in conformity with Plato's thought. For we know the Platonic Socrates only through Plato. The *Apology of Socrates* is as much a Platonic writing as any other Platonic writing. The *Apology of Socrates* is even a Platonic *dialogue*, the dialogue of Socrates with the people of Athens (37a7). It is a Platonic work of art, and not a report. We must pass through Plato's thought in order to understand the thought of the Platonic Socrates. And Plato has presented his thought exclusively in works of art, and not in treatises. What must one understand by a work of art? We remind ourselves of the story told in praise of the Greek painter—that he painted grapes so perfectly that birds flew to peck at them. The man who told this story characterized the work of art by two features. It is an imitation of something, and the imitation creates the delusion that it is the thing imitated. The imitation is perfect if it makes one forget the delusion. The delusion consists in the disregard of something essential, the abstraction from something essential. Painted grapes cannot be eaten, to say nothing of the fact that they are not three-dimensional. But grapes are not painted for the sake of birds. The abstraction from something essential which characterizes the work of art serves the purpose of bringing out something more essential, of heightening something more essential. In works like the Platonic dialogues abstraction is made in the first place from visibility. We merely hear people talk. We do not, strictly speaking, see them. And secondly, abstraction is made from chance. Everything happening in the work is meaningful or necessary. The abstraction from the visible and the fortuitous serves the purpose of making us concentrate on the audible and the necessary, on the necessity of the speech and in the speech.

The problem of the Platonic dialogue is, in a way, insoluble. There exists no Platonic utterance about the meaning of the Platonic dialogues. Still, Plato's Socrates gives us a most important hint when he speaks of the essential defect of all writings. A writing, as distinguished from a wise speech, says the same things to all men. The essential defect of writings is inflexibility. Since Plato, in contradistinction to Socrates, did produce writing, one is entitled to assume that the Platonic dialogues are meant to be writings which are free from the essential defect of writings. They are writings which, if properly read, reveal themselves to possess the flexibility of speech, and they are properly read if the necessity of every part of them becomes clear. The Platonic dialogues do say, and they are meant to say, different things to different men. This thought, which can be developed in great detail without too great difficulty, has only one defect. As it was stated, at any rate, it is based on the premise that Plato's Socrates is Plato's spokesman. Yet what entitles us to accept that premise? Socrates is not always Plato's spokesman. He is not Plato's spokesman in the *Timaeus*, the *Critias*, the *Sophist*, the *Statesman*, the *Parmenides*, and the *Laws*. What does Plato signify by making Socrates a silent listener to other men's speeches? As long as we do not know this we cannot have clarity regarding Socrates' alleged spokesmanship. Certainly Plato never said that his Socrates is his spokesman. When speaking of dramas, as distinguished from narratives, his Socrates says that in a drama the author conceals himself (Republic 392cff.): that is to say, the author does not say a word in his own name, and the Platonic dialogue is a sort of drama. In the case of Shakespeare, for instance, who would dare to say that according to Shakespeare life is a tale told by an idiot, full of sound and fury, signifying nothing? Everyone would say that these are the words, not of Shakespeare, but of Macbeth, and no conclusion whatever as to Shakespeare's holding the view expressed by these words can be drawn from the fact that Shakespeare wrote these words. Perhaps one can even prove that Shakespeare did not hold the view by considering the character of the speaker and the situation of the

speaker when he uttered them. Perhaps the action of the play refutes Macbeth's utterances. Perhaps the dramatic poet reveals his
thought exclusively by the play as a whole, by the action, and not
by speech, that is to say, the speeches of his characters. This much
we can say safely, that the distinction between speeches and
deeds, and the implication that the deeds are more trustworthy
than the speeches, is basic for the understanding of works like the
Platonic dialogues. The deeds are the clue to the meaning of the
speeches. More precisely, perhaps, the unthematic, that which is
not in the center of attention of the speakers as speakers, is the
clue to the thematic, to that which is in the center of attention of
the speakers as speakers. No doubt it is paradoxical to say that an
utterance of the Platonic Socrates is no more revealing of Plato's
thought than the quoted utterance of Macbeth is of the thought of
Shakespeare. Let us then retract this paradoxical suggestion, and
let us take Plato's Socrates as Plato's spokesman. But this will be
of no help, for Plato's Socrates is famous for his irony. To have
a spokesman who is famous for his irony is tantamount to having no spokesman at all. Irony means primarily dissimulation. It
comes to mean noble dissimulation. The superior man who is
aware of his superiority is "ironical in his relations to the many,"
says Aristotle. That is to say, he does not let his inferiors feel their
inferiority, or his superiority. He conceals his superiority. But if his
superiority consists in wisdom, his noble dissimulation must consist in concealing his wisdom, that is to say in presenting himself
as less wise than he is, or in not saying what he knows. And given
the fact that there is a great variety of types of unwisdom, his irony
will consist in speaking differently to different kinds of people.
Irony comes to mean to answer general questions differently when
speaking to different kinds of people, as well as never answering,
but always raising, questions.

The beginning of understanding of the Platonic dialogues is
wonder. Wonder means here not merely admiration of beauty, but
also and above all perplexity, recognition of the sphinx-like character of the Platonic dialogues. To begin with, we have no other
clue than the outward appearance which one must try to describe.
To begin with, the Platonic dialogue is one big question mark, and
nothing else. But, fortunately, there are many Platonic dialogues.
The very manyness and variety is an articulation of the theme,
Platonic dialogue, and hence sheds some light. The student of the
Platonic dialogues is in the position of a zoologist confronted by
an unknown species, or rather genus, of animals. His first task is

to classify in accordance with the most obvious, with the visible appearance. I mention three classifications which are evidently necessary. In the first place, there is a distinction between Socratic and non-Socratic dialogues, between dialogues in which Socrates conducts the conversation and dialogues in which someone other than Socrates conducts the conversation. Secondly, there is a distinction between performed and narrated dialogues, the performed dialogues looking like dramas. In the performed dialogues there is no bridge between the characters of the dialogue and the reader. In the narrated dialogues a participant in the dialogue gives an account of the conversation to a nonparticipant, and hence also to us, the reader. In a narrated dialogue the narrator, who may be Socrates himself, can tell us the reason why he said what he said to a participant, as well as his observations regarding the participants which he could not with propriety make to the participants. For instance, if the *Republic* were not a narrated dialogue, we could not know that at a given moment Thrasymachus was red in his face, not because he was ashamed, but because he was hot from the day. In a narrated dialogue Socrates can make us into people who are in the know together with him, or even into his accomplices. Thirdly, there is a distinction between voluntary and compulsory dialogues; voluntary dialogues are dialogues which Socrates spontaneously seeks, while compulsory dialogues are dialogues which Socrates cannot with propriety avoid.

If we look at Plato's *Apology of Socrates* from this point of view we see that this dialogue between Socrates and the Athenian people, or his accusers, is a performed and compulsory dialogue. Socrates did not spontaneously seek this conversation, nor does he tell us the reason why he says what he said, or his observations regarding the participants, which he could not with propriety make to the participants' face. We would have to turn to the *Gorgias*, for instance, in order to find an answer to the question regarding this background of the *Apology of Socrates*. There we find that Socrates explains that in his position as an accused he was in the position of a physician accused by the cook before a tribunal of children that he did not give them the nice candies which they would like to have (*Gorgias* 521e–522e); this is something which he could not with propriety say of the Athenians in the *Apology of Socrates*. Accordingly we note that the way in which the Platonic Socrates presents himself in his performed and compulsory conversation with the Athenian people assembled differs from the way in which the Platonic Socrates is presented by Plato in the dialogues taken as a whole. The *Apology of Socrates* makes us expect to find Socrates presented as engaged in conversations in the marketplace with anybody who just happened to be there. But the Platonic Socrates in deed, as distinguished from his compulsory self-presentation in public, is extremely selective. He talks with youths who are promising, with sophists, rhetoricians, rhapsodes, or soothsayers, on very rare occasions with retired generals or politicians, and still more rarely with ordinary citizens as such. He is famous, or ridiculed, for using the example of shoemakers and other craftsmen, but in contradistinction to Xenophon's Socrates, the Platonic Socrates never has a discussion with a craftsman. He always speaks about shoemakers, but never with shoemakers. On the other hand we never find him engaged as a mature man in a conversation with a man who is not clearly his inferior. He is silently present when Timaeus explains the cosmos, and he silently observes the Eleatic Stranger training Thaeatetus or the young Socrates. It is true, in the *Parmenides* we find Socrates engaged in a conversation with Parmenides, but there Parmenides is clearly the superior, Socrates still being very young. To summarize, the Platonic Socrates, outside of the Platonic Socrates' self-presentation in his sole public speech, converses only with people who are not common people, who in one way or other belong to an elite, although never to the elite in the highest sense; in short, he converses with inbetween people. The Platonic dialogue refutes the Platonic Socrates' public self-presentation.

This observation induces us to pay the greatest attention, to begin with, to the *Republic*. The *Republic* is the only dialogue narrated by Socrates which is compulsory. Socrates is compelled, not indeed by the Athenian *demos*, but by some young companions, to stay in the Piraeus, and this compulsory stay supplies the occasion for an extensive conversation on justice, in the course of which Socrates founds a perfectly just city, not in deed, but in speech. Before considering any Platonic dialogue, one must consider the fact that there are many Platonic dialogues, or that Plato's work consists of many dialogues because it imitates the manyness, the variety, the heterogeneity, of being. The imitation is not a simple reproduction. The individual Platonic dialogue is not a chapter from the *Encyclopaedia of the Philosophical Sciences* or from a system of philosophy, nor is it the product of an occasion or the relic of a stage of Plato's development. The individual dialogue is characterized less by its subject matter than by the manner in which it treats the subject matter. Each dialogue treats its subject matter by means of a specific abstraction, and hence a specific distortion. For instance, the *Euthyphro* deals with piety while being silent about the soul, or in abstraction from the phenomenon of the soul.

To understand a dialogue means, therefore, to recognize the principle guiding the specific abstraction which characterizes the dialogue in question. This principle is revealed primarily by the setting of the dialogue: its time, place, characters, and action. The discussion taking place in a dialogue is made necessary primarily not because of the subject matter, but because of the setting in which the dialogue takes place. It is reasonable to expect that the setting was chosen by Plato as most appropriate with a view to the subject matter, but on the other hand what Plato thought about the subject matter comes to our sight first through the medium of the setting. As for the setting of the *Republic:* the conversation takes place in the Piraeus, the harbor of Athens, the seat of Athens' naval and commercial power, in the house of a wealthy resident alien, on a day in which a new and strange religious procession took place for the first time. The surroundings are then at the opposite pole from old and patrician Athens, which lives in the spirit of the ancestral. The surroundings bespeak what in the light of the tradition would appear as political decay. Yet Piraeus had also another connotation. There are in the *Republic* ten companions, mentioned by name. Ten in the Piraeus. This is a reminder of the rule of the Thirty Tyrants, during which there were ten men in control of the Piraeus. We are thus reminded of the attempt, with which Plato was himself somehow connected, to put down the democracy and restore an oligarchic or aristocratic regime. Yet the characters of the *Republic* have nothing in common with the oligarchic reaction. The family of Cephalus, in whose house the conversation takes place, as well as Niceratus, were victims of the Thirty Tyrants. Just as the chief interlocutors in Plato's dialogue on courage are defeated generals, and the chief interlocutors in his dialogue on moderation are future tyrants, at any rate some of the individuals in his dialogue on justice are innocent victims of a rebellion made in the name of justice. The restoration which Socrates performs in the *Republic* is then not likely to be a political restoration; it rather will be a restoration on a different plane. The spirit of this Socratic restoration is indicated by the fact that Socrates and the other participants, from uptown Athens, are kept in the Piraeus by the promise of dinner, as well as of a torch race in honor of a goddess. But we hear nothing further about either the torch race or the dinner. Torch race and dinner are replaced by a conversation on justice. The feeding of the body is replaced by the feeding of the soul. The very extended conversation on justice constitutes in itself a training in self-control regarding the pleasures and even the needs of the body, or it constitutes an act of asceticism. When Thomas More wrote an imitation of the *Republic*, his much less ascetic *Utopia*, he arranged that the description of his perfect commonwealth be given after luncheon.

The antagonist of Socrates in the *Republic* is Thrasymachus, the rhetorician. As becomes clear from a brief exchange between a follower of Thrasymachus and a follower of Socrates, by which the discussion between Thrasymachus and Socrates is interrupted, Thrasymachus starts from the quite unparadoxical view that the just is identical with the legal. Since what is legal or not depends in each case on the decision of the lawgiver or the government, the just is then identical with the will of the stronger. The manner in which Thrasymachus behaves—he forbids the saying of certain things, or forbids the giving of certain answers; he demands a fine from Socrates, for payment of which Plato's brother vouches, just as Plato himself vouches for a payment of another kind demanded from Socrates on the day of his accusation—reminds us of the behavior of the city of Athens towards Socrates. The thesis of Thrasymachus, that the just is the legal, is the thesis of the actual polis, which does not permit an appeal beyond its laws. In a sense Thrasymachus is the polis. He plays the polis. He is able to play the polis because he possesses the art of rhetoric. Socrates succeeds easily in crushing and in silencing Thrasymachus, but Thrasymachus continues to play a role in the *Republic* after he has been silenced. At the beginning of the fifth book there occurs a scene which reminds us of the scene with which the *Republic* opens. In both scenes we have a deliberation ending in a decision, an imitation of the action of the city. But whereas in the first deliberation, or decision, Thrasymachus does not take part, he does take part in the second. By the beginning of the fifth book Thrasymachus has become a member of the city. The restoration of the city in speech includes the integration of Thrasymachus into the city. The restoration of justice on the new plane requires the help of Thrasymachus' art, the art of rhetoric.

In Aristophanes' *Clouds*, we may recall, Socrates had been responsible for the revelation of the weakness of the Just Speech. The Just Speech was weak because it was based principally on mythology, on the stories told about the gods. The gods, the alleged guardians of justice, were manifestly unjust. If Socrates is to show the strength of the Just Speech, and this is naturally his primary function in the *Republic,* he must therefore wholly divorce justice from mythology, from all ancient hearsay or tradition. The Platonic Socrates shows, then, in deed the strength of the Just Speech, but he shows the strength of an entirely new, novel, unheard of Just Speech. The Platonic Socrates transcends the generally accepted and impure notion of justice, according to which justice consists in giving to everyone what is his due; for a man's due is determined by custom, law, or positive law, and there is no necessity that the positive law itself be just. What the positive law declares to be just is as such just merely by virtue of positing, of convention; therefore one must seek for what is just intrinsically, by nature. We must seek a social order which as such is intrinsically just, the polis which is in accordance with nature. Of such a city there is no example. It is wholly novel. It must be founded in order to be. In the *Republic* it is founded in speech.

Yet what guidance do we possess after we have been compelled to question the view that justice consists in giving everyone his due? According to the generally accepted view, justice is not merely the habit of giving everyone what is due to him; it is also meant to be beneficial. We shall then say that justice is the habit of giving to everyone what is good for him. According to Aristotle the first impression he received from the *Republic* is the philanthropic character of the scheme presented therein. If justice is the habit of giving to everyone what is good for him, justice is the preserve of the wise. For just as the physician alone knows what is truly good for the body of a man, only the wise man, the physician of the soul, knows what is truly good for the whole man. Furthermore, justice so understood—as the habit of giving to everyone what is good for him—is utterly selfless. It is selfless devotion to others, pure serving of others, or serving of the whole. Since in a just city everyone is supposed to be just in the sense that he be dedicated to the service of others, no one will think of himself, of his own happiness, of his own. Total communism, communism regarding property, women, and children, is merely the institutional expression of justice. But is the well-being of the whole not identical with the well-being of all its members? In other words, why is everyone to dedicate himself entirely to the polis? The answer is this. The good city is the necessary and sufficient condition for the highest excellence or virtue of each according to his capacity. The just city is a city in which being a good citizen is simply the same as being a good man. Everyone is to dedicate himself, not to the pursuit which is most pleasant or attractive to him, but to that which makes him as good a man as possible. Yet justice implies some reciprocity of giving and taking. The just city is then the city in which everyone does that which he is by nature fitted to do, and in which everyone receives that which is by nature good, rather than attractive or pleasant, for him. The just city is a perfectly rational society. Nothing is fair or noble, nothing is even sacred or holy, except what is useful for that city—that is to say, in the last resort, for the greatest possible perfection or virtue of each member. To mention only the most shocking and striking example, the family and the sacred prohibitions against incest between brothers and sisters must give way to the demands of eugenics. The whole scheme presupposes on every point the absolute rule of the wise, or of the philosophers. But how are the wise to find obedience on the part of the unwise? This, you see, is the same problem which we found in Xenophon. The required obedience would not be forthcoming without the use of force. Therefore the few wise need the support of a fairly large number of loyal auxiliaries. But how can the wise secure the loyalty of the auxiliaries, who as such are not wise? The wise rule the auxiliaries by persuasion, and by persuasion alone. For in the good city the auxiliaries will not be hampered by the laws. Persuasion is not demonstration. The unwise, and especially the auxiliaries, are persuaded by means of a noble deception. Even the rational society, the society according to truth and nature, is not possible without a fundamental untruth.

That fundamental untruth consists of two parts. Its first part consists in the replacement of the earth as the common mother of all men, and therewith of the fraternity of all men, by a part of the earth, the land, the fatherland, the territory, and the fraternity of only the fellow citizens. The first part of the fundamental untruth consists then in assigning the natural status of the human species to a part of the human species, the citizens of a given city. The second part of the fundamental untruth consists in ascribing divine origin to the existing social hierarchy, or, more generally stated, in identifying the existing social hierarchy with the natural hierarchy; that is to say, even the polis according to nature is not simply natural, or even the most rational society is not simply rational. Hence the crucial importance for it of the art of persuasion. This difficulty recurs in an even sharper form when the question is raised as to how one can transform an actual polis into the best polis. This transformation would be wholly impossible if the citizens of an actual polis—that is to say, men who have not undergone the specific education prescribed in the *Republic* for the citizens of the best city—could not be persuaded to bow to the rule of the philosophers. The problem of the best city would be altogether insoluble if the multitude were not amenable to persuasion by the philosophers. It is in the context of the assertion that the multitude is persuadable by the philosophers that Socrates declares that he and Thrasymachus have just become friends. Thrasymachus must be integrated into the best city because the best city is not possible without the art of Thrasymachus. To the best of my knowledge the only student of the *Republic* who has understood this crucial fact was Alfarabi, an Islamic philosopher who flourished around 900 and who was the founder of medieval Aristotelianism. According to Alfarabi the way of Socrates, which is appropriate only for the philosophers dealing with the elite, must be combined with the way of Thrasymachus, which is appropriate for the philosophers dealing with the multitude. The first reason why the noble delusion is required is the tension between the impossibility of a universal political society on the one hand—universal is meant here literally, embracing all human beings—and the essential defect of the particular or closed political society on the other. The particular or closed political society conflicts with the natural fraternity of all men. Political society in one way or another draws an arbitrary line between man and man. Political society is essentially exclusive or harsh. The discussion of justice in the first book of the *Republic* may be said to culminate in the suggestion that the just man does not do any harm to anyone. Pursuing this line of thought, we arrive at the conclusion that justice is universal beneficence. But this whole line of thought is dropped silently, yet not unnoticeably, in Socrates' strong speech on behalf of justice. The guardians of the just city are compared to dogs who are gentle to their acquaintances, or friends, and harsh to enemies, or strangers. In this way Plato makes his Socrates express the same view which Xenophon expresses by indicating that he, the pupil of Socrates, was as good at guiding gentlemen by praise as he was at beating the base into obedience. Both the Xenophontic and the Platonic Socrates have understood the essential limitation of reason and of speech generally, and therewith the nature of political things.

As I have indicated, the action of the *Republic* consists in Socrates' first bringing into the open his latent conflict with Thrasymachus, then in his silencing Thrasymachus, and finally in reconciling Thrasymachus by assigning him an important, if subordinate, place in the best city. To express it somewhat differently, the action of the *Republic* centers on the strength and the weakness of rhetoric. In the course of the conversation the expectation from rhetoric is greatly increased. To begin with it is only expected that the people who have already grown up in the best city and have been educated in its ways will believe in the noble lie. Later on it is expected that the people of an actual city can be persuaded of the need to submit to the rule of the philosophers. Only on the basis of this expectation does it make sense to say that evils will not cease from the city if the philosophers do not become kings. That the philosophers can become kings depends on their ability to persuade the multitude of their ability to be kings. But at the end of this part of the *Republic,* which is its central part, the condition of political bliss is drastically reformulated. Political bliss will follow, not if the philosophers become kings, but when the philosophers have become kings, and if they have rusticated everyone older than ten, and if they bring up the children without any influence whatever of the parents on the children. Socrates does not even try to show that the multitude can ever be persuaded to submit to the rule of the philosophers with the understanding that the philosophers will expel the multitude from the city and keep only the children in the city. The majority of men cannot be brought by persuasion alone to undergo what they regard as the greatest misery for the rest of their days so that all future generations will be blessed. There are absolute limits to persuasion, and therefore the best city as sketched in the *Republic* is not possible. The best city would be possible if a complete clean sweep could be made, yet there is always a powerful heritage which cannot be swept away and whose power can only be broken by the sustained effort of every individual by himself. The best city would be possible only if all men could become philosophers, that is to say, if human nature were miraculously transformed.

Now, the best city was founded in speech in order to prove the strength of the Just Speech. Hence it would seem to follow that not only the traditional Just Speech but the novel Just Speech as well is weak, or that Aristophanes was right. The Platonic Socrates provides against this conclusion by conceiving of the justice of the city as being strictly parallel to the justice of the individual, and vice versa. Accordingly he defines justice as doing one's job, or rather as doing one's job well. A being is just if all its significant parts do their jobs well. In order to be truly just it is not necessary that a man should do well the job which he would have to fulfill in the perfectly just city. It suffices if the parts of his soul do their jobs well, if his reason is in control and his subrational powers obey his reason. But this is strictly possible only in the case of a man who has cultivated his reason properly, that is to say, in the case of the philosopher. Hence the philosopher, and only the philosopher, can be simply just, regardless of the quality of the city in which he lives; and, vice versa, the nonphilosopher will not be simply just, regardless of the quality of the city in which he lives. Socrates speaks less of doing one's job well than simply of doing one's job, which has a common meaning of minding one's own business, not to be a busybody, or to lead a retired life. To lead the just life means to lead a retired life, the retired life *par excellence*, the life of the philosopher. This is the manifest secret of the *Republic*. The justice of the individual is said to be written in small letters, but the justice of the city is in large letters. Justice is said to consist in minding one's business, that is to say, in not serving others. Obviously the best city does not serve other cities. It is self-sufficient.

Justice is self-sufficiency and hence is philosophy. Justice thus understood is possible regardless of whether the best city is possible or not. Justice thus understood has the further advantage that the question as to whether it is worthy of being chosen for its own sake cannot arise. Whereas justice in the vulgar sense can well be a burden, the philosopher's minding his own business, that is to say, his philosophizing, is intrinsically pleasant. To exaggerate somewhat for the sake of clarity, in the best city the whole is happy, and no individual is happy, since the philosophers are burdened with the duties of administration. Outside of such a city the philosophers as philosophers are happy. At this point we may begin to understand what the distinction between compulsory and voluntary dialogues means, and why the *Republic* is the only dialogue narrated by Socrates which is compulsory. But all this does not mean more than that the individual is capable of a perfection of which the city is not capable.

Political life derives its dignity from something which transcends political life. This essential limitation of the political can be understood in three different ways. According to Socrates the transpolitical to which the political owes its dignity is philosophy, or *theoria*, which, however, is accessible only to what he calls good natures, to human beings who possess a certain natural equipment. According to the teaching of revelation the transpolitical is accessible through faith, which does not depend on specific natural presuppositions, but on divine grace or God's free election. According to liberalism the transpolitical consists in something which every human being possesses as much as any other human being. The classic expression of liberal thought is the view that political society exists above all for the sake of protecting the rights of man, the rights which every human being possesses regardless of his natural gifts or his achievements, to say nothing of divine grace.

To return to the argument of the *Republic*, by realizing the essential limitations of the political, one is indeed liberated from the charms of what we now would call political idealism, or what in the language of Socrates might have to be called the charm of the idols, the imaginative presentation of justice—with the understanding, however, that it is better not to be born than never to have felt that charm. But the liberation from that charm will not weaken but strengthen the concern for political life, or political responsibility. Philosophy stands or falls by the city. Hence Plato devoted his most extensive work, the *Laws*, which is *the* political work of Plato, to politics. And the *Laws* presents the best city which is possible for beings who are not gods nor sons of gods, whereas the *Republic* is Plato's presentation, not of the best city, but, in the guise of such a presentation, his exposition of the *ratio rerum civilium*, of the essential character of political things, as Cicero has wisely said (*De Republica* 2.52). This being so, it is remarkable that the Platonic character who is the chief interlocutor in the *Laws* is not Socrates. In the light of everything that has been said before, this fact forces us to raise the pardoxical question: is not Aristophanes' presentation of Socrates confirmed in a decisive respect by Plato? This question can be answered without any paradoxes. The Platonic Socrates, as distinguished from the Aristophanean Socrates, is characterized by *phronesis*, by practical wisdom. He is so far from being blind to political things that he has realized their essential character, and he acts consistently in accordance with this realization.

It is, then, of the essence of political things to be below that perfection of which the individual is capable. If the perfection of the individual is the ceiling which the city never reaches, what is the flooring beneath which the city cannot fall without becoming inhuman or degraded? The Platonic Socrates begins his discussion of these minimum requirements when he describes the first city, that city which Glaucon calls the city of pigs but which Socrates calls the true city, the city which is nothing but city. This is a city which does nothing but satisfy the primary wants, the wants of the body—food, clothing, and shelter—and in which nothing good or evil that goes beyond these elementary things has yet emerged. It is a state of innocence which, because it is innocent, is so easily lost; it is a state of decency, a state characterized, not by virtue, but by simplicity and good-naturedness, and by the absence of the need for government. In the moment the human faculty is developed, the need for government arises; for, to say the least, there is no necessity whatever that the faculties should develop in the right direction. The need for government is identical with the need for restraint and the need for virtue. Virtue thus understood is required for the sake of living together; it is the flooring beneath which the city cannot fall without becoming degraded. This kind of virtue is called by Plato popular or political virtue. We may call it utilitarian virtue. Its rationale, or root, to repeat, is the need of the city.

Yet there is another root of virtue and hence another kind of virtue: genuine virtue. The Socratic formula for genuine virtue is: virtue is knowledge. This is another manifest secret of the Platonic as well as of the Xenophontic Socrates. The formula means what it says. Virtue in the strict sense is nothing but knowledge or understanding, and vice in the strict sense is nothing but ignorance—knowledge or ignorance of the *akra physeos*, of the peaks of being. This virtue in the strict sense both presupposes and produces the other virtues—courage, moderation, and justice. If we may use the Aristotelian (i.e., not Platonic) term, "moral virtue," we can state the view of the Platonic Socrates as follows. The "moral virtues" have two different roots. The ends for the sake of which they exist are the city on the one hand and the life of the mind on the other. To the extent to which the moral virtues are rooted only in the needs of society they are only popular or political virtues, and they are acquired only by habituation. As such they have no solidity. A man who has lived in a well-ordered city as a good citizen, participating in virtue by habituation and not by philosophy, chooses the greatest tyranny for his next life, as Plato states towards the end of the *Republic* (619b–d). Popular or political virtue is acquired by habituation in accordance with a reasoning or calculation, the starting point of which is the need for society or the needs of the body, whereas the philosopher is *inclined* to virtue and does not need a calculation for that. In our century Bergson has spoken of the two roots of morality, one of them being the city, the other being the open or universal society. What Bergson said about the first root is in fundamental agreement with the Socratic teaching. All the more striking is the disagreement regarding the second root. The place occupied in Socrates' thought by philosophy is occupied in Bergson's thought by the open and universal society inspired by a kind of mysticism.

Yet if morality has two radically different roots, how can there be a unity of morality, how can there be a unity of man, and how is it possible that the moral requirements of society on the one hand and the moral requirements of the life of the mind on the other agree completely, or at any rate to a considerable extent? The unity of man consists in the fact that he is that part of the whole which is open to the whole, or, in Platonic language, that part of the whole which has seen the ideas of all things. Man's concern with his openness to the whole is the life of the mind. The dualism of being a part while being open to the whole, and therefore in a sense being the whole itself, is man. Furthermore, society, and the whole simply, have this in common, that they are both wholes which transcend the individual, in using the individual to rise above and beyond himself. All nobility consists in such rising above and beyond oneself, in such dedicating oneself to something greater than oneself.

We shall tentatively say that the question of the unity of man is discussed in the *Republic* in the form of the question of the unity of the human soul. This implies that the *Republic* abstracts from the body. Every dialogue, I suggest, is characterized by a specific abstraction from something most relevant to the subject matter discussed. The abstraction characteristic of the *Republic* is the abstraction from the body. The characteristic political proposal of the *Republic* is complete communism. But the body constitutes the absolute limit to communism; man cannot, strictly speaking, share his body with anybody else, whereas he can well share his thoughts and desires with others. The same abstraction from the body can be observed in the discussion of the equality of men and women in the *Republic*, where the difference between men and women is treated as if it had the same status and significance as the difference between men who are baldheaded and men who are not baldheaded. The same intention is revealed by the provisions of the *Republic* regarding children. The blood relation between children and parents, this bodily relation, is to be rendered invisible. Also, and above all, the argument of the *Republic* as a whole is based on the parallelism of the individual man and the polis, but this parallelism between man and the polis is soon replaced by the parallelism between the individual's soul and the polis. The body is silently dropped. We recall here Plato's failure to provide for the dinner promised at the beginning of the conversation. Furthermore, we understand from here the fact that Socrates almost forgets to mention among the studies to be pursued by future philosophers the field of solid geometry, geometry of bodies. Last but not least, we mentioned the exaggeration of the rhetorical power of the philosophers, which is only the reverse side of the abstraction from the bodily power of the philosophers to force the non-philosophers. At any rate, the question of the unity of man is discussed in the *Republic* in the form of the question of the unity of the soul. The question arises because of the evident necessity to admit the essential difference between intelligence or reason on the one hand and the subrational powers of the soul on the other. The question of the unity of man thus becomes the question of the bond between the highest and the lowest in the human soul.

In the *Republic* Plato suggests a partition of the soul into three parts, reason, spiritedness, and desire. Of the two subrational parts spiritedness is the highest, or noblest, because it is essentially obedient to reason, whereas desire revolts against reason. To use the terms employed by Aristotle in his *Politics* in a kindred context, reason rules spiritedness politically or royally, by persuasion, whereas it rules desire despotically, by mere command. It appears, then, that spiritedness is the bond between the highest and the lowest in man, or that which gives man unity. We shall venture to say that the characteristically human, the human-all-too-human, is spiritedness. The word which is translated by spiritedness, *thymos* or *thymoeides,* has originally a much broader meaning, and this meaning occurs also in the Platonic dialogues. We may say that spiritedness is a Greek equivalent of the Biblical "heart." Especially in the *Republic* Plato prefers the narrow meaning by opposing spiritedness and desire, whereas desire, of course, belongs as much to *thymos* in the original sense, to the heart, as does spiritedness. To understand Plato's preference, especially in the *Republic,* we start from the fact that desire includes eros, erotic desire in the highest and lowest sense. Spiritedness in the sense of the *Republic* is radically distinguished from eros. It is anerotic or anti-erotic.

By assigning to spiritedness a higher status than to desire, Plato depreciates eros. This depreciation appears most clearly in two facts. When Plato indicates in the second book the needs for the satisfaction of which men live in society, he mentions food and drink but is silent about procreation. When he describes in the ninth book the tyrant he presents him as absolutely under the sway of eros, as eros incarnate. The tyrant, however, is injustice incarnate, or the incarnation of that which is destructive of the city. Spiritedness, we should then say, as opposed to eros is meant to be the political passion. It is for this reason that Xenophon presents his Cyrus, the most successful of all rulers, as a thoroughly unerotic man. Yet how can this be understood? Unerotic spiritedness, the political passion, shows itself as a desire for victory, superiority, rule, honor, and glory. But is the political passion not also, and even primarily, attachment to the polis, to the fatherland, and hence love? Is not the model of the guardian, or the citizen, the dog who loves his acquaintances or friends? But precisely this model shows that the guardian or citizen must also be harsh to the noncitizen or stranger. The political passion, then, cannot be understood merely as attachment. The harsh, exclusive element is equally essential to patriotism. This harshness is not essential to eros because two human beings can love one another without being harsh to others. This harshness is not essential to eros but is supplied by spiritedness. There remains a greater difficulty. Spiritedness shows itself as desire for victory, superiority, rule, honor, and glory. Is it then not also a kind of desire? With what right can it be distinguished from desire, or even opposed to it? The answer is implied in the traditional distinction between the concupiscible and the irascible, a distinction which is the outgrowth of the Platonic distinction between desire and spiritedness. But the Platonic distinction is not identical with the traditional distinction. I have spoken of the twofold root of morality, the needs of society, which are ultimately the needs of the body, and the needs of the mind. To these two kinds of needs there correspond two kinds of desires. Desire is directed toward a good, the good simply, but spiritedness, of which anger is the most obvious form, is directed towards a goal as difficult to obtain. Spiritedness arises out of the desire proper being resisted or thwarted. Spiritedness is needed for overcoming the resistance to the satisfaction of the desire. Hence spiritedness is a desire for victory. Whereas eros is primarily the desire to generate human beings, spiritedness is the derivative willingness to kill and to be killed, to destroy human beings.

Being secondary in comparison with desire, spiritedness is in the service of desire. It is essentially obedient, while looking more masterful than anything else. But as such it does not know what it should obey, the higher or the lower. It bows to it knows not what.

It divines something higher; it is *aidos*, reverence. Yet qua essentially deferential it is of higher dignity than the bodily desires, which lack that deference. The spirited man is, as it were, always on the lookout, or on the search, for something for which he can sacrifice himself. He is prepared to sacrifice himself and everything else for anything. He is as anxious to honor as he is to be honored. While being most passionately concerned with self-assertion, he is at the same time and in the same act most self-forgetting. Since spiritedness is undetermined as to the primary end, the goods of the body or the good of the mind, it is in a way independent of, or oblivious to, those goods. As such, spiritedness is neutral to the difference between the two kinds of objects of desire—the goods of the body and the good of the mind. It is therefore radically ambiguous, and therefore it can be the root of the most radical confusion. Spiritedness thus understood is that which makes human beings interesting. It is therefore the theme of tragedy. Homer is the father of tragedy because his theme in the *Iliad* is the wrath of Achilles, and in the *Odyssey* the *thwarted* return of Odysseus. Spiritedness is the region of ambiguity, a region in which the lower and the higher are bound together, where the lower is transformed into the higher, and vice versa, without a possibility of a clear distinction between the two. It is the locus of morality in the ordinary sense of the term.

Philosophy is not spirited. When joining issue with the atheists in the tenth book of the *Laws*, the philosopher addresses them explicitly without spiritedness. Spiritedness must be subservient to philosophy, whereas desire, eros, in its highest form *is* philosophy. Here we touch on the point of the deepest agreement between Plato and Aristophanes. As desire for superiority, spiritedness becomes in the case of sensible men the desire for recognition by free men. It is therefore essentially related to political liberty, hence to law, and hence to justice. Similarly, as essentially deferential, it is a sense of shame, which as such bows primarily to the ancestral, the primary manifestation of the good. For both reasons it is essentially related to justice. Spiritedness in its normal form is a zeal for justice, or moral indignation. This is the reason why, in Plato's dialogue on justice, the *Republic*, spiritedness is presented as the bond through which man is one. And the action of the *Republic* can be said to consist in first arousing spiritedness or the virtue belonging to it—that is to say, zeal dedicated to nonunderstood justice, that is, what we now mean by political idealism—and then in purging it. By understanding spiritedness we understand the fundamental ambiguity of moral indignation, which easily turns into vindictive-ness or punitiveness. The ambiguity of spiritedness is not ex-hausted, however, by the ambiguity of moral indignation. It shows itself most strikingly in the shift from justified indignation to un-justified indignation. No one has stated this more directly than Shakespeare in Hamlet's soliloquy. Hamlet enumerates seven things which make life almost impossible to bear. Almost all of them are objects of moral indignation, the oppressor's wrong and so on, but in the center he mentions the pangs of despised love. The justified indignation about injustice shifts insensibly into the unjustified indignation about unrequited love. This is perhaps the deepest secret of spiritedness and therefore at least one of the deepest secrets of Plato's *Republic*.

The *Republic* could not show the purification of spiritedness, that purification which consists in its submission to philosophy, without making spiritedness the center, the center of man. The world of the *Republic* is a world of spiritedness, unpurified and purified. In other words, the *Republic* abstracts from *charis*, grace— in the classic sense, in which it is essentially akin to eros. The world of spiritedness is not the world of *charis* or eros. How these two worlds are related in Plato's view, whether they are not related as *charis* and *anangkē*, as grace and compulsion: this question co-incides with the question of the relation between the *Republic* and the *Symposium*, between the most compulsory and the most vol-untary of the Platonic dialogues.

Concluding Lecture

These lectures take place under the shadow of the contemporary collapse of rationalism. This collapse induces us to consider the whole issue of rationalism. The first step in this inquiry, to the extent to which it is an empirical inquiry, is the question of the origin of rationalism. For a number of reasons this question can be identified with the problem of Socrates, or the problem of classical political philosophy in general. It is no doubt of the ut-most importance to contrast classical political philosophy with the philosophic alternatives to it which are presented by modern po-litical philosophy. But before one can do that one must have under-stood classical political philosophy by itself. I limit myself to the question concerning the character and claim of classical political philosophy, to the question concerning the problem which it tried to solve, concerning the obstacle it tried to overcome. That problem and that obstacle appeared clearly in Aristophanes' presentation of Socrates. Socrates is unpolitical because he lacks self-knowledge. He does not understand the political context within which philosophy exists. He is unaware of the essential difference between philosophy and the polis. He does not understand the political in its specific character. This is because he is unerotic and amusic. To this accusation Xenophon and Plato give one and the same reply. Socrates is political and erotic. He understands the political in its nonrational character. He realizes the critical importance of *thymos*, of spiritedness, as the bond between the philosophers and the multitude. He understands the political in its specific character. In fact, no one before him has done so. For he is the first to grasp the significance of the *idea*, of the fact that the whole is characterized by articulation into classes or kinds, whose character can be understood only by thought, and not by sense perception.

Whatever we may think of the adequacy of this reply, in one point the reply is manifestly inadequate. It does not reply to the charge that Socrates was amusic.

According to a widespread view, the opposite, or the opponent, of classical political philosophy is sophistry, the teaching and the practice of the Greek sophists. This view deserves the reputation which it enjoys. A single superficial reading of the first book of the *Republic*, of the *Gorgias*, or of the *Protagoras* is sufficient for producing it. In the nineteenth century this view came to be understood as follows. Classical political philosophy is related to the sophists as German idealism, especially Hegel, is to the theorists of the French revolution, and in particular to the French *philosophes*. Both the adherents and enemies of the principles of 1789 have adhered, and still adhere, to this view. Liberals are inclined to favor the sophists, and conservatives are inclined to favor classical political philosophy. The most up-to-date and hence most simplistic version of this view no longer asserts a merely proportional equality, but asserts instead a simple equality (see Eric Havelock, *The Liberal Temper in Greek Politics* [New Haven, 1957]). For the view that classical political philosophy is related to the sophists as German idealism is to the theorists of the French revolution implied that there is a fundamental difference between all classical thought and all modern thought, and therefore that there is only an analogy between modern liberalism and the sophistic doctrines. Now, however, we are told that the sophists simply were liberals or theorists of democracy. It is necessary to know this opinion and to examine it carefully, for it embodies the most powerful obstacle to an understanding of either classical political philosophy or of the sophists. But this is not the proper place for such an examination (see L. Strauss, "The Liberalism of Classical Political Philosophy," chap. 3 of *Liberalism Ancient and Modern* [New York, 1968]).

Here I limit myself to the following remarks. Plato's criticism of the sophists is directed less against the teaching peculiar to the sophists than against a specific way of life. He had in mind a phenomenon similar to that which is known to us by the name of "the intellectuals," a most ambiguous phenomenon. For the name intellectual conceals the decisive difference between those who cultivate their intellect for its own sake and those who do it for the sake of gain, power, or prestige. In other words, intellectual is a merely external description, a description good enough perhaps for certain bureaucratic purposes, say, tax declarations. Intellectuals are men who earn their living by writing and reading, yet not by writing and reading tax declarations, for example, but something ill-defined. Intellectuals form a profession, but in all other professions there are standards allowing the profession to distinguish between, say, physicians and fake physicians. There exists no such possibility in the profession of intellectuals. One could perhaps say that the profession of intellectuals is distinguished from all other professions by the vagueness, as well as the enormous extent, of its claims. Its ambiguity, born of confusion, increases confusion, and therefore it is a menace—not to morality, but to clarity.

To return to the sophists, in the very *Republic* (492aff.) Plato defends the sophists against the common charge that they are corrupters of the young. The young are corrupted, Plato says, not—as the many charge—by the sophists, but by the many themselves who make that charge, or by the polis, as it actually is and always will be. The sophists are mere imitators of the polis and of the politicians. Gorgias and Polus in the *Gorgias* and Thrasymachus in the *Republic* are rhetoricians. Classical political philosophy is opposed, not to another political philosophy, but to rhetoric, that is to say, to autonomous rhetoric, or to the view that the highest art, the political art, is rhetoric. This view was indeed based on a philosophy, but on a philosophy which excluded the possibility of political philosophy. Plato has given a clear sketch of this philosophy in the tenth book of the *Laws*. It started from the premise that the fundamental phenomena are bodies, whereas soul and mind are merely derivative. It arrived at the conclusion that justice, or right, is in no way natural or in accordance with nature, but *is* only by virtue of convention or of opinion. Hence, in principle, any convention, any opinion, or, as they say today, any value system, is as good as any other. There is no nature, no truth, in this kind of thing, and therefore there cannot be a science of these things. The true art or science dealing with such matters is the art of influencing opinions with a view to one's interest, that is to say, the art of rhetoric. But in the *Republic,* at any rate, Plato speaks much less emphatically of the enmity between philosophy and rhetoric than of the enmity between philosophy and poetry. This enmity is so grave because the poets—and not the rhetoricians or the sophists—abuse the philosophers as "bitches barking at their master" (607b). The great alternative to classical political philosophy is poetry.

Let me state at the outset how in my opinion Plato settles the quarrel between philosophy and poetry. He emphasizes the need for the noble delusion; he therewith emphasizes the need for poetry. Philosophy as philosophy is unable to provide these noble delusions. Philosophy as philosophy is unable to persuade the nonphilosophers or the multitude; it is unable to charm them. Philosophy needs, then, poetry as its supplement. Philosophy requires a ministerial poetry. This implies Plato quarrels only with autonomous poetry. If he is to convince us, he must show that nothing which is admirable in poetry is lost if poetry is understood as ministerial.

In the *Republic* Plato discusses poetry twice. The first discussion, in the second and third books, precedes the discussion of philosophy. The discussion is in more than one respect prephilosophic. The second discussion, in the tenth book, follows the discussion of philosophy. The first discussion takes place between Socrates and Adeimantus, whose characteristic is moderation or sobriety, not to say austerity, rather than courage and erotic desire, and who has shown a profound dissatisfaction with what the poets teach regarding justice. The second discussion takes place between Socrates and Glaucon, whose characteristic is courage and erotic desire rather than sobriety or austerity. The second discussion of poetry promises to be infinitely more daring than the first.

The prephilosophic discussion of poetry is identical with the discussion of the education of the nonphilosophic soldiers. The first theme of that discussion is myth, or untrue speeches to be told to children. The makers of myth are the poets. The poets are entirely unconcerned with whether their stories are fit to be told to children, that is to say, to immature human beings regardless of their age. The distinction between fit and unfit stories has therefore to be made by people other than the poets, by the political authorities, in the best case by the wise founders of the best city. The political authorities must be concerned with whether the stories are conducive to the goodness of men and citizens. They are not concerned, it seems, with their poetic qualities. As regards the poetic qualities, the poets are likely to be better judges than the political authorities. The political authorities must supervise and censor the poets. In particular they must compel the poets to present the gods in such a way that the gods can be models of human and civic excellence. The presentation must be left to the poets. The task imposed on the poets is formidable. It suffices to think of Aphrodite as a model of civic excellence, not to say of a housewife. The founders of the city can lay down the outline, or the general principles, of what Adeimantus calls "theology." Socrates mentions two such principles. The gods must be presented as the cause only of good and not of evil. And the gods must be presented as simple, and as never deceiving. Adeimantus has no difficulty whatever in accepting the first proposition, but he is somewhat perplexed by the second proposition. The reason for this appears later on in the same context. For it appears that the only noble motive for deceiving is that implied in the function of ruling. If the gods rule men, how can they avoid the necessity of deceiving men for man's benefit? But the most striking rule laid down by Socrates is the prohibition against presenting the terrors of death and the suffering from the loss of a man's dearest. The poets are not permitted to state in public what they alone can state adequately when everyone else is made speechless through suffering, grief, or sorrow. They must write poetry on the principle that a good man, by virtue of his self-sufficiency, is not made miserable by the loss of his children, his brothers, or his friends. The poets may present the lamentations of inferior women and still more inferior men, so that the best part of the young generation will learn to despise lamentation.

Autonomous poetry gives expression to the passions by poetically imitating the passions; it consecrates the passions. Ministerial poetry, on the other hand, helps men in learning to control the passions. It is necessary to consider this contention also as a reply to Aristophanes. According to Aristophanes the poets are wise men who as such teach justice. Plato denies that claim. Poetry weakens the respect for right in the very act of teaching right. The poets present with sympathy and force the powers in man which make man act against right and against propriety. Appealing to the claim raised by Aristophanes, Plato demands that the poets be teachers of justice pure and simple, that they not give their audience any relief, so to speak, from this salutary teaching. Poets must be nothing but the severe and austere servants of justice. Plato turns the tables on Aristophanes; he draws all the conclusions from Aristophanes' indictment of Euripides in the *Frogs* and turns them against Aristophanes. Especially convincing, or amusing, is the critique of comedy as such in the name of the polis, a critique which occupies the center of the respective discussions. The imitation of men who ridicule one another and use foul language against one another, whether they are sober or drunk, is not to be permitted in the just city. The levity fostered by comedy is bound to counteract any lessons of justice which the comedy may otherwise convey. All the devices of comedy—slander, obscenity, blasphemy, and parody—are explicitly or implicitly rejected by Plato.

In spite or because of all this, no doubt is left as to the necessity of poetry. Yet there is likewise no doubt left, and in fact it is explicitly stated, that the permitted poetry is rather austere and therefore less delightful than the best excluded poetry. We are expected to abandon something of great worth for the sake of justice. What we shall miss is most clearly stated in the discussion of the Homeric verse in which Achilles expresses his contempt for his chief, the king Agamemnon. Hearing such insults of rulers by subjects, Socrates says, "is not conducive to obedience at any rate" (390a). And he adds, "if it yields some other pleasure, this would in no way be surprising." Now what that other pleasure is appears from a brief consideration of the verse in question, which reads, "You drunkard, who possess the eyes of a dog and the heart of a deer" (*Iliad* 1.225). The pleasure we derive from hearing this verse is twofold. In the first place it is a most perfect insult which can be hurled against a king or a captain. He has the heart of a deer; he thinks only of flight. But a deer is a noble, graceful animal; therefore he is compared to a dog, to the eyes of a dog, to an ignoble, slavish, crawling expression. But a dog can attack and fight back; therefore he is compared to a deer, which can only run away, and so on. It is a perfect circle. Secondly, it is an insult hurled by a noble subject against an unworthy king. It expresses a noble feeling, the feeling of indignation, about the rule of unworthy men, about the oppression of born rulers by merely factual rulers. Socrates understandingly deplores that we should have to miss such gems. We shall have to miss, above all, all tragedy and comedy, for, says Socrates, in the best city each man must dedicate himself entirely to one job, and the dramatic poet must imitate and hence, in a sense, be many different kinds of people. In particular no one must and can be both a comic and a tragic poet (395a). This latter point is suggested by the same Socrates who, when he speaks, not to the puritan Adeimantus, but to a comic and a tragic poet, compels them to admit that the good comic poet is also a good tragic poet, and vice versa (*Symposium* 223d). It is suggested by the same Socrates who demands that in the just city one kind of man, the highest kind according to him, must have two jobs, that of the philosopher and that of the administrator, and who demands of all other men that they perform a single job, or mind their own business, but urges the comic poets "not to mind their business, but to be serious" (452c). We are therefore not surprised to see that Socrates leaves an opening for another discussion, for a completely different discussion, of poetry by saying, "We must obey our present argument until someone persuades us by another, more beautiful, argument" (388e). The necessity for such a reopening of the discussion appears from the simple consideration that one cannot teach control of the passions if one does not know the passions, and one cannot convince other people of one's knowing the passions unless one is able to present, to imitate, to express, the passions. In accordance with this, Plato himself imitates the passions; even the meanest capacities can see this in the case of Plato's presentation of Thrasymachus' anger in the first book of the *Republic*. Plato's deed contradicts his speech, or, rather, it contradicts the speech of his Socrates, or, to be still more precise, it contradicts the speech of Plato's Adeimantus. We are then in need of another argument, a more beautiful argument, regarding poetry.

The first step in that argument is dictated by the most obvious flaw of the first argument, of the first round, as it were, in the contest between Plato and the poets. In the first argument we were not told what poetry is. The crucial question "what is" was not even raised regarding poetry. Poetry came to sight as the making of myths, or untrue tales about gods, demons, heroes, and the things in Hades. As such, poetry was subjected to political control, to pruning in the name of justice or morality. Henceforth poetry must tell edifying stories rather than charming stories. But in the course of the argument it became unclear whether the canons with which poetry must comply in presenting the gods and the things in Hades consist of untrue or of true opinions about the gods and the things in Hades. One cannot leave it, then, at considering poetry from the point of view of the city, or of morality. The ultimate judgment on morality will depend on how poetry is related to truth.

The first discussion of poetry takes place at the earliest possible moment in the founding of the best city. The second, and in a sense final, discussion of poetry takes place after the completion of the political part of the *Republic*. For the political part of the *Republic* is not concluded, as some people seem to think, somewhere in the fifth book when the subject of philosophy comes to the fore. The discussion of philosophy in the *Republic* is a part of the political argument. Philosophy is introduced in the *Republic* as a mere means for establishing the good city. Hence Aristotle, the most competent interpreter of Plato that ever was, does not even refer to the rule of the philosophers in his summary and criticism of the *Republic*. The political part of the *Republic* ends at the end of the ninth book. At that place it has become perfectly clear that the best city as described before is not only impossible but, in a sense, even irrelevant. "It makes no difference," Socrates says there, whether the best city, or justice presented in speech, "exists, or will exist," on earth or in heaven, for it is certain that it can exist within the soul of the individual (592b).

The great question which must still be settled concerns the possible rewards for justice and punishments for injustice, either during life or after death. The final discussion of poetry introduces the discussion of the rewards for justice and the punishments for injustice. At the beginning of the final discussion of poetry Socrates says that the necessity of rejecting especially dramatic poetry has in the meantime become so much clearer, for in the meantime the difference between the various kinds or forms of the soul has been brought out. By this he does not merely mean the exposition regarding the tripartite division of the soul into the reasoning, the spirited, and the desiring part. He means also, and above all, the various forms of badness of the soul, the timocratic, oligarchic, democratic, and tyrannical forms which have been discussed in the eighth and ninth books. Only after the philosophic analysis of both goodness and badness of the soul has been completed can the final discussion of poetry take place. For poetry is as concerned with the goodness and badness of the soul as is philosophy. Only now, in the second and final discussion of poetry, does Socrates raise the question "what is" regarding poetry, or, more precisely, regarding imitation. Imitation, we learn, is the production of appearances which look like the original but are not the original. For example, a painted bed is not a bed in which one can sleep, like the bed made by the carpenter. Yet even the bed made by the carpenter is not the true bed. The true bed is the idea of the bed, the model with a view to which the carpenter makes visible and tangible beds. There are, then, three beds, the true bed, i.e., the bed in nature, which is made by God; the visible bed made by the carpenter; and the painted bed made by the painter. The painter does not reproduce the true proportions of the bed; he produces the bed as it appears perspectively. He imitates not the visible bed but the phantasm of the bed. Imitation is then the reproduction of something which is at the third remove from nature or truth. It is the imitation of a phantasm of something which in its turn is modelled after the truth, or in imitation of the truth. Now in order to imitate the phantasm, the mere appearance, one does not have to know the original, the thing itself, truth. The poet, for example, who presents a general does not know the general in his generalship. He does not possess the art of the general.

Up to this point the poet is compared by Socrates to other makers or producers. Hence the relation of the poet to the philosopher remains obscure. Socrates replaces therefore the triad of makers—God, carpenter, painter—by the triad: user of the bed, carpenter, painter; and he contends, generalizing from this, that the only one who possesses genuine knowledge, that is to say, the only one who can judge things from the point of view of goodness, is a user, the man who does not make or produce at all. Hence, we conclude, poetry is at the third remove not only from the truth but from philosophy as well. The common craftsmen are superior in wisdom and understanding to the poets (similarly, in *Phaedrus* 248d–e, even the lovers of bodily toil or of gymnastic training are ranked superior to the poets).

What does this extreme and absurd description and denigration of poetry signify? It cannot be simply absurd, for the men who listen to Socrates or answer his somewhat leading questions are as intelligent as I or most of you, and not one of them protests. Philosophy, it appears, is concerned with nature, that is to say, with the forms, or the ideas. Poetry, however, is said to imitate artifacts. Even the ideas are here presented as artifacts. The very summit and cause of the world of poetry, the ideas, consists of artifacts. For the poets do not possess knowledge of the nature of things. They imitate only opinions. They imitate opinions especially regarding virtue, or they imitate phantasms of virtue, and therefore also opinions about and phantasms of the divine. They imitate the human things as they appear in the light of opinion, of authoritative opinion. Or, to use a Platonic image, poetry lives in the world of artificiality because it belongs entirely to the cave, to the city. Poetry praises and blames what the city, what society, praises or blames. The city praises and blames what it has been taught to praise and blame by its legislator or founder. The legislator lays down the moral order of the city by looking at the idea of justice, just as a carpenter makes a bed by looking with his mind's eye at the model of a bed. The poet remains within the boundaries drawn by the legislator. He therefore imitates the legislator, who in his turn imitates in some way or another the idea of justice.

Nietzsche has perhaps unwittingly given a perfect interpretation of what Plato conveys. The artists, Nietzsche says, have at all times been the valets of a morality or a religion (*The Gay Science*, no. 1). But, as Nietzsche knew, for a valet there is no hero. If the poets are the valets of a morality, they are in the best position to know the defects which their master conceals in public and in daytime. The poets, that is to say, the decent ones among them, come indeed to sight as valets of the morality to which they are subject. In truth, however, they are the severest critics of any established morality or any established order. When Plato criticizes (in the tenth book of the *Republic*) the poets as imitators of imitators, he criticizes the poets as he had constituted them, as he himself had made them in his first critique of poetry in the second and third books of the *Republic*. For there he had subjected the poets to the city and its order against the nature of poetry. After he has completed the political part of the *Republic*, he takes away the last remaining part of the scaffolding by letting us divine the nature of poetry.

This interpretation of the teaching of the *Republic* regarding poetry is confirmed by the teaching conveyed through Plato's *Laws*. In the thematic discussion of poetry in the second book of the *Republic* it is made clear that poetry is necessarily subject to political or moral control. The legislator must persuade or compel the poets to present only good men, to teach that only the good are happy and only the bad are miserable. But in the *Laws*, where an old Athenian tries to convince an old Spartan and an old Cretan of the desirable character of wine-drinking, it is made clearer than in the *Republic* that morality is not the only criterion with which poetry must comply. There are standards of poetic excellence which must also be considered. Grace or pleasure in their way are as important as morality, and of this element the poets themselves are the best judges. That is to say, Plato did not favor ill-written pious tracts. The relation between legislator and poet is entirely reversed, however, in a later discussion in the *Laws*, in the fourth book, where the problem of legislation in the strict and narrow sense comes to the fore. The first question here is, how should the legislator state his laws? Should he state them simply as mere commands, relying entirely on compulsion and force, or should he state the laws doubly, that is to say, both as mere commands and justifying them by a proem or a prelude which persuades men of the wisdom of the laws? The double statement is much to be preferred. Yet this doubleness or duplicity is not sufficient, for the audience to be persuaded is not homogeneous or uniform. Very roughly, every audience consists of an intelligent and an unintelligent part. The prelude to the law must therefore fulfill a dual function. It must persuade the intelligent on the one hand and the unintelligent on the other. Yet intelligent people are sometimes persuaded by different arguments from those that persuade unintelligent people, and the difference may very well go so far as to become a contradiction. The author of a prelude must then be a man of great versatility and flexibility. He must be a man who has learned to speak differently to different kinds of people, and who shows his competence in this respect by his ability to make different kinds of people speak differently. This man cannot be the legislator as legislator, for the province of the legislator is simple and unambiguous speech, saying the same thing to all.

Who then is the man who can write the proper prelude? Plato introduces the discussion of preludes by making his spokesman address the legislator "on behalf of the poets" (*Laws* 719b). He refers first to the ancient myth according to which the poets speak through inspiration and hence do not know what they say. But then he goes on to say that the irrationality of the poet consists, not in his ignorance of what he says, but in self-contradiction. Since the poet imitates human beings, he creates characters of contradictory moods who contradict one another, and in this way—in *this* way—he contradicts himself without knowing which of the contradictory statements is true and which is false. The philosopher goes on to identify himself with the poet. In other words, the poet does not truly contradict himself. He speaks ambiguously by impersonating contradictory characters, so that one cannot know which, if any, of the characters through which he speaks comes closest to what he thinks. The legislator on the other hand must speak unambigously and simply. But this is no easy matter. The legislator wishes, for example, that funerals be moderate, but what a moderate funeral is depends very much on the means of the people to be buried, whether they are rich or poor or of moderate means. Each station has its peculiar dignity. No one appreciates that peculiar dignity better than the poet, who can praise with equal felicity the tomb of excessive grandeur, the simple tomb, and the modestly adorned tomb because the poet knows best and interprets best the moods of the rich, the poor, and the inbetween people. If the legislator wishes then to legislate intelligently for human things, he must understand the human things, and he is helped in acquiring that understanding by sitting at the feet of the poets, for the poets, we may add, understand the human things not only as they appear in the light of the law, or established morality, but as they are in themselves. The poet rather than the legislator knows men's souls. Since it is the poet who teaches the legislator, the poet is so far from being the valet of a theology or of a morality that he is rather the creator of them. According to Herodotus, Homer and Hesiod created what we would call Greek religion. Plato has expressed this thought as clearly as he could in his simile of the cave. The cave-dwellers, that is to say, we humans, see nothing other, that is to say, nothing higher, than shadows of artifacts, especially of reproductions of men and other living beings moving around on high. We do not see the human beings who make and carry these artifacts. But as is shown clearly by Plato's demand for the noble delusion, he himself is far from disapproving altogether of the poet's activity. In principle the poets do exactly the same thing as Plato himself.

The discussion of poetry in the *Laws* leads us to realize that according to Plato the poets possess genuine knowledge of the soul, and therefore that poetry is *psychologia kai psychagogia*, understanding of the soul and guiding of the soul, just like philosophy itself—more precisely, just like Platonic philosophy itself, for not every philosophy is psychology in the Platonic sense. The necessary although not sufficient condition for philosophy being psychology in the Platonic sense is that the soul is not regarded as derivative from body or as secondary in relation to the body. A materialistic philosophy is indeed radically different from poetry. It would need poetry, understanding of the life of the soul as we know it as human beings, only in the form of a dubious sentimental supplement. We see this clearly today when poetry appears as the only refuge from a psychology and a sociology which are unable to articulate human life in its fullness and depth because they are constitutionally ignorant of the differences between the noble and the base—for that psychology and that sociology are of materialistic origin. Platonic philosophy, on the other hand, which regards the soul as the primary phenomenon and the body as derivative, has the same subject matter as poetry. This cannot be literally true, of course, for philosophy is concerned with the whole, with all things, and not everything is soul, the soul of man. Philosophy is necessarily also concerned with that which is not soul, with body, and number, and the relation of the soul to these other things. But Plato characteristically entrusts the treatment of that other thing to the stranger Timaeus, who presents cosmology, a mathematical physics, as a likely tale. The core, or the *archē*, the initiating principle, of Platonic philosophy is the doctrine of the soul, and this core, or *archē*, is identical with the theme of poetry. Yet is it not obvious that even Platonic philosophy treats its subject in an entirely different manner than does poetry? The poet sets forth his vision of the soul; he does not try to prove that vision or to refute alternative visions. His organ is a vision with the mind's eye (*nous*), not reasoning (*logismos*). Therefore poetry expresses itself in poems—epic, dramatic, or lyric—whereas philosophy expresses itself in treatises. In the treatise proper names do not occur except accidentally. Treatises are "impersonal." They are not lifeless, but what lives in them, or what dies in them, what undergoes various kinds of fate in treatises, is not human beings but *logoi*, assertions with their accompanying reasoning. Plato refers frequently to this life and fate of the *logoi*, most clearly perhaps in the *Phaedo*, where Socrates expresses the fear that his *logoi*, let us say his assertions, might die, that is to say, prove to be refutable. Yet the primary theme of the *Phaedo* is not the death of Socrates' *logoi* but the death of Socrates himself. More generally stated, it is not true that Platonic philosophy expresses itself in the form of treatises. Platonic philosophy is incompatible with the form of the treatise. It expresses itself in the form of the dialogue, of a kind of drama, of imitation. Not only is the subject matter of poetry the same as that of the fundamental part of Platonic philosophy, but likewise the treatment is fundamentally of the same character in both cases. Neither the Platonic dialogue nor the poetic work is autonomous; both are ministerial, both serve to lead men to the understanding of the human soul.

But is this not a preposterous assertion? Did we not admit that the poet sets forth his vision of the human soul without supporting reasoning and without refuting alternative visions, whereas Plato does nothing, so to speak, except present his supporting reasoning and refute alternative visions? Homer's vision of the soul strikingly differs, so it seems, from Dante's, and both poets' visions strikingly differ again from Shakespeare's. The very question as to which vision is the most adequate cannot be raised, let alone answered, in the element of poetry. However, the reasoning is in Plato's dialogues integrated into the human drama. The reasoning is frequently, not to say always, faulty—deliberately faulty, as it should be within an imitation of human life. And on the other hand, with what right can one say that Shakespeare, Dante, and Homer were not able to support their visions of the human soul by reasoning? They did not set forth that reasoning, surely. Nor did Plato. Plato indicates that Homer's poems contain hidden, unexpressed thoughts (*Republic* 378d). These thoughts include Homer's reasoning. Furthermore, one might say that every human phenomenon has its two sides, a poetic and a nonpoetic side. For example, love has its poetic and its medical side. Philosophy alone will consider both. But this is obviously not true. Think of the way in which Goethe presented in *Faust* the two sides of love by contrasting Faust's and Mephistopheles' remarks on Faust's love for Gretchen. Poetry does justice to the two sides of life by splitting itself, as it were, into tragedy and comedy, and precisely Plato says that the true poet is both a tragic and a comic poet. Finally, philosophy is said to appeal only to our understanding, not to our passion, whereas poetry works primarily on our passion. This would be true if philosophy were entirely a science like mathematics. But philosophy in the Platonic sense is a solution, and in fact *the* solution, to *the* human problem, the problem of happiness. Philosophy is therefore not merely a teaching, but a way of life. Therefore the presentation of philosophy is meant to affect, and in fact affects, our whole being, just as poetry, and perhaps more than poetry. In the words of Plato, "We ourselves to the best of our power are the authors of the tragedy which is at once the fairest and the best" (*Laws* 817b).

Is there then no difference whatever between Platonic philosophy and poetry, or rather between the Platonic dialogue and other poetry? Other poetry, or what we ordinarily mean by poetry simply, does not imitate, Plato says in the tenth book of the *Republic*, the sensible and quiet or reposed character, but it prefers the multicolored and complicated characters which as such are more interesting and therefore the natural themes of poetry. The theme of poetry is not the simply good man or the good life. But is there a simply good man? Will the good man not feel grief at the loss of his son, for instance? Will he not be torn between his grief and his duty, and hence be twofold and not simple? Socrates says (604a), "When left alone I believe he will dare to utter many things which he would be ashamed of if another would hear them, and he will do many things which he would not consent to have another see him doing." That which the good man cannot help feeling, but which he conceals from others, is the major theme of poetry. Poetry expresses with adequacy and with propriety what the non-poet cannot express adequately and with propriety. Poetry legitimately brings to light what the law forbids bringing to light. Poetry alone gives us relief from our deepest suffering just as it deepens our happiness. Yet we must understand the expression "the good man" not only in the common sense but also and above all in the Platonic sense. Virtue is knowledge. The good man in the Platonic sense is the philosopher. It goes without saying that the philosopher is not an individual like myself, or like other professors of political philosophy or of philosophy *tout court* or *tout long*.

By saying that poetry does not present the good man and the good life, Plato means, then, that poetry does not present the philosopher—the thinker and the life of thought. I quote from the *Phaedrus* (247c): "The superheavenly place has not yet been praised and will never be properly praised by any of the poets here," that is to say, by any of the poets in the ordinary and narrow sense. But is not the poet too a thinker? And does not poetry present also the poet as poet, for example, Hesiod in his *Works and Days*, Dante, and Shakespeare in his *Tempest*, to say nothing of Aristophanes? Still, it is not essential to poetry that it should present the poet. And while Plato presents the life of thought in order to instill his readers with love of the life of thought, or to call them to the philosophic life, poetry does not present poetry in order to induce its hearers to become themselves poets. But be this as it may, poetry as poetry presents men inferior to the philosopher and ways of life inferior to the philosophic life. Poetry presents ways of life characterized by a fundamental choice which excludes philosophy as the solution to the human problem, the problem of happiness. For according to Plato as well as Aristotle, to the extent to which the human problem cannot be solved by political means it can be solved only by philosophy, by and through the philosophic way of life. Plato too presents men who are not good, or who are, then, bad, but he does this only to present all the more clearly the character of the good man, and this is his chief theme. Poetry, however, presents only human beings for whom the philosophic life is not a possibility. From Plato's point of view the life which is not philosophic is either obviously incapable of solving the human problem, or else it does solve the human problem in a wholly inadequate or absurd manner. In the first case it is the theme of tragedy. In the second case it is a theme of comedy. From here we may understand why it is according to nature that philosophy delegate to poetry a ministerial function, a function which philosophy itself cannot fulfill. Poetry presents human life as human life appears if it is not seen to be directed toward philosophy. Autonomous poetry presents nonphilosophic life as autonomous. Yet by articulating the cardinal problem of human life as it comes to sight within the nonphilosophic life, poetry prepares for the philosophic life. Poetry is legitimate only as ministerial to the Platonic dialogue, which in its turn is ministerial to the life of understanding. Autonomous poetry is blind in the decisive respect. It lives in the element of imagination and of passion, of passionate images, of passion expressing itself in images which arouse passion and yet modify passion. It ennobles passion and purifies passion. But autonomous poetry does not know the end for the sake of which the purification of passion is required.

Part III
The Dialogue between Reason and Revelation

8

On the *Euthyphron*

The subject matter of the *Euthyphron* is piety. For more than one reason, the *Euthyphron* does not tell us what Plato thought about piety. It certainly does not transmit to us his final or complete view of piety. Still, the work transmits to us an important part of Plato's analysis of piety. Thus, by studying the *Euthyphron* we shall not learn more than part of the truth, as Plato saw it, a partial truth, which is necessarily also a partial untruth. Yet we can be certain that we shall never find the truth about piety as Plato saw it, except after having understood and digested the half-truth that is presented to us not so much in the *Euthyphron* as through the *Euthyphron*. The half-truth presented to us through the *Euthyphron* does not belong to the common type of half-truth. The most common type of half-truth tells us the commonly accepted opinions. The half-truth presented through the *Euthyphron* is not a generally accepted half-truth. It is unpopular. Since it is unpopular, it is irritating. An irritating half-truth is in one respect superior to the popular half-truth. In order to arrive at the irritating half-truth we must make some effort. We must think. Now, it is most unsatisfactory if we are first forced to think and then receive no other reward than an irritating provisional result. Plato gives us two kinds of comfort: first, thinking itself may be said to be the most satisfying activity regardless of the character of the result. Secondly, if we should believe that the result is more important than the way to the result, Plato's moral character is the guarantee that the final result, or what he regarded as the complete account of piety, would be absolutely satisfactory and in no way irritating.

The *Euthyphron* is a conversation between Euthyphron and Socrates about piety. Three definitions of piety are suggested, and all three of them prove to be insufficient. Having arrived at the end of the dialogue, we are perplexed with regard to piety. We do not know what piety is. But does not everyone know what piety is? Piety consists in worshipping the ancestral gods according to ancestral customs. This may be true, but piety is supposed to be a virtue. It is supposed to be good. But is it truly good? Is worshipping gods according to ancestral custom good? The *Euthyphron* does not give us an answer. It would be more accurate to say that the discussion presented in the *Euthyphron* does not give us an answer. But the discussion presented in any Platonic dialogue is only part of the dialogue. The discussion, the speech, the *logos*, is one part; the other part is the *ergon*, the deeds, the action, what is happening in the dialogue, what the characters do or suffer in the dialogue. The *logos* may end in silence, and the action may reveal what the speech conceals. The conversation between Socrates and Euthyphron takes place after Socrates has been accused of impiety. The dialogue abounds with references to this fact, this action. It forces us, therefore, to wonder, Was Socrates pious? Did Socrates worship the ancestral gods according to ancestral custom? The *Euthyphron* then gives us a twofold presentation of piety: first, a discussion of what piety is; secondly, a presentation of the problem of Socrates' piety. These two subjects seem to belong to two entirely different orders. The question of what piety is, is philosophical. The question of whether Socrates was pious seems to belong to the realm of gossip rather than to that of philosophy. Yet while this is true in a sense, it misses the decisive point. For the philosophic question is whether piety in the sense defined is a virtue. But the man who has all the virtues to the degree to which a human being is capable of having all the virtues is the philosopher. Therefore, if the philosopher is pious, piety is a virtue. But Socrates is a representative of philosophy. Hence, if Socrates is pious, piety is a virtue. And if he is not pious, piety is not a virtue. Therefore, by answering the gossipy question of whether Socrates was pious, we answer the philosophic question regarding the essence of piety. Then let us see whether we can learn anything from the *Euthyphron* regarding Socrates' piety.

Socrates is accused of impiety; he is suspected of impiety. Now, Euthyphron, who is a soothsayer, is an expert in piety, and he is convinced that Socates is innocent. Euthyphron vouches for Socrates' piety. But Euthyphron does not know what piety is. Still, if we assume that piety consists in worshipping the ancestral gods according to ancestral customs, everyone could see whether Socrates was pious, whether Socrates did or did not worship the ancestral gods according to ancestral customs. Euthyphron, in spite of his philosophic incompetence, could be a good witness as regards the decisive fact. But the truth is that Euthyphron is not likely to pay much attention to what human beings do. Above all, Euthyphron's own piety is, to say the least, open to suspicion. Therefore, let us dismiss Euthyphron's testimony and see what we ourselves can observe.

We hear from Socrates' own mouth that, both prior to his accusation and after it, he regards it as important to know the divine things. Apparently in consequence of Socrates' quest for knowledge about the divine things, the accuser thought that Socrates was an innovator, that is to say, a producer of error. The accuser naturally thought that he himself knew the truth. He charged Socrates, in fact, with ignorance of the truth about the divine things. The charge presupposed that Socrates' alleged or real ignorance was careless, but that ignorance could not be criminal except if truth about the divine things was easily accessible to every Athenian citizen. This would indeed be the case if the truth about the divine things were handed down to everyone by ancestral custom. Was Socrates criminally ignorant of the divine things? He seems to grant that he is ignorant of the divine things. But he seems to excuse his ignorance by the difficulty of the subject matter. His ignorance is involuntary, and therefore not criminal. Now, if Socrates was ignorant of the divine things, he did not believe in what tradition or ancestral custom told him, as well as everyone else, about the divine things. He did not regard those tales as knowledge. As a matter of fact, he suggests that one ought not to assent to any assertion of any consequence before having examined it. He makes it rather clear that the ancestral reports about the ancestral gods are not more than bare assertions. If Socrates was really ignorant, radically ignorant, he did not even know whether the ancestral gods exist. How then could he worship the ancestral gods according to ancestral customs? If Socrates was really ignorant, and knew that he was really ignorant, he could not possibly be pious. Of course, he could still go through the motions of worship; he could outwardly conform. But this conformity would no longer be pious, for how can a sensible man worship beings whose very existence is doubtful? Socrates' outward conformity would not have been due to any fear of the gods, but only to being ashamed of what human beings might think of nonconformance, or to the fear of bad reputation. Fear of bad reputation is fear of reputation for badness. People who did not believe in the ancestral gods were thought to be simply bad men, men capable of every kind of wickedness, and this stigma attached especially to philosophers. In the circumstances, Socrates would seem to have been forced to conform outwardly, if not for his own sake, at any rate for the sake of philosophy. Still, if Socrates conformed outwardly, how could people know that he was not pious? They could know it from what he said. But did Socrates say everything he thought to every human being? He himself feared that he was believed to say profusely everything he knew to every real man, out of philanthrophy, and to say it not only without receiving pay, but even gladly paying money, if he had any, provided people would only listen to him. We have the impression that what the Athenians really resented was not so much his cleverness, or the deviationist character of his thought, as his alleged missionary zeal. His real crime, the crime that killed him, was then not so much his impiety as his apparent philanthropy, or what is called in the charge his "corrupting the young."

Hitherto, we have taken at its face value what Socrates said concerning his ignorance with regard to the divine things. But if we look again into the *Euthyphron* we find that Socrates is in fact not altogether ignorant in this respect. Towards the end of the conversation, he says that all good things which he has have been given by the gods. Earlier in the conversation he indicates that he loathes the current stories about the gods committing unjust actions or their having dissensions and fights with each other, and that he does not believe that these tales are true. He seems to believe he knows that the gods are both good and just and therefore both the givers of all good things, and only of good things, to man and incapable of fighting with each other. But precisely this knowledge would make him impious; for the current tales about the gods which he rejected were not merely the invention of good painters, but also the invention of good poets. It is much more important that they supplied the rationale of important elements of the ancestral worship. The fact that he did not accept the current tales about the fights among the gods would explain why he was accused of impiety. He himself suggests this explanation. But did he profusely say to every real man that these tales are untrue? Was he guilty of excessive philanthropy?

In his conversation with Euthyphron he does nothing of the kind. He does not go beyond indicating an unbelief in regard to these tales, or his being displeased with these tales. He says that he accepts the tales with some feeling of annoyance. In addition, he did not seek the conversation with Euthyphron. He did not approach Euthyphron with the intention of enlightening him. On the contrary, the conversation is forced upon him by Euthyphron. Without Euthyphron's initiative, Euthyphron might never have heard that one could or should doubt the current tales about the gods. Socrates does not show a trace of missionary zeal.

To this, one might make the following objection. In the second book of the *Republic*, Socrates develops his theology at great length. But, in the first place, the characters with whom Socrates talks in the *Republic*, and even the audience which is present, are a select group. Euthyphron does not belong to the same type of man. He belongs, firstly, to the majority of Athenians who condemned Socrates to death. And, secondly, in the *Republic* Socrates does not explicitly mention, as he does in the parallel in the *Euthyphron*, the fact that the wrong notions of the gods were, as it were, embodied in the official cult of the city of Athens. The outspoken criticism in the *Republic* is directed against the poets, who were private men, and not against ancestral custom.

I draw this provisional conclusion. Socrates was indeed impious in the sense of the charge. But he was not guilty of that excessive philanthropy of which he feared he might be thought to be guilty. I have said the conversation with Euthyphron was forced upon Socrates. Certainly Socrates did not seek that conversation. The reference to Socrates' favorite haunt at the beginning of the dialogue is most revealing. That reference reminds us of the openings of the *Charmides* and the *Lysis*, where Socrates himself describes how gladly he sought those places where he could converse with the young. Socrates does not gladly talk to Euthyphron. He talks to him because he cannot help it, out of duty, or because he thought it was just to do so. This conversation was an act of justice. Socrates shows by deed that he is just. Here the deed bears out the implicit testimony of Euthyphron. Whereas Socrates' impiety remains, to say the least, doubtful, his justice becomes perfectly evident.

But what is justice? According to Euthyphron, justice, in the strict sense, seems to be identical with skillfully tending human beings. By virtue of such skillful tending, or herding, human beings are benefited or become better. Whatever may have been the success of Socrates' skillfully tending Euthyphron, he is certainly depicted trying hard to make Euthyphron better by showing him, who believes himself to be extremely wise, that he is extremely stupid. By trying to make him somewhat reasonable, by thus acting justly, by trying to make people better, Socrates believes he acts prudently. For every sane man would want to live among good, and hence helpful, persons, rather than among bad, and hence harmful, persons. But just as a man who tries to appease vicious dogs might be bitten by them, or just as a father who takes away harmful toys from a child might provoke the child's anger, Socrates, in trying to better people, might have provoked their resentment and thus have come to grief. Was it then prudent of him even to attempt to better the Athenians? In spite of this difficulty, Socrates' attempt was rewarding to him and to his friends, and ultimately even to us. For in talking to people, however silly, he was learning, he was studying human nature. Without this study the Platonic dialogues could never have been written.

But let us come back to the main issue, Socrates' impiety. Socrates was impious because he knew, or believed he knew, that the ancestral reports about the ancestral gods which underlay ancestral custom are wrong. This knowledge is perfectly compatible with the possibility that Socrates was ignorant in regard to the divine things. He may have had sufficient knowledge of the divine things to know that the current tales about the gods are untrue, and therefore that the worship of the ancestral gods according to ancestral customs is not good, or, if you wish, that to worship the ancestral gods according to ancestral custom is not true piety. But he may not have had sufficient knowledge of the divine things to know what true piety positively is. In that case, he could not know whether he was truly pious or not. And assuming that other men are not likely to be wiser than Socrates, no man could know whether Socrates was pious or not. In that case one could say no more than that he ought not to have been punished for impiety. I personally believe that this would have been a wise decision. It is just possible that this is the most obvious message of the *Euthyphron:* that it would be wonderful if the crime of impiety could be wiped off the statue books. But from Plato's point of view that message could not express more than a pious wish, a wish that cannot be fulfilled.

Let us now turn to a somewhat more exact analysis of the *Euthyphron.* Let us first try to establish the place of the *Euthyphron* within the cosmos of the Platonic dialogues. The *Euthyphron* deals with piety, i.e., with one particular virtue. It belongs therefore together with the *Laches,* which deals with courage, with the *Charmides,* which deals with moderation, and with the *Republic,* which deals with justice. Now, there are four cardinal virtues—courage, moderation, justice, and wisdom. There is no Platonic dialogue devoted to wisdom (which, I add, is only true if you assume that the *Theages* is spurious, because the *Theages* is devoted to wisdom). Instead we have a Platonic dialogue on piety. Is then wisdom to be replaced by piety? The dialogue in which the four cardinal virtues are set forth most clearly is the *Republic*. In the *Republic* Socrates seems rather to replace piety by wisdom. When speaking of the nature of the philosopher, i.e., on the most exalted level of the discussion of morality in the *Republic*, Socrates does not even mention piety. In spite or because of this, there is no Platonic dialogue devoted to wisdom. Yet wisdom is a kind of science, and there is a dialogue devoted to science, the *Theaetetus*. Now, the *Euthyphron* and the *Theaetetus* belong together, not merely because they deal with particular virtues, but also because they are contemporaneous: the two conversations take place about the same time, after the accusation and before the condemnation. They belong to the end of Socrates' life. Accordingly, they contain explicit references by Socrates to his father and his mother, or, more precisely, to the skill of his father and the skill of his mother, or still more precisely, to the skill of his ancestor on his father's side and the skill of his mother. He compares his own skill to the skill of his mother. He denies that his own skill has any kinship with the skill of his ancestor on his father's side, with the skill of Daedalus. The relation of his own skill to the ancestral, to the paternal, remains doubtful. His attitude toward the ancestral or paternal remains doubtful.

The *Euthyphron* deals with piety, and it leaves open the question of what piety is. The *Theaetetus* deals with science, and it culminates therefore in a description of the philosophic life. That description in its turn culminates in the thesis that one must try to flee from here thither as quickly as possible; but that flight is assimilation to God as far as it is possible. And that assimilation consists in becoming just and pious, together with becoming prudent. Here in this most solemn and central passage (almost literally central), the question of whether piety is a virtue is answered in the affirmative. Yet this passage is not altogether free from ambiguity, as would appear from a consideration of the context. One cannot settle any Platonic question of any consequence by simply quoting Plato. This much about the place of the *Euthyphron* within the cosmos of the Platonic dialogues.

The aged Socrates is accused of impiety by young Meletus. Euthyphron takes Socrates' side against Meletus. But Euthyphron, the young Euthyphron, has accused his own aged father of impiety. Euthyphron's action parallels Meletus' action, the young man accusing the aged one. Euthyphron occupies a middle position between Socrates and Meletus. What kind of man is he? What kind of man is he who is the only interlocutor in Plato's only dialogue dealing with piety?

Euthyphron is well-disposed towards Socrates, and he is a boaster. He is a harmless boaster. There is a connection between his boasting and his harmlessness. What makes him side with Socrates? Socrates has a power of divination, the demonic thing that happened to him. And Euthyphron is a professional diviner. Both Euthyphron and Socrates are different. Both have superior gifts, superior gifts of the same kind. On account of this superiority, they are envied by the many. Euthyphron believes that he and Socrates are in the same boat.

Euthyphron is a diviner. He boasts that he has superior knowledge of divine things. Because he has such knowledge, he can predict the future in an infallible manner. Yet the people will laugh at him as at a madman. They do not take him seriously. They regard him as harmless. But he is so certain of his superiority that such ridicule does not affect him. He is proud to appear to be mad. For he knows somehow that the divine is bound to appear as madness to those who have at best only human wisdom. He speaks of himself and the gods in the same breath. He draws a line between himself and human beings. He is certain that only an expert in the divine things, a man like him, can be pious. By implication he denies the ordinary citizens the possibility of being pious. He has a great contempt for the many. He keeps the most marvelous part of his knowledge for himself, or for an elite. He conceals his wisdom. He does not conceal, however, his claim to wisdom. Therefore, he is sometimes driven to reveal his wisdom too. One does not know whether he conceals his wisdom voluntarily or because it does not find any takers. Being versed in the divine things, he despises the human things; hence, he knows next to nothing of human things. He seems to believe that all conflicts are conflicts about principles, about values. He does not seem to be aware that most conflicts presuppose agreement as to principles, that most conflicts arise from the fact that different men regard the same thing as good and want to have it each for himself. He seems to believe that men who are accused of a crime defend themselves by denying the principle that criminals ought to be punished, instead of by denying the fact that they committed the crime. Euthyphron is harmless, within the limits of his knowledge of divine things. If this knowledge should force him to harm human beings, he will not for a moment hesitate to do so. He would not hesitate for a moment to accuse of impiety even his father or mother, his brother or sister, his children, his wife, or his friends. He stands in striking contrast to Socrates, who would not accuse anyone of anything. At the beginning of the conversation Euthyphron believes that he is in the same boat as Socrates. Socrates draws his attention to the fact that whereas Euthyphron is ridiculed on account of his superior gift, Socrates is persecuted on account of his. Socrates suggests, as an explanation of this difference, that Euthyphron conceals his wisdom and therefore is safe, whereas Socrates is thought to broadcast his wisdom and therefore is in danger. At this point there does not seem to be another difference between Socrates and Euthyphron than that Euthyphron is more reticent than Socrates.

After Euthyphron has proudly told the surprised Socrates of his feat, which consists in accusing his own father of impiety, and Socrates has indicated a doubt in regard to the wisdom of this act, Euthyphron might seem to become aware that he is wiser than Socrates. Whereupon, Socrates suggests that he wishes to become a pupil of Euthyphron, who claims to know everything about the divine things, in order thus to bring about his acquittal of the charge of impiety. He suggests more particularly that he would like to use Euthyphron as a lightning protector against Meletus' bolts. He wishes to hide behind Euthyphron's back and his well-concealed wisdom. He draws Euthyphron's attention to the fact that by teaching Socrates Euthyphron is going to leave the sheltered position which Euthyphron enjoyed hitherto. All this does not make any impression on Euthyphron. All this does not make him realize that he is not in the same boat as Socrates, or that a gulf separates him from Socrates. He becomes aware of this gulf only after Socrates has indicated his doubt of the truth of the current tales about the gods. For after this he (however unwittingly) puts Socrates into the same category as the many. From that point on he knows that Socrates is not in the same boat as himself. Yet he still apparently regards Socrates, in contradistinction to the many, as educable, i.e., as willing to listen to Euthyphron's wisdom. Socrates, however, disappoints his expectations. Very curiously, Socrates is chiefly interested in less worthy, less divine, and, in fact, trivial subjects. He is much more interested in the definition of piety than in wondrous stories about what the gods did or what they demand of man. Socrates seems to have a desire for a kind of knowledge which Euthyphron does not regard very highly. He condescends, however, to gratify this desire.

In the sequel it dawns upon Euthyphron that he might lose his lawsuit, which, after all, he would have to win on earth before a human jury, before a jury consisting of the many, but Euthyphron pays too little attention to human things to be upset by that prospect. On the contrary, Socrates' strange familiarity with human things, and with the manner in which the low conduct their low affairs, has convinced Euthyphron that Socrates belongs with the many, not only for the time being but altogether; that Socrates is not educable, that his unwillingness to listen to Euthyphron's wisdom is due to his incapacity to understand that wisdom. Socrates, in a word, is a worldling. Somewhat later, Socrates succeeds in bringing it home to Euthyphron that he grossly contradicts himself. Although he knows that self-contradiction is a bad thing, and although he appeals to the principle of self-contradiction when arguing against others, Euthyphron is in no way perplexed by the weakness of his own speech. In fact, he would seem to have expected something like it. His self-contradiction merely proves to him that he cannot say or express to Socrates what he thinks or has an awareness of. How indeed can one express experiences like those of which Euthyphron can boast to someone who has never tasted the divine things? Is one not bound to contradict oneself when trying to communicate the incommunicable? Still later, Euthyphron almost openly refuses to tell Socrates the true secrets regarding the divine things, although Socrates urges him to do so. He suggests that Socrates must rest satisfied with the simple verities which even the vulgar know sufficiently. Socrates' strange remark regarding these simple verities—they concern sacrifices and prayers—apparently reveals to Euthyphron an abyss of ignorance in Socrates. When Socrates asks Euthyphron shortly before the end of the conversation not to regard him as unworthy, he is quite serious to the extent that he is convinced that Euthyphron does regard him as unworthy. The conversation comes to an end because Euthyphron gives it up as hopeless, and he gives up the conversation as hopeless because he has learned in the course of the conversation that Socrates is a hopeless case. Euthyphron is immune to Socrates' conversational skill. He suffers as little change during the conversation as Socrates himself. He learns in his own way something about Socrates, just as Socrates learns in his way something about Euthyphron. This is all. In a sense, then, he is really in the same boat as Socrates. For the singularity which we have mentioned amounts to a fundamental similarity. Euthyphron is a caricature of Socrates. Just as Socrates, Euthyphron transcends the dimension of the ordinary arts and virtues. But whereas Socrates goes over from the ordinary arts and virtues to philosophy, Euthyphron goes over from them to a spurious kind of knowledge of the divine things. Euthyphron, as it were, replaces philosophy by a spurious kind of knowledge of the divine things. Although Euthyphron believes himself to be superior to both Meletus and Socrates, he in fact occupies a middle position between Meletus and Socrates. We must now try to define that middle position.

Meletus accused Socrates of not believing in the gods in which the city believes. Meletus identifies himself with the belief of the city. Meletus calls Socrates before the tribunal of the city. Meletus identifies himself with what we may call the orthodox view. What the orthodox position is will become somewhat clearer after we have clarified Euthyphron's deviation. Euthyphron himself knows that he is different, that he deviates from what "the human beings" regard as pious. What does he understand by piety? In his first answer to Socrates' question as to what the pious is, he gives a formally defective answer. He gives an example instead of a definition. His second answer is formally adequate, and so is his third and last answer. But neither the second nor the third answer expresses that view of piety which underlies the formally defective first answer. Only the first answer has a direct relation to Euthyphron's taste, to his action, to his accusation of his father. Only the first answer is a speech of Euthyphron in harmony with Euthyphron's deed, with his life, with the principle animating his life. It is therefore the only answer given by Euthyphron which throws a light on that view of piety which is characteristic of him. Plato has killed three birds by making Euthyphron express his true piety in a formally defective answer. In the first place, he thus characterizes Euthyphron as insufficiently trained. Secondly, he thus lets us see that Euthyphron never made fully clear to himself the full meaning of his deviation from the orthodox or accepted view. And thirdly, he thus prevented a real discussion of the real issue. No solution to the problem of piety can be given in the circumstances, and no solution to the problem of piety shall be given lest the reader be prevented from seeking the solution for himself. What then would be a formally adequate expression of that view of piety which Euthyphron indicates in his first and formally defective answer?

We shall say: piety consists in doing what the gods do. And we shall contrast this view with the orthodox view, according to which piety consists in doing what the gods tell us to do. For to worship the ancestral gods according to ancestral customs means, since the custom must ultimately be conceived of as divinely instituted, to do what the gods tell us to do. Euthyphron expresses his view of piety by deed, rather than by speech. Contrary to ancestral custom, he accuses his father of impiety. Yet piety is said to consist in worshipping the ancestral gods according to ancestral custom. His deed amounts to a denial of the accepted view. His deed expresses the view that piety consists in doing what the gods do. Euthyphron's view of piety is heretical. Or, to use a more up-to-date term, it is deviationist. This can be easily seen from the following considerations. According to the orthodox view, piety consists chiefly, not to say exclusively, in praying and sacrificing. But the gods do not pray and sacrifice. By imitating the gods or the actions of the gods, by doing what the gods do, one will not pray or sacrifice. The gods are not pious. By imitating the gods, one ceases to be pious. A more adequate formulation of Euthyphron's view would therefore be that what pleases the gods is men's doing what the gods do, and therefore that what pleases the gods is something entirely different from the pious. But Euthyphron shrinks from admitting to himself this implication of his view. In his second answer, he identifies the pious with what is pleasing to the gods. Yet Socrates shows him that what he really means is that the pious and what is pleasing to the gods are altogether different things. It is true Socrates shows this to Euthyphron in a somewhat different manner than I just indicated, but we shall gradually see that Socrates' explicit argument is only the apparently simplified but in fact the immensely telescoped formulation of his implicit argument. Euthyphron holds, then, the view that piety consists in doing what the gods do. How does he know what the gods do? From what the human beings believe about the gods: from what the human beings agree upon in regard to the gods, from the current tales about the gods which he takes to be true. But those current tales also say that men ought not to do what the gods do, but rather what the gods tell men to do. Euthyphron's position is therefore untenable. The authority to which he appeals refutes him. He ought to return to orthodoxy.

But can one return to orthodoxy? Can one accept a position which is based on mere tales? Yet, if we abandon the tales, what can we say about the gods and about piety? Still, we divine that the gods are superhuman beings, and therefore that the highest human type gives us an inkling of what the gods might be. But the highest human type is the wise man. The analogy of the wise man will therefore be the best clue at our disposal in regard to the gods. Now, the wise man loves more the people who do what he does than those people who merely do what he tells them to do and do not do what he does. Accordingly, we may then be inclined to think, considering that we understand by "gods" superhuman beings, that the gods do not rule at all by telling people what they should do, or by issuing commands. However this may be, the analogy of the wise man, which is our only guide to knowledge of the gods, or of what would please the gods, leads us to realize that Euthyphron's view of piety is a halfhearted attempt to transcend the orthodox view of piety in the direction of a higher view. Euthyphron does occupy a middle position between Meletus and Socrates. It is impossible to return to Meletus. We have no choice but to go forward to Socrates.

The direction of the road and even the end of the road is indicated by Euthyphron's halfway position and by the difficulty with which it is beset. Yet Euthyphron's view is superior to the orthodox view, and Euthyphron knows it. His boasting is not altogether unfounded. Euthyphron transcends the orthodox view because he has aspired to something higher than is visualized by the many. Yet he has no right to this observation. He really is a boaster. Euthyphron contradicts himself by saying that what pleases the gods is the pious and by meaning that what pleases the gods is not the pious. To solve the contradiction, one must leave it at simply denying the identity of what pleases the gods and the pious. One must have the courage of holding the view that one cannot please the gods except by being impious in the sense in which the city understands impiety. Or, more precisely, one must have the courage to be impious in a certain manner. In what manner? Euthyphron had meant that it is pleasing to the gods if men do what the gods do. But the different gods do different and even opposite things. By pleasing one god, one will displease the other. It is impossible to please the gods if the different gods are pleased by different things, if the different gods disagree with each other, if they fight with each other. Euthyphron admits this in a way. He is doing what the best and justest god, Zeus, does. He chooses the justest god out of the many gods for his model. But in order to make this choice, he must know justice. He must know what justice is. He must know the idea of justice. For the justest god is the god that imitates the idea of justice most perfectly. But if one knows the idea of justice, there is no reason why one must imitate the most perfect imitation of the idea of justice. Why not imitate the idea of justice itself? There is no reason for imitating any god. Imitating the gods, doing what the gods do because the gods do it, and hence piety, proves to be superfluous. We must go a step further and say there is no need for any gods. If we doubt the current tales about the gods, if we try to think for ourselves, we are led to the conclusion that what general opinion assigns to the gods actually belongs to the ideas. The ideas replace the gods. From here we can understand and judge Meletus' charge.

Meletus is right to this extent. Socrates really does not believe in the gods of the city. And he really introduces different beings. But Meletus is wrong in assuming that the different beings which Socrates introduces are gods or demonic things. In fact they are the ideas. If we want to speak of gods, we would have to say that the different gods which Socrates introduced are the ideas. One can also say that Meletus erred grossly in speaking of Socrates' introducing novel things. For the ideas, being prior to any beings which imitate the ideas, are prior to any gods. They are the first things, the oldest things. Following a clue given by Euthyphron, Socrates formulates Meletus' charge as follows: Socrates is accused of making gods (the Greek, *poiein*, "inventing"). Socrates' defense can be stated as follows. Socrates is the only one who recognizes as first things such beings as can in no sense be conceived of as having been made and as making other things. His view is the radically unpoetic view, poetic in the sense of "making." His accuser was a poet. If one were to deny that the first things are the ideas, one would be forced to say that the first things are the gods, and that the gods made the ideas (tenth book of the *Republic*). One would be forced to conceive of the first things as making or productive beings. The alternative suggested by the Euthyphron is so extreme that one would be very glad if it could be avoided. How can it be avoided? Let us return to the point where Euthyphron unwittingly left the right way.

Euthyphron had denied that doing what the gods do is superior to doing what the gods tell or command us to do. But he became perplexed when he realized that the different gods do different things, opposite things. He was forced to choose among the gods, and therefore he had to appeal to a principle of choice or preference. That principle proved to be the idea of justice, i.e., something which is superior to the gods. But is there no way of choosing among the conflicting gods without having recourse to the ideas, without undermining piety? Indeed there is. From the point of view of ancestral custom, the good is identical with the ancestral, with the old. The best gods will be therefore the oldest gods. In order to find out what the oldest god is, we do not have to refer to any ideas. We simply have to consult the records of the past. If we accept the current stories as such records, we learn that the oldest god is Uranos, the grandfather of Zeus. The only possible way of being pious in the sense of doing what the gods do, the only way of being safely pious along Euthyphron's lines, is to do what Uranos did, or to imitate Uranos. But what did Uranos do? He hurt or damaged his children. He damaged the young. In Greek the saying is, he corrupted the young. That is to say, precisely by corrupting the young would Socrates be pious. Or the other way around, the pious Socrates chooses the only pious way, picking the oldest god as his model, and therefore corrupts the young. Yet Uranos is not only a personal god, he is also heaven. And we know from other personal dialogues that virtue can be identified with imitating heaven. Meletus, on the other hand, who accuses the aged Socrates, and more particularly Euthyphron, who tries to destroy his own aged father, both imitate Zeus, a relatively young god. They are impious. In addition they are inconsistent, for Zeus did not respect the old gods. Hence not Meletus and Euthyphron, who respect the old gods, but Socrates, who does not respect the old gods, imitates Zeus. Socrates seems to be pious from every point of view except that of simple orthodoxy.

One may say that these are jokes. These statements are certainly exposed to quite a few difficulties, one of them being that while Uranos may be said to be the oldest god, he certainly is not the oldest divinity. Certainly Mother Earth is older than Uranos. And Socrates would probably not admit that a man's virtue is incompatible with imitating a female god or a female being in general. Was not his own skill a woman's skill? Let us therefore repeat our question: can we not avoid the alternative, either the ideas or the gods? In other words, why is it necessary to assert the primacy of the ideas? The *Euthyphron* suggests an alternative. Either the highest beings are fighting gods, or else the highest beings are ideas. If one denies the primacy of the ideas, one arrives at the belief in fighting gods. Why? Why do the gods fight? Ultimately, because they do not know. But knowledge, genuine knowledge, is the knowledge of the unchangeable, of the necessary, of intelligible necessity, of the ideas. That of which knowledge is knowledge, is prior. The ideas are prior to knowledge of the ideas. There cannot be knowledge if there is no primacy of the ideas. Therefore if one denies the primacy of the ideas, one denies the possibility of knowledge. If the ideas are not the primary beings, the primary beings or the first things cannot be knowing beings. Their action must be blind. They will collide; they will fight. In other words, if the primary beings are the gods, and not the ideas, whatever is good or just will be good or just because the gods love it, and for no other reason, for no intrinsic reason. The primary act is not knowledge or understanding but love without knowledge or understanding, i.e., blind desire. But is this alternative not overcome in monotheism? It is impossible to decide this question on the basis of the *Euthyphron*, in which I believe the singular "God" never occurs. Still the *Euthyphron* seems to suggest that even the oldest god must be conceived of as subject to the ideas. It is true that if there is only one God, there is no difficulty in thinking that piety consists in imitating God. One must know that God is good or just or wise, i.e., that God complies with the rules of justice. If that rule were subject to God, or dependent on God, or made by God, if it could be changed by God, it could no longer serve as a standard. God must be thought to be subject to a necessity, an intelligible necessity, which he did not make. If we deny this, if we assume that God is above intelligible necessity, or not bound by intelligible necessity, he cannot know in the strict sense, for knowledge is knowledge of the intelligible and unalterable necessity. In that case, God's actions would be altogether arbitrary. Nothing would be impossible to him. For example, he could create other gods, and the many gods, who, of course, cannot have knowledge, would fight.

If piety is superfluous, if the gods are superfluous, why then do almost all men believe that piety is necessary and that the gods are necessary? Why do men need gods? The answer to this question is suggested in the discussion of the third definition of piety. According to that definition, piety consists in tending the gods. More precisely, piety consists in a kind of tending of the gods which is similar to that which slaves practice towards their masters, in prostrating oneself and doing the master's bidding. Piety is a kind of serving. Socrates interprets it as follows. Piety is an art of serving, a serving art, a ministering art. As such it necessarily serves a ruling or architectonic art. Piety presupposes then that the gods are practitioners of the ruling art. But every art is productive of something. What then does the gods' ruling art produce—while using human arts as its ministerial arts? Euthyphron merely answers, the gods produce many fine things. He refuses to explain to an uninitiated man like Socrates what these many fine things are. And there can be no doubt that the many fine things which Euthyphron has in mind would not have satisfied Socrates, but Socrates also says in the context that by answering the question as to what the products of the gods' ruling arts are, one would have reached an adequate understanding of piety. The examples which Socrates gives in the immediate context make it clear what he regards as the specific product of the art of the gods. Socrates uses generalship and farming as examples of the ministering art. The fine things which men try to acquire and produce by generalship and farming are victory and good harvest. Yet generalship and farming are not enough for producing victory and good harvest. For these arts cannot guarantee the outcome, and the outcome is, in these arts, the only thing that matters. Whether the outcome of the use of generalship and of farming be good or bad depends upon chance. Chance is that which is in no way controllable by art or knowledge, or predictable by art or knowledge. But too much depends on chance for man to be resigned to the power of chance. Man makes the irrational attempt to control the uncontrollable, to control chance. Yet he knows that he cannot control chance. It is for this reason that he needs the gods. The gods are meant to do for him what he cannot do for himself. The gods are the engine by which man believes he can control chance. He serves the gods in order to be the employer of gods, or the lord of gods.

Yet there is one particular art, the most architectonic of all human arts, whose outcome particularly depends on chance and which absolutely requires gods or piety as its complement. This is the legislative art. The legislative art is concerned with the just, the noble, and the good, i.e., with objects regarding which genuine knowledge is much more difficult than regarding numbers, measures, and weights. The legislative art is therefore the natural domain of disagreement. The primary object of the legislative art is the just. And it is as a part of justice that piety is defined in the third and last definition. Piety is justice towards the gods, just as justice in the narrower sense is justice towards men. Justice towards men is good. We have already seen that. What is doubtful is the status of piety, or justice towards the gods. It would seem that the need for piety can best be understood from the deficiency or the limitation of justice towards men. Now, the most serious deficiency of justice towards men is that it does not have sufficient sanction in the eyes of irrational people. It is this sanction that is supplied by piety and by the gods. But in order to fulfill this function, piety must be in the service of justice in the narrower sense. Justice in the narrower sense is primarily law-abidingness, or obedience to the law. Piety therefore must be a part of justice in this

sense, that it must be a part of obedience to law. But law is primarily ancestral custom. Therefore piety stands or falls by obedience
to ancestral custom. It is here that Socrates agrees with orthodoxy
over against the heretic, Euthyphron. Euthyphron disobeys ancestral custom by accusing his own father of impiety. Socrates shows
Euthyphron *ad hominem* that he has no right to disobey ancestral
custom. Now, no wonder that he appears to Euthyphron as one of
the people, as a vulgar man. We may say that both the orthodox
and Socrates have common sense, whereas Euthyphron lacks common sense. By this I mean that a society is possible on both orthodox and Socratic principles, whereas a society is not possible on
Euthyphron's principles. For society is not possible if ancestral custom is not regarded as sacred as far as practice is concerned. It is
for this reason that Plato insisted on the necessity of laws punish-
ing impiety. Liberals like ourselves are tempted to argue against
Plato upon the basis of Plato's own testimony. Does not Plato show
us that in the eyes of all men of common sense, of both the many
and of Socrates, Euthyphron is a ridiculous human being? And is
not the ridiculous a harmless deficiency? Why then not tolerate
Euthyphron? But I hasten back to the dialogue.

The *Euthyphron* is a very paradoxical dialogue. So indeed is
every Platonic dialogue. The specific paradox of the *Euthyphron*
consists in this. The normal procedure in a Platonic dialogue of the
type to which the *Euthyphron* belongs is that the interlocutor first
gives a definition which expresses the most common view on the
subject under discussion and then gradually is led to a higher
view. But the first definition suggested in the *Euthyphron* is in the
decisive respect superior to the last definition, which merely formulates the popular view of piety, meaning, piety consists in sacrifice and prayer. More generally expressed, whereas the normal
procedure in the Platonic dialogues is ascent from the lower to the
higher, the procedure followed in the *Euthyphron* is descent from
the higher to the lower. One can explain this paradox in two different ways. In the first place, Euthyphron the heretic must be
brought back to where he belongs, namely, to orthodoxy or to conformity. In the second place, the *Euthyphron* is an unusually radical
dialogue. It suggests the most uncompromising formulation of the
problem of piety. Therefore, the structure of this dialogue has this
character: *A*, exposition of the truth; *B*, explanation of the basic
error. Shortly before the end of the dialogue, Socrates compares
Euthyphron to Proteus. Proteus was a wily sea-god who could
only with great difficulty be seized. He could turn into all kinds

of shapes: bearded lions, dragons, leopards, huge boars, liquid water, branching trees. Euthyphron resembles Proteus because he cannot easily be seized, but changes his position all the time. Moreover, Euthyphron resembles Proteus because Proteus is unerring: he can tell all the secrets of the gods. Now, Socrates tries to seize Euthyphron, to force him to tell the truth. Who tried to seize Proteus in the myth, to force him to tell the truth? Menelaus. Just as Euthyphron imitates Proteus, Socrates imitates Menelaus. Socrates resembles Menelaus. What does Socrates have in common with Menelaus? Menelaus is the husband of Helen, just as Socrates is the husband of Xanthippe. This does not lead very far. Let us see in what context, or for what reason, Menelaus tried to seize Proteus (*Odyssey* 4.351ff.). Menelaus himself says, "At the river of Egypt, eager as I was to hasten hither, the gods still held me back because I did not make the offering due. And the gods wish us ever to be mindful of their precepts." Menelaus tried to seize Proteus because only Proteus could tell him how he could get out of the trouble into which he had come because he did not make the offering due. Socrates tried to seize Euthyphron because only Euthyphron could tell him how he could get out of the trouble into which he had come because he did not make the offerings due. It seems that this state of things throws some light on Socrates' last word to Crito in the *Phaedo*, "We still owe Aesculapius a cock," as one might well understand the passage. However this may be, Socrates failed where Menelaus succeeded. The reason is obvious. Socrates did not ask his Proteus what he, Socrates, should do, but he asked him a purely theoretical question: What is piety?

I said at the beginning that the *Euthyphron* conveys to us an irritating half-truth. That irritating half-truth is that piety is superfluous and that the gods are superfluous except for the many. Why is it a half-truth? Because we know that the gods exist. Not indeed the gods of the city of Athens, but the living gods. How do we know it? By demonstration. By demonstration starting from what phenomena? From the phenomena of motion, of self-motion, of life, of the soul. Plato has indicated the half-truth character of the message conveyed through the *Euthyphron* by never using that word, the term "soul." Through the emphasis on the ideas and the silence about the soul, Plato creates the appearance that there is no place for the gods. Plato probably would have justified this half-truth by the consideration that the ideas are at any rate above the soul.

In conclusion, I would like to say a word about what might have been offensive to some of you, the somewhat jocular character of the argument, the argument that is devoted to the most serious of all subjects. I remind you of the end of the *Banquet*, which I take to mean that philosophy fulfills singlehandedly the highest function of both comedy and tragedy. Both the traditional and current interpretations of Plato may be said to bring out the tragic element in Plato's thought, but they neglect the comic element except where it hits one in the face. Many reasons can be given for this failure. I mention only one. Modern research on Plato originated in Germany, the country without comedy. To indicate why the element of comedy is of crucial importance in Plato I read to you a few lines from the only Platonist I know of who had an appreciation of this element, Sir Thomas More. I quote: "For to prove that this life is no laughing time, but rather the time of weeping we find that our saviour himself wept twice or thrice, but never find we that he laughed as much as once. I will not swear that he never did, but at the leastwise he left us no example of it. But on the other side, he left us example of weeping" (*Dialogue of Comfort Against Tribulation*, chap. 13). If we compare what More said about Jesus with what Plato tells us about Socrates, we find that "Socrates laughed twice or thrice, but never find we that he wept as much as once." A slight bias in favor of laughing and against weeping seems to be essential to philosophy. For the beginning of philosophy as the philosophers understood it is not the fear of the Lord, but wonder. Its spirit is not hope and fear and trembling, but serenity on the basis of resignation. To that serenity, laughing is a little bit more akin than weeping. Whether the Bible or philosophy is right is of course the only question which ultimately matters. But in order to understand that question one must first see philosophy as it is. One must not see it from the outset through Biblical glasses. Wherever each of us may stand, no respectable purpose is served by trying to prove that we eat the cake and have it. Socrates used all his powers to awaken those who can think out of the slumber of thoughtlessness. We ill follow his example if we use his authority for putting ourselves to sleep.

9

How to Begin to Study
Medieval Philosophy

We raise the question of how to study medieval philosophy. We cannot discuss that question without saying something about how to study earlier philosophy in general, and indeed about how to study intellectual history in general.

In a sense, the answer to our question is self-evident. Everyone admits that, if we have to study medieval philosophy at all, we have to study it as exactly and as intelligently as possible. As exactly as possible: we are not permitted to consider any detail, however trifling, unworthy of our most careful observation. As intelligently as possible: in our exact study of all details, we must never lose sight of the whole; we must never, for a moment, overlook the wood for the trees. But these are trivialities, although we have to add that they are trivialities only if stated in general terms, and that they cease to be trivialities if one pays attention to them while engaged in actual work: the temptations to lose oneself in curious and unexplored details on the one hand, and to be generous as regards minutiae on the other, are always with us.

We touch upon a more controversial issue when we say that our understanding of medieval philosophy must be historical understanding. Frequently people reject an account of the past, not simply as unexact or unintelligent, but as unhistorical. What do they mean by it? What ought they to mean by it?

According to a saying of Kant, it is possible to understand a philosopher better than he understood himself (*Critique of Pure Reason*, B370). Now, such understanding may have the greatest merits; but it is clearly not historical understanding. If it goes so far as to claim to be *the* true understanding, it is positively unhistorical. The most outstanding example of such unhistorical interpretation which we have in the field of the study of Jewish medieval philosophy is Hermann Cohen's essay on Maimonides' ethics

("Charakteristik der Ethik Maimunis," in *Jüdische Schriften*, 3 vols. [Berlin, 1924], 3.221–89). Cohen constantly refers statements of Maimonides, not to Maimonides' center of reference, but to his own center of reference; he understands them not within Maimonides' horizon, but within his own horizon. Cohen had a technical term for his procedure: he called it "idealizing" interpretation. It may justly be described as the modern form of allegoric interpretation. At any rate, it is professedly an attempt to understand the old author better than he understood himself. Historical understanding means to understand an earlier author exactly as he understood himself. Everyone who has ever tried his hand at such a task will bear me out when I say that this task is an already sufficiently tough assignment in itself.

The attempt to understand a philosopher of the past better than he understood himself presupposes that the interpreter considers his insight superior to the insight of the old author. Kant made this quite clear when suggesting that one can understand a philosopher better than he understood himself. The average historian is much too modest a fellow to raise such an enormous claim in so many words. But he is in danger of doing so without noticing it. He will not claim that his personal insight is superior to that of, e.g., Maimonides. But only with difficulty can he avoid claiming that the collective insight available today is superior to the collective insight available in the twelfth century. There is more than one historian who in interpreting, say, Maimonides tries to assess the contribution of Maimonides. His contribution to what? To the treasure of knowledge and insight which has been accumulated throughout the ages. That treasure appears to be greater today than it was, say, in the year of Maimonides' death. This means that when speaking of Maimonides' "contribution" the historian has in mind the contribution of Maimonides to the treasure of knowledge or insight as it is available today. *Hence, he interprets Maimonides' thought in terms of the thought of the present day.* His tacit assumption is that the history of thought is, generally speaking, a progress, and that therefore the philosophic thought of the twentieth century is superior to, or nearer *the* truth than, the philosophic thought of the twelfth century. I contend that this assumption is irreconcilable with true historical understanding. It necessarily leads to the attempt to understand the thought of the past *better* than it understood itself, and not *as* it understood itself. For it is evident that our understanding of the past will tend to be more adequate, the more we are interested in the past; but we cannot be seriously interested, i.e., passionately interested, in the past, if we know beforehand that the present is, in the most important respect, superior to the past. It is not a matter of chance that, generally speaking, the historical understanding of the continental romantics, of *the* historical school, was superior to the historical understanding of eighteenth-century rationalism; it is a necessary consequence of the fact that the representatives of the historical school did not believe in the superiority of their time to the past, whereas the eighteenth-century rationalist believed in the superiority of the Age of Reason to all former ages. Historians who start from the belief in the superiority of present-day thought to the thought of the past feel no necessity to understand the past by itself: they understand it as only a preparation for the present. When studying a doctrine of the past, they do not ask primarily, What was the conscious and deliberate intention of its originator? They prefer to ask, What is the contribution of the doctrine to our beliefs? What is the meaning, unknown to its originator, of the doctrine from the point of view of the present? What is its meaning in the light of later developments? Against this approach, the historical consciousness rightly protested in the name of historical truth, of historical exactness. The task of the historian of thought is to understand the thinkers of the past exactly as they understood themselves, or to revitalize their thought according to their own interpretation of it. To sum up this point: the belief in the superiority of one's own approach, or of the approach of one's time, to the approach of the past is fatal to historical understanding.

We may express the same thought somewhat differently as follows. The task of the historian of thought is to understand the thought of the past exactly as it understood itself; for to abandon that task is tantamount to abandoning the only practicable criterion of objectivity in the history of thought. It is well known that the same historical phenomenon is interpreted in very different ways by different periods, different generations, and different types of men. The same historical phenomenon appears in different lights at different times. New human experiences shed light on old texts. No one can foresee how, e.g., the Bible will be read one hundred years hence. Observations such as these have led some people to adopt the view that the claim of any one interpretation to be *the* true interpretation is untenable. Yet the observations in question do not justify such a view. For the infinite variety of ways in which a given text can be understood does not do away with the fact that the author of the text, when writing it, understood it in one way only. The light in which the history of Samuel and Saul appears on the basis of the Puritan revolution, for example, is not the light in which the author of the Biblical history understood that history. And *the* true interpretation of the Biblical history in question is the one which restates and makes intelligible the Biblical history as understood by the Biblical author. Ultimately, the infinite variety of interpretations of an author is due to conscious or unconscious attempts to understand the author better than he understood himself; but there is only one way of understanding him as he understood himself.

To return to the point where I left off: the belief in the superiority of one's own approach, or of the approach of one's time, to the approach of the past is fatal to historical understanding. This dangerous assumption, which is characteristic of what one may call progressivism, was avoided by what is frequently called historicism. Whereas the progressivist believes that the present is superior to the past, the historicist believes that all periods are equally "immediate to God." The historicist does not want to judge the past, by assessing the contribution of each person, for example, but rather seeks to understand and to relate how things have actually been, *"wie es eigentlich gewesen ist"* (Leopold von Ranke, *Geschichten der Römanischen und Germanischen Völker von 1492 bis 1535,* Preface), and in particular how the thought of the past has been. The historicist has at least the intention to understand the thought of the past exactly as it understood itself. But he is constitutionally unable to live up to his intention. For he knows, or rather he assumes, that, generally speaking and other things being equal, the thought of all epochs is equally true, because every philosophy is essentially the expression of the spirit of its time. Maimonides, for example, expressed the spirit of his time as perfectly, as, say, Hermann Cohen expressed the spirit of *his* time. Now, all philosophers of the past claimed to have found *the* truth, and not merely the truth for their time. The historicist, however, asserts that they were mistaken in believing so. And he makes this assertion the basis of his interpretation. He knows a priori that the claim of Maimonides, to teach *the* truth, the truth valid for all times, is unfounded. In this most important respect, the historicist, just as his hostile brother the progressivist, believes that his approach is superior to the approach of the thinkers of old. The historicist is therefore compelled, by his principle if against his intention, to try to understand the past better than it understood itself. He merely repeats, if sometimes in a more sophisticated form, the sin for which he blames the progressivist so severely. For, to repeat, to understand a serious teaching, one must be seriously interested in it; one must take it seriously. But one cannot take it seriously if one knows beforehand that it is "dated." To take a serious teaching seriously, one must be willing to consider the possibility that it is simply true. Therefore, if we are interested in an adequate understanding of medieval philosophy, we must be willing to consider the possibility that medieval philosophy is simply true, or, to speak less paradoxically, that it is superior, in the most important respect, to all that we can learn from any of the contemporary philosophers. We can understand medieval philosophy only if we are prepared to learn something, not merely *about* the medieval philosophers, but *from* them.

It remains true, then, that if one wants to understand a philosophy of the past, one must approach it in a philosophic spirit, with philosophic questions: one's concern must be primarily, not with what other people have thought about the philosophic truth, but with the philosophic truth itself. But if one approaches an earlier thinker with a question which is not *his* central question, one is bound to misinterpret, to distort, his thought. Therefore, the philosophic question with which one approaches the thought of the past must be so broad, so comprehensive, that it permits of being narrowed down to the specific, precise formulation of the question which the author concerned adopted. It can be no question other than the question of *the* truth about the whole.

The historian of philosophy must then undergo a transformation into a philosopher, or a conversion to philosophy, if he wants to do his job properly, if he wants to be a competent historian of philosophy. He must acquire a freedom of mind which is not too frequently met with among the "professional" philosophers: he must have as perfect a freedom of mind as is humanly possible. No prejudice in favor of contemporary thought, even of modern philosophy, of modern civilization, of modern science itself, must deter him from giving the thinkers of old the full benefit of the doubt. When engaging in the study of the philosophy of the past, he must cease to take his bearings by the modern signposts with which he has grown familiar since his earliest childhood; he must try to take his bearings by the signposts which guided the thinkers of old. Those old signposts are not immediately visible: they are concealed by heaps of dust and rubble. The most obnoxious part of the rubble consists of the superficial interpretations by modern writers, of the cheap clichés which are offered in the textbooks and which seem to unlock by one formula the mystery of the past. The signposts which guided the thinkers of the past must be recovered before they can be used. Before the historian has succeeded in recovering them, he cannot help being in a condition of utter bewilderment, of universal doubt: he finds himself in a darkness which is illumined exclusively by his knowledge that he knows nothing. When engaging in the study of the philosophy of the past, he must know that he embarks on a journey whose end is completely hidden from him: he is not likely to return to the shore of his time as the same man who left it.

True historical understanding of medieval philosophy presupposes that the student is willing to take seriously the claim of the medieval philosophers that they teach *the* truth. Now, it may justifiably be objected, is this demand not most unreasonable? Medieval philosophy is based, generally speaking, on the natural science of Aristotle: has that science not been refuted once and for all by Galileo, Descartes, and Newton? Medieval philosophy is based on an almost complete unawareness of the principles of religious toleration, of the representative system, of the rights of man, of democracy as we understand it. It is characterized by an indifference (touching on contempt) to poetry and history. It seems to be based on a firm belief in the verbal inspiration of the Bible and in the Mosaic origin of the oral Law. It stands and falls with the use of a method of Biblical interpretation as unsound as the allegoric interpretation. In brief, medieval philosophy arouses against itself all convictions fostered by the most indubitable results of modern science and modern scholarship.

Nor is this all. Medieval philosophy may have been refuted by modern thought, and yet it could have been an admirable and highly beneficial achievement for its time. But even this may be questioned. A strong case can be made for the view that the influence of philosophy on medieval Judaism was far from being salutary. Most of you will have read the remarkable book by Dr. Gershom Scholem, *Major Trends in Jewish Mysticism* (New York, 1961). Dr. Scholem contends that from the point of view of Judaism, i.e., of rabbinical Judaism, the Kabbala is by far superior to Jewish medieval philosophy. He starts from the observation that

> both the mystics and the philosophers completely transform the structure of ancient Judaism. . . . [But] the philosopher can only proceed with his proper task after having successfully converted the concrete realities of Judaism into a bundle of abstractions. By contrast, the mystic refrains from destroy-

ing the living structure of religious narrative by allegorizing it. . . . The difference becomes clear if we consider the attitude of philosophy and Kabbalah respectively to the two outstanding creative manifestations of Rabbinical Jewry: Halakhah and Aggadah, Law and Legend. It is a remarkable fact that the philosophers failed to establish a satisfactory and intimate relation to either. . . . The whole world of religious law remained outside the orbit of philosophic inquiry, which means of course, too, that it was not subjected to philosophic criticism. . . . For a purely historical understanding of religion, Maimonides' analysis of the origin of the *mitswoth*, the religious commandments, is of great importance, but he would be a bold man who would maintain that his theory of the *mitswoth* was likely to increase the enthusiasm of the faithful for their actual practice. . . . To the philosopher, the Halakah either had no significance at all, or one that was calculated to diminish rather than to enhance its prestige in his eyes. . . . The Aggadah . . . represents a method of giving original and concrete expression to the deepest motive-powers of the religious Jew, a quality which helps to make it an excellent and genuine approach to the essentials of our religion. However, it was just this quality which never ceased to baffle the philosophers of Judaism. . . . Only too frequently their allegorizations are simply . . . veiled criticism. (Ibid., pp. 23, 26, 28–31)

Scholem does not leave it at suggesting that our medieval philosophers were, qua philosophers, blind to the deepest forces of the Jewish soul; he suggests also that they were blind to the deepest forces of the soul of man as man. Philosophy, he says, turned "its back upon the primitive side of life, that all-important region where mortals are afraid of life and in fear of death, and derive scant wisdom from rational philosophy" (ibid., p. 35). The Kabbalists, on the other hand, "have a strong sense of the reality of evil and the dark horror that is about everything living. They do not, like the philosophers, seek to evade its existence with the aid of a convenient formula" (ibid., p. 36).

We ought to be grateful to Dr. Scholem for his sweeping and forceful condemnation of our medieval philosophy. It does not permit us to rest satisfied with that mixture of historical reverence and philosophic indifference which is characteristic of the prevailing mood. For Scholem's criticism, while unusually ruthless, cannot be said to be paradoxical. In fact, to a certain extent, Scholem merely says quite explicitly what is implied in the more generally accepted opinion on the subject. The central thesis underlying the standard work on the history of Jewish philosophy, Julius Guttman's *Philosophies of Judaism*, is that our medieval philosophers abandoned, to a considerable extent, the Biblical ideas of God, world, and man in favor of the Greek ideas, and that the modern Jewish philosophers succeed much better than their medieval predecessors in safeguarding the original purport of the central religious beliefs of Judaism. In this connection we might also mention the fact that Franz Rosenzweig considered Hermann Cohen's *Religion of Reason Out of the Sources of Judaism* to be definitely superior to Maimonides' *Guide of the Perplexed*.

Criticisms such as these cannot be dismissed lightly. Nothing would be more impertinent than to leave things at a merely dialectical or disputative answer. The only convincing answer would be a real interpretation of our great medieval philosophers. For it would be a grave mistake to believe that we dispose already of such an interpretation. After all, the historical study of Jewish medieval philosophy is of fairly recent origin. Everyone working in this field is deeply indebted to the great achievements of Salomon Munk, David Kaufmann, and Harry A. Wolfson in particular. But I am sure that these great scholars would be the first to admit that modern scholarship has not yet crossed the threshold of such works as Halevi's *Cuzari* and Maimonides' *Guide*: we are still in a truly preliminary stage. But quite apart from this perhaps decisive consideration, the critical remarks quoted can be answered to a certain extent without raising the gravest issue. Dr. Scholem takes it for granted that our medieval philosophers intended to express, or to interpret, in their philosophic works, the living reality of historical Judaism, or the religious sentiments or experiences of the pious Jew. Their real intention was much more modest, or much more radical. The whole edifice of the Jewish tradition was virtually, or even actually, under attack from the side of the adherents of Greek philosophy. With all due caution necessitated by our insufficient information about what happened in the Hellenistic period of Jewish history, one may say that the Middle Ages witnessed the first, and certainly the first adequate, discussion between these two most important forces of the Western world: the religion of the Bible and the science or philosophy of the Greeks. It was a discussion, not between ethical monotheism and paganism, i.e., between two religions, but between religion as such and science or philosophy as such: between the way of life based on faith and obedience and a way of life based on free insight, on human wisdom, alone. What were at stake in that discussion were not so much the religious sentiments or experiences themselves, as the elementary and inconspicuous *presuppositions* on the basis of which those sentiments or experiences could be more than beautiful dreams, pious wishes, awe-inspiring delusions, or emotional exaggerations. It was very well for the Kabbalist Moses of Burgos to say that the philosophers end where the Kabbalists begin (see Scholem 1961, p. 24). But does this not amount to a confession that the Kabbalist as such is not concerned with the *foundations* of belief, i.e., with the only question of interest to the philosopher as philosopher? To deny that this question is of paramount importance is to assert that a conflict between faith and knowledge, between religion and science, is not even thinkable, or that intellectual honesty is nothing to be cared for. And to believe that the specific experiences of the mystic are sufficient to quell the doubts raised by science or philosophy is to forget the fact that such experiences guarantee the absolute truth of the Torah in no other way than that in which they guarantee the absolute truth of the Christian dogma or of the tenets of Islam; it means to minimize the importance of the doctrinal conflicts among the three great monotheist religions. In fact, it was the insoluble character of those doctrinal conflicts which engendered, or at any rate strengthened, the impulse toward philosophic studies. (It is perhaps not altogether insignificant that Jewish philosophy has proved to be much more impervious to the influence of the Christian dogma than the Kabbala.) One may say of, course—and this is the implication of the view taken by Guttmann and Rosenzweig in particular—that modern Jewish philosophy has discussed the question of faith and knowledge, of religion and science, in a much more advanced, in a much more mature, way than medieval Jewish philosophy. At the root of all our internal difficulties is, after all, the conflict between the traditional Jewish beliefs and, not Aristotelian metaphysics, but modern natural science and modern historical criticism. And this conflict is being discussed, of course, not by medieval Jewish philosophy, but by modern Jewish philosophy. Yet there is another side to this picture. Modern Jewish philosophy from Moses Mendelssohn to Franz Rosenzweig stands and falls with the basic premises of modern philosophy in general. Now, the superiority of modern philosophy to medieval philosophy is no longer so evident as it seemed to be one or two generations ago. Modern philosophy led to a distinction, alien to medieval philosophy, between philosophy and science. This distinction is fraught with the danger that it paves the way for the admission of an unphilosophic science and of an unscientific philosophy: of a science which is a mere tool, and hence apt to become the tool of any powers, of any interests that be, and of a philosophy in which wishes and prejudices have usurped the place belonging to reason. We have seen modern philosophy resigning the claim to demonstrable truth and degenerating into some form of intellectual autobiography, or else evaporating into methodology by becoming the handmaid of modern science. And we are observing every day that people go so far in debasing the name of philosophy as to speak of the philosophies of vulgar imposters such as Hitler. This regrettable usage is not accidental: it is the necessary outcome of the distinction between philosophy and science, of a distinction which is bound to lead eventually to the separation of philosophy from science. Whatever we might have to think of neo-Thomism, its considerable success among non-Catholics is due to the increasing awareness that something is basically wrong with modern philosophy. The old question, discussed in the seventeenth century, of the superiority of the moderns to the ancients, or vice versa, has again become a topical question. It has again become a *question;* only a fool would presume that it has already found a sufficient answer. We are barely beginning to realize its enormous implications. But the mere fact that it has again become a question suffices for making the study of medieval philosophy a philosophic, and not merely a historical, necessity.

I would like to stress one point which is of particular significance for the right approach to medieval philosophy. The development of modern philosophy has led to a point where the meaningfulness of philosophy or science as such has become problematic. To mention only one of its most obvious manifestations: there was a time when it was generally held that philosophy or science is, or can, or ought to be the best guide for social action. The very common present-day talk of the importance and necessity of political myths alone suffices to show that, at any rate, the social significance of philosophy or science has become doubtful. We are again confronted with the question, Why philosophy? or, Why science? This question was in the center of discussion in the beginnings of philosophy. One may say that the Platonic dialogues serve no more obvious purpose than precisely this one: to answer the question, Why philosophy? or, Why science? by justifying philosophy or science before the tribunal of the city, the political community. In fundamentally the same way, our medieval philosophers are compelled to raise the question, Why philosophy? or,

Why science? by justifying philosophy or science before the tribunal of the law, or the Torah. This most fundamental question of philosophy, the question of its own legitimacy and necessity, is no longer a question for modern philosophy. Modern philosophy was from its beginning the attempt to replace the allegedly wrong philosophy or science of the Middle Ages by the allegedly true philosophy or science. It did not raise any longer the question of the necessity of philosophy or science itself; it took that necessity for granted. This fact alone can assure us, from the outset, that medieval philosophy is distinguished by a philosophic radicalism which is absent from modern philosophy, or that it is, in the most important respect, superior to modern philosophy.

It is then not altogether absurd that we should turn from the modern philosophers to the medieval philosophers with the expectation that we might have to learn something from them, and not merely about them.

The student of medieval philosophy is a modern man. Whether he knows it or not, he is under the influence of modern philosophy. It is precisely this influence which makes it so difficult—and, to begin with, even impossible—really to understand medieval philosophy. It is this influence of modern philosophy on the student of medieval philosophy which makes an *un*historical interpretation of medieval philosophy, to begin with, inevitable. The understanding of medieval philosophy requires then a certain emancipation from the influence of modern philosophy. And this emancipation is not possible without serious, constant, and relentless reflection on the specific character of modern philosophy. For knowledge alone can make men free. We modern men understand medieval philosophy only to the extent to which we understand modern philosophy in its specific character.

This cannot possibly mean that the student of medieval philosophy must possess a complete knowledge of all important medieval and modern philosophies. The accumulation of such a vast amount of knowledge, of factual information, if at all possible, would reduce any man to a condition of mental decrepitude. On the other hand, it is impossible for any genuine scholar to rely on those *fables convenues* about the difference between medieval and modern thought which have acquired a sort of immortality by migrating from one textbook to another. For even if those clichés were true, the young scholar could not know that this is the case: he would have to accept them on trust. There is only one way of combining the duty of exactness with the equally compelling duty of comprehensiveness: one must start with detailed observations at strategic points. There are cases, for example, in which a medieval work has served as a model for a modern work: by a close comparison of the imitation with its model, we may arrive at a clear and lively firsthand impression of the characteristic difference between the medieval approach and the modern approach. As an example one could mention Ibn Tufayl's *Hayy ibn Yuqdhân* and Defoe's *Robinson Crusoe*. Defoe's work is based on the Latin translation, made in the seventeenth century, of the work of the Arabic philosopher. Both works deal with the question of what a solitary human being can achieve with his natural powers, without the help of society or civilization. The medieval man succeeds in becoming a perfect philosopher; the modern man lays the foundation of a technical civilization. Another type of strategic point is represented by modern commentaries on medieval texts. A comparison of Mendelssohn's commentary on Maimonides' *Treatise on Logic* with the Maimonidean text itself could well perform the function of an entering wedge into our subject. The third type would be detailed modern polemics against medieval teachings, such as Spinoza's critique of Maimonides' teaching and method in the *Theologico-Political Treatise*. By observing what theses of Maimonides are misunderstood or insufficiently understood by Spinoza, one is enabled to grasp some of the specifically modern prejudices which, to begin with, prevent us—at least as much as they did Spinoza—from understanding Maimonides. Yet all examples of the three types mentioned are open to the objection that they may mislead the unwary student into taking the difference between these specific modern and medieval philosophies for *the* difference between modern philosophy as such and medieval philosophy as such.

To grasp that general difference, there is, I think, no better way than a precise comparison of the most typical divisions of philosophy or science in both the Middle Ages and the modern period. It is easy to compile a list of the philosophic disciplines which are recognized today, from the curricula of present-day universities, or from the title pages of systems of philosophy composed in the nineteenth and twentieth centuries. Compare that list with, say, Alfarabi's or Avicenna's division of philosophy. The differences are so big, they are so appallingly obvious, that they cannot be overlooked even by the most shortsighted person; they are so obtrusive that they compel even the most lazy student to think about them. One sees at once, for instance, that there do not exist in the Middle

Ages such philosophic disciplines as aesthetics or philosophy of history, and one acquires at once an invincible and perfectly justified distrust of the many modern scholars who write articles or even books on medieval aesthetics or on medieval philosophy of history. One becomes interested in the question: when did the very terms "aesthetics" and "philosophy of history" appear for the first time? One learns that they made their first appearance in the eighteenth century; one starts reflecting on the assumptions underlying their appearance—and one is already well on one's way. Or take the absence of a discipline called "philosophy of religion" from medieval philosophy. How many books and pamphlets have been written on Jewish philosophy of religion in the Middle Ages—on something, that is, which strictly speaking does not exist! Something must be basically wrong with all these books and pamphlets. In the place of our modern philosophy of religion, we find in medieval philosophy theology as a philosophic discipline, *natural* theology as it was formerly called. There is a world of difference between natural theology, the doctrine of God, and philosophy of religion, the analysis of the human attitude toward God. What is the meaning of that difference? What does it mean that the greatest work of medieval Christianity is entitled "Summa *Theologica*," whereas the greatest work of the Reformation is entitled "Institutio Christianae *Religionis?*" And what does it mean that Maimonides excludes the discussion of religious subjects from his *Guide?* This is exactly the type of questions with which one has to start in order to arrive eventually at a true, exact, historical understanding of medieval philosophy.

Many scholars consider the type of questions which I have mentioned as pedantic, not to say bureaucratic. They would argue as follows: why should we not describe a medieval philosopher's remarks on poetry, e.g., as his contribution to aesthetics? The medieval philosopher would have considered those remarks as belonging to poetics, or to ethics, or perhaps even to political science. He conceived of poetry as an essentially purposeful activity, as an activity destined to please by instructing or to instruct by pleasing. He conceived of poetics as a technical art destined to teach how to make good poems, etc. He considered poetry essentially subservient to ulterior purposes such as moral improvement. In short, he had a terribly narrow view of poetry. Thanks to our modern philosophers, we know better: we know that poetry is something existing in its own right, and that aesthetics, far from teaching a poet how to make poems, is the analysis of poetic productivity and of aesthetic enjoyment or appreciation or understanding. The modern view being so manifestly superior to the medieval view, why should we hesitate for a moment to refer the medieval philosopher's remarks on poetry to *our* center of reference, and hence to describe them as belonging to aesthetics? Well, this is precisely the mental habit which makes impossible historical understanding of medieval philosophy. If we know from the outset that the medieval view of the matter is wrong or poor, we should not waste our time in studying it; or if someone does not mind wasting his time, he simply will not command the intellectual energy required for truly understanding a view for which he cannot have any real sympathy. Since I mentioned this example of aesthetics versus poetry, I may be permitted to add that the medieval view of poetry ultimately goes back to Plato's *Republic,* i.e., to the work of a man who cannot be accused of having had a monkish lack of sense of beauty.

The implication of the point I have been trying to make is that terminology is of paramount importance. Every term designating an important subject implies a whole philosophy. And since, to begin with, one cannot be certain which terms are important and which terms are not, one is under an obligation to pay the utmost attention to any term which one reads, or which one uses in one's presentation. This naturally brings us to the question of translations. There is no higher praise for a translation of a philosophic book than that it is of utmost literalness, that it is *in ultimitate literalitatis,* to avail myself of the Latinity of those wonderful medieval translators whose translations from the Arabic into Hebrew or from either language into Latin infinitely surpass most modern translations, although their Latin in particular is frequently *in ultimitate turpitudinis.* It is difficult to understand why many modern translators have such a superstitious fear of translating literally. It leads to the consequence that a man who has to rely entirely on modern translations of philosophic works is unable to reach a precise understanding of the thought of the author. Accordingly, even the poorest linguists (such as the present speaker) are compelled to read the originals. This was not so in the Middle Ages. Medieval students of Aristotle who did not know a word of Greek are by far superior as interpreters of Aristotle to modern scholars who possess a simply overwhelming knowledge of Greek antiquities. This superiority is decisively due to the fact that the medieval commentators disposed of most literal translations of the Aristotelian text and that they stuck to the text and the terminology of the text.

The foregoing remarks apply to the study of medieval philosophy in general. Now let us turn to Jewish medieval philosophy in particular. Medieval Jewish philosophy consists broadly of two types, an earlier type which flourished in an Islamic environment, and a more recent type which emerged in a Christian environment. I shall limit myself to the older type, which is more interesting from the point of view of our methodological question, to say nothing of other considerations. There are specific difficulties obstructing our understanding of Arabic-Jewish philosophy, as well as of the Islamic philosophy on which it is dependent. History of philosophy, as distinguished from doxography, is an outgrowth of the modern world. Its program was stated for the first time by Francis Bacon. Originally it was considered as something outside of philosophy proper, as a pursuit for antiquarians rather than for philosophers: it became an integral part of philosophy in the nineteenth century only, owing to Hegel in particular. History of philosophy, being an outgrowth of Christian Europe, has a congenital inclination to take its bearings as regards the study of medieval philosophy by the standards of Christian or Latin scholasticism. The student of medieval philosophy, as a modern man, is prevented, by the influence of modern philosophy on his thought, from understanding medieval philosophy if he does not coherently reflect on the difference between modern and medieval philosophy. Similarly, the student of Islamic and Jewish philosophy, who as a historian of philosophy participates in a tradition of Western origin, is prevented by that tradition from understanding Islamic and Jewish philosophy if he does not coherently reflect on the difference between Christian scholasticism and Islamic-Jewish philosophy.

One has to start from the difference between Judaism and Islam on the one hand and Christianity on the other. For the Jew and the Moslem, religion is primarily not, as it is for the Christian, a faith formulated in dogmas, but a law, a code of divine origin. Accordingly, *the* religious science, the *sacra doctrina,* is not dogmatic theology, *theologia revelata,* but the science of the law, *halaka* or *fiqh.* The science of the law thus understood has much less in common with philosophy than has dogmatic theology. Hence the status of philosophy is, as a matter of principle, much more precarious in the Islamic-Jewish world than it is in the Christian world. No one could become a competent Christian theologian without having studied at least a substantial part of philosophy; philosophy was an integral part of the officially authorized and even required training. On the other hand, one could become an absolutely competent halakist or faqih without having the slightest knowledge of philosophy. This fundamental difference doubtless explains the possibility of the later complete collapse of philosophic studies in the Islamic world, a collapse which has no parallel in the West in spite of Luther. It explains why, as late as 1765, the Ashkenasic Jew Mendelssohn felt compelled to offer a real apology for recommending the study of logic, and to show why the prohibition against the reading of extraneous or profane books does not apply to the study of works of logic. It explains at least partly why Maimonides' *Guide* in particular never acquired the authority enjoyed by Thomas Aquinas's *Summa Theologica*. Nothing is more revealing than the difference between the beginnings of these two most representative works. The first article of Thomas's great *Summa* deals with the question as to whether theology is necessary apart from, and in addition to, the philosophic disciplines: Thomas defends theology before the tribunal of philosophy. Maimonides' *Guide*, on the other hand, is especially devoted to the science of the law, if to the *true* science of the law; it opens in the form of a somewhat diffuse commentary on a Biblical verse; it opens as a defense of philosophy before the tribunal of traditional Jewish science rather than as a defense of traditional Jewish science before the tribunal of philosophy. Can one even imagine Maimonides opening the *Guide* with a discussion of the question as to whether the halaka is necessary in addition to the philosophic disciplines? Maimonides' procedure is illustrated by a treatise of his contemporary Averroës, the explicit purpose of which is the legal justification of philosophy: it discusses in legal terms, in terms of the Islamic law, the question as to whether the study of philosophy is permitted or forbidden or commanded. Philosophy was clearly on the defensive, not so much perhaps in fact, but certainly as far as the legal situation was concerned. There is more than one parallel to Averroës' argument in Jewish literature.

The problematic status of philosophy in the Jewish Middle Ages finds its most telling expression in the use of the terms "philosophy" and "philosopher." We take it for granted that men such as Maimonides and Halevi were philosophers, and we call their respective books without hesitation philosophic books. But, by doing so, do we act in agreement with their view of the matter? In their usage, philosopher designates normally a man whose beliefs are fundamentally different from those of the adherents of any of the three monotheist religions, whether he belongs nominally to one of these religions or not. The philosophers as such are supposed to form a group, a sect, fundamentally distinguished from the sect of the Jews, that of the Muslims, and that of the Christians. By calling thinkers such as Halevi and Maimonides "philosophers," we implicitly deny that there is a problem in the very idea of a Jewish philosopher or of Jewish philosophy. But of nothing were these men more deeply convinced than of this: that Jewish philosophy is, as such, something problematic, something precarious.

Now let us consider the other side of the picture. The official recognition of philosophy in the Christian world doubtless had its drawbacks. That recognition was bought at the price of the imposition of strict ecclesiastical supervision. The precarious position of philosophy in the Islamic-Jewish world, on the other hand, guaranteed, or necessitated, its private character, and therewith a higher degree of inner freedom. The situation of philosophy in the Islamic-Jewish world resembles in this respect its situation in classical Greece. It has often been said that the Greek city was a totalitarian social order: it comprised and regulated, not only political and legal matters proper, but morality, religion, tragedy, and comedy as well. There was, however, one activity which was, in fact and in theory, essentially and radically private, transpolitical, and transsocial: philosophy. The philosophic schools were founded, not by authorities civil or ecclesiastical, but by men without authority, by private men. In this respect, I said, the situation of philosophy in the Islamic world resembles the Greek situation rather than the situation in Christian Europe. This fact was recognized by the Islamic-Jewish philosophers themselves: elaborating on a remark of Aristotle, they speak of the philosophic life as a radically private life: they compare it to the life of a hermit.

Religion is conceived by Muslims and Jews primarily as a law. Accordingly, religion enters the horizon of the philosophers primarily as a political fact. Therefore, the philosophic discipline dealing with religion is not philosophy of religion, but political philosophy or political science. The political science in question is a specific one: Platonic political science, the teaching of Plato's *Republic* and of his *Laws*. No difference between Islamic-Jewish philosophy on the one hand and Christian scholasticism on the other is more palpable than this: whereas the classic of political science in the Western world was Aristotle's *Politics*, the classics of political science in the Islamic-Jewish world were the *Republic* and the *Laws*. In fact, Aristotle's *Politics* was unknown to the Islamic-Jewish world, and the *Republic* and the *Laws* made their appearance in Christian Europe not before the fifteenth century.

The Islamic law as well as the Jewish law is, of course, considered a divine law, a law given by God to men by the intermediary of a prophet. The prophet is interpreted by Alfarabi, Avicenna, and Maimonides in terms of the Platonic philosopher-king: as the founder of the perfect political community. The doctrine of prophecy as such is considered by these philosophers a part of political science. Avicenna describes Plato's *Laws* as the standard work on prophecy. This view of the essentially political character of prophecy influences the very plan of Maimonides' *sepher ha-mizvot* and of his *sepher ha-madda*. Its implications appear from Maimonides' remark that the neglect of the arts of war and of conquest in favor of astrology led to the destruction of the Jewish state.

The difference between Islamic-Jewish philosophy and Christian scholasticism shows itself most clearly in the field of practical philosophy. As regards theoretical philosophy, both Islamic-Jewish philosophy and Christian scholasticism build on substantially the same tradition. But in political and moral philosophy the difference is fundamental. I have mentioned the absence of Aristotle's *Politics* from the Islamic-Jewish world. Equally significant is the absence from it of the Roman literature, of Cicero and the Roman Law in particular. This leads to the consequence that the doctrine of natural law, so characteristic of Christian scholasticism, and indeed of Western thought up to the end of the eighteenth century, is completely lacking in Islamic-Jewish philosophy: it appears in some later Jewish writers only under the influence of Christian thought. It is true, the Islamic theologians, the *mutakallimûn*, had asserted the existence of rational laws which were practically identical with what were called natural laws in the Occident; but the Islamic-Jewish philosophers reject this view altogether. The rules of conduct which are called by the Christian scholastics natural laws and by the *mutakallimûn* rational laws are called by the Islamic-Jewish philosophers generally accepted opinions. This view appears in the Christian Middle Ages only at their fringes, as it were, in the teaching of Marsilius of Padua, the most energetic medieval opponent of clerical claims.

This leads me to the last point which I would like to make in order to indicate the extent and bearing of the difference separating Islamic-Jewish philosophy from Christian scholasticism, and in order to justify my contention that a genuine understanding of Islamic-Jewish philosophy must be based on constant awareness of that difference. That school of Christian scholasticism which was most deeply influenced by Islamic philosophy was Latin Averroism. Latin Averroism is famous for its doctrine of the double truth, for its assertion that a thesis may be true in philosophy but false in theology and vice versa. The doctrine of the double truth does not occur in Averroës himself or in his predecessors. Instead, we find in Islamic philosophy a relatively ample use of the distinction between exoteric teachings, based on rhetorical arguments, and esoteric teaching, based on demonstrative or scientific arguments. Up to now, students of Islamic philosophy have not paid sufficient attention to this distinction, which is evidently of absolutely decisive importance. For if the true, scientific teaching is an esoteric, a secret, teaching, we have no right to be as certain as we are accustomed to be that the public teaching of the Islamic philosophers is their real teaching. We would have to acquire a special technique of reading: a technique not necessary for the understanding of books which set forth the views of their authors directly, without any concealment or circumlocution. It would be wrong to trace the esotericism in question to certain spurious phenomena of dying antiquity: its origin has to be sought in Plato himself, in the doctrine of the *Phaedrus* concerning the superiority of oral teaching to teaching by writings, in the doctrine of the *Republic* and the *Laws* concerning the necessity of noble lies, and, above all, in the literary technique used by Plato himself in all his works. One may safely say that before this Platonism of the Islamic philosophers has been duly studied, our understanding of Islamic philosophy rests on extremely shaky foundations. Similar considerations apply to the Jewish philosophy which is dependent on Islamic philosophy. Everyone who has read the *Guide* knows how emphatically Maimonides insists on the secret character of his own teaching: he warns his reader from the outset that he has set forth only the chapter headings of the secret teaching, and not the chapters themselves. In the *Cuzari*, we are confronted with a similar situation: the final conversion of the Cuzari to Judaism is the consequence of his listening to a highly secret interpretation of the secret teaching of the *sepher yeszira*. It was with a view to phenomena such as these that I ventured to say that our understanding of medieval philosophy is still in a truly preliminary stage. In making this remark I do not minimize the debt which we owe to Wolfson and Isaac Heinemann in particular, who have spoken on the peculiar literary technique of earlier philosophers on various occasions. What is required, beyond the general observations, is a coherent and methodic application of those observations to the actual interpretation of the texts. Only after this interpretation has been completed will we be in a position to judge of the value, of the truth, of our medieval philosophy. For the time being, it is good policy to suspend our judgment and to learn from these great teachers. For there are many important lessons which modern man can learn only from premodern, from unmodern, thinkers.

10
Progress or Return?

I

The title of these lectures indicates that progress has become a problem—that it could seem as if progress has led us to the brink of an abyss, and that it is therefore necessary to consider alternatives to it. For example, to stop where we are, or else, if this should be possible, to return. Return is the translation for the Hebrew word *t'shuvah*. *T'shuvah* has an ordinary and an emphatic meaning. Its emphatic meaning is rendered in English by "repentance." Repentance is return, meaning the return from the wrong way to the right one. This implies that we were once on the right way before we turned to the wrong way. Originally we were on the right way; deviation or sin or imperfection is not original. Man is originally at home in his Father's house. He becomes a stranger through estrangement, through sinful estrangement. Repentance, return, is homecoming.

I remind you of a few verses from the first chapter of Isaiah. "How is the faithful city become a harlot! It was full of judgment, righteousness lodged in it. But now murderers. . . . Therefore, saith the Lord . . . I will restore thy judges as at first and thy counsellors as at the beginning. Afterwards thou shalt be called the city of righteousness, the faithful city." Repentance is return; redemption is restoration. A perfect beginning—the faithful city—is followed by defection, decline, sin; and this is followed by a perfect end. But the perfect end is the restoration of the perfect beginning: the faithful city at the beginning and at the end. At the beginning, men did not roam a forest left to themselves, unprotected and unguided. The beginning is the Garden of Eden. Perfection resides in the beginning—in the beginning of time, the oldest time. Hence perfection is sought derivatively in the old time—in the father, the father of fathers, the patriarchs. The patriarchs are the divine chariot which Ezekiel saw in his vision. The great time—the classic time—is in the past: first the period of the desert, later the period of the temple. The life of the Jew is the life of recollection. It is at the same time a life of anticipation, of hope, but the hope for redemption is restoration—*restituto in integro*. "Their children shall be as aforetime" (*Jeremiah* 30:20). Redemption consists in the return of the youngest, the most remote from the past, the most future ones, so to speak, to the pristine condition. The past is superior to the present. This thought is, then, perfectly compatible with hope for the future. But does the hope for redemption—the expectation of the Messiah—not assign a much higher place to the future than to the past, however venerable?

This is not unqualifiedly true. According to the most accepted view, the Messiah is inferior to Moses. The messianic age will witness the restoration of the full practice of the Torah, part of which was discontinued owing to the destruction of the Temple. Belief in the Torah was always the way in Judaism, whereas messianism frequently became dormant. For example, as I learn from Gershom Scholem, kabbalism prior to the sixteenth century concentrated upon the beginning; it was only with Isaac Luria that kabbalism began to concentrate upon the future—upon the end. Yet even here, the last age became as important as the first. It did not become more important. Furthermore (I quote Scholem), "by inclination and habit, Luria was decidedly conservative. This tendency is well expressed in persistent attempts to relate what he had to say to older authorities." For Luria, "salvation means actually nothing but restitution, re-integration of the original whole, or *Tikkun*, to use the Hebrew term. . . . For Luria, the appearance of the Messiah is nothing but the consummation of the continuous process of Restoration. . . . The path to the end of all things is also the path to the beginning" (*Major Trends in Jewish Mysticism* [New York, 1961] pp. 256, 268, 274). Judaism is a concern with return; it is not a concern with progress. "Return" can easily be expressed in biblical Hebrew; "progress" cannot. Hebrew renderings of "progress" seem to be somehow artificial, not to say paradoxical. Even if it were true that messianism bespeaks the predominance of the concern with the future, or of living toward the future, this would not affect in any way the belief in the superiority of the past to the present. The fact that the present is nearer in time to the final redemption than is the past does not mean, of course, that the present is superior in piety or wisdom to the past, especially to the classic past.

Today, the word *t'shuvah* has acquired a still more emphatic meaning. Today, *t'shuvah* sometimes means, not a return which takes place within Judaism, but a return to Judaism on the part of many Jews who, or whose fathers, had broken with Judaism as a whole. That abandonment of Judaism—that break with Judaism— did not understand itself, of course, as a defection or desertion, as leaving the right way; nor did it understand itself as a return to a truth which the Jewish tradition in its turn had deserted; nor even merely a turn to something superior. It understood itself as progress. It granted to the Jewish tradition, as it were, that Judaism is old, very old, whereas it itself had no past of which it could boast. But it regarded this very fact, the antiquity of Judaism, as a proof of its own superiority and of Judaism's inadequacy. For it questioned the very premise underlying the notion of return, that premise being the perfect character of the beginning and of the olden times. It assumed that the beginning is most imperfect and that perfection can be found only in the end—so much so that the movement from the beginning toward the end is in principle a progress from radical imperfection toward perfection. From this point of view, age did not have any claim whatsoever to veneration. Antiquity rather deserved contempt, or possibly contempt mitigated by pity.

Let us try to clarify this issue somewhat more fully by contrasting the life characterized by the idea of return with the life characterized by the idea of progress. When the prophets call their people to account, they do not limit themselves to accusing them of this or that particular crime or sin. They recognize the root of all particular crimes in the fact that the people have forsaken their God. They accuse their people of rebellion. Originally, in the past, they were faithful or loyal; now they are in a state of rebellion. In the future they will return, and God will restore them to their original place. The primary, the original or initial, is loyalty; unfaithfulness, infidelity, is secondary. The very notion of unfaithfulness or infidelity presupposes that fidelity or loyalty is primary. The perfect character of the origin is a condition of sin—of the thought of sin. Man who understands himself in this way longs for the perfection of the origin, or of the classic past. He suffers from the present; he hopes for the future.

Progressive man, on the other hand, looks back to a most imperfect beginning. The beginning is barbarism, stupidity, rudeness, extreme scarcity. Progressive man does not feel that he has lost something of great, not to say infinite, importance; he has lost only his chains. He does not suffer from the recollection of the past. Looking back to the past, he is proud of his achievements; he is certain of the superiority of the present to the past. He is not satisfied with the present; he looks to future progress. But he does not merely hope or pray for a better future; he thinks that he can bring it about by his own effort. Seeking perfection in a future which is in no sense the beginning or the restoration of the beginning, he lives unqualifiedly toward the future. The life which understands itself as a life of loyalty or faithfulness appears to him as backward, as being under the spell of old prejudices. What the others call rebellion, he calls revolution or liberation. To the polarity faithfulness-rebellion, he opposes the polarity prejudice-freedom.

To repeat, the contemporary return to Judaism succeeds a break with Judaism which eventually, or from the beginning, understood itself as a progress beyond Judaism. That break was effected in a classic manner by a solitary man—Spinoza. Spinoza denied the truth of Judaism: Judaism, which includes, of course, the Bible, is a set of prejudices and superstitious practices of the ancient tribes. Spinoza found in this mass of heterogeneous lore some elements of truth, but he did not consider this as peculiar to Judaism. He found the same elements of truth in paganism as well. Spinoza was excommunicated by the Jewish community in Amsterdam. He ceased to regard himself as a Jew. He has sometimes been accused of having been hostile to Judaism and to Jews. I do not find that he was more opposed to Judaism than to Christianity, for example, and I do not find that he was hostile to Jews. He acquired a strange, or perhaps not so strange, neutrality in regard to the secular conflict between Judaism and Christianity. Looking at the Jews and the Jewish fate from this neutral point of view, he even made some suggestions as to the redemption of the Jews. One suggestion is almost explicit. After having asserted that the Jews have not been elected in any other sense than that in which the Canaanites too had been elected earlier, and that therefore the Jews have not been elected for eternity, he tries to show that their survival after the loss of the land can be explained in a perfectly natural manner. In this context, he makes the following remark: "If the foundations of their religion did not effeminate their minds, I would absolutely believe that they might again restore their state, under auspicious circumstances, considering the fact that human things are mutable" (*Theologico-Political Treatise*, chap. 3 near the end). This means that the hope for divine redemption is altogether baseless. The sufferings of the exiles are altogether meaningless. There is no guarantee whatsoever that these sufferings will ever cease. But the first condition for entertaining any reasonable hope for the end of the exile is that the Jews should get rid of the foundations of their religion, that is to say, of the spirit of Judaism. For that spirit, Spinoza thought, is adverse to warlike enterprise and to the energy of government. As far as I know, this is the earliest suggestion of a purely political solution to the Jewish problem: the substitution of a purely political solution for the miracle of redemption toward which men can contribute, if at all, only by a life of piety. This is the first inkling of unqualifiedly political Zionism. But Spinoza intimated still another solution. In his *Theologico-Political Treatise*, he sketched the outline of what he regarded as a decent society. That society, as described by him, can be characterized as a liberal democracy. Incidentally, Spinoza may be said to be the first philosopher who advocated liberal democracy. Spinoza still regarded it as necessary to underwrite liberal democracy with a public religion or a state religion. Now, it is very remarkable that that religion, that state religion, which was emphatically not a religion of reason, was neither Christian nor Jewish. It was neutral in regard to the differences between Judaism and Christianity. Furthermore, Spinoza claimed to have proved, on the basis of the Bible, that the Mosaic law was binding only for the period of the Jewish commonwealth. If one considers these two facts, first, that the state religion is neutral in regard to the differences between Judaism and Christianity, and second, that the Mosaic law is no longer binding, one is entitled to say that Spinoza laid the foundation for another purely political solution of the Jewish problem: for the alternative to political Zionism, the solution known as assimilationism.

In Spinoza's liberal democracy, Jews do not have to become baptized in order to acquire full citizen rights. It is sufficient if they accept the extremely latitudinarian state religion, and they may then forget about the Mosaic law. In this neutral atmosphere, the sufferings of the exiles could be expected to wither away. Spinoza has merely intimated the two classical alternatives which followed from the radical break with Judaism. The practical consequences were fully developed in the course of the nineteenth century. But when they were exposed to the test of practice, they led into certain difficulties.

On the premise of assimilationism, Jewish suffering—suffering for Judaism—becomes meaningless. That suffering is merely the residue of a benighted past, a residue which will cease in proportion as mankind makes further progress. But the results were somewhat disappointing. The decrease of the power of Christianity did not bring about the expected decrease of anti-Jewish feeling. Even where legal equality of the Jews became a fact, it contrasted all the more strongly with the social inequality which continued. In a number of countries, legal inequality and the cruder forms of social inequality gave way to subtler forms of social inequality, but the social inequality did not for this reason become less of a hardship. On the contrary, sensitivity increased with social ascent. Our ancestors had been immune to hatred and contempt because it merely proved to them the election of Israel. The uprooted, assimilated Jew had nothing to oppose to hatred and contempt except his naked self. Full social equality proved to require the complete disappearance of the Jews as Jews—a proposition which is impracticable, if for no other reason, then at least for the perfectly sufficient one of simple self-respect. Why should we, who have a heroic past behind and within us, which is not second to that of any other group anywhere on earth, deny or forget that past? (That past which is all the more heroic, one could say, since its chief characters are not the glitter and trappings of martial glory and of cultural splendor, although it does not lack even these.) Assimilation proved to require inner enslavement as the price of external freedom. Or, to put it somewhat differently, assimilationism seemed to lead the Jews into the bog of philistinism, of shallow satisfaction with the most unsatisfactory present: a most inglorious end for a people which had been led out of the house of bondage into the desert with careful avoidance of the land of the Philistines: "and it came to pass when Pharaoh had let the people go, that God led them not through the way of the land of the Philistines, although that was near" (Exodus 13:17). It is always near. Once progress was indeed achieved, hatred of the Jews could no longer present itself among educated or half-educated people as hatred of the Jews. It had to disguise itself as anti-Semitism, a term invented by some bashful German or French pedant of the nineteenth century. It is certainly a most improper term. The shock administered by the continued existence of social inequality and by the emergence of anti-Semitism, especially in Germany and France, proved to be a fair warning for what was going to happen in Germany, especially between 1933 and 1945.

Those European Jews who realized that assimilation was no solution to the Jewish problem and looked out for another purely human or political solution turned to political Zionism. But political Zionism led to difficulties of its own. The basic idea underlying purely political Zionism was not Zionist at all. It could have been satisfied by a Jewish state anywhere on earth. Political Zionism was already a concession to the Jewish tradition. Those who were seeking a solution of the Jewish problem other than the disappearance of the Jews had to accept not only the territory hallowed by Jewish tradition but its language, Hebrew, as well. They were forced to accept, furthermore, Jewish culture. "Cultural" Zionism became a very powerful rival of political Zionism. But the heritage to which cultural Zionism had recourse rebelled against being interpreted in terms of "culture" or "civilization," meaning, as an autonomous product of the genius of the Jewish people. That "culture" or "civilization" had its core in the Torah, and the Torah presents itself as given by God, not created by Israel. Thus the attempts to solve the Jewish problem by purely human means ended in failure. The knot which was not tied by man could not be untied by man. I do not believe that the American experience forces us to qualify these statements. It is very far from me to minimize the difference between a nation conceived in liberty and dedicated to the proposition that all men are created equal, and the nations of the old world, which certainly were not conceived in liberty. I share the hope in America and the faith in America, but I am compelled to add that that faith and that hope cannot be of the same character as that faith and that hope which a Jew has in regard to Judaism and which the Christian has in regard to Christianity. No one claims that the faith in America and the hope for America are based on explicit divine promises.

The attempt to solve the Jewish problem has failed because of the overwhelming power of the past. The experience of that power by a generation which had become forgetful of that power is part of what is sometimes called the discovery of history. The discovery was made in the nineteenth century. As a discovery, it consisted in the realization of something which was not realized previously: that the acceptance of the past or the return to the Jewish tradition is something radically different from mere continuation of that tradition. It is quite true that Jewish life in the past was almost always more than a continuation of a tradition. Very great changes within that tradition have taken place in the course of the centuries. But it is also true that the change which we are witnessing today, and which all of us are participating in, in one way or the other, is qualitatively different from all previous changes within Judaism.

Let me try to clarify that difference. Those who today return to Judaism do not assert that, say, Spinoza was altogether wrong.

They accept at least the principle of that Biblical criticism which was regarded as the major offense of Spinoza. Generally speaking, those who today return to Judaism admit that modern rationalism, to use this vague term, had a number of important insights which cannot be thrown overboard and which were alien to the Jewish tradition. Therefore, they modify the Jewish tradition consciously. You only have to contrast that with the procedure of Maimonides in the twelfth century, who, when introducing Aristotelian philosophy into Judaism, had to assume that he was merely recovering Israel's own lost inheritance. These present-day Jews who return to the tradition try to do in the element of reflection what traditionally was done unconsciously or naively. Their attitude is historical rather than traditional. They study the thought of the past as thought of the past and therefore as not necessarily binding on the present generation as it stands. But still, what they are doing is meant to be a return—that is to say, the acceptance of something which was equally accepted by the Jewish tradition. Thus the question arises as to the relative importance of these two elements: the new element and the unchanged element, the new element being the fact that present-day Judaism is forced to be what has been called "postcritical." Are we wiser than our ancestors in the decisive respect, or only in a subordinate respect? In the first case, we still would have to claim that we have made decisive progress. But if the insights implied in the "postcritical" character of present-day Judaism are only of a subordinate character, the movement which we are witnessing can justly claim to be a return. Now, this movement of return would not have had the effect which it has had, but for the fact that, not only among Jews but throughout the Western world more generally, progress has become a matter of doubt. The term "progress" in its full and emphatic meaning has practically disappeared from serious literature. People speak less and less of "progress" and more and more of "change." They no longer claim to know that we are moving in the right direction. Not progress but the "belief" in progress, or the "idea" of progress as a social or historical phenomenon, is a major theme for the present-day student of society. A generation or so ago, the most famous study on this subject was entitled *The Idea of Progress*. Its opposite number in present-day literature is entitled *The Belief in Progress*. The substitution of belief for idea is in itself worthy of note. Now, to understand the crisis of the belief in progress, we must first clarify the content of that belief.

What is progress? Progress, in the emphatic sense, presupposes that there is something which is simply good, or the end, as the goal of progress. Progress is change in the direction of the end. But this is only the necessary, not the sufficient, condition of the idea of progress. A sign of this is the notion of the Golden Age which also presupposes a notion of the simply good; but that simply good, that end, is here located in the beginning. The end of man, the simply good, must be understood in a specific manner if it is to become the basis of the idea of progress. I suggest that the end of man must be understood primarily as perfection of the understanding in such a manner that the perfection of the understanding is somehow akin to the arts and crafts. It has always been controversial whether man's beginning was perfect or imperfect, but both parties to the controversy admitted that the arts and the crafts, and certainly their perfection, do not belong to man's beginning. Therefore, the answer to the question of the perfection or imperfection of man's beginning depends upon how the question of the value of the arts and crafts is decided. At any rate, the idea of progress presupposes that there is the simply good life and that the beginning of life is radically imperfect. Accordingly, we find in Greek science or philosophy a full consciousness of progress: in the first place, of progress achieved; and its inevitable concomitant, looking down on the inferiority or the weakness of the ancients; and as regards future progress, Aristotle himself noted: "In the art of medicine, there is no limit to the pursuit of health, and in the other arts there is no limit to the pursuit of their several ends. For they aim at accomplishing their ends to the uttermost" (*Politics* 1257b25–28). The possibility of infinite progress, at least in certain respects, is here stated. Yet *the* idea of progress is different from the Greek conception of progress. What is the relative importance of fullfillment, on the one hand, and future progress on the other? The most elaborate statements on progress seemed to occur in Lucretius and Seneca, where the possibility of infinite progress in the sciences and arts was clearly stated. Yet Lucretius was an Epicurean, and Seneca was a Stoic, which means they both presupposed that the fundamental issue had been settled already, either by Epicurus or by the Stoa. No future progress, then, in the decisive respect was envisioned. Generally speaking, it seems that in classical thought the decisive questions were thought to have been answered as far as they can be answered. The only exception of which I know is Plato, who held that the fulfillment proper, namely full wisdom, is not possible, but only the quest for wisdom, which in Greek means philosophy. He also insisted that there are no assignable limits to that quest for wisdom, and therefore it follows from Plato's notion that indefinite progress is possible in principle.

Hitherto I have spoken of intellectual progress. What about social progress? Are they parallel? The idea that they are necessarily parallel, or that intellectual progress is accompanied in principle by social progress, was known to the classics. We find there the idea that the art of legislation, which is the overarching social art, progresses like any other art. Yet Aristotle, who reports this doctrine (*Politics* 1268b26ff.), questions this solution, and he notes the radical difference between laws and arts or intellectual pursuits. More generally stated, or more simply stated, he notes the radical difference between the requirements of social life and the requirements of intellectual life. The paramount requirement of society is stability, as distinguished from progress.

If I may summarize this point, in the classical conception of progress, it is clearly admitted that infinite intellectual progress in secondary matters is theoretically possible. But, we must add immediately, it is not practically possible. For according to the one school, the visible universe is of finite duration; it has come into being and will perish again. As for those holding the other view, that the visible universe is eternal, they asserted, especially Aristotle (*Politics* 1269a5–8), that there are periodic cataclysms which will destroy all earlier civilizations. Hence, eternal recurrence of the same progressive process, followed by decay and destruction. Now, what is distinctive in the classical conception as compared to the modern? I see two points. First, there is lacking in the classical conception the notion of a guaranteed parallelism between intellectual and social progress; secondly, there is in the modern conception no necessary end of the progressive process through telluric or cosmic catastrophes.

As to the first point—the guaranteed parallelism between social and intellectual progress—in the classical statements about progress, the emphasis is upon intellectual progress rather than on social progress. The basic idea can be stated as follows: science or philosophy is the preserve of a small minority, of those who "have good natures," as they called it, or who "are gifted," as we say. Their progress, the progress of this tiny minority, does not necessarily affect society at large—far from it. It was this thought which was radically challenged in the seventeenth century, at the beginning of modern philosophy and with the introduction of the crucial notion of the idea of method. Method brings about the levelling of the natural differences of the mind, and methods can be learned in principle by everyone. Only discovery remains the preserve of the few. But the acquisition of the results of the discovery, and especially of the discovery of methods, is open to all. And there is a very simple proof: mathematical problems which formerly could not be solved by the greatest mathematical geniuses are now solved by high-school students; the level of intelligence—that was the conclusion—has been enormously raised; and since this is possible, there is a necessary parallelism between intellectual and social progress.

As for the second point—the guarantee of an infinite future on earth not interrupted by telluric catastrophes—we find this thought fully developed in the eighteenth century. The human race had a beginning but no end, and it began about seven thousand years ago (the thinker I have in mind did not accept the Biblical chronology). Hence, since mankind is only seven thousand years old, it is still in its infancy. An infinite future is open, and look what we have achieved in this short span—compared with infinity—of seven thousand years! The decisive point is then this: there is a beginning and no end. Obviously the argument presupposes a beginning; otherwise you cannot figure out this infinite progress. The origin of this idea—a beginning but no end—could perhaps be found in Plato's dialogue *Timaeus*, if one takes that literally. Yet Plato certainly admitted regular telluric catastrophes. The source, I think, has to be found in a certain interpretation of the Bible, which we find, for example, in Maimonides, where you have the beginning—the creation—and no end, and cataclysms are excluded, not by natural necessity, but by the covenant of God with Noah. Yet precisely on the basis of the Bible, the beginning cannot be imperfect. Moreover, such additional important notions as the power of sin and of the need for greater redemption counter the effect of the notion of progress necessarily. Then again, in the Bible the core of the process from the beginning to the end is not progress. There is a classic past, whether we seek it at Mount Sinai or in the patriarchs or wherever else. Furthermore, and quite obviously, the core of the process as presented in the Bible is not intellectual-scientific development. The availability of infinite time for infinite progress appears, then, to be guaranteed by a document of revelation which condemns the other crucial elements of the idea of progress. Progress in the full and emphatic sense of the term is a hybrid notion.

This difficulty explains why the idea of progress underwent a radical modification in the nineteenth century. I quote one specimen:

> Truth can no longer be found in a collection of fixed dogmatic propositions . . . but only in the process of knowing, which process ascends from the lower to ever higher stages. . . . All those stages are only perishable phases in the endless development from the lower to the higher. . . . There is no final absolute truth and no final absolute stage of the development. Nothing is imperishable except the uninterrupted process of becoming and perishing, of the endless ascent from the lower to the higher. . . . We do not have to consider here the question as to whether this view agrees with the present state of natural science, for at present natural science predicts a possible end to the existence of the earth and a certain end to the inhabitability of the earth. Natural science therefore assumes today that human history consists not only of an ascending, but also of a descending, process. However this may be, we are certainly still rather remote from the point where decline begins to set in. . . .

That statement was made by Friedrich Engels, the friend and co-worker of Karl Marx (*Ludwig Feuerbach und der Ausgang der deutschen klassischen Philosophie*, ed. H. Hayek, p. 6). Here we see infinite progress proper is abandoned, but the grave consequences of that are evaded by a wholly incomprehensible and unjustifiable "never mind." This more recent form of the belief in progress is based on the decision just to forget about the end, to forget about eternity.

The contemporary crisis of Western civilization may be said to be identical with the climactic crisis of the idea of progress in the full and emphatic sense of the term. I repeat, that idea consists of the following elements: the development of human thought as a whole is a progressive development; certainly the emergence of modern thought since the seventeenth century marks an unqualified progress beyond all earlier thought. There is a fundamental and necessary parallelism between intellectual and social progress. There are no assignable limits to intellectual and social progress. Infinite intellectual and social progress is actually possible. Once mankind has reached a certain stage of development, there exists a solid floor beneath which man can no longer sink. All these points have become questionable, I believe, to all of us. To mention only one point, perhaps the most massive one, the idea of progress was bound up with the notion of the conquest of nature, of man making himself the master and owner of nature for the purpose of relieving man's estate. The means for that goal was the new science. We all know of the enormous successes of the new science and of technology which is based on it, and we all can witness the enormous increase of man's power. Modern man is a giant in comparison to earlier man. But we have also to note that there is no corresponding increase in wisdom and goodness. Modern man is a giant of whom we do not know whether he is better or worse than earlier man. More than that, this development of modern science culminated in the view that man is not able to distinguish in a responsible manner between good and evil—the famous "value judgment." Nothing can be said responsibly about the right use of that immense power. Modern man is a blind giant. The doubt of progress led to a crisis of Western civilization as a whole, because in the course of the nineteenth century the old distinction between good and bad, or good and evil, had been progressively replaced by the distinction between progressive and reactionary. No simple, inflexible, eternal distinction between good and bad could give assurance to those who had learned to take their bearings only by the distinction between progressive and reactionary, as soon as these people had become doubtful of progress.

The substitution of the distinction between progressive and reactionary for the distinction between good and bad is another aspect of the discovery of history, to which I referred before. The discovery of history, to state this very simply, is identical with the substitution of the past or the future for the eternal—the substitution of the temporal for the eternal. Now, to understand this crisis of Western civilization, one cannot leave it at understanding the problematic character of the idea of progress, for the idea of progress is only a part, or an aspect, of a larger whole, of what we shall not hesitate to call modernity. What is modernity? A hard question, which cannot be discussed here in detail. However, I would like to offer one or two somewhat rambling considerations. First, one might remember the decisive steps which led up to the contemporary crisis of Western civilization, and to those who are familiar with these things I must apologize for the superficiality of what is now offered in brief; but I think it is important to recall these things nevertheless. Therefore regard this as a stenogram, not as an analysis.

Western civilization has two roots: the Bible and Greek philosophy. Let us begin by looking at the first of these elements, the Bible, the Biblical element. Modern rationalism rejected Biblical theology and replaced it by such things as deism, pantheism, and atheism. But in this process, Biblical morality was in a way preserved. Goodness was still believed to consist in something like justice, benevolence, love, or charity; and modern rationalism has generated a tendency to believe that this Biblical morality is better preserved if it is divorced from Biblical theology. Now this was, of course, more visible in the nineteenth century than it is today; it is no longer so visible today because one crucial event happened around 1870 or 1880: the appearance of Nietzsche. Nietzsche's criticism can be reduced to one proposition: modern man has been trying to preserve Biblical morality while abandoning Biblical faith. That is impossible. If the Biblical faith goes, Biblical morality must go too, and a radically different morality must be accepted. The term which Nietzsche used is "the will to power." Nietzsche meant it in a very subtle and noble manner, yet the crude and ignoble way in which it was later understood is not altogether independent of the radical change of orientation he suggested.

As for the other major component of Western civilization, the classical element, that is, the idea of philosophy or science, that too began to change. In the seventeenth century, a new philosophy and a new science began to emerge. They made the same claims as all earlier philosophy and science had done, but this seventeenth-century revolution produced something which had never existed before—Science with a capital S. Originally the attempt had been made to replace traditional philosophy and science by a new philosophy and a new science; but in the course of a few generations it appeared that only a part of the new philosophy and science was successful and, indeed, amazingly successful. No one could question these developments (e.g., Newtonian physics). But only a part of the new science or philosophy was successful, and then the great distinction between philosophy and science, which we are all familiar with, came into being. Science is the successful part of modern philosophy or science, and philosophy is the unsuccessful part—the rump. Science is therefore higher in dignity than philosophy. The consequence, which you know, is the depreciation of all knowledge which is not scientific in this peculiar sense. Science becomes the authority for philosophy in a way perfectly comparable to the way in which theology was the authority for philosophy in the middle ages. Science is *the* perfection of man's natural understanding of the world. But then, certain things took place in the nineteenth century, e.g., the discovery of non-Euclidean geometry and its use in physics, which made it clear that science cannot be described adequately as the perfection of man's natural understanding of the world, but rather as a radical modification of man's natural understanding of the world. In other words, science is based on certain fundamental hypotheses which, being hypotheses, are not absolutely necessary and which always remain hypothetical. The consequence was again drawn most clearly by Nietzsche: science is only one interpretation of the world among many. The scientific interpretation of the world has certain advantages, but that of course does not give it any ultimately superior cognitive status. The last consequence stated by some men in our age is as you know: modern science is in no way superior to Greek science, as little as modern poetry is superior to Greek poetry. In other words, even science, with its enormous prestige— a prestige higher than any other power in the modern world—is also a kind of giant with feet of clay, if you consider its foundations. As a consequence of this chain of scientific development the notion of a rational morality, the heritage of Greek philosophy, has, to repeat myself, lost its standing completely; all choices are, it is argued, ultimately nonrational or irrational.

II

The immediate cause of the decline of the belief in progress can perhaps be stated as follows: the idea of progress in the modern sense implies that once man has reached a certain level, intellectual and social or moral, there exists a firm level of being, below which he cannot sink. This contention, however, is empirically refuted by the incredible barbarization which we have been so unfortunate as to witness in our century. We can say that the idea of progress, in the full and emphatic sense of the term, is based on wholly unwarranted hopes. You can see this even in many critics of the idea of progress. One of the most famous critics of the idea of progress prior to the First World War was the Frenchman Georges Sorel, who wrote a book, *The Delusions of Progress*. But strangely, Sorel declared that the decline of the Western world was impossible because of the vitality of the Western tradition. I think that we have all now become sufficiently sober to admit that whatever may be wrong in Spengler—and there are many things wrong in Spengler—the very title, in the English translation especially, of the work *The Decline of the West* is more sober, more reasonable, than these hopes which lasted so long.

This barbarization which we have witnessed and which we continue to witness is not altogether accidental. The intention of the modern development was, of course, to bring about a higher civilization, a civilization which would surpass all earlier civilizations. Yet the effect of the modern development was something else. What has taken place in the modern period has been a gradual corrosion and destruction of the heritage of Western civilization. The soul of the modern development, one may say, is a peculiar realism, consisting in the notion that moral principles and the appeal to moral principles—preaching, sermonizing—are ineffectual, and therefore that one has to seek a substitute for moral principles which would be much more efficacious than ineffectual preaching. Such substitutes were found, for example, in institutions or in economics, and perhaps the most important substitute is what was called "the historical process," meaning that the historical process, is, in a way, a much more important guarantee for the actualization of the good life than what the individual could or would do through his own efforts. This change shows itself, as already noted, in the change of general language, namely, in the substitution of the distinction between progressive and reactionary for the distinction between good and bad—the implication being that we have to choose and to do what is conducive to progress, what is in agreement with the historical trends, and that it is indecent or immoral to be squeamish in such adaptations. Once it became clear, however, that historical trends are absolutely ambiguous and therefore cannot serve as a standard, or, in other words, that to jump on the bandwagon or the wave of the future is not more reasonable than to resist those trends, no standard whatever was left. The facts, understood as historical processes, indeed do not teach us anything regarding values, and the consequence of the abandonment of moral principle proper was that value judgments came to have no objective support whatsoever. To spell this out with the necessary clarity—although one knows this from the study of the social sciences—the values of barbarism and cannibalism are as defensible as those of civilization.

I have spoken of modernity as of something definite and hence knowable. An analysis of this phenomenon is out of the question here, as goes without saying. Instead I would like briefly to enumerate those characteristic elements of modernity which are particularly striking, at least to me. But I must make one observation in order to protect myself against gross misunderstanding. A modern phenomenon is not characterized by the fact that it is located, say, between 1600 and 1952, because premodern traditions of course survived and survive. And more than that, throughout the modern period, there has been a constant movement against this modern trend, from the very beginning. One phenomenon which is very well known, perhaps unduly well known, is the quarrel between the ancients and moderns at the end of the seventeenth century, which in its most well-known form was concerned with the relatively unimportant question of whether the French drama of the seventeenth century was really comparable to the classical drama. The real quarrel between the ancients and moderns did not concern the drama, of course, but concerned modern science and philosophy. There was a resistance to modern science from the very beginning: the greatest man in English letters who represented this was Swift; but then you have it again very strongly in German classicism in the second half of the eighteenth century; and then indeed in the nineteenth century this movement, this countermovement, was completely pushed to the wall as a great intellectual movement. But in a way, of course, the tradition still persisted. So having made clear that by modernity I do not mean something which is simply chronological, let me now indicate what I think are the most striking elements of modernity in a purely enumerative fashion without attempting an analysis.

The first characteristic feature of modern thought as modern thought, one can say, is its anthropocentric character. Although apparently contradicted by the fact that modern science with its Copernicanism is much more radically antianthropocentric than earlier thought, a closer study shows that this is not true. When I speak of the anthropocentric character of modern thought, I contrast it with the theocentric character of Biblical and medieval thought and the cosmocentric character of classical thought. You see this most clearly if you look at modern philosophy, which, while it does not have the general authority which modern science has, is nevertheless a kind of conscience or consciousness of modern science. One has only to look at the titles of the most famous books of modern philosophy to see that philosophy is, or tends to become, analysis of the human mind. You could also see this same trait easily, but that would be too laborious, by looking at which philosophic disciplines emerged in modern times that were unknown to earlier philosophy: all are parts of the philosophy of man or of the human mind. The underlying idea, which shows itself not in all places clearly but in some places very clearly, is that all truths, or all meaning, all order, all beauty, originate in the thinking subject, in human thought, in man. Some famous formulations: "We know only what we make"—Hobbes. "Understanding prescribes nature its laws"—Kant. "I have discovered a spontaneity, little known previously, of the monads of the thoughts"—Leibniz. To give you a very simple popular example, certain human pursuits which were formerly called imitative arts are now called creative arts. One must not forget that even the atheistic, materialistic thinkers of classical antiquity took it for granted that man is subject to something higher than himself, e.g., the whole cosmic order, and that man is not the origin of all meaning.

Connected with this anthropocentric character is a radical change of moral orientation, which we see with particular clarity in the fact of the emergence of the concept of rights in the precise form in which it was developed in modern social thought. Generally speaking, premodern thought put the emphasis on duty, and rights, as far as they were mentioned at all, were understood only as derivative from duties and subservient to the fulfillment of duties. In modern times, we find the tendency, again not always expressed with the greatest clarity but definitely traceable, to assign the primary place to rights and to regard the duties as secondary, if, of course, very important. This is connected with another fact: in the crucial period of the seventeenth century, where the change becomes most visible, it is understood that the basic right coincides with a passion. The passions are in a way emancipated, because in the traditional notion the passion is subordinate to the action, and the action means virtue. The change which we can observe throughout the seventeenth century in all the most famous revolutionary thinkers is that virtue itself is now understood as a passion. In other words, a notion that virtue is a controlling, refraining, regulating, ordering attitude towards passion—think of the image in Plato's *Phaedrus,* the horses and the charioteer—is given up when virtue itself is understood as a passion. This leads to another change which becomes manifest only at a somewhat later stage, namely, that freedom gradually takes the place of virtue; so that in much present-day thought you find, not that freedom is the same as license (that it is not goes without saying), but that the distinction between freedom and license takes on a different meaning, a radically different meaning. The good life does not consist, as it did according to the earlier notion, in compliance with a pattern antedating the human will, but consists primarily in originating the pattern itself. The good life does not consist of both a what and a how, but only of a how. To state it somewhat differently, and again repeating that I am only enumerating, man has no na-

ture to speak of. He makes himself what he is; man's very humanity is acquired. That is granted, I think, in many quarters; that is,
what is absolutely stable are certain so-called biological character-
istics and perhaps some very elementary psychological character-
istics, the character of perception, etc. But all interesting things are
not modelled on a pattern antedating human action, but are a
product of human activity itself. Man's very humanity is acquired.

And this leads me to the third point, which became fully clear
only in the nineteenth century, and which is already a kind of cor-
rective of this radical emancipation of man from the superhuman.
It became ever more clear that man's freedom is inseparable from
a radical dependence. Yet this dependence was understood as itself a product of human freedom, and the name for that is history.
The so-called discovery of history consists in the realization, or in
the alleged realization, that man's freedom is radically limited by
his earlier use of his freedom, and not by his nature or by the
whole order of nature or creation. This element is, I think, increasing in importance: so much so that today one tends to say that the
specific character of modern thought is "history," a notion which
in this form is, of course, wholly alien to classical thought or to any
premodern thought (Biblical thought as well, naturally). If I had
the time I would try to show that precisely in this so-called histo-
ricization of modern thought the problem of modernity becomes
most visible from a technical point of view, and a technical point
of view has a peculiarly convincing character, at least to a certain
type of person. But I leave it at that.

The crisis of modernity on which we have been reflecting leads
to the suggestion that we should return. But return to what? Obviously, to Western civilization in its premodern integrity, to the
principles of Western civilization. Yet there is a difficulty here, because Western civilization consists of two elements, or has two
roots, which are in radical disagreement with each other. We may
call these elements, as I have done elsewhere, Jerusalem and Athens, or, to speak in nonmetaphorical language, the Bible and
Greek philosophy. This radical disagreement today is frequently
played down, and this playing down has a certain superficial justification, for the whole history of the West presents itself at first
glance as an attempt to harmonize, or to synthesize, the Bible and
Greek philosophy. But a closer study shows that what happened,
and has been happening in the West for many centuries, is not a
harmonization but an attempt at harmonization. These attempts
at harmonization were doomed to failure for the following reason:

each of these two roots of the Western world sets forth one thing as the one thing needful, and the one thing needful proclaimed by the Bible is incompatible, as it is understood by the Bible, with the one thing needful proclaimed by Greek philosophy, as it is understood by Greek philosophy. To put it very simply and therefore somewhat crudely, the one thing needful according to Greek philosophy is the life of autonomous understanding. The one thing needful as spoken by the Bible is the life of obedient love. The harmonizations and synthesizations are possible because Greek philosophy can use obedient love in a subservient function, and the Bible can use philosophy as a handmaid; but what is so used in each case rebels against such use, and therefore the conflict is really a radical one. Yet this very disagreement presupposes some agreement. In fact, every disagreement, we may say, presupposes some agreement, because people must disagree about something and must agree as to the importance of that something. But in this case the agreement is deeper than this purely formal one.

Now, what, then, is the area of agreement between Greek philosophy and the Bible? Negatively we can say, and one could easily enlarge on this position, that there is a perfect agreement between the Bible and Greek philosophy in opposition to those elements of modernity which were described above. They are rejected explicitly or implicitly by both the Bible and Greek philosophy. But this agreement is, of course, only an implicit one, and we should rather look at the agreement as it appears directly in the texts. One can say, and it is not misleading to say, that the Bible and Greek philosophy agree in regard to what we may call, and we do call in fact, morality. They agree, if I may say so, regarding the importance of morality, regarding the content of morality, and regarding its ultimate insufficiency. They differ as regards that x which supplements or completes morality, or, which is only another way of putting it, they disagree as regards the basis of morality.

I will give you first a brief statement, a reminder rather, of the agreement. Now, some people assert that there is a radical and unqualified opposition between Biblical morality and philosophic morality. If one heard certain people speak, one would believe that the Greek philosophers did nothing but preach pederasty, whereas Moses did nothing but curb pederasty. These people must have limited themselves to a most perfunctory reading of a part of Plato's *Banquet* or of the beginning of the *Charmides;* they cannot have read the only work in which Plato set forth specific prescriptions for human society, namely, Plato's *Laws;* and what Plato's *Laws*

(835cff.) say about this subject agrees fully with what Moses says. Those theologians who identified the second table of the Decalogue, as the Christians call it, with the natural law of Greek philosophy were well-advised. It is as obvious to Aristotle as it is to Moses that murder, theft, adultery, etc., are unqualifiedly bad (*Ethics* 1107a9ff.). Greek philosophy and the Bible agree as to this, that the proper framework of morality is the patriarchal family, which is, or tends to be, monogamous, and which forms the cell of a society in which the free adult males, and especially the old ones, predominate. Whatever the Bible and philosophy may tell us about the nobility of certain women, in principle both insist upon the superiority of the male sex. The Bible traces Adam's Fall to Eve's temptation. Plato traces the fall of the best social order to the covetousness of a woman (*Republic* 549c–d). Consisting of free men, the society praised by the Bible and Greek philosophy refuses to worship any human being. I do not have to quote the Bible, for I read it in a Greek author who says, "You worship no human being as your Lord, but only the gods," and he expresses an almost Biblical abhorrence of human beings who claim divine honors. The Bible and Greek philosophy agree in assigning the highest place among the virtues, not to courage or manliness, but to justice. And by justice both understand, primarily, obedience to the law. The law that requires man's full obedience is in both cases not merely civil, penal, and constitutional law, but moral and religious law as well. It is, in Biblical language, the guidance, the Torah, for the whole life of man. In the words of the Bible, "It is your life," or "It is the tree of life for those who cling to it" (Proverbs 3:18); and in the words of Plato, "The law effects the blessedness of those who obey it" (see *Laws* 718b). Its comprehensiveness can be expressed by saying, as Aristotle does, "What the law does not command, it forbids" (*Ethics* 1138a8); and that, substantially, is the Biblical view as well, as is shown by such commandments as "Thou shall eat and be full" (Leviticus 25:19) and "Be fruitful and multiply" (Genesis 1:28). Obedience to a law of this kind is more than ordinary obedience; it is humility. No wonder that the greatest prophet of the Bible, as well as the most law-abiding among the Greeks, is praised for his humility. Law and justice, thus understood, are divine law and divine justice. The rule of law is fundamentally the rule of God, theocracy. Man's obedience or disobedience to the law provokes divine retribution. What Plato says in the tenth book of the *Laws* about man's inability to escape from divine retribution is almost literally identical with certain verses of

Amos and Psalm 139. In this context, one may even mention, and without apology I think, the kinship between the monotheism of the Bible and the monotheism toward which Greek philosophy is tending, and the kinship between the first chapter of Genesis and Plato's *Timaeus*. But the Bible and Greek philosophy agree not merely regarding the place which they assign to justice, the connection between justice and law, the character of law, and divine retribution. They also agree regarding the problem of justice, the difficulty created by the misery of the just and the prospering of the wicked. One cannot read Plato's description in the second book of the *Republic* of the perfectly just man who suffers what would be the just fate of the most unjust man without being reminded of Isaiah's description of him who has done no violence, neither was any deceit in his mouth, yet who was oppressed and afflicted and brought as a lamb to the slaughter (Isaiah 53:7). And just as Plato's *Republic* ends with restoring all kinds of prosperity to the just, the Book of Job ends with the restoration to the just Job of everything he had temporarily lost.

Now, in the course of these extremely summary remarks, I have tacitly replaced morality by justice, understanding by "justice" obedience to the divine law. This notion, the divine law, it seems to me is the common ground between the Bible and Greek philosophy. And here I use a term which is certainly easily translatable into Greek as well as into Biblical Hebrew. But I must be more precise. The common ground between the Bible and Greek philosophy is the problem of divine law. They solve that problem in a diametrically opposed manner.

Before I speak of the root of their difference, I would like to illustrate the fundamental antagonism between the Bible and Greek philosophy by enumerating some of its consequences. I have indicated the place of justice in both the Bible and Greek philosophy. We may take Aristotle's *Ethics* as the most perfect, or certainly the most accessible, presentation of philosophic ethics. Now, Aristotle's *Ethics* has two foci, not one: one is justice; the other, however, is magnanimity or noble pride. Both justice and magnanimity comprise all other virtues, as Aristotle says, but in different ways. Justice comprises all other virtues insofar as the actions flowing from them relate to other men; magnanimity, however, comprises all other virtues insofar as they enhance the man himself. Now, there is a close kinship between Aristotle's justice and Biblical justice, but Aristotle's magnanimity, which means a man's habitual claiming for himself great honors while he deserves these honors, is alien to the Bible. Biblical humility excludes magnanimity in the Greek sense. There is a close relation between the magnanimous man and the perfect gentleman. There occur a few, very few, gentlemen and ladies in the Bible—I hope that this remark is not understood as a criticism of the Bible. There is Saul, who disobeys a divine command and by doing so does the noble thing—he spares his brother, King Agag, and destroys only what is vile and refuse. For this he was rejected by God, and Agag was hewn to pieces by the prophet Samuel before the Lord. Instead of Saul, God elected David, who did a lot of things a gentleman would not do, who was one of the greatest sinners, but at the same time one of the greatest repenters, who ever lived. There is a gentleman, Jonathan, who was too noble to compete with his friend David for kingship in Israel. There is a lady, Michal, the wife of David, who saw David leaping and dancing before the Lord; she despised him in her heart and ridiculed him for having shamelessly compromised his royal dignity by leaping and dancing before the riffraff, but she was punished by God with sterility. I need not dwell on the obvious connection between the Biblical rejection of the concept of a gentleman and the Biblical insistence on man's duties to the poor. The Greek philosophers were very far from being vulgar worshippers of wealth—must I say so? Socrates lived in thousandfold poverty, as he himself says, and he failed to see why a horse can be good without having money, whereas a man cannot. But they held that, as far as the general run of men is concerned, virtue presupposes a reasonable economic underpinning. The Bible, on the other hand, uses poor and pious or just as synonymous terms. Compared with the Bible, Greek philosophy is heartless in this as well as in other respects. Magnanimity presupposes a man's conviction of his own worth. It presupposes that man is capable of being virtuous, thanks to his own efforts. If this condition is fulfilled, consciousness of one's shortcomings or failings or sins is something which is below the good man. Again I quote Aristotle: "Sense of shame [which is such consciousness of human failing] befits young men who cannot yet be fully virtuous, but not men of mature age who are free not to do the wrong thing in the first place" (Ethics 1128b1off.). Or, to quote the remark made by one twentieth-century gentlemen about another, "Disgrace was impossible because of his character and behavior." The Greek philosophers differed as to whether man can become fully virtuous, but if some deny this possibility, as Socrates does, they merely replace self-satisfaction, the self-admiration of the virtuous man, by

the self-satisfaction or self-admiration of him who steadily progresses in virtue. Socrates does not imply, as far as the happy few
are concerned, that they should be contrite, be repentant, or express a sense of guilt. Man's guilt was indeed the guiding theme
of tragedy. Hence Plato rejects tragedy from his best city. (I do not
say that this is the whole story; that this is only a part of the story
you see from the fact that tragedy is replaced by songs praising the
virtuous). And according to Aristotle, the tragic hero is necessarily
an average man, not a man of the highest order. Moreover, it
should be noted that tragedy is composed and performed for the
benefit of the multitude. Its function is to arouse the passions of
fear and pity while at the same time purging them.

Now, fear and pity are precisely the passions which are necessarily connected with the feeling of guilt. When I become guilty,
when I become aware of my being guilty, I have at once the feeling
of pity toward him whom I have hurt or ruined and the feeling of
fear of him who avenges my crime. Humanly speaking, the unity
of fear and pity combined with the phenomenon of guilt might
seem to be the root of religion. God, the king or the judge, is the
object of fear; and God, the father of all men, makes all men brothers and thus hallows pity. According to Aristotle, without these
feelings, which have to be purged by tragedy, the better type
of man is liberated from all morbidity and thus can turn whole-
heartedly to noble action. Greek philosophy has frequently been
blamed for the absence from it of that ruthless examination of one's
intentions which is the consequence of the Biblical demand for pu-
rity of the heart. "Know thyself" means for the Greeks, know what
it means to be a human being, know what is the place of man in
the universe, examine your opinions and prejudices, rather than,
search your heart. This philosophic lack of depth, as it is called,
can consistently be maintained only if God is assumed not to be
concerned with man's goodness or if man's goodness is assumed
to be entirely his own affair. The Bible and Greek philosophy
agree, indeed, as to the importance of morality or justice and as to
the insufficiency of morality, but they disagree as to what completes morality. According to the Greek philosophers, as already
noted, it is understanding or contemplation. Now, this necessarily
tends to weaken the majesty of the moral demands, whereas humility, a sense of guilt, repentance, and faith in divine mercy,
which complete morality according to the Bible, necessarily
strengthen the majesty of the moral demands. A sign of this is the
fact that contemplation is essentially a transsocial or asocial possi-

bility, whereas obedience and faith are essentially related to the community of the faithful. To quote the Jewish medieval thinker, Yehuda Halevi, "The wisdom of the Greeks has most beautiful blossoms, but no fruits," with fruits here meaning actions (*Divan*, 2 vols., ed. Heinrich B. Brody [Berlin, 1899 (vol. 1) and 1909 (vol. 2)], 2.166). That asocial perfection which is contemplation normally presupposes a political community, the city, which accordingly is considered by the philosophers as fundamentally good, and the same is true of the arts, without whose services, and even model, political life and philosophic life are not possible. According to the Bible, however, the first founder of a city was the first murderer, and his descendants were the first inventors of the arts. Not the city, not civilization, but the desert, is the place in which the Biblical God reveals himself. Not the farmer Cain, but the shepherd Abel, finds favor in the eyes of the Biblical God.

The force of the moral demand is weakened in Greek philosophy because in Greek philosophy this demand is not backed up by divine promises. According to Plato, for example, evil will never cease on earth, whereas according to the Bible the end of days will bring perfect redemption. Hence the philosopher lives in a state above fear and trembling as well as above hope, and the beginning of his wisdom is not, as in the Bible, the fear of God, but rather the sense of wonder; Biblical man lives in fear and trembling as well as in hope. This leads to a peculiar serenity in the philosopher, which I would like to illustrate here by only one example which I think is not wholly accidental. The prophet Nathan seriously and ruthlessly rebukes King David for having committed one murder and one act of adultery. I contrast that with the way in which a Greek poet-philosopher (in Xenophon's *On Tyranny*) playfully and elegantly tries to convince a Greek tyrant who has committed an untold number of murders and other crimes that he would have derived greater pleasure if he had been more reasonable. I think I can illustrate the difference also by two other characteristic events or accounts. Think of the account of the Akedah—the binding of Isaac—in the story of Abraham. There the crucial point is that Abraham obeys an unintelligible command; the command is unintelligible because he has been promised that his name would be called through Isaac and in the descendants of Isaac, and now he is asked to slaughter that son. Yet Abraham obeys the command unhesitatingly. The only analogy in Greek philosophy of which I can think would be the example of Socrates, who is, or believes at least that he has been, commanded by Apollo to something, and yet the action consists not in unhesitating obedience, but in examining an unintelligible saying of Apollo.

Now, after these illustrations, what is the difference? The principles were clarified in the medieval discussion, in the heyday of theological discussion; Maimonides especially, in the *Guide of the Perplexed*, is probably the greatest analyst of this fundamental difference. The issue as he stated it was as follows: philosophy teaches the eternity of the world, and the Bible teaches creation out of nothing. This conflict must be rightly understood, because Maimonides is primarily thinking of Aristotle, who taught the eternity of the visible universe. But if you enlarge that and apply it not only to this cosmos, to this visible universe in which we live now, but to any cosmos or chaos which might ever exist, certainly Greek philosophy teaches the eternity of cosmos or chaos; whereas the Bible teaches creation, implying creation out of nothing. The root of the matter, however, is that only the Bible teaches divine omnipotence, and the thought of divine omnipotence is absolutely incompatible with Greek philosophy in any form. And I think one can even trace that back to the very beginnings of Greek literature—though technically much beyond philosophy—to the passage in the *Odyssey* (10.302) where Hermes shows Odysseus a certain herb which he could use for protecting himself and his fellows against Circe. Now, in this context, the gods can do everything, the gods are omnipotent, one can say, but it is very interesting what this concept means in this context. Why are the gods omnipotent? Because they know the natures of all things, which means, of course, they are not omnipotent. They know the natures of things which are wholly independent of them, and through that knowledge they are capable of using all things properly. In all Greek thought, we find in one form or the other an impersonal necessity higher than any personal being; whereas in the Bible the first cause is, as people say now, a person. This is connected with the fact that the concern of God with man is absolutely, if we may say so, essential to the Biblical God; whereas that concern is, to put it very mildly, a problem for every Greek philosopher. Stated somewhat differently, what is now called religious experience is underlined in the Bible and is understood by the Bible as genuine experience; whereas from the point of view of the Greek philosophers, this religious experience is a questionable interpretation—I take the example of Plato—a questionable interpretation of experience of the soul as an all-pervasive principle (see *Laws* 10).

We must try, as far as it is possible, to understand this antagonism. It can well be questioned whether what I am going to say can in truth be called an attempt at understanding, and so you can take it as a kind of illustration from the point of view of, say, social science. In order to clarify this antagonism, it is proposed that we go back to the common stratum between the Bible and Greek philosophy, to the most elementary stratum, a stratum which is common, or can be assumed to be common, to all men. How can we find that? I think it is easier to start from philosophy, for the simple reason that the question which I raise here is a scientific or philosophic question. We have to move in the element of conceptual thought, as it is called, and that is of course the element of Greek philosophy. With a view to this fact, I would like to state the issue more precisely. What distinguishes the Bible from Greek philosophy is the fact that Greek philosophy is based on this premise: that there is such a thing as nature, or natures—a notion which has no equivalent in Biblical thought. It should be noted that there is no Hebrew-Biblical term for nature, the Hebrew word being derived very indirectly from a Greek word which is an equivalent of "nature," *charakter, teva* in Hebrew. So the issue from this point of view would be this: we have to go back behind that discovery or invention of nature. We have to try to discern what we may call the prephilosophical equivalent of nature, and, by starting from that, perhaps we can arrive at a purely historical understanding of the antagonism we are analyzing. Let me add, parenthetically, another point. Philosophy is the quest for principles, meaning—and let us be quite literal—for the beginnings, for the first things. This is, of course, something common to philosophy and myth, and I would suggest for the time being that philosophy, as distinguished from myth, comes into being when the quest for the beginnings is understood in the light of the idea of nature.

Now what is the prephilosophic equivalent of nature? I think we can find the answer to this question in such notions as "custom" or "way." This answer occurred to me, very simply, as a result of reading Maimonides, who knew the true roots of which I speak very well indeed. In the beginning of his great legal work, the *Mishneh Torah*, in the first section, the "Hilchot Yesodei ha-Torah," "Laws Regarding the Foundations of the Torah," chapter 4, he speaks of the four elements. Before he introduces the term nature, he speaks first of the custom or way—the custom of fire, and the way of earth; somewhat later he refers to the nature of water. And this insight goes, I think, to the root of the problem. The rubrics "custom" and "way" are Biblical notions and are, of course, also to be found in Greek sources. Moreover, I would assume, until the contrary has been proven, that these ideas are really universal ones. People in all times and places have observed that things behave in a regular manner, that they have customs of behaving and ways of behaving. Take, for example, a Biblical expression, *derech nashim*, the way of women, menstruation, or in Greek an expression such as *boskematōn dikē*, the custom of beasts, meaning the same as the nature of beasts. Or again, in Biblical Hebrew, the word *mishpat* means the custom or the law of a thing as reflected in its regular behavior. In this context it is clear that no distinction is made between the custom of dogs and the custom of the Philistines; for example, a Philistine regularly behaves in his way, and the dog regularly behaves in his way. You can also take lions and Hebrews, if you think I employ only poor examples. So things have regular behavior, customs or ways. I have also learned from a Hindu student that the Hindy term *dharma*, which is usually translated as "religion," means custom or way, and can refer to such things as the custom or way of iron, of trees, and of whatnot. And since the custom or way of human beings is, of course, the Hindu religion, it means derivatively, if most importantly, what is according to religion.

If we now assume that this idea of the "way" is really the prephilosophical equivalent of nature, we have immediately to add this very obvious observation: that there is one way, among the many ways, which is particularly important, and that is the way of the group to which one belongs—our way. Now, our way is, of course, the right way. And why is it right? The answer: because it is old, and because it is one's own, or, to use the beautiful expression of Edmund Burke, because it is "home-bred and prescriptive" (*Letters on a Regicide Peace* 4). We can bring it all together under the term "ancestral." Hence the original notion is that the ancestral is identical with the good. The good is necessarily ancestral, which implies, since man was always a thinking being, that the ancestors were superior. If this were not the case, in what sense would the ancestral be good? The ancestors are superior, and therefore the ancestors must be understood, if this notion is fully thought through, as gods or sons of gods, or pupils of gods. In other words, it is necessary to consider the right way as the divine law, *theos nomos*. Whether this conclusion is always reached is, of course, uninteresting to us, because we admit the possibility that sometimes people do not think with sufficient penetration; but in those places where they did they arrived at this understanding.

Unfortunately, the divine law, the *theos nomos*, to use the Greek image, leads to two fundamental alternatives: one is the character of Greek philosophy; the other is the character of the Bible. Now, why is the divine law problematic? The answer is all too familiar: i.e., the variety of divine laws. We find everywhere such orders claiming to be divine, and these orders are not only different from each other—that would not technically be a difficulty, because different gods could have assigned different codes to different tribes—but they contradict each other. In every code of this kind, there are some elements which claim to be universal. One only has to read Herodotus to get very beautiful examples of conflicting claims: one tribe burned the dead, and the other tribe buried them. Now, the alternative burial custom was not only looked upon as a different folklore, a different cultural pattern, but as an abomination. So we may say that different laws contradict each other, and they contradict each other especially regarding what they say about the first things, because no early code, written or unwritten, is thinkable without a preamble which explains the obligations involved and which provides an account of the first things. Given this variety and this contradictory character of the various allegedly divine codes, it becomes necessary to transcend this whole dimension, to find one's bearings independently of the ancestral, or to realize that the ancestral and the good are two fundamentally different things despite occasional coincidences between them.

There is, too, the basic question of how to find one's bearings in the cosmos. The Greek answer fundamentally is this: we have to discover the first things on the basis of inquiry. We can note two implications of what inquiry means here. In the first place, inquiry implies seeing with one's own eyes as distinguished from hearsay; it means observing for oneself. Secondly, the notion of inquiry presupposes the realization of the fundamental difference between human production and the production of things which are not manmade, so that no conclusion from human production to the production of nonmanmade things is possible except if it is first established by demonstration that the visible universe has been made by thinking beings. This implication, I think, is decisive: it was on the basis of the principles of Greek philosophy that what later became known as demonstrations of the existence of God or gods came into being. This is absolutely necessary, and that is true not only in Aristotle, but in Plato as well, as you see, for example, from the tenth book of the *Laws*. An ascent from sense perception and reasoning on sense data, an ascent indeed guided, according to Plato and Aristotle, by certain notions, leads upwards; and everything depends on the solidity of the ascending process, on the demonstration. The quest for the beginning, for the first things, becomes now the philosophic or scientific analysis of the cosmos; the place of the divine law, in the traditional sense of the term, where it is a code traced to a personal God, is replaced by a natural order, which may even be called, as it was later to be called, a natural law—or at any rate, to use a wider term, a natural morality. So the divine law, in the real and strict sense of the term, is only the starting point, the absolutely essential starting point, for Greek philosophy, but it is abandoned in the process. And if it is accepted by Greek philosophy, it is accepted only politically, meaning for the education of the many, and not as something which stands independently.

To understand the Biblical notion in the sense of understanding to which I refer, one can say this: the Bible, Biblical thought, clings to this notion that there is one particular divine law; but it contends that this particular divine law is the only one which is truly divine law. All these other codes are, in their claim to divine origin, fraudulent. They are figments of man. Since, however, one code is accepted, then no possibility of independent questioning arises or is meant to arise. Now, what, then, is it that distinguishes the Biblical solution from the mythical solution? I think it is this: that the author or authors of the Bible were aware of the problem of the variety of the divine laws. In other words, they realized, and I am now speaking not as a theologian but as a historian, they realized what are the absolutely necessary conditions if one particular law should be *the* divine law. How has one to conceive of the whole if one particular, and therefore contingent, law of one particular, contingent tribe is to be the divine law? The answer is: it must be a personal God; the first cause must be God; He must be omnipotent, not controlled and not controllable. But to be knowable means to be controllable, and therefore He must not be knowable in the strict sense of the term. Thus in the language of later thought, of already Graecified thought, God's essence is not knowable; as the Bible says, one cannot see God's face. But this is not radical enough, and the divine name given in Exodus, which literally translated means, "I shall be what I shall be," is the most radical formulation of that. It is just the opposite of the Greek notion of essence, where it means the being is what it is and was and will be. But here the core, one could say, is inaccessible; it is absolutely free: God is what he shall be. It is a free God, unpredictable.

Why then can man trust Him? Answer: only because of the covenant. God has freely bound himself, but all trust depends on trust in God's word, in God's promise; there is no necessary and therefore intelligible relation; and, needless to say, this covenant is not a free covenant, freely entered into by originally independent partners; it is a covenant which, according to the Bible, God commanded man to perform.

To complete this extremely sketchy picture by a few points, I would like to say this. There is no doubt that the Greek philosophers of the classical period did not know the Bible, and it is, I think, generally admitted that the authors of the Bible did not know the Greek philosophers. But the extraordinary fact is that if one studies both the Greek philosophers and the Bible a little more carefully, one sees that in both sources of Western thought the alternative was, if I may say so, divined. Even in Aristotle you will find passages where he speaks of certain very crude notions in Greece which pointed fundamentally to what we know in the Bible in a more developed form, e.g., the notion that maybe it is bad to devote oneself to the philosophical rebellion against God.

By way of comparison, now, consider the perfect agreement, as to the decisive Biblical message, between the first account of creation and the second account of creation, the account which culminates in the story of the Fall. The same notion underlies the account in the first chapter, the depreciation of heaven, and the prohibition against the eating of fruit of the tree of knowledge of good and evil. For the knowledge of good and evil means, of course, not one special branch of knowledge—as is shown by the fact that in God's knowing of the created things, the verse always ends, "And He saw that it was good." The completed thing, the complete knowledge of the completed thing, is knowledge of the good, the notion being that the desire for, striving for, knowledge is forbidden. Man is not meant to be a theoretical, a knowing, a contemplating being; man is meant to live in childlike obedience. Needless to say, this notion was modified in various ways in the later tradition, but it seems to me that the fundamental thought was preserved, if we disregard some marginal developments.

What then is the principle underlying the seemingly changed attitude of later times? I think we can understand this from the Bible itself. You recall that the story of the Fall is followed by the account of Cain and later on by the genealogy of Cain, where the city and the arts are assigned to this undesirable branch of mankind; and yet later on we find that there is a very different attitude toward the city and the arts: think of the holy city of Jerusalem, and of the arts which Bezalel used in adorning the Temple, etc. I think we find the clearest discussion of this issue later on, in the discussion of kingship, of the institution of human kingship in Israel, in the first book of Samuel, where we see what the general trend of the Biblical solution is. Fundamentally, the institution of human kingship is bad—it is a kind of rebellion against God, as are the polis and the arts and knowledge. But then it becomes possible, with divine dispensation, that these things, which originate in human rebellion, become dedicated to the service of God and thus become holy. And I think that this is the Biblical solution to the problem of human knowledge: human knowledge, if it is dedicated to the service of God, and only then, can be good; and perhaps, in that sense, it is even necessary. But without that dedication it is a rebellion. Man was *given* understanding in order to understand God's commands. He could not be freely obedient if he did not have understanding. But at the same time this very fact allows man to emancipate the understanding from the service, from the subservient function for which it was meant, and this emancipation is the origin of philosophy or science from the Biblical point of view. And so the antagonism between them. Even if you take as your model, e.g., so-called Jewish medieval philosophy, you will still find that this difficulty is very noticeable.

Yet the meaning of philosophy is obscured by a number of facts; and therefore we must dwell upon it for a moment. The obscuration, I believe, is ultimately due to the fact that in the discussions regarding the relation of theology and philosophy, philosophy is identified with the completed philosophic system: in the Middle Ages, of course, primarily with Aristotle—by which I do not mean to say that Aristotle had a system, although it is sometimes believed that he had—but certainly with Hegel in modern times. That is, of course, one very special form of philosophy: it is not the primary and necessary form of philosophy. I have to explain that.

In a medieval work, the *Cuzari* (5.14) by Yehuda Halevi, we find this statement: "Socrates says to the people, 'I do not reject your divine wisdom, I simply do not understand it. My wisdom is merely human wisdom.'" Now in the mouth of Socrates, as in this apothegm, "human wisdom" means imperfect wisdom or the quest for wisdom, that is to say, philosophy. Since Socrates realizes the imperfection of human wisdom, it is hard to understand why he does not go from there to divine wisdom. The reason implied in this text is this: as a philosopher, he refuses assent to anything which is not evident to him, and revelation is for him not more than an unevident, unproven possibility. Confronted with an unproven possibility, he does not reject; he merely suspends judgment. But here a great difficulty arises, which one can state as follows: it is impossible to suspend judgment regarding matters of utmost urgency, regarding matters of life and death. Now, the question of revelation is evidently of utmost urgency. If there is revelation, unbelief in revelation or disobedience to revelation is fatal. Suspense of judgment regarding revelation would then seem to be impossible. The philosopher who refuses to assent to revelation because it is not evident therewith rejects revelation. But this rejection is unwarranted if revelation is not disproved. Which means to say that the philosopher, when confronted with revelation, seems to be compelled to contradict the very idea of philosophy by rejecting without sufficient grounds. How can we understand that? The philosophic reply can be stated as follows: the question of utmost urgency, the question which does not permit suspense, is the question of how one should live. Now, this question is settled for Socrates by the fact that he is a philosopher. As a philosopher, he knows that we are ignorant of the most important things. The ignorance, the evident fact of this ignorance, evidently proves that quest for knowledge of the most important things is the most important thing for us. Philosophy is then evidently the right way of life. This is, in addition, according to him, confirmed by the fact that he finds his happiness in acquiring the highest possible degree of clarity which he can acquire. He sees no necessity whatever to assent to something which is not evident to him. And if he is told that his disobedience to revelation might be fatal, he raises the question, What does fatal mean? In the extreme case, it would be eternal damnation. Now, the philosophers of the past were absolutely certain that an all-wise God would not punish with eternal damnation or with anything else such human beings as are seeking the truth or clarity. We must consider later on whether this reply is quite sufficient. At any rate, philosophy is meant, and that is the decisive point, not as a set of propositions, a teaching, or even a system, but as a way of life, a life animated by a peculiar passion, the philosophic desire, or eros. Philosophy is not understood as an instrument, or a department, of human self-realization. Philosophy understood as an instrument or as a department is, of course, compatible with every thought of life, and therefore also with the Biblical way of life. But this is no longer philosophy in the original sense of the term. This has been greatly obscured, I believe, by the Western development, because philosophy was certainly in the Christian Middle Ages deprived of its character as a way of life and became just a very important compartment.

I must therefore try to restate why, according to the original notion of philosophy, philosophy is necessarily a way of life and not a mere discipline, even if the highest discipline. I must explain, in other words, why philosophy cannot possibly lead up to the insight that another way of life apart from the philosophic one is the right one. Philosophy is the quest for knowledge regarding the whole. Because it is essentially a quest, because it is not able ever to become wisdom (as distinguished from philosophy), philosophy finds that the problems are always more evident than the solutions. All solutions are questionable. Now, the right way of life cannot be fully established except by an understanding of the nature of man, and the nature of man cannot be fully clarified except by an understanding of the nature of the whole. Therefore, the right way of life cannot be established metaphysically except by a completed metaphysics, and therefore the right way of life remains questionable. But the very uncertainty of all solutions, the very ignorance regarding the most important things, makes quest for knowledge the most important thing, and therefore makes a life devoted to it the right way of life. So philosophy in its original and full sense is, then, certainly incompatible with the Biblical way of life. Philosophy and the Bible are the alternatives, or the antagonists in the drama of the human soul. Each of the two antagonists claims to know or to hold the truth, the decisive truth, the truth regarding the right way of life. But there can be only one truth: hence, conflict between these claims, and necessarily conflict among thinking beings; and that means, inevitably, argument. Each of the two opponents has tried for millenia to refute the other. This effort is continuing in our day, and in fact it is taking on a new intensity after some decades of indifference.

III

Now I have to say a few words about the present-day argument. The present-day argument in favor of philosophy, we can say, is practically nonexistent because of the disintegration of philosophy. I have spoken on a former occasion of the distinction between philosophy and science, as understood today—a distinction which necessarily leads to a discrediting of philosophy. The contrast between the lack of results in philosophy and the enormous success of the sciences brings this about. Science is the only intellectual pursuit which today successfully can claim to be the perfection of the human understanding. Science is neutral in regard to revelation. Philosophy has become uncertain of itself. Just one quotation, a statement of one of the most famous present-day philosophers: "Belief in revelation is true, but not true for the philosopher. Rejection of revelation is true for the philosopher, but not true for the believer." Let us then turn to the more promising present-day argument in favor of revelation. (I shall not waste words on the most popular argument which is taken from the needs of present-day civilization, the present-day crisis, which would simply amount to this: that we need today, in order to compete with communism, revelation as a myth. Now this argument is either stupid or blasphemous. Needless to say, we find similar arguments also with Zionism, and I think this whole argument has been disposed of in advance a long time ago by Dostoevski in *The Possessed*.)

Now, the serious argument in favor of revelation can be stated as follows: there is no objective evidence whatever in favor of revelation, which means there is no shred of evidence in favor of revelation except, first, the experience, the personal experience, of man's encounter with God, and secondly, the negative proof of the inadequacy of any nonbelieving position. Now, as to the first point—there is no objective evidence in favor of revelation except the experience of one's encounter with God—a difficulty arises. Namely, what is the relation of this personal experience to the experience expressed in the Bible? It becomes necessary to distinguish between what the prophets experience, what we may call the call of God or the presence of God, and what they said—and this latter would have to be called, as it is today called by all nonorthodox theologians, a human interpretation of God's action. It is no longer God's action itself. The human interpretation cannot be authoritative. But the question arises, is not every specific meaning attached to God's call or to God's presence a human interpretation? For example, the encounter with God will be interpreted in radically different manners by the Jew on the one hand and by the Christian on the other, to say nothing of the Muslim and others. Yet only one interpretation can be the true one. There is therefore a need for argument between the various believers in revelation, an argument which cannot help but allude somehow to objectivity. As for the second point—the negative proof of the inadequacy of any nonbelieving position—that is usually very strong insofar as it shows the inadequacy of modern progressivism, optimism, or cynicism, and to that extent I regard it as absolutely convincing.

But that is not the decisive difficulty. The decisive difficulty concerns classical philosophy, and here the discussions, as far as I know them, do not come to grips with the real difficulty. To mention only one point, it is said that classical philosophy is based on a kind of delusion which can be proved to be a delusion. Classical philosophy is said to be based on the unwarranted belief that the whole is intelligible. Now, this is a very long question. Permit me here to limit myself to saying that the prototype of the philosopher in the classical sense was Socrates, who knew that he knew nothing, who therewith admitted that the whole is not intelligible, who merely wondered whether by saying that the whole is not intelligible we do not admit to having some understanding of the whole. For of something of which we know absolutely nothing, we could of course not say anything, and that is the meaning, it seems to me, of what is so erroneously translated by the intelligible, that man as man necessarily has an awareness of the whole. Let me only conclude this point. As far as I know, the present-day arguments in favor of revelation against philosophy are based on an inadequate understanding of classical philosophy.

Now, to find our bearings, let us return to a more elementary stratum of the conflict. What is truly significant in the present-day argument will then become clearer, and we shall understand also the reasons for the withdrawal from objectivity in the argument in favor of revelation in present-day theology. The typical older view regarding revelation and reason is today accepted fully only by the Catholic Church and by Orthodox Jews and orthodox Protestants. I shall speak of course only of the Jewish version. The question is, how do we know that the Torah is from Sinai, or is the word of the living God? The traditional Jewish answer is primarily that our fathers have told us, and they knew it from their fathers, an uninterrupted chain of a reliable tradition, going back to Mount Sinai. If the question is answered in this form, it becomes inevitable to wonder, is the tradition reliable? I will mention only one specimen from the earlier discussion. At the beginning of his legal code, Maimonides gives the chain of tradition from Moses down to Talmudic times, and there occurs the figure of Ahijah the Shilonite, who is said to have received the Torah from King David and also is introduced as a contemporary of Moses who had received the Torah from Moses. Now, whatever Maimonides may have meant by the insertion of this Talmudic story, from our point of view it would be an indication of the fact that this chain of the tradition, especially in its earlier parts, contains what today are called "mythical," that is to say unhistorical, elements. I shall not dwell on the very well-known discrepancies in the Bible. The question of who wrote the Pentateuch was traditionally answered, as a matter of course, by, "Moses," so much so that when Spinoza questioned the Mosaic origin of the Torah it was assumed that he denied its divine origin. Who wrote the Pentateuch: Moses himself, or men who knew of the revelation only from hearsay or indirectly? The details are of no interest to us here; we have to consider the principle.

Is a historical proof of the fact of revelation possible? A historical proof of the fact of revelation would be comparable to the historical proof of the fact, say, of the assassination of Caesar by Brutus and Cassius. That is demonstrably impossible. In the case of historical facts proper, or historical facts in the ordinary sense of the term, there is always evidence by impartial observers or by witnesses belonging to both parties. For example, here, friends and enemies of Caesar. In the case of revelation, there are no impartial observers. All witnesses are adherents, and all transmitters were believers. Furthermore, there are no pseudo-assassinations or pseudo-wars, but there are pseudo-revelations and pseudo-prophets. The historical proof presupposes, therefore, criteria for distinguishing between genuine and spurious revelation. We know the Biblical criterion, at least the decisive one in our context: a prophet cannot be a genuine prophet if he contradicts the preceding classic revelations, the Mosaic revelation. Therefore the question is how to establish the classic revelation.

The usual traditional answer was: miracles. But here the difficulty arises in this form: miracles as miracles are not demonstrable. In the first place, a miracle as a miracle is a fact of which we do not know the natural causes, but our ignorance of the cause of a given phenomenon does not entitle us to say it cannot have been produced by any natural cause, but only supernaturally. Our ignorance of the power of nature—that is Spinoza's phrasing of the argument—our ignorance of the power of nature disqualifies us from ever having recourse to supernatural causation. Now, this argument in this form is not quite adequate, for the following reason: while our knowledge of the power of nature is certainly very limited, of certain things we know, or at least men like Spinoza believed to know, that they are impossible by nature. I mention only the resurrection of a dead man, to take the strongest example, which Spinoza would admit could never have taken place naturally. Therefore the argument taken from the ignorance of the power of nature is supplemented by the following argument: that it might be possible theoretically to establish in given cases that a certain phenomenon is miraculous, but it so happens that all these events regarding which this claim is made are known only as reported, and many things are reported which have never happened. More precisely, all miracles which are important, certainly to the Jew and even to the Protestant (the case of Catholicism is different), took place in a prescientific age. No miracle was performed in the presence of first-rate physicists, etc. Therefore, for these reasons, many people today say, and it was also said by certain famous theologians of the past, that miracles presuppose faith; they are not meant to establish faith. But whether this is sufficient, whether this is in accordance with the Biblical view of miracles, is a question. To begin with, one could make this objection: that if you take the story of the prophet Elijah on Carmel, you see that the issue between God and Baal is decided by an objective occurrence equally acceptable to the sense perception of believers and unbelievers.

The second ordinary traditional argument in favor of revelation is the fulfillment of prophecies. But I need not tell you that this again is open to very great difficulties. In the first place, we have the ambiguity of prophecies, even in cases of unambiguous prophecies. For example, the prophecy of Cyrus in the fortieth chapter of Isaiah is today generally taken to be a prophecy after the event, the reasoning being that such a prophecy would be a miracle if established; but it is known only as reported, and therefore the question of historical criticism of the sources comes in.

Much more impressive is the other line of the argument, which proves revelation by the intrinsic quality of revelation. The revealed law is the best of all laws. Now, this, however, means that the revealed law agrees with the rational standard of the best law; but if this is the case, is then the allegedly revealed law not in fact the product of reason, of human reason, the work of Moses and not of God? Yet the revealed law, while it never contradicts reason, has an excess over reason; it is suprarational, and therefore it cannot be the product of reason. That is a very famous argument, but again we have to wonder what does suprarational mean? The supra has to be proved, and it cannot be proved. What unassisted reason sees is only a nonrational element, an element which, while not contradicting reason, is not in itself supported by reason. From the point of view of reason, it is an indifferent possibility: possibly true, possibly false, or possibly good, possibly bad. It would cease to be indifferent if it were proved to be true or good, which means if it were true or good according to natural reason. But again, if this were the case, it would appear to be the product of reason, of human reason. Let me try to state this in more general terms. The revealed law is either fully rational—in that case it is a product of reason—or it is not fully rational—in that case it may as well be the product of human unreason as of divine super-reason. Still more generally, revelation is either a brute fact, to which nothing in purely human experience corresponds—in that case it is an oddity of no human importance—or it is a meaningful fact, a fact required by human experience to solve the fundamental problems of man—in that case it may very well be the product of reason, of the human attempt to solve the problem of human life. It would then appear that it is impossible for reason, for philosophy, to assent to revelation as revelation. Moreover, the intrinsic qualities of the revealed law are not regarded as decisive by the revealed law itself. Revealed law puts the emphasis not on the universal, but on the contingent, and this leads to the difficulties which I have indicated before.

Let us now turn to the other side of the picture; these things are, of course, implied in all present-day secularism. Now, all these and similar arguments prove no more than that unassisted human reason is invincibly ignorant of divine revelation. They do not prove the impossibility of revelation. Let us assume that revelation is a fact, if a fact not accessible to unassisted reason, and that it is meant to be inaccessible to unassisted reason. For if there were certain knowledge, there would be no need for faith, for trust, for true obedience, for free surrender to God. In that case, the whole refutation of the alleged rejection of the alleged objective historical proofs of revelation would be utterly irrelevant. Let me take this simple example of Elijah on Carmel: were the believers in Baal, whom Elijah or God convinced, impartial scientific observers? In a famous essay, Francis Bacon made a distinction between idolators and atheists and said that the miracles are meant only for the conviction, not of atheists, but of idolators, meaning of people who in principle admit the possibility of divine action. These men were fearing and trembling, not beyond hope or fear like philosophers. Not theology, but philosophy, begs the question. Philosophy demands that revelation should establish its claim before the tribunal of human reason, but revelation as such refuses to acknowledge that tribunal. In other words, philosophy recognizes only such experiences as can be had by all men at all times in broad daylight. But God has said or decided that he wants to dwell in mist. Philosophy is victorious as long as it limits itself to repelling the attack which theologians make on philosophy with the weapons of philosophy. But philosophy in its turn suffers a defeat as soon as it starts an offensive of its own, as soon as it tries to refute, not the necessarily inadequate proofs of revelation, but revelation itself.

Now there is today, I believe, still a very common view, common to nineteenth- and twentieth-century freethinkers, that modern science and historical criticism have refuted revelation. I would say that they have not even refuted the most fundamentalistic orthodoxy. Let us look at that. There is the famous example which played such a role in the nineteenth century and, for those of us who come from conservative or orthodox backgrounds, in our own lives: the age of the earth is much greater than the Biblical reports assume. But this is obviously a very defective argument. The refutation presupposes that everything happens naturally; but this is denied by the Bible. The Bible speaks of creation; creation is a miracle, *the* miracle. All the evidence supplied by geology, paleontology, etc., is valid against the Bible only on the premise that no miracle intervened. The freethinking argument is really based on poor thinking. It begs the question. Similarly, as regards textual criticism—the inconsistencies, repetitions, and other apparent deficiencies of the Biblical text: if the text is divinely inspired, all those things mean something entirely different from what they would mean if we were entitled to assume that the Bible is a merely human book. Then they are just deficiencies, but otherwise they are secrets.

Historical criticism presupposes unbelief in verbal inspiration. The attack, the famous and very effective attack, by science and historical criticism on revelation is based on the dogmatic exclusion of the possibility of miracles and of verbal inspiration. I shall limit myself to miracles, because verbal inspiration itself is one miracle. Now, this attack, which underlies all the scientific and historical arguments, would be defensible if we knew that miracles are impossible. Then we would indeed be able to draw all these conclusions. But what does that mean? We would have to be in possession of either a proof of the nonexistence of an omnipotent God, who alone could do miracles, or of a proof that miracles are incompatible with the nature of God. I see no alternative to that. Now the first alternative—a proof of the nonexistence of an omnipotent God—would presuppose that we have perfect knowledge of the whole, so, as it were, we know all the corners, and that there is no place for an omnipotent God. In other words, the presupposition is a completed system. We have the solution to all riddles. And then I think we may dismiss this possibility as absurd. The second alternative—namely, that miracles are incompatible with the nature of God—would presuppose human knowledge of the nature of God: in traditional language, natural theology. Indeed, the basis, the forgotten basis, of modern free thought is natural theology. When the decisive battles were waged, not in the nineteenth century, but in the eighteenth and seventeenth, the attempted refutation of miracles, etc., was based on an alleged knowledge of the nature of God—natural theology is the technical name for that.

Let us sketch the general character of this argument. God is the most perfect being. This is what all men mean by God, regardless of whether He exists or not. Now, the philosophers claim that they can prove the incompatibility of revelation and of any other miracle with divine perfection. That is a long story, not only in the seventeenth and eighteenth centuries but of course also in the Middle Ages. I will try to sketch this argument by going back to its human roots. Fundamentally, the philosophic argument in natural theology is based on an analogy from human perfection. God is the most perfect being. But we know perfection empirically only in the form of human perfection, and human perfection is taken to be represented by the wise man or by the highest human approximation to the wise man. For example, just as the wise man does not inflict infinite punishment on erring human beings, God, still more perfect, would do so even less. A wise man does not do silly or purposeless things; but to use the miracle of verbal inspiration, for example, in order to tell a prophet the name of a pagan king who is going to rule centuries later, would be silly. This—or something of this kind—is the argument underlying these things. To this I would answer as follows: God's perfection implies that he is incomprehensible. God's ways may seem to be foolish to man; this does not mean that they are foolish. Natural theology would have to get rid, in other words, of God's incomprehensibility in order to refute revelation, and that it has never done.

There was one man who tried to force the issue by denying the incomprehensibility of God's essence, and that man was Spinoza. (May I say this in passing: that I have leaned very heavily in my analysis of these things on Spinoza.) One can learn much from

Spinoza, who is the most extreme, certainly, of the modern critics of revelation, not necessarily in his thought but certainly in the expression of his thought. I like to quote the remark of Hobbes—as you know, a notoriously bold man—who said that he had not dared to write as boldly as Spinoza. Now, Spinoza says, "We have adequate knowledge of the essence of God," and if we have that, God is clearly fully comprehensible. What Spinoza called the adequate knowledge of the essence of God led to the consequence that miracles of any kind are impossible. But what about Spinoza's adequate knowledge of the essence of God? Let us consider that for one moment, because it is really not a singular and accidental case. Many of you will have seen Spinoza's *Ethics*, his exposition of that knowledge. Spinoza's *Ethics* begins, as you know, with certain definitions. Now these definitions are in themselves absolutely arbitrary, especially the famous definition of substance: substance is what is by itself and is conceived by itself. Once you admit that, everything else follows from that; there are no miracles possible then. But since the definitions are arbitrary, the conclusions are arbitrary. The basic definitions are, however, not arbitrary if we view them with regard to their function. Spinoza defines by these definitions the conditions which must be fulfilled if the whole is to be fully intelligible. But they do not prove that these conditions are in fact fulfilled—that depends on the success of Spinoza's venture. The proof lies in the success. If Spinoza is capable of giving a clear and distinct account of everything, then we are confronted with this situation. We have a clear and distinct account of the whole, and, on the other hand, we have obscure accounts of the whole, one of which would be the Biblical account. And then every sane person would prefer the clear and distinct account to the obscure account. That is, I think, the real proof which Spinoza wants to give. But is Spinoza's account of the whole clear and distinct? Those of you who have ever tried your hand, for example, at his analysis of the emotions, would not be so certain of that. But more than that, even if it is clear and distinct, is it necessarily true? Are its clarity and distinctness not due to the fact that Spinoza abstracts from those elements of the whole which are not clear and distinct and which can never be rendered clear and distinct? Now, fundamentally, Spinoza's procedure is that of modern science according to its original conception—to make the universe a completely clear and distinct, a completely mathematizable, unit.

Let me sum this up: the historical refutation of revelation (and I say here that this is not changed if you take revelation in the most fundamentalist meaning of the term) presupposes natural theology, because the historical refutation always presupposes the impossibility of miracles, and the impossibility of miracles is ultimately guaranteed only by knowledge of God. Now, a natural theology which fills this bill presupposes in its turn a proof that God's nature is comprehensible, and this in its turn requires completion of the true system, or of the true or adequate account of the whole. Since such a true or adequate, as distinguished from a merely clear and distinct, account of the whole is certainly not available, philosophy has never refuted revelation. Nor, to come back to what I said before, has revelation, or rather theology, ever refuted philosophy. For from the point of view of philosophy, revelation is only a possibility; and secondly, man, in spite of what the theologians say, can live as a philosopher, that is to say, untragically. It seems to me that all these attempts (made, for example, by Pascal and by others) to prove that the life of philosophy is fundamentally miserable presuppose faith; these arguments are not acceptable and possible as a refutation of philosophy. Generally stated, I would say that all alleged refutations of revelation presuppose unbelief in revelation, and all alleged refutations of philosophy presuppose faith in revelation. There seems to be no ground common to both and therefore superior to both.

If one were to say, colloquially, the philosophers have never refuted revelation and the theologians have never refuted philosophy, that would sound plausible, considering the enormous difficulty of the problem from any point of view. And to that extent we may be said to have said something very trivial; but to show that it is not quite trivial, I submit to you this consideration in conclusion. And here when I use the term philosophy, I use it in the common and vague sense of the term where it includes any rational orientation in the world, including science and what-have-you, common sense. If the foregoing is so, philosophy must admit the possibility of revelation. Now, that means that philosophy itself is possibly not the right way of life. It is not necessarily the right way of life, not evidently the right way of life, because this possibility of revelation exists. But what then does the choice of philosophy mean under these conditions? In this case, the choice of philosophy is based on faith. In other words, the quest for evident knowledge rests itself on an unevident premise. And it seems to me that this difficulty underlies all present-day philosophizing, and that it is this difficulty which is at the bottom of what in the social sciences is called the value problem: that philosophy or science, however you might call it, is incapable of giving an account of its own necessity. I do not think I have to prove that showing the practical usefulness of science, natural and social science, does not, of course, prove its necessity at all. I mean I shall not speak of the great successes of the social sciences, because they are not so impressive; but as for the great successes of the natural sciences, we in the age of the hydrogen bomb have the question completely open again whether this effort is really reasonable with a view to its practical usefulness. That is, of course, not the most important consideration theoretically, but one which has practically played a great role.

However this may be, it seems to me that this antagonism must be considered by us in action. That is to say: it seems to me that the core, the nerve, of Western intellectual history, Western spiritual history, one could almost say, is the conflict between the Biblical and the philosophic notions of the good life. This was a conflict which showed itself primarily, of course, in arguments— arguments advanced by theologians on behalf of the Biblical point of view and by philosophers on behalf of the philosophic point of view. There are many reasons why this is important, but I would like to emphasize only one: it seems to me that this unresolved conflict is the secret of the vitality of Western civilization. The recognition of two conflicting roots of Western civilization is, at first, a very disconcerting observation. Yet this realization has also something reassuring and comforting about it. The very life of Western civilization is the life between two codes, a fundamental tension. There is therefore no reason inherent in Western civilization itself, in its fundamental constitution, why it should give up life. But this comforting thought is justified only if we live that life, if we live that conflict. No one can be both a philosopher and a theologian, nor, for that matter, some possibility which transcends the conflict between philosophy and theology, or pretends to be a synthesis of both. But every one of us can be and ought to be either one or the other, the philosopher open to the challenge of theology or the theologian open to the challenge of philosophy.

Notes

Introduction

1. Reprinted in Leo Strauss, *On Tyranny* (Ithaca: Cornell University Press, 1968).

2. See esp. chap. 13 of C. B. Macpherson, *Democratic Theory* (Oxford: Oxford University Press, 1973), and chap. 13 of Leo Strauss, *Studies in Platonic Political Philosophy* (Chicago: University of Chicago Press, 1983).

3. *Marxism and the Existentialists* (New York: Harper & Row, 1969), pp. 84ff.

4. Hans-Georg Gadamer, *Truth and Method* (New York: The Seabury Press, 1975), pp. 482–91; the letters exchanged between Strauss and Gadamer and between Strauss and Löwith were later published in *The Independent Journal of Philosophy* 2:5–12 (1978) and 4:105–119 (1983). See also Strauss's discussion of Löwith in *What is Political Philosophy?* (Glencoe: The Free Press, 1959), pp. 268–70.

5. "Ermeneutica e pensiero classico in Leo Strauss," reprinted in *Quarto contributo alla storia degli studi classici et del mondo antico* (Rome: Edizioni di Storia e Letteratura, 1969), pp. 117–28.

6. Brian Barry, *Political Argument* (London: Routledge and Kegan Paul, 1965), p. 290.

7. See, for example, Mr. Burnyeat's later, repeated attacks on Strauss in the *New York Review of Books:* 30 May, 10 October, and 24 October 1985; 24 April 1986; 31 March 1988.

8. Stephen Holmes, in *APSR* 73:113–28 (1979)—quote is from p. 113; and Stanley Rothman, in *APSR* 56:341–52 (1962)—quote is from p. 352.

9. J. G. Gunnell, in *APSR* 72:122–34 (1978)—quote is from p. 123.

10. J. G. A. Pocock, in *Political Theory* 3:384–401 (1975).

11. S. B. Drury, in *Political Theory* 13:315–37 (1985).

12. The chapter is reprinted from the proceedings of the conference: Leonard D. White, ed., *The State of the Social Sciences* (Chicago: University of Chicago Press, 1956), pp. 415–25 (© 1956 by the University of Chicago); I have omitted a few words at the beginning and later on that refer to the program of the conference.

13. In Helmut Schoeck and J. W. Wiggins, eds., *Relativism and the Study of Man* (Princeton: Van Nostrand, 1961), pp. 135–57. I have omitted some portions of the original essay that were redundant in the light of chapters one and three of the present volume.

14. It originally appeared in the journal *Social Research,* in February, 1945; reprinted with permission.

15. Previously published as "Exoteric Teaching," in *Interpretation: A Journal of Political Philosophy* 14 (1986), pp. 51–59; reprinted with permission.

16. *The City and Man* (Chicago: Rand McNally, 1964), chapter 3, sections 1 and 10, and "Greek Historians," *The Review of Metaphysics* 21, no. 4 (1968): 656–66.

17. The lecture from which a small portion was taken was previously published as "The Mutual Influence of Theology and Philosophy," in Hebrew translation in *Iyyun: Hebrew Philosophical Quarterly* 5:110–26 (1954), and in English in *The Independent Journal of Philosophy* 3:111–18 (1979); the other two lectures were previously published as "Progress or Return? The Contemporary Crisis in Western Civilization," *Modern Judaism* 1:17–45 (1981). Reprinted with permission.

Chapter Four

1. Note the procedure of Aristotle in *Politics* 1280a7–1284b34 and 1297a6–7; also Plato *Eighth Letter* 354a1–5 and 352c8ff., and *Laws* 627d11–628a4.

2. See Xenophon *Memorabilia* 4.6.14–15 and context; also Aristotle *Athenian Constitution* 28.5; also the remark by Hume (in his essay "Of the Original Contract"): "but philosophers, who have embraced a party (if that be not a contradiction in terms) . . ." The difference between the classical political philosopher and the present-day political scientist is illustrated by Macaulay's remark on Sir William Temple: "Temple was not a mediator. He was merely a neutral." Compare de Tocqueville, *De la démocratie en Amérique* [Preface, end]: "J'ai enterpris de voir, non pas autrement, mais plus loin que les partis."

3. Xenophon *Memorabilia* 3.6.2; Thucydides 1.138. See also Plato *Lysis* 209d5–210b2, and *Republic* 494c7–d1. One of the purposes of the *Menexenus* is to illustrate the "transferable" character of political science: a sufficiently gifted foreign woman is as capable as Pericles, or more capable than he, to compose a most solemn speech to be delivered on behalf of the city of Athens.

4. Plato *Protagoras* 319a1–2, and *Timaeus* 19e; also Aristotle *Nicomachean Ethics* 1181a12ff. as well as *Politics* 1264b33–34 and 1299a1–2; Isocrates *Nicocles* or, *The Cyprians* 9; Cicero *De oratore* 3.57.

5. Aristotle *Nicomachean Ethics* 1141b24–29 (compare 1137b13); also Plato *Gorgias* 464b7–8, and *Minos* 320c1–5; Cicero *Offices* 1.75–76. The classical view was expressed as follows by Rousseau, who still shared it, or rather restored it: "s'il est vrai qu'un grand prince est un homme rare, que sera-

ce d'un grand législateur? Le premier n'a qu'à suivre le modèle que l'autre doit proposer" (*Contrat social* 2.7).

6. Consider Plato *Laws* 630b8–c4 and 631d–632d, and Aristotle *Nicomachean Ethics* 1180a33ff. and 1109b34ff. as well as *Politics* 1297b37–38; cf. Isocrates *To Nicocles* 6 and Montesquieu, *Esprit des Lois*, beginning of the twenty-ninth book. On the difference between political science proper and political skill see Thomas Aquinas's commentary on Aristotle's *Ethics* 6, lectio 7, and also Alfarabi's *Enumeration of the Sciences*, chapter 5.

7. Not to mention the fact that the authors of the *Politics* and the *Cyropaedia* were "strangers" when they wrote those books. See *Politics* 1273b27–32.

8. Aristotle *Politics* 1300b36–39; Rousseau *Contrat social* 2.9.

9. Letter to John Adams, 28 October 1813.

10. See Aristotle *Nicomachean Ethics* 1094b18ff.; Xenophon *Memorabilia* 4.2.32ff.

11. See Aristotle *Politics* 1265a17ff. and 1325b33–40; Plato *Laws* 857e8–858c3; Cicero *Republic* 1.33.

12. See Plato *Laws* 739b8ff., and the beginning of the fourth book of Aristotle's *Politics*.

13. Aristotle *Nicomachean Ethics* 1135a4–5.

14. Plato *Republic* 427c2–3, 470e4ff. and 499c7–9; see also *Laws* 739c3 (compare *Republic* 373e with *Phaedo* 66c5–7), also *Theaetetus* 175a1–5, *Politicus* 262c8–263a1, *Cratylus* 390a, *Phaedo* 78a3–5, and *Laws* 656d–657b and 799aff.; also *Minos* 316d.

15. *Cyropaedia*, 1.1–2, 3.1.38–40; compare 2.2.26.

16. Hegel, *Vorlesungen ueber die Geschichte der Philosophie*, ed. Michelet-Glockner, 1:291: "Wir werden ueberhaupt die praktische Philosophie nicht spekulativ werden sehen, bis auf die neuesten Zeiten." See also Schelling, *Studium Generale*, ed. Glockner, 94–95.

17. See Aristotle *Nicomachean Ethics* 1095b4–6 and 1140b13–18; Cicero *Laws* 1.37–39.

18. Plato *Gorgias* 521d7; Aristotle *Nicomachean Ethics* 1094b11 and 1130b26–29 (*Rhetoric* 1356a25ff.).

19. Aristotle *Nicomachean Ethics* 1142a1–2 (compare 1177a25ff.), and *Metaphysics* 982b25–28; Plato *Republic* 620c4–7 and 549c2ff., and *Theaetetus* 172c8ff. and 173c8ff. See also Xenophon *Memorabilia* 1.2.47ff. and 2.9.1.

20. Aristotle *Nicomachean Ethics* 1181b15, 1141a20–b9, 1155b2ff., and 1177b30ff. Compare the typical disagreement between the philosopher and the legislator in Plato's *Laws* 804b5–c1 with his *Meno* 94e3–4 and *Apologia Socratis* 23a6–7 (also *Republic* 517d4–5, *Theaetetus* 175c5, and *Politicus* 267e9ff.). Compare also Xenophon *Memorabilia*, 1.1.11–16, and Seneca *Naturales Quaestiones* 1, beginning.

21. Plato *Republic* 519b7–d7; compare 521b7–10.

22. Plato *Republic* 520b2–3 and 494a4–10, *Phaedo* 64b, and *Apologia Socratis* 23d1–7. Compare Cicero *Tusculanae disputationes* 2.1.4 and *De officiis* 2.1.2, and Plutarch *Nicias* 23.

23. Xenophon, *Memorabilia* 4.6.15.

24. Aristotle *Politics* 1275b25 (compare J. F. Gronovius's note to Grotius *De jure belli*, Prolegomena, § 44) and *Nicomachean Ethics* 1171a15–20; Polybius 5.33.5; see also Locke, *Essay Concerning Human Understanding*, 3.9.3, 22. Note especially the derogatory meaning of "political" in the term "political virtue": Plato *Phaedo* 82a10ff. and *Republic* 430c3–5, and Aristotle *Nicomachean Ethics* 1116a17ff.

25. Aristotle *Eudemian Ethics* 1221a1ff.

26. Aristotle *Nicomachean Ethics* 1117b23ff. and *Rhetoric* 1.5.6. See also Plato *Laws* 630cff. and 963e, and *Phaedrus* 247d5–7; Xenophon *Memorabilia* 4.8.11 (compare his *Apologia Socratis* 14–16); Thomas Aquinas *Summa theologica* 2.2 qu. 129 art. 2 and qu. 58 art. 12.

27. See, for example, Aristotle *Politics* 1258b8ff., 1279b11ff., and 1299a28ff.

Chapter Five

1. Zeller, *Aristotle and the Earlier Peripatetics*, tr. Costelloe and Muirhead (London, 1897), 1:120ff.

2. See Lessing, *Werke*, ed. Petersen and von Olshausen, 6:21–60 ("Ernst und Falk") and 21:138–189 (the two other treatises mentioned). Compare also Lessing's "Ueber eine zeitige Aufgabe" (24:146–153). "Ernst und Falk" has been translated as "Lessing's *Ernst and Falk, Dialogues for Freemasons*, A Translation with Notes," by Chaninah Maschler, in *Interpretation* 14:1 (Jan. 1986): 1–49.

3. Lessing's exotericism was recognized to a certain extent by Gottfried Fittbogen, *Die Religion Lessings* (Leipzig, 1923), 60 ff. and 79ff. Fittbogen did not, however, see the most important implications of his valuable remarks, since his interpretation of Lessing was based on a Kantian or post-Kantian view of the meaning of philosophy.

4. "*Falk:* Weisst du, Freund, dass du schon ein halber Freimaeurer bist? . . . denn du erkennst ja schon Wahrheiten, die man besser verschweigt. *Ernst:* Aber doch sagen *koennte*.
Falk: Der Weise *kann* nicht sagen, was er besser verschweigt."
Second Dialogue, in Lessing, *Werke* 6:31.
(Falk: Do you realize, friend, that you're already half a free-mason? . . . For you recognize truths that are better left unsaid.
Ernst: Yes, but they *could* be said.
Falk: The wise man *can* not say what he had better leave unsaid.)
Cf. p. 21 of Maschler trans.

5. In the Third Dialogue (p. 40 = p. 28 of Maschler trans.), it is explicitly stated that only such shortcomings of even the best political constitution have been explicitly mentioned as are evident even to the most shortsighted eye. This implies that there are other shortcomings of political life as such which are not evident to "shortsighted eyes."

6. The contradiction between the statement made at the beginning that free-masonry is always in existence and the statement made toward the end that free-masonry came into being at the beginning of the eighteenth century enables us to see that free-masonry is an ambiguous term.

7. Lessing, *Werke* 21:147. Cf. Plato *Theaetetus* 180c7–d5 with *Protagoras* 316c5–317c5 and 343b4–5.

8. Lessing, *Werke* 21:160. Cf. also the remarks about "believing" on pp. 184, 187, and 189.

9. In a private conversation, published only after his death, Lessing said to F. H. Jacobi about Leibniz: "Es ist bei dem groessten Scharfsinn oft sehr schwer, seine eigentliche Meinung zu entdecken" (Even for the most penetrating, it is often very difficult to discover his true meaning) (*Werke* 24:173).

10. Compare Clemens Alexandrinus *Stromata* 5.58 (365 Staehlin ed.).

11. For a similar example of Lessing's way of expressing himself, see his *Briefe antiquarischen Inhaltes* 7 (*Werke* 27:97ff.).

12. F. Schleiermacher, *Platons Werke* (Berlin: 1804), 1.1.20.

13. "Das geheime . . . [ist] nur beziehungsweise so" (What is secret . . . [is] only relatively so) (ibid., 12); "die eigentliche Untersuchung wird mit einer anderen, nicht wie mit einem Schleier, sondern wie mit einer ange-wachsenen Haut ueberkleidet, welche dem Unaufmerksamen, *aber auch nur diesem*, desjenige verdeckt, was eigentlich soll beobachtet oder gefun-den werden, dem Aufmerksamen aber nur noch den Sinn fuer den innern Zussamenhang schaerft und laeutert" (the real investigation is clothed with another—not as if with a veil, but as if with a skin growing around it—which conceals from the inattentive, *but only from him,* what ought to be noticed or discovered, while clarifying and sharpening for the attentive his sense of the inner cohesion) (ibid., 20, italics mine).

14. *Republic* 518c–e, 521e, and 619c–d. See also *Phaedo* 69a–c.

15. That reason can be discovered by an analysis of statements such as the following: "Knowledge of the essence of reason is ethics"; "The ordi-nary distinction between offensive and defensive wars is quite empty" (*Philosophic Ethics,* sections 60, 276).

16. Cf. the remarks of the young Lessing, on the relevant passage in Gellius (20.5), in the tenth *Literaturbrief* (*Werke* 4:38).

17. Another statement about the crisis which Lessing underwent when he was about forty occurs in the *Briefe antiquarischen Inhalts* 54 (*Werke* 27:250).

18. See, e.g., von Olshausen in his introduction to *Werke* 24:41ff. Com-pare also Jacobi's letter to Hamann of 30 December 1784: "Als [Lessings] *Erziehung des Menschengeschlechts . . .* von einigen fuer eine nicht unchrist-liche Schrift, beinahe fuer eine Palinodie Angesehen wurde, stieg sein Aerger ueber die Albernheit des Volks bis zum Ergrimmen" (When [Less-ing's] *Education of the Human Race . . .* was seen by some not to be an un-Christian writing, but to be almost the opposite, his irritation over the

idiocy of people grew to the point of fury) (F. H. Jacobi, *Werke* [Leipzig, 1812] 1:398).

19. Compare von Olshausen (in Lessing, *Werke* 1:44ff.), who, however, rejects this conclusion on the basis of "internal reasons."

20. See, e.g., the following headings of sections: "Of the separation of arts and professions" and "Of the corruption incident to polished nations."

21. The influence of Ferguson's mitigated Rousseauism on Lessing can be seen from a comparison of the following quotations, on the one hand, with what Lessing says, on the other, in "Ernst und Falk" on the obvious reasons for the necessary imperfection of all civil societies. Ferguson says in part 1, sections 3 and 4: "The mighty engine which we suppose to have formed society, only teaches it to set its members at variance, or to continue their intercourse after their bonds of affection were broken." "The titles of fellow-citizens and countrymen, unopposed to those of alien and foreigner, to which they refer, would fall into disuse, and lose their meaning." "It is vain to expect that we can give to the multitude of a people a sense of union among themselves, without admitting hostility to those who oppose them." See also part 4, section 2: "If the lot of a slave among the ancients was really more wretched than that of the indigent labourer and the mechanic among the moderns, it may be doubted whether the superior orders who are in possession of consideration and honours, do not proportionately fail in the dignity which befits their condition."

22. Jacobi, *Werke* 2:334 ("Etwas das Lessing gesagt hat"). Jacobi quotes in that article Ferguson's *Essay* extensively.

23. Jacobi, *Werke* 3:469. See Lessing's "Gespraech ueber die Soldaten und Moenche" (*Werke* 24:159).

24. He writes in the seventy-first *Literaturbrief* (*Werke* 4:197), after having quoted a statement of Leibniz in praise of criticism and the study of the classics: "Gewiss, die Kritik von dieser Seite betrachtet, und das Studium der Alten bis zu dieser Bekanntschaft [with Plato, Aristotle, Archimedes, and Apollonius] getrieben, ist keine Pedanterei, sondern vielmehr das Mittel, wodurch Leibniz der geworden ist, wer er war, und *der einsige Weg*, durch welchen sich ein fleissiger und denkender Mann ihm naehern kann" (Certainly, criticism considered from this point of view, and the study of the ancients pursued to this level of familiarity [with Plato, Aristotle, Archimedes, and Apollonius], is not Pedantry, but much rather the means whereby Leibniz became who he was—and is *the only way*, through which a diligent and thinking man can approach him) (italics mine). Ten years later (1769) he says in his *Brief antiquarischen Inhalts* 45 (*Werke* 27:218): "Wir sehen mehr als die Alten; und doch duerften viellecht unsere Augen schlechter sein als die Augen der Alten: die Alten sahen weniger als wir; aber ihre Augen, ueberhaupt zu reden, moechten leicht schaerfer gewesen sein als unsere.—Ich fuerchte, dass die ganze Vergleichung der Alten und Neuern hierauf hinauslaufen duerfte" (We see more than the ancients; and yet perhaps our eyes may be worse than the

eyes of the ancients: the ancients saw less than we see; but their eyes, especially for reading, may well have been sharper than ours—I am afraid, that the entire comparison of Ancients and Moderns must flow from this).

Bibliography
Suggested Further Readings in the
Works of Leo Strauss

Chapter One: Social Science and Humanism

"What Is Political Philosophy?" chapter 1 of *What Is Political Philosophy? and Other Studies* (Glencoe, Illinois: The Free Press, 1959).

"An Epilogue," in *Essays on the Scientific Study of Politics*, ed. Herbert J. Storing (New York: Holt, Rinehart, and Winston, 1962); reprinted as chapter 8 of *Liberalism Ancient and Modern* (New York: Basic Books, 1968).

"What Is Liberal Education?" and "Liberal Education and Responsibility," chapters 1 and 2 of *Liberalism Ancient and Modern*.

Chapter Two: "Relativism"

Introduction to *Natural Right and History* (Chicago: University of Chicago Press, 1953).

"Natural Right and the Distinction between Facts and Values," chapter 2 of *Natural Right and History*.

"The Liberalism of Classical Political Philosophy" and "Perspectives on the Good Society," chapters 3 and 10 of *Liberalism Ancient and Modern*.

"Political Philosophy and History," chapter 2 of *What Is Political Philosophy? and Other Studies*.

"On Collingwood's Philosophy of History," *Review of Metaphysics* 5 (1952): 559–86.

Chapter Three: An Introduction to Heideggerian Existentialism

"Natural Right and the Historical Approach," chapter 1 of *Natural Right and History*.

"Philosophy as Rigorous Science and Political Philosophy," chapter 1 of *Studies in Platonic Political Philosophy* (Chicago: University of Chicago Press, 1983).

"Kurt Riezler," chapter 10 of *What Is Political Philosophy? and Other Studies*.

279

"Correspondence with Hans-Georg Gadamer Concerning *Warheit und Methode*," *The Independent Journal of Philosophy* 2 (1978): 5–12.

Chapter Four: On Classical Political Philosophy

"On a New Interpretation of Plato's Political Philosophy," *Social Research* 13:3 (1946): 326–67.
"The Origin of the Idea of Natural Right," and "Classic Natural Right," chapters 3 and 4 of *Natural Right and History.*
"What Is Political Philosophy?" chapter 1 of *What Is Political Philosophy? and Other Studies.*
Introduction to Leo Strauss and Joseph Cropsey, eds., *History of Political Philosophy* (3d ed., Chicago: University of Chicago Press, 1987).

Chapter Five: Exoteric Teaching

"Persecution and the Art of Writing," chapter 2 of *Persecution and the Art of Writing* (Glencoe, Ill.: The Free Press, 1952).
"On a Forgotten Kind of Writing," chapter 9 of *What Is Political Philosophy? and Other Studies.*

Chapter Six: Thucydides: The Meaning of Political History

"On Thucydides' War of the Peloponnesians and the Athenians," chapter 3 of *The City and Man* (Chicago: Rand McNally, 1964).
"Greek Historians," *Review of Metaphysics* 21 (1968): 656–66.
"Preliminary Observations on the Gods in Thucydides' Work," chapter 4 of *Studies in Platonic Political Philosophy.*

Chapter Seven: The Problem of Socrates

"On Aristotle's *Politics*," and "On Plato's *Republic*," chapters 1 and 2 of *The City and Man.*
On Tyranny, Revised and Enlarged Edition ["A Study of Xenophon's *Hiero*, Alexandre Kojève's Critique of that Study, and the Author's Reply"] (Glencoe, Ill.: The Free Press, 1963).
Socrates and Aristophanes (New York: Basic Books, 1966).
Xenophon's Socratic Discourse (Ithaca: Cornell University Press, 1970).
Xenophon's Socrates (Ithaca: Cornell University Press, 1972).
"Plato's *Apology of Socrates* and *Crito*," and "On the *Euthydemus*," chapters 2 and 3 of *Studies in Platonic Political Philosophy.*

Chapter Eight: On the *Euthyphron*

"On the *Minos*," in T. L. Pangle, ed., *The Roots of Political Philosophy: Ten Forgotten Socratic Dialogues* (Ithaca: Cornell University Press, 1987).

The Argument and the Action of Plato's "Laws" (Chicago: University of Chicago Press, 1975).

Chapter Nine: How to Begin to Study Medieval Philosophy

Persecution and the Art of Writing.

Philosophy and Law: Essays Toward the Understanding of Maimonides and His Predecessors, translated by Fred Baumann (New York: Jewish Publication Society, 1987).

Spinoza's Critique of Religion, translated by Elsa M. Sinclair (New York: Schocken Books, 1965).

"Marsilius of Padua," in *History of Political Philosophy.*

"Farabi's Plato," in *Louis Ginzberg Jubilee Volume* (New York: American Academy for Jewish Research, 1945); reprinted in Arthur Hyman, ed., *Essays in Medieval Jewish and Islamic Philosophy* (New York: KTAV Publishing House, 1977).

"On Natural Law," chapter 6 of *Studies in Platonic Political Philosophy.*

Chapter Ten: Progress or Return?

"Perspectives on the Good Society," chapter 10 of *Liberalism Ancient and Modern.*

Introduction to *The City and Man.*

"Jerusalem and Athens: Some Preliminary Reflections," chapter 7 of *Studies in Platonic Political Philosophy.*

"The Mutual Influence of Theology and Philosophy," *The Independent Journal of Philosophy* 3 (1979): 111–18.

"Introductory Essay," for Hermann Cohen's *Religion of Reason Out of the Sources of Judaism,* translated by Simon Kaplan (New York: Frederick Ungar, 1972), reprinted as chapter 15 of *Studies in Platonic Political Philosophy.*

"On the Interpretation of Genesis," with a French translation, in *L'Homme: Revue française d'anthropologie* 21:1 (1981): 5–36.

"On Natural Law," chapter 6 of *Studies in Platonic Political Philosophy.*

Index of Names

Adams, Henry, 32, 76
Aeschylus, 107, 108, 110, 112, 122
Albo, Joseph, xxxiv
Algazel, xxxiii–xxxiv
Alfarabi, xxxiii, 159, 218, 224, 273 n. 6
Apollonius, 276 n. 24
Archimedes, 276 n. 24
Arendt, Hannah, xxiv
Aristippus, 141
Aristophanes, xx, xxxii, 103–26, 129–30, 133, 156–57, 160, 162, 167, 169, 172–73, 182
Aristotle, xii, xv, xix–xx, xxix, 6–7, 28, 34, 37, 38–39, 57, 63, 73, 74, 107, 112, 126, 157, 163, 165, 175, 182, 212, 220, 223, 234, 235, 236, 247, 252, 255–56, 257, 258, 272 nn. 1, 2, 4, 5, 273 nn. 6, 7, 8, 10, 11, 12, 13, 17, 18, 19, 20, 274 nn. 24, 25, 26, 27, 276 n. 24
Aron, Raymond, ix
Austen, Jane, 134
Averroës, xxxiii–xxxiv, 222, 224–25
Avicenna, xxxiii, 218, 224

Bacon, Francis, xxi, 221, 265
Barry, Brian, x
Bergson, Henri, 163–64
Berlin, Isaiah, xxviii, 13–18
Bloom, Allan, x
Bryce, James, 4
Burke, Edmund, 254
Burnet, John, 127–28
Burnyeat, M. F., x, xi

Calvin, John, 219
Cassirer, Ernst, 28
Cervantes, Miguel de, 119
Cicero, xv, 128, 162, 224, 272 nn. 4, 5, 273 nn. 11, 17, 22
Clemens Alexandrinus, 275 n. 10
Cohen, Hermann, xxxv–xxxvi, 28, 207–8, 210
Collingwood, R. G., 34

Dante, 181, 182
Defoe, Daniel, 218
Descartes, René, xxi, 71, 212
Dewey, John, 22
Diogenes Laertius, 135
Dostoevski, Fyodor, 72, 261
Drury, S. B., xi

Engels, Friedrich, 21, 238
Epicurus, 27
Euripides, 73, 103, 107, 108, 110, 112, 113–14, 120, 122, 125, 173

Farabi. See Alfarabi
Ferguson, Adam, 70
Fittbogen, Gottfried, 274 n. 3

Gadamer, Hans-Georg, ix
Galileo, 212
Goethe, Johann Wolfgang von, 33, 181
Gronovius, J. F., 274 n. 24
Grotius, Hugo, 274 n. 24
Guttman, Julius, 214, 215

283